SAN ANSELMO LIBRARY
110 TUNSTEAD AVENUE
SAN ANSELMO, CA 9496

SAN ANSELMO LIBRARY

O9-BTZ-549

DISCARDED

APR 1 6 2002

DATE DUE

MAY 1 7 2002	JAN 0 3 2011
AUG 0 3 2002	JAN 0 3 2011
AUG 0 3 2002	
AUG 2 8 2002 R	
OCT 0 5 2002	
OCT 3 0 2002	
11/15	
DEC 2 8 2002	
MAR 2 4 2003	
APR 1 3 2005	
JAN 0 3 2006	
FEB 1 1 2006	
JAN 0 6 2007	

Brodart Co.   Cat. # 55 137 001   Printed in USA

ALSO BY EDWARD A. GARGAN

China's Fate: A People's Turbulent Struggle with Reform and Repression,
1980–1990

The River's Tale

The River's Tale

A Year on the Mekong

Edward A. Gargan

Alfred A. Knopf New York 2002

This Is a Borzoi Book
Published by Alfred A. Knopf

Copyright © 2002 by Edward A. Gargan

Maps copyright © 2002 by George Colbert

All rights reserved under International and Pan-American Copyright Conventions.
Published in the United States by Alfred A. Knopf, a division of Random House, Inc.,
New York, and simultaneously in Canada by Random House of Canada Limited,
Toronto. Distributed by Random House, Inc., New York.

www.aaknopf.com

Knopf, Borzoi Books, and the colophon are registered trademarks of
Random House, Inc.

Grateful acknowledgment is made to the following for permission to reprint
previously published material:

Georges Borchardt, Inc. and *Carcanet Press Limited:* Poem "Into the Dusk-Charged Air"
from *Rivers and Mountains* by John Ashbery, copyright © 1962, 1963, 1964, 1966 by John
Ashbery. Rights in the United Kingdom from *The Mooring of Starting Out* administered
by Carcanet Presss Limited, London. Reprinted by permission of Georges Borchardt, Inc.,
on behalf of the author and Carcanet Press Limited.

Leiber & Stoller Music Publishing: Excerpt from "Love Potion #9" by Jerry Leiber and
Mike Stoller, copyright © 1959 by Jerry Leiber Music and Mike Stoller Music,
copyright renewed. All rights reserved. Reprinted by permission of Leiber & Stoller
Music Publishing.

Wisdom Publications: Excerpts from the *Warrior Song of King Gesar* by Douglas J. Penick,
copyright © 1996 by Douglas J. Penick. Reprinted by permission of Wisdom Publications,
199 Elm Street, Somerville, Massachusetts, 02144, www.wisdompubs.org.

Library of Congress Cataloging-in-Publication Data
Gargan, Edward A.
The river's tale : a year on the Mekong / Edward A. Gargan.
p.   cm.
Includes bibliographical references and index.
ISBN 0-375-40584-4 (alk. paper)
1. Asia, Southeastern—Description and travel.   2. China—Description and travel.
3. Mekong River—Description and travel.   4. Mekong River Delta—
Description and travel.   I. Title.
DS522.6 .G37 2002
915.904'53—dc21   2001038056

Manufactured in the United States of America

First Edition

All photographs are by the author

For my parents,
for whom travel was learning,
and to the woman I loved

Running water never disappointed.
Crossing water always furthered something.
Stepping stones were stations of the soul.

SEAMUS HEANEY, "CROSSINGS"

Contents

A Note on Names and Places

Romanizing the languages that are spoken along the Mekong is for the most part no easy task. In the case of Tibetan I have eschewed the strict orthography of Tibetology and have adopted a more generally accessible romanization used in nonacademic works. All Chinese names and places are rendered in pinyin, the romanization system used in mainland China. For Laotian terms and names I have discarded diacritical markings and used a slightly more simplified spelling than is customarily employed by Western scholars. In the case of Cambodian names and terms I have used the romanization adopted by David Chandler, the leading historian of modern Cambodia. Burmese place names are rendered in the commonly accepted romanization. For both Thai and Vietnamese terms and names I have dropped accents and diacritical markings. Finally, in some instances, I have changed the names and identifying details of certain people to protect their identity.

E.A.G.

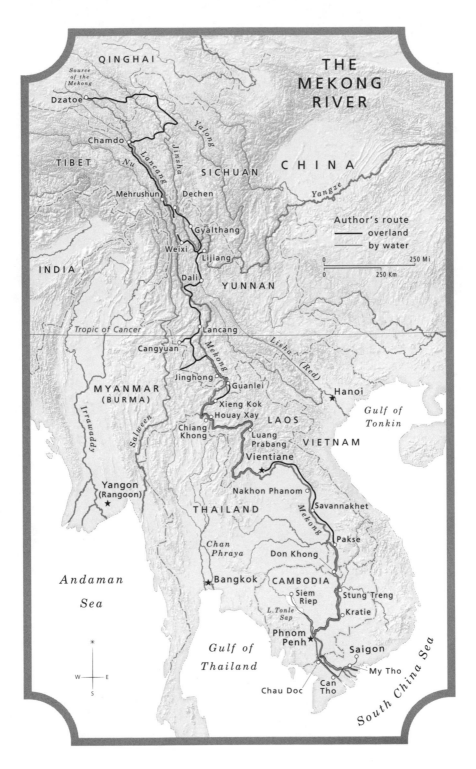

THE
MEKONG
RIVER

QINGHAI

Source of the Mekong

Dzatoe

Chamdo

TIBET

Nu

Lancang

Jinsha

Yalong

SICHUAN

CHINA

Mehrushun

Dechen

Yangze

Gyalthang

Weixi

Lijiang

Dali

YUNNAN

Author's route
— overland
— by water

0   250 Mi
0   250 Km

Tropic of Cancer

Lancang

Cangyuan

Mekong

Lisha (Red)

Jinghong

Guanlei

Hanoi

MYANMAR
(BURMA)

Xieng Kok

Houay Xay

LAOS

*Gulf of
Tonkin*

Irrawaddy

Salween

Chiang
Khong

Luang
Prabang

Vientiane

VIETNAM

Yangon
(Rangoon)

Nakhon Phanom

Savannakhet

THAILAND

Mekong

Pakse

*Chan
Phraya*

Don Khong

*Andaman

Sea*

Bangkok

CAMBODIA

Siem
Riep

*L. Tonle
Sap*

Stung Treng

Kratie

Phnom
Penh

Saigon

*Gulf of
Thailand*

Chau Doc

Can
Tho

My Tho

South China Sea

W   E
S

The River's Tale

Introduction

One evening, as a great orange lozenge of sun plopped into the jungle to the west, my vessel of the week, a canoe-narrow, wood-plank cargo boat painted the green favored by the trams in Boston, edged into the shoreline somewhere in northern Laos. There were no lights on either side of the fat, lazy meander of darkening brown water, and just a clutter of bamboo thatched huts scattered up on the high riverbank. Another cargo boat, a larger, tubbier wooden craft of the kind often used to haul grain from village to town in a country with few roads, was cozied up to the shore snout first. A torpid heat laced with the tang of burning vegetation weighed on us.

It had been a long day chugging down the Mekong River from Luang Prabang, the old royal capital of Laos, a day of endless arguments with the boatman, a wretched, hollow-cheeked scamster who had relieved me of some 800,000 kip, about $160, with the promise to convey me in clattering splendor for three days downriver to Vientiane, the country's capital. Barely two hours out of Luang Prabang, the boatman, named Pheng, steered his vessel alongside a floating gas station, one of the occasional pit stops along the river where diesel fuel is served up from steel oil drums. After filling his tank with the lollipop-red fluid he informed me that the boat engine was broken and he could go no farther. I told him to fix it. He told me he couldn't. We repeated this pas de deux for some time. Under a devastating sun, deep in an empty landscape, I succumbed to months of frustrations and uncharitably raised my voice, angry that my careful arrangements to travel the Mekong were once again collapsing and that my shark-eyed boatman was intent on ripping me off. Shouted exchanges and desultory silences came and went. After once more urging me to hang out at the gas pump and wait for another boat, the boatman finally conferred with his engine boy, a blind teenager who sat in the rear of the eighty-foot-long boat next to the pile of iron and steel that passed for an engine. A few clangs with a well-used wrench later, the boat's engine belched a cloud of black smoke and then chundered to life. We were off again.

The rest of the day's voyage proceeded in a similar vein, the boatman wailing about his failing engine as he swigged tea from a glass jar—tea brewed with the silty water of the Mekong itself—and yanked a cord that ran back to a bell that hung over the head of the engine boy, one ring for neutral, two for forward and three for reverse. I squatted on a plank that was jammed between the cabin walls up front, next to the boatman. Ahead of us the Mekong flowed, its broad, caramel-colored flanks rubbing against sandbanks and forest, massaging great fields of heavy granite boulders the size of suburban American houses. From time to time a clutter of huts, like jumbled, yawning haystacks, would peek over the riverbank, or a few bare-chested men would drag a fishing net in a wide loop to try and corral the little fish that dashed up the river. But mostly, we crept through deep silence.

Relentless beneath us, keeping us afloat, was water that first issued from mountains some 1,750 miles away, high up in the northern Tibetan plateau in China's Qinghai Province. It had taken me about five months to reach this point, about midway in a journey along a river that crashes down from Tibet through six Asian countries—China, Burma, Laos, Thailand, Cambodia and Vietnam; seven if you regard Tibet itself as a separate, but occupied, nation—before releasing itself in a vast deltic splay into the South China Sea. For much of this century, the countries washed by the Mekong's waters have figured heavily in Western imagination and history, an imagination too often bathed in reverie and wistfulness, and a history too often soaked in blood.

Colonialism has long been banished from the region; the region's wars are over, although scars remain all too visible on the people and on the face of the land itself. A web of Western modernity, its cultures, economy and politics are settling, not always easily, across much of Asia. The Mekong slices through this history, its residue and prospects. Along it, Internet cafés sprout in dirt-streeted towns, sometimes only a few miles from thatched-hut villages that have never had electricity. Plodding mule trains caravaning sacks of opium move through Burma, then across isolated borders into China for processing and shipment to eager Western consumers. More than three miles above sea level, Tibetan Khamba horsemen lathered in yak butter and adorned in silver and amber jewelry gallop across endless grasslands rising from the river's pebbled shores, herding yaks as their ancestors did for ages before them; while two thousand miles to the south, Vietnamese cosmetics salesmen in short-sleeved white shirts, tan slacks and sandals scoot about on Hondas, fanning out across the river's delta to hundreds of villages and towns, hawking American beauty shampoos and face soaps.

Yet the Mekong no more binds Asia together than does a wider notion of a shared Asianness, an idea bandied about by the proponents of authoritarianism (from Singapore, Hong Kong and Malaysia), who claim to find some deeper meaning in a grab bag of aphorisms ladled out under the rubric "Asian values." A Tibetan monk would find little to say to a Thai insurance agent, even though at sunrise both wake next to the Mekong River, and both are Buddhist. Indeed, as the Mekong scythes its way through mountains and slithers past rice paddies, the river itself is called by many names on its three-thousand-mile journey to the sea: to the Vietnamese, it is the Cuu Long; Tonle Thom, Tonle Sap or Tonle Thuc to the Khmer; Mae Nam Khong to the Thai and Laotians; Lancang Jiang to the Chinese; and to the Tibetans, Dzachu.

For much of my life I have been consumed by Asia, initially as a doctoral student in medieval Chinese history at the University of California, Berkeley—an experience of intellectual intensity and depth, but at a tactile level, somewhat anemic—and for much of the last fifteen years as a correspondent for the *New York Times*. Even before my passage into the groves of academe, however, Asia had intruded into my life, as it did into the lives of virtually all young men in college during the years of the Vietnam War, or what the Vietnamese not surprisingly call the American War. My closing teenage years and early twenties were spent largely organizing protest activities against the war, and when I finally reached Berkeley at the rather latterly age of twenty-five, I was more than ready to immerse myself in what my father, an historian of modern France, invariably called "the life of the mind." What compelled me at the time were the pleasures of ninth- and tenth-century Tang poetry and the complexities of urbanization in the Sung dynasty, 320 years of prosperity, intellectual accomplishment, invasion by the Mongols and dissolution that ended in 1278.

Scholarship demands passion. My father had it. My advisers at Berkeley, particularly Frederick Wakeman, did as well. But there was, to my mind, an element of passionlessness about the eight-hour days tucked into my carrel at the East Asian Library, hemmed in by towers of navy blue, cloth-covered boxes of block print classical histories. Perhaps it wasn't the absence of passion as much as what I sensed as a lack of immediacy, a distancing (certainly in temporal terms) from the scent of Asia, the tumult of street life, the feel of its fabrics and pottery and land, the breath of societies recovering from war, searching for democracy, figuring out how to get enough to eat, trying to preserve themselves. These are all very fundamental and broad questions, and I wanted to get below them somehow. Journalism offered a way in—"journalism as the first draft of history," as is so often repeated—and some of it allowed me to dig where I wanted, follow paths I chose, talk to prime ministers, prostitutes, priests, moviemakers, poets, India's untouchables. There was an exhilaration about mixing my academic background with my unrestrained nosiness in a part of the world that offered few certainties, relentless challenges and rewards of discovery, understanding, friendships and some accomplishment. I relished moving through worlds few Americans knew intimately, struggling to bring a sense of coherence to these places in my work, a coherence mingled with my own feel for the heft of history, a cultural ease and an Irish intolerance for the blarney.

Fifteen years in China, India and Hong Kong, however, also took a toll. Constant travel to meet deadlines, breaking stories and the demands of editors, as well as the ephemeral nature of newspaper journalism itself, seemed always to leave a tang of incompleteness in my work. Pace was dictated by the rigors of the newspaper, not by the rhythm of a place, a story, someone's tale. The chance to spend another few days in a village, time to wander without clear purpose, to sit and learn, was stunted by the voracious appetite of the newspaper; as an editor insisted to me once, "it's a daily newspaper."

Equally true of newspaper journalism is its rigorous adherence to standards of what some call "objectivity," which is mostly a way of saying that one reports on events, people and places in a dispassionate and fair manner, in a way that reflects balance and an absence of prejudice. There are dips into analytical waters, but opinions (and passion) are confined to the opinion pages. Still, my opinions hardened, a cynicism about almost everything flourished, from the venality and duplicity of governments (particularly well honed in Asia) to the sanctimoniousness of American policymakers, and the articles I filed for the newspaper began to have a feel of tissuelike durability. I became restless with the quotidian nature of my work. Finally, in middle age, intent on following my own muse, my own sense of the important, the riveting, the bizarre, the hysterically funny, the tragic, the romantic, I set out to understand Asia in a way I never had before.

Traveling through Asia for many years had occasionally flung me glancingly against the Mekong River, a river that for years had figured heavily in the journalism of the Vietnam War but since then had retreated somewhat from popular imagination. It was not the first river that drew me in; the Congo, the Ganges, the Nile all beckoned me at different times. Rivers are inherently interesting, both as geographical phenomena and as metaphors for larger questions. They mold landscapes, sunder them with gaping canyons, nurture inland fisheries, lavish the bounty of the lands they travel through onto vast fertile deltas. Historically they have been the earliest and the most basic of trade routes, sources of food (and, of course, drinking water), a place to wash, a splashy frolic for children. Civilizations have emerged next to rivers, in China, India, Europe, Africa and the Middle East. Rivers are sacred in some places—India's Ganges, for example—and are abused and remade in others, like the Columbia in the American northwest. And as much as they sustain life, they also bring death and destruction; regularly the Yangze in central China swells beyond its banks, inundating villages, sweeping away lives in violent, uncontrollable, muddy torrents. Rivers are gentle and ferocious, placid and mean. They trigger conflict—Bangladesh and India still haggle over water rights to the Ganges. They delineate boundaries everywhere. They provide architects with opportunities for grandeur—Tower Bridge in London, the Brooklyn Bridge in New York. And, in their infant form, they provide middle-aged fly fishermen with places to craft pop philosophies about life and casting for fish. They are the stuff of metaphor and fable, poetry and painting.

Rivers move. They come from somewhere and head toward oceans and seas. They flow past societies and civilizations, mute witness to human events. For me, rivers are magnetic. I can sit and watch the water move past for hours. They are places of contemplation—contemplation about the river itself to be sure, but also a place to reflect on the passage of time, of life, of experience. And so I set out to weave together my passion for Asia with a longing to travel at my own speed, to wander as I wished, to find a river that would pull me through Asia and open itself to me. That river is the Mekong.

In a real sense, a Mekong journey is a voyage through the heart of Asia's complexity, amid a blizzard of languages, from the tongue spoken by the largest number of people in the world, Chinese, to a language shared by scarcely thousands, the Wa of southwestern Yunnan, across economies of utter deprivation and despair as well as those of affluence and promise, and among cultures under seige, as in Tibet, to those all but pulverized, as in Cambodia, to those content and self-confident, as in Thailand. Even the great thread that follows the river from its source to its exhausted release from Vietnam, the beliefs and practice of Buddhism, is in reality two great traditions that found their way from India on different historical currents. For some people along the Mekong, life is a daily struggle to wrench enough food from pallid soil to survive, while for others a daily chore is pondering which among two dozen sparkling chrome wheels is jazzy enough for a new pickup truck. At certain places along the river, the world is no bigger than a village, with the river a highway that carries people dashing by to places unknown. Elsewhere, the river has become little more than a tourist site, with commerce and life turned toward the macadam of yellow-striped highways.

The Mekong is no easy river. In swathes of Tibet and Yunnan, the river thunders through gorges, loud and violent; here it is untouchable, unreachable. A thousand miles to the south, it waltzes among hundreds of limestone outcrops and islands bushy with coconut palms, and pink-gray dolphins arch and blow in its gentle ripples. For China, the Mekong is a new source of energy, with two immense hydroelectric dams channeling its flow through massive turbines as the river lakes up behind the soaring concrete walls. For Laotians, it is still the country's principal transport route, a toilet for those along the river, and a bathtub and drinking water supply for the thousands of boatmen that ply it. In Vietnam, it is harbor and fishery, a web of canals and channels for vegetable sellers in wooden longboats, a prairie for duck herders in pirogues, the backroads of a good deal of the southern quarter of the country.

The Mekong both unites and divides as it journeys south. It links the apple merchants of Sichuan to consumers in Thailand, and the loggers of Laos to the lumber mills in Yunnan. But it is a barrier as well, its broad expanse walling off Thailand from Laos, a watery no-man's-land between the bright lights, the boisterous politics and the blossoming economy of Thailand and the dark impoverishment—economic, political and intellectual—of Laos.

Some of this I knew before I began my journey along the river, but much I was yet to discover. In one sense, the essential reason for any voyage like this is to see the river, and the societies that adhere to its watershed, through the eyes of the people themselves. In another sense, however, there was a deeper personal purpose. During my late teens and early twenties, when my activism against American involvement in the war in Vietnam, Laos and Cambodia led me to leave college for several years of full-time antiwar organizing, I spent a couple of years in a federal prison for refusing to fight in that war. But as a student, my sense of the war and southeast Asia was somewhat intangible, as indeed it was for most Americans, filtered through the lens of television cameras, the accounts in newspapers. Now, I hoped, this journey through the Mekong watershed would lend some substance and meaning to those years, and cast light for me on what victory, if that is what it was, over American forces brought the people of the region. I knew, of course, the broad outlines of the quarter century since the last Americans left Saigon, but it was a disembodied knowledge. I wanted to see for myself.

And there was in this trip as well a desire to reflect upon the broader meanings of my peripatetic fifteen years in Asia, to find a way to mesh my years of scholarship with those of my hands-in-the-dirt journalism. I sought to let Asia roll around inside me in ways it never had—and to make something of it, something more profound, more deep, more lasting than I had as a journalist. In daily journalism, too often one is driven by the subject of each story; questions are framed around discrete issues (and sometimes for stories I found of little or no interest). Now, I wanted to let the people I met tell the stories they wanted, show me their lives in their own way, sing me songs; I wanted to be able to get drunk, or lie at the bottom of a boat, my belly stuffed with boat-cooked chicken, without having to scamper back to some hotel to file frantically yet another newspaper story. I wanted, in short, to write about Asia from a longer, larger perspective.

The Mekong scours some of the saddest history of recent years. In Tibet, the Chinese government has imposed a reign of political and cultural terror—there is no other word for it—that has brought Tibetan society and its Buddhism to a crossroads; Tibet's survival very likely depends on whether the Communist party in China endures. If it does, Tibet's future as a coherent society is in jeopardy. It is a broken country. Laos and Cambodia, broken as well, are both victims of the Vietnam War; two decades later, Cambodia is still attempting to find a way past nearly four years of genocide. For Americans, it is difficult to conceive the horrors that have been visited on these societies, but it is those devastations that have shaped the mentalities of much of modern Asia. As I traveled I wanted to hear the tales of survivors, the tales of suffering and endurance. I wanted to hear the voices of those who had been imprisoned in Vietnam, who had fled the Khmer Rouge, who had returned warily to Tibet. Those are the voices that make up some of the cacophony that is Asia's mosaic. Equally, I wanted to wander into the hills of northern Tibet and yak about yaks with a nomad, sit with monks in the old Lao royal town of Luang Prabang, check out the nightlife in reviving Saigon.

An historical shadow stretches as well across Asia. For much of the last two centuries the West has laid its hand and purpose on the region. In the nineteenth century, the French came as explorers and conquerors, and today faint footprints of their passage remain. But the footprints of the Americans are deeper and reach farther, whether in the physicality of their bomb craters, the unexploded bombs that still kill and maim or the Americanized English fluency of many Saigonese. A quarter of a century after the Vietnam War, the world has become a much smaller place, more tightly bound together than ever in history, in bindings manufactured in New York and London, Paris and Frankfurt. Foreign capital moves with unprecedented ease; a shift in mood toward Asia by bankers on Wall

Street or in London's City can, and did in 1997, catapult Asia into a deep recession. From the widest of historical lenses, one can see the face of Asia today in many respects as the product of the two titanic struggles of this century, World War II and the collapse of the Soviet Union, and the subsequent triumph of Western, and primarily American, economic practices, political values and cultural aspirations. This is a story told along the Mekong.

For a year I pursued, as well, an adventure, the challenge, simply put, of traveling the length of the Mekong River itself, the world's ninth longest. There is no certain trail along the Mekong; I was to learn this early and be reminded of it daily. There are no boat schedules, no bus routes, indeed, sometimes no roads. In the river's cornucopia of languages, I stumbled along in Chinese, French and English, three among dozens of tongues spoken by the 60 to 100 million people who inhabit the river's watershed. I planned, and the plans crumbled like dried leaves. I drove for days along precipices only to have the road blocked by a collapsed mountainside. I gasped for air at sixteen thousand feet and watched mosquitoes feast on my feet in the Mekong Delta. At the South China Sea, I noted on my handheld global positioning system that the Mekong pushed, reddish-brown, into the sea 1,824 miles from its source; as the river runs it is closer to 3,050 miles.*

Inevitably a journey like this, one that consumed a significant part of my life, stirred a mix of conflicting emotions. Alone much of the time—alone in the sense that I was without companionship—there were moments of intense isolation, moments that in retrospect approached despair. Being stranded at China's border with Laos after four months, and after no contact for a very long time with anyone I knew, sitting on a clay bluff over the Mekong, I was about as disconsolate as I have ever been. It was not so much the physical discomfort, which at times approached the gruesome, but the depth of the solitude that raised questions for me about a life that in many respects has been rootless for nearly two decades. Yes, there is a genuine emotional and intellectual rush that comes from travel and discovery,

---

* Most writers on the Mekong have traditionally assessed the length of the river as about 2,600 miles. In 1997, however, geographers at the Yunnan Institute of Geography in Kunming remeasured the river from its source to the many mouths of the Mekong Delta that spill into the South China Sea and determined its length to be 4,880 kilometers, or 3,050 miles.

not in the sense of the nineteenth-century French explorers, of "getting there first," but in understanding, in seeing societies change, adapt, create, struggle, survive. And there is the rush of travel itself, a "wind in the hair" sensation that comes from hefting a backpack and heading into what is truly the unknown.

Yet, somewhat paradoxically, as I traveled the river day in and day out, it was sometimes impossible to think very much about Asia itself. Each day presented its own little battles—where to find something to eat, where to find a boat, where to sleep, where am I?—and it was not easy to avoid becoming submerged in the details of getting through the day. And in the thick air of that dusky evening in Laos as we crawled toward a shadowed and empty embankment, I reflected mostly on my meager meal—a stew of remarkably boney fish chunks and tubers in a brown sauce of uncertain provenance over white rice of truncated, rounded grains—concocted over a kerosene flame by the boatman, and the squadrons of mosquitoes on combat missions that regularly cruised by. I was not, it is true, utterly happy. I unrolled my sleeping bag and chose an almost-nail-free bit of planking on which to sleep while the occasional thunk of the larger cargo boat next door punctuated the murmured conversation of the two boat-men. And then, just as I was dropping off, I heard from the next boat, from a plastic boom box, the opening chords of a 1964 tune by the Searchers. I hummed along:

> *I took my troubles down to Madame Rue*
> *You know that gypsy with the gold-capped tooth*
> *She's got a pad down on 34th and Vine*
> *Sellin' little bottles of Love Potion Number 9. . . .*

One

The Dzachu

Tibet is high and its land is pure.
Its snowy mountains are at the head of everything,
The sources of innumerable rivers and streams,
It is the center of the sphere of the gods.

A TIBETAN HYMN

As I spread my blanket-sized map of northwestern China on the dining table in the comfort of Hong Kong, I ran my finger west through Qinghai Province, across the thick paper, tracing the route I hoped to take over the coming days. Past Xining, the provincial capital, west to Jyekundo (in small type) and then farther on. A faint red line marking the narrowest and least maintained of the region's roads expired at a small dot labeled Dzatoe. Beyond Dzatoe, a spidery map trace of blue—the Dzachu, or Mekong—extended into a ganglia of tributaries, streams and rivulets, to the very sources of the river itself.

I found it difficult to visualize what those faint weaving blues and reds really represented, what tales they told, what they felt like, how many of my bones would bruise over these purported roads. Many years before, at least a decade earlier, I had been to Xining, an arid and remote place and the closest city with air service to the Mekong's source, but never beyond the city limits; it was there I was to fly to begin this journey. As I loaded my backpack—a sackful of lightweight clothing, a heavy sweater for the frigid nights, a sleeping bag (for where there were no hotels) and a thermal blanket to go with it, a satchel with a razor, toothbrush, assorted antibiotics and vitamins, a pair of decent binoculars, a camera, a basic satellite global positioning system (GPS) device that could tell me where I was, how high, and how fast I was moving, a clutch of maps and a few good books—I did so with an uncomfortable mix of emotions: anxiety over the unknown; eagerness at the possibilities that lay ahead; some self-doubt at the very burden of spending a year mostly by myself on a river I scarcely knew heading into lands I had never seen. As a correspondent for the *Times* for many years, I had more often than not found myself in cushy hotels on my travels, unworried about costs, cosseted in the certainties of an institutional structure that worried about my well-being and that was available in emergencies to yank me out of desperate situations. This was different. This was me and the river.

Ahead of me, for at least a couple of months, lay travel in Tibet, and what had been Tibet before China hived off chunks of it and tacked them onto neighboring Chinese provinces. China's rulers, ethnic Hans, communist in name, authoritarian in instinct, have been wary of allowing foreigners in Tibet. In 1987, when I was on a reporting trip to Tibet, a spontaneous revolt against Chinese rule erupted in Lhasa, leaving several monks dead, a Chinese police station torched and hundreds of other Tibetans shipped off to prisons. While I and several colleagues attempted to report on those events, we were rounded up by state security police and ordered out of Tibet; China did not then and does not now want the world to see the manner of its subjugation of Tibet and still sharply regulates visits there. That day, waiting for the plane that would take me out of Tibet, I was suddenly dragged from among my colleagues and arrested by the police for what they said was "beating up a policeman," a rather laughable accusation given my lamentable pugilistic skills and rather slight build. I was hustled into a concrete chamber where, after reading the charge to me (which was dutifully videotaped and recorded by a note taker), they issued me a document in Tibetan and Chinese replete with a half dozen decorous red stamps warning me not to repeat my crime; today, opulently framed, it hangs on the wall of my home. As I prepared to head back toward Tibet now, I harbored apprehensions about what this trip to the region might hold if the police wondered about a lone foreigner wandering in remote areas. At the same time though, I knew, because I had been to China many times in the last decade, that restrictions over foreigners traveling in the country had eased substantially. I also knew that there was not much to be gained from worrying about what I could not control.

It was typically sweltering in Hong Kong as I headed west and north, first to Guangzhou, and then by Xinjiang Airlines to Xining. As cities go, Xining is among the most forlorn, an expanse of 1950s Socialist-era blockhouse architecture squatting on China's desolate northwestern plains. I told myself that this Mekong journey would truly begin, not on an airplane, but above the river itself on a hill, or in a valley of yaks, or with my toes in a rushing stream of the river's first waters. I had difficulty imagining precisely what I would find, but my more immediate concern was to find a bus to Jyekundo, twenty-two hours away, where I would meet an old friend from the Tibetan plateau of northern Yunnan, a former Buddhist monk, scholar of Buddhist scriptures and adventurer, Dakpa Kelden. For a time, we would travel together.

A clapperless blue bell hung overhead, immense, flawless, infinitely clear. Stapled to it like the nub end of a rivet flared a white-yellow sun, naked and small. A range of stegosaurus-bladed mountain peaks rimmed a velvety, baize green sea of rolling hills. On some hillocks, at a distance measured in exhausting hours, like a bag of spilled coffee beans on sparse carpet, herds of stoop-shouldered yaks gnawed at the tough, crew-cut grass. High up a hill, whipped by an insistent wind, clean and cold in high August, a huddle of three black tents clung resolutely to a barren, treeless perch. Smoke seeped from a tent peak, only to be instantly scrubbed away by the wind's stiff brush.

In the distance ran a dirt-and-stone track that crept between the nearest town and this place on the vast Tibetan plateau. The town, Tibetans know it as Dzatoe, brags not much more than a string of cement-and-mud buildings, only a handful reaching two stories. It straddles a runwaylike main street of sturdy concrete where a few motorcycles race up and down, heading nowhere. An occasional battered, open-backed truck rumbles in from Xining, forty-eight hours away. Dzatoe is the last commercial outpost before Qinghai Province melts into limitless, roadless miles of mountainous plateau, grassy hill lands and a tangled filigree of streams and rivers.

On Chinese maps, this plateau is shown as deep within Qinghai Province, although no Chinese, save a sprinkling of Communist officials, live outside the capital or the towns and villages in the far east of the province. The south and west of Qinghai were once the northern reaches of Tibet proper, but the province now exists not as any cultural or linguistic entity in its own right—it has no cuisine of its own, no dialect, no local costume or custom—but as a Chinese administrative unit, one of the country's most impoverished, and home to much of China's vast prison gulag.

Several hours past Dzatoe, on a stony, unmapped track, the aging Japanese four-wheel drive I shared with Dakpa and a lackadaisical Tibetan driver jolted along shin-deep ruts and skirted gashlike fissures that cracked the earth. We had hugged the river, now the faint rust brown color of unfired pottery, thirty or so yards wide, as it serpentined across the grasslands from the hills ahead. Then I saw those three black tents, lashed to the earth by a cat's cradle of ropes and cording. Below us, on a mesa of scrub grass that ran to the river, yaks chawed the short, tough grass and, if they were lucky, the rare cluster of gerbera daisies that sometimes sequinned the grasslands. I told Dakpa we should stop here—or perhaps better—start here. The car uttered a faint gasp when the driver turned the engine off.

Dakpa and I started our hike up the hill, he far more acclimated to the enervating effects of altitude than I. (For those who have not been raised at altitude, the thin oxygen over time has a progressively debilitating effect, and in serious cases can bring illness and death.) Very quickly, my heart was beating with a manic thump that I imagined augured ill, or worse; I ran regularly, but no amount of running prepares one for the

Dakpa Kelden, a Tibetan friend, at the early waters
of the Dzachu, the Tibetan name for
the Mekong River

effects of oxygen depletion at altitude. My pocket GPS device put us above 15,500 feet, nearly three miles above the surface of the placid South China Sea, into which the Mekong runs. As we trekked up the hill, small brown marmots popped from tunnels to assess our intentions. A great lammergeier eagle beat through the thin air above us, the silence sliced by the *shyup, shyup, shyup* of its huge wings. The marmots vanished.

We managed our way over the last rise to the nomads' encampment and suddenly a black-and-tan mastiff hurtled toward us, its teeth bared as it loosed what struck me more as a lionine than doglike roar, until the chain linked to its collar tautened abruptly, yanking the beast backward. It continued barking, testing the perimeter of its chain, eyeing us meanly. All Tibetan nomads have guard dogs, and all of them react ferociously to strangers, Dakpa told me. Standing cautiously just beyond the hound's orbit, Dakpa called toward the tents. A tent flap raised and an older, wizened man emerged, his shoulder-length gray hair disordered. He hesitated before ordering the dog back to the tents, where it immediately padded.

He stared at us for a time. "Come," he said finally, "sit here," gesturing to a couple of logs squared around an extinct fire. The dog's commotion had roused everyone, and—men, women, children and infants in arms appeared from the three large black tents, tents woven from the thickest

yak wool. A tent flap snapped and a small boy bolted into the open in a
ragged checked shirt and muddied khaki trousers, a Chicago Bulls hat
clamped askew on his head. A young woman in a high-collared, Chinese-
style blue satin jacket nursed an infant as she squatted in front of us.
Another woman in a brown wool robe placed in our hands steaming bowls
of yak butter tea, a concoction of tea, salt and yak butter that is churned in
a narrow wooden tube with a long-handled plunger. It is an acquired taste.

In parts of Tibet, a common ditty is sometimes sung about yak butter
tea (for Tibetans, a *dre* is a female, *yak* a male), as Dakpa did as he noisily
slurped his:

> *One, the best tea from China,*
> *Two, the pure* dre *butter of Tibet,*
> *Three, the white salt from the northern plains,*
> *All three meeting in the copper pot.*
> *Yet, how the tea is brewed*
> *Is up to you, O tea maker. . . .*

Dakpa and the old man—he gave his name as Phon Dza, the head of
what he later told us was a clan of three families—sat and talked, Dakpa of
his life in the far northwest of Yunnan, the old man listening, chewing on
the bit of a long-stemmed pipe. "It's not like here," Dakpa said, "with you
and your yaks. I have no yaks." The old man nodded, twin tendrils of
smoke leaking from his nose. "We all live in a town now," Dakpa went on.
"Even though it is Tibetan, there are Chinese there now. And we are
rebuilding our monastery." Phon Dza listened as Dakpa continued
describing a Tibetan land so different from his own, nodding from time to
time. Then he interrupted. "No yaks?" he asked. "Really no yaks?" Yes,
said Dakpa. As we sat on small Tibetan rugs, which the women had bundled out of the tents, the infant Dzachu, the seeds of the Mekong,
uncoiled across the plateau beneath us, already brusque in its passage.
Phon Dza, a man of calm and patience, his face hewn sharply with pronounced cheekbones and a high, clear brow, told us that he had always
lived within sight of the Dzachu and had traveled with his herds in these
mountains and pastures for sixty-eight years.

"In all, there are twelve of us here," he said, "my five children, three
with wives, brothers, sisters and children." He rearranged his legs on the
rug, blew across the surface of his tea bowl to push the film of greasy but-

Phon Dza, a sixty-eight-year-old nomadic herder,
sitting above the early waters of the Dzachu

ter from the surface of the tea and drank. His rough blue wool pants and pajama-like, flap-collared shirt had not been washed in some time, nor had the clothes of the family who sat around us. Cleanliness means different things in the mountains, with yak butter used for grooming hair and on the face as a block against the wind and cold. Dakpa rendered Phon Dza's Tibetan into English.

"All of my children are working with yaks. Some go to the mountains to collect caterpillar fungus to sell in the town." High in the mountains, the fragile, hidden fungus that is prized as a delicacy and for its purported medicinal virtues is gathered and sold to traders in nearby towns. Even so, like many nomadic herders, Phon Dza is often on the margins of the monetary economy. "If many people go out and look, in one season maybe we can get one kilo. But often we cannot find that much. For one kilo, we can get ten thousand to fifteen thousand yuan," the equivalent of between $1,220 and $1,830, "depending on the quality. But we cannot be sure we can gather even a kilo every year. Sometimes the fungus does not grow, or we cannot find it." Still, for anyone here, such a sum is an immense amount of money. "We also sell yak meat and yak butter in town. For a kilo of butter, we get twenty yuan," or $2.40. "We have to buy barley to get *tsampa*"—the flour milled from barley that is the staple grain of

Tibetans—"wheat, tea, everything. We sell what we can." Unlike other regions of Tibet, the altitude is too high here for barley to flourish, and so it must be trucked in from lower climes. Below us and higher on steeply rising mountainsides, Phon Dza's herds chewed their way through the late summer grasses.

It is the yaks—huge, woolly, cowlike creatures with shaggy brows and deep black eyes—that are the lifeblood of nomadic herders. The herders' large tents are woven from the thickest yak hair. Butter from the yak is a food, the requisite flavoring for tea, a cosmetic, the fuel for votive lamps. Even the bushy pom-pom of a yak tail is used as a fly whisk. And, of course, yak meat is a staple in the diet. "Yaks," Phon Dza said simply, "are our life."

Some Tibetans tell this story of how the yak came to Tibet: Many, many years ago water buffaloes plodded through India, relatively content, and all was well. One day, one of the water buffaloes said to his friend, "I want to go north on an errand. Could I borrow your furry coat?" His companion said yes. The water buffalo trekked north through the Himalayas to the Tibetan plateau. When he arrived there and looked around, he liked it so much he decided to stay. Which is why, the legend goes, water buffaloes are virtually hairless, and the yak is covered in a warm, dense coat of wool. The Dalai Lama himself, we're told, when asked what he missed most about Tibet, replied at once, "Yaks."

Every few years, Phon Dza travels to the nearest big town, Jyekundo, the prefectural seat, a grotty place of scarcely twenty thousand people, either to its annual summer festival of horsemanship, drinking and not inconsiderable wagering, or to buy things not available in Dzatoe, or to try and get a better price for his summer's gathering of caterpillar fungus. The journey usually takes five or six days each way. But though Jyekundo offers the closest thing to urban life on this bit of the Tibetan plateau—it has electricity, and karaoke parlors—he still does not like the town, its people or its pace. "It is so crowded. There are too many people. Too many. You cannot see the mountains. And there are no yaks. But here is beautiful. It is perfect here."

He gestured toward a mountain that loomed to the west, a jagged peak, distinct from its neighbors in its spiky silhouette and solitary majesty. "This mountain is our protector," he explained. "We call it Ware Nechok, the holiest place of the lord protector. Maybe this is not its proper name. I don't know. This is the name our family gives to the mountain." He turned his head and pointed to the river beneath us. "And the Dzachu gives us life."

Tibet is the nursery of most of Asia's great rivers. Near where we sat, at least in terms of direct-line miles—the journey is arduous—the sources of the Yangze, the Yellow and the Salween spill from this plateau. Asia's other major rivers, the Indus, the Brahmaputra and tributaries to the Ganges, tumble from the mountains elsewhere in Tibet. Much of the region here is uncharted, roadless and, to me, that rarest of qualities, timeless.*

Though neither Phon Dza nor any of the members of his family have traveled more than one hundred miles or so from the traditional grazing grounds for their herds, through legend and folklore they know that these rivers emanate from their lands. Our conversation wandered, and Phon Dza began to recite stanzas from the oral epic of Gesar, the mythological king and warrior of the state of Ling, a place said to be near here and the heartland for the Khambas, the people of Kham, or eastern Tibet. The epic of Gesar tells of endless feats of heroism, battles to recover his wife, kidnapped by the rival king of Hor (now called Uighurs) and miraculous events of courage and daring, as well as the ceaseless irritation of a nagging aunt in visions and dreams; to this day nomadic fathers, who are almost always illiterate here, recite long passages of the legend from memory to their children. Stanzas are often invoked as well to punctuate any debate or conversation, lines that lend both clarity and broader wisdom to any discussion. Early on, the epic says this:

> Noble lords and ladies, brave warriors,
> Know me as I am, the one who has been foretold.
> It has been written in prophecies, and you know it in your hearts;
> I am Gesar, King of Ling,
> Who brings prosperity, dignity and joy,
> Who destroys cowardice, delusion and slavery,
> I am Gesar, Lion King of Ling,

---

* In September 1999, after I had journeyed to the Tibetan plateau, a team of American and Chinese geologists traveled close to the source and then rafted back to Dzatoe. Their work has produced the first accurate maps of the fault and fold lines on the upper plateau, work that goes a great way in explaining the course of the Mekong River as it flows from its headwaters.

The great conqueror and the great healer.
I am the light of your darkness,
The food of your hunger, and the scourge of your corruption.
I hold the sword of truth in one hand,
And the medicine of peace in the other.
The time of my kingdom is now.

Dakpa, whose roots on the southeastern edge of the Tibetan plateau and non-Khamba heritage placed him at a disadvantage in this recitation duel, laughed aloud as Phon Dza spun tales easily and mirthfully. Out-done, Dakpa offered a stanza from the epic of Gesar about the river we had come to follow.

Dzachu, Machu, Brichu soom,
Gyuksa tsawa kaka re,
Dzomsa gyatso dhing la re.

Denma, Pala, Ghaden soom,
Kyesa sacha kaka re,
Zoomsa Lingyu tamo re.

Phon Dza beamed. Dakpa paused and then offered the translation and interpretation: " *'Dzachu, Machu, Brichu soom . . .'* means 'Mekong, Yel-low, Yangze rivers three, although their sources are in different places, the three rivers melt into the same sea.' *'Denma, Pala, Ghaden soom . . .'* means 'Denma, Pala, Ghaden three'—these are three knights—'although born of different mothers, they meet together in Ling,' the kingdom of Gesar." The simple stanzas embody both the sense that Tibet is the mother of the world's rivers, as known to the chroniclers of Gesar, and that these knights are the core of the great Ling lineages, the clans that dominate the Gesar epic. For Phon Dza, and for the Khamba who inhabit the mountains and pasturelands here, the Gesar, more even than the abstruse complexities of Tibetan Buddhist texts, is the central fable in their lives, an epic that predates Buddhism and recounts all that was true and magisterial in Tibetan history, and it carries in it as well a lingering vision of what life could yet be, one that is purely Tibetan, one that is not Chinese.

Although Phon Dza admitted he had never been to the places where the Dzachu first comes from the earth, and believed that he would never in this life see them, he said that like all who live along the river, he revered them. "There are," he said, "two sources of the Dzachu. We call one Chugo Tashi Khenba," roughly, Auspicious Omniscient Source, "and we call one Dzanak Chugo," or Black Source. "In the summer the high lamas go to the sources and offer prayers. The lamas spend one night at each source to pray. They pray for all the people. The two sources keep the people alive. The lamas pray for the river to keep flowing. When they go, the lamas burn incense and put up prayer flags."

Phon Dza's eyes wandered toward the river's elbow, and then he said: "The source, it is a sacred place."

For me, that place, the exact source, that bit of earth where the first waters of the Mekong emerge, was in itself unimportant. Rather, the importance of the river's source in the life of the people who live here is what carried meaning. Though we were seated here nearly seventy miles from the geographic birth of the Mekong, I sensed that this was my source. This place, I felt, was as good as any for the beginning of my journey, this green bosomy slope where the Mekong first filters into the consciousness and purpose of people's lives. For Phon Dza, it was life; it was where his yaks went to drink, an icy highway into Dzatoe during winter, a swimming hole for the children in summer (albeit a very chilly one), a river of legend, a thing of beauty.

In truth, as Phon Dza recounted, his life has not always been as his father's had been. For two decades, from around 1960 into the 1980s, Communist officials, in various guises, depending, he supposed, on which political faction was ascendant in the capital, forced nomads into communes where herds were shared and worked collectively, meals taken together for a time and Communist indoctrination—"teachings," he called it derisively—were a daily ritual. It was in vain, he laughed, although his weathered face betrayed a hint of sadness. "Nobody believes the Chinese," he said. "But what can we do? We are poor people. We have no way to fight armies. We are just yak herders." To this day, he said, many yaks are still owned by the government, a remnant of the days of collectivism, and a practice, I hazarded, of dubious legality. He equivocated some when asked the size of his own herd—the government tries to levy a tax based on herd sizes—but Dakpa guessed it was about sixty, with additional yaks under his care belonging to the government.

"Now they leave us alone," Phon Dza said, a weariness, and some confusion, I suppose, setting in at questions about things he assumed everybody knew. "Myself, I don't know any Chinese people. This is not their place." There is in the solitude of nomadic life a pace, a rhythm, a sensibility that is not easily accessible to the outsider. Even Dakpa, who spent many years in a Tibetan monastery and who is a master of three Tibetan dialects, admitted that he found it hard to keep a conversation flowing. Long pauses would seep into our conversation, normally after Phon Dza replied to a question, moments of silence that were never uncomfortable and were clearly inherent to the pattern of life here.

There was no sign, spoken or visible, just a feeling that Phon Dza had said all he wanted to: Dakpa sensed before I did that our visit should end. We rose from the rugs, thanked Phon Dza for the tea and our talk and headed down the hill. Never once, in our hours with him, did anyone else from his family speak.

As we tramped down the hill to our car, there was around us a profound silence unlike almost anything I have felt. The Dzachu was too far away for its flow to be heard, and there were no yaks near us. Unlike the quiet of a cave, which always struck me as a silence that forcefully pushes in on you, like strapping pillows to each ear, the silence of the Tibetan plateau was deep and boundless, stretching into an infinite, unscarred blue that domed over us. It took me a moment to hear this silence, to be startled by its all-embracing totality. As Dakpa and I stood still on the grassy hillside, where there was none of the background noise of the daily life I knew— the buzz of computers, the grumble of an engine, a child's laugh, the rattle of a chain-link fence, the bark of a dog, the whine of an airplane, the bell of a trolley, the slam of a distant door, the sound of a page turning—the silence was at once empty and full, a sensation of utter absence and yet overwhelming presence, something strangely whole.

We resumed walking, our feet crunching in the short grass. Here and there, clumps of tall iron grass sprouted, each blade tough as plastic binding and a yard or more long. Tiny blue and white wildflowers speckled pies of yak dung. A field mouse, perhaps what is called the high-mountain mouse, scampered by and an unruly flock of tiny birds picked at the ground farther down. A couple of yaks, their coats thick and matted in anticipation of the coming winter, lifted their heads from the grass and eyed our descent, unmoving and unmoved by our passing.

This hill was the beginning of my journey, a place new for me, although I was not unfamiliar with Tibet itself. I knew after many years living in

China that Chinese culture, its political rigidities and cultural chau-
vinisms, had bludgeoned Tibet in ways irreparable. More than a decade
before, on several trips to central Tibet, I had visited the great monasteries in and around Lhasa and seen the effects of whiplike political
vengeance against Tibetans and their fidelity to their faith and to the
Dalai Lama. In much of central Tibet, where there had been hundreds
upon hundreds of monasteries, there was nothing more than pocked and
stumpy earthen ramparts, eroded walls of prayer halls and monks' chambers, seemingly a scene from antiquity, not, as they were, the remains of a
very recent rampage of destruction. I wondered at the time how or
whether recovery from such devastation was possible. As I prepared to follow the Mekong, to hear this river's tale, I would see.

At the bottom of the hill I stopped again, this time to watch the
river as it curled by, and reflected on the journey ahead. Phon
Dza and his family, at one end of this great river, lived lives that
had been shaken by Chinese occupation, but had emerged to live much
as their ancestors had—simple lives by our urban lights, but lives harsh,
unforgiving, bound by seasonal rhythms. Yet there was a kind of purity
to their existence that is not easily dismissed, not in the cloying or
precious "back-to-nature" sense, but in its enduring quality, in the sense
that their lives are a strand in a bruised and battered culture, a culture
China wants to scrub away, installing its hollow shell in museums and in
rigorously policed Tibetan monasteries, mummifying Tibet for curious
onlookers.

Much of the trip ahead would be through fractured or dying cultures,
through societies that had turned on themselves or been savaged by outsiders. Much of the trip, though, would be, I hoped, a window into how
cultures draw the wagons into a circle, as it were, to preserve themselves.
Not all, I suspected, would be successful, but others would have managed
to survive. On the hill where Phon Dza lived, no Chinese has probably
ever walked, and yet China stakes its claim to his hill, his home, his life.
That claim, and its consequences, have led to four decades of bloodshed
and oppression in Tibet, the exile of its spiritual leader, the kidnapping
and disappearance of what Tibetans believe to be the incarnation of the
second-ranking lama, and the flight of virtually the entire learned assembly of senior monks. But for Phon Dza, the land, his family, his yaks, the

river, shape a world of meaning that is not so easily erased. I was buoyed by his toughness, by the receding sight of his three black tents on that hill.

It was late afternoon when we reached Dzatoe. A few kerosene lanterns inside buildings were already lit. A solitary power line ran into the town from the east, but it had been cut long ago. The broad arrow of concrete slicing down Dzatoe's core was empty, except for a few children rolling a car tire down the center line. At the western edge of town, a small concrete bridge hung over a rush of the river.

On the bridge, a group of young men, loafing, flicking pebbles, watching women in their long *chuba*—a fleece-lined robe made snug at the waist often with a belt and carefully tooled silver buckle—wore brilliant red, black and white baseball caps; emblazoned on the front of each were the words *Chicago Bulls*. As successful and renowned as Chicago's basketball team was, I wondered how its popularity had seeped across the Tibetan plateau so effortlessly, particularly to a place notable for its lack of electricity.

"Tchee-khaa-ghhoo-bools," pronounced one young man, holding his cap in front of his panoramic mirrored sunglasses in an attempt to read the unfamiliar letters. "Tchee-khaa-ghhoo-bools," he repeated. And what, I asked, did he believe the "bools" to be? He shook his head, the long hair of his Khamba heritage spilling down to his shoulders. "I don't know. What is it?" he murmured in Tibetan, Dakpa shaping his words into English. I offered a summary of basketball and the notion that there were teams of men in the United States who played this game, many of whom made millions of dollars tossing an inflated ball through a steel hoop. The young man squeezed his brow in skeptical furrows but carefully repositioned his cap on his head. "One day," he explained, "a truck came with piles of clothes and bags of hats, just like these. Everybody has a hat like this." His friends nodded at this, carefully adjusted the rake of their caps so that the brims yawed jauntily to port or starboard, and then they sauntered over to a row of outdoor pool tables arrayed at one end of the bridge. Pool is the one game that appears to have swept across China, into even its most remote corners. Although few tables are without rips in the felt, cues are often warped and tipless, and the balls are dented and chipped, young men—never women, it seems—can be seen rocketing balls into pockets hour after hour at roadside pool halls in a haze of cigarette smoke.

Commerce in Dzatoe, a settlement of just a couple of thousand people, was rudimentary. Merchants, often women, laid out their wares on a plastic sheet alongside the road: cooking woks, knives and black iron cleavers, locks, hammers, Buddhist amulets, gray-brown wool sweaters, glass bottles, Chinese-made batteries, maybe a thermos bottle or two, horse bridles, piles of diminutive iron horseshoes, white ceramic bowls, lengths of chain, packs of cigarettes, green Chinese police jackets, stacks of "Tchee-khaa-ghhoo-bools" caps. Nomads drift into town, selling yak butter, yak-wool blankets, yak meat and yak-skin leather straps. A few shopfronts along the main street offered a bit wider selection of goods, including basic Chinese-manufactured clothing in a startling range of grays.

A military garrison butts up against the main street as well, and a handful of buzz-cut soldiers hung white T-shirts on lines and shuffled about a cement courtyard in rubber flip-flops. Like many towns in Tibet, Chinese rule is ensured by both the army and contingents of secret police, although to the Tibetans they are the not-so-secret police, who monitor anti-Chinese sentiment and activity. Since 1959, when the Dalai Lama, Tibet's spiritual and political leader, was forced into exile in India ahead of a massive Chinese invasion, there has been sporadic resistance to Chinese occupation, some armed, most merely nonviolent protest. In the late 1980s, marches by Buddhist monks were bloodily suppressed, some monks and nuns killed, many imprisoned and others forced to flee into exile. China's surveillance of Tibet's monasteries dramatically increased, and monks were forced to attend political reeducation classes. Political monitors were stationed at all monasteries, restrictions were placed on the number of new novices and all pictures of the Dalai Lama were banned. Here in Dzatoe, however, remoteness has entailed less attention from Chinese authorities. While unhappiness and anger over China's occupation of their land remains pervasive, most Tibetans in this region are nomads and are more concerned with their herds of yaks and sheep. China is something very far away.

Dzatoe is the first town on the Mekong, and it is a spiritless, desolate outpost. Perhaps early remote towns in the American West resembled this place, at least in terms of their isolation and the rigors of life. Dzatoe itself exudes no breath of adventure or future; much of the time, lonely towns along stagecoach lines in the American West must have shared this sense of estrangement from any greater beyond. This is not a place of beginnings, more a dead-end, the last dot on a map before it blurs into an uncharted realm of mountains, ravines and the birth of rivers. At least this is what it must feel like for a Chinese unfortunate enough to be sent here. For Tibetans, though, it is a gateway, if a fairly ramshackle one, to the world beyond. For young men of daring and means, there are 100 c.c. motorcycles to be had. At makeshift, one-room theaters, there are images of the outside world on televisions and videocassette recorders powered by car batteries. There is beer to drown sorrows, and higher-octane liquor for a price. And for the gastronomically adventurous, there is rice.

A short gambol from the most elegant hostelry in town, a ten-room truck-stop guest house where we rented two grime-smeared, cement-walled rooms, the owner of a small restaurant welcomed us, ushering us into a room soupy with cigarette smoke. Presciently, Dakpa that morning had asked him to chill several bottles of beer in the frigid waters of the Dzachu so that we would be spared the warm beer that is customarily consumed, warm because there are no refrigerators and more importantly because that is how beer has always been drunk here. Like pool tables, beer is ubiquitous in China and Tibet, under a myriad of labels and in a rather alarming spectrum of palatability. The evening's beverage was Yellow River Beer.

At a round table next to ours, a group of local officials well into their cups were loudly toasting one another over glass thimbles of clear Chinese *gaoliang*, a distilled sorghum-based liqueur of considerable potency. Our host sent a young boy down to the river to retrieve our beer, which he plopped unceremoniously on the table in a plastic string bag, river water running copiously over the wood-topped surface. I was drained by the trek up the mountain, far more so than Dakpa, who seemed invigorated by the pile of potatoes and wok-fried yak meat that was delivered to the table. In this land where rice is not grown, there was even a bowl of rice, although the grains were crumpled and tasteless. Very quickly, even before we had made it through a helping of food, glasses of *gaoliang* appeared on our table and the expectant faces of the officials next to us were plastered with uncoordinated grins. Courtesy, certainly more than desire, required a toast and a quick shot of the liqueur. It seemed, however, that one was not enough.

The loudest of the voices at the neighboring table was that of a Tibetan in a Mao-style blue jacket, who noisily scraped his chair over to our table, swiveled unsteadily to reach behind him for the bottle and insisted we join him in one more toast. He wore huge-lensed glasses that lent him a fish-eyed cast. His jacket was unbuttoned and rumpled, but he displayed a surprising talent for filling the glass thimbles without spilling a drop, despite his utter drunkenness. "You are a foreign friend," he announced to the restaurant. I agreed I was foreign. "You must drink with us." And so, against my better judgment and habits, I did. "My name is Gyaltsen Sangpo," he informed us. "I am the chief of animal husbandry here." And with that, he poured himself another drink and shot it back in an effortless motion.

In Tibet, low-level government jobs are usually held by locals who have displayed at least a measure of fealty to China. In Lhasa, Tibet's capital, even some of the most senior positions are filled by ethnic Tibetans, although the policies they advocate and implement are dictated by Beijing. But Sangpo was a very big man in Dzatoe, the chief of all things involving yaks. After a respite in the drinking, I managed to ask him a question that had occurred to me earlier in my conversation with Phon Dza. How many yaks did the government own? I wanted to know. "Yaks," he bellowed in Chinese, not Tibetan, "yaks. The government owns no yaks." A younger colleague, also Tibetan, leaned over and loudly whispered in his ear. "Yes, yes, yes . . . ," he said. "There are some yaks with no owners but they are taken care of by yak herders." Were not, I wondered, these technically government-owned yaks? "These yaks are under the control of the government, but they are not owned by the government," he answered, a reply of a somewhat elusive logic. It did appear, however, that vestiges of the collective economy of more than two decades ago remained here, although it seemed confined to yaks.

Across China the state has withdrawn from large sectors of the economy. In major industrial centers like Shenyang in Manchuria, huge factories remain state-owned, inefficient and often bankrupt by any sensible accounting standard. But almost everywhere, private enterprise has flourished in businesses as diverse as cosmetics and dot-coms, pharmaceuticals and diesel engine manufacturing, factories churning out Christmas ornaments and those making camping gear, toys, laptop computers and a thousand other products. Here in Dzatoe, the government has little presence or effect, apart from a handful of petty officials and the army garrison; there is not even a bank.

Sangpo helped himself to one more thimble and rose from our table, but not before scribbling his name and his position in my notebook. He then carefully, and with some pride, wrote down his phone number, adjusted his Mao jacket and retreated into the blackness outside. (In a place with no electricity, I failed to understand how a phone could work.)

In a faint dawn glow the following morning, as I prepared to leave Dzatoe and accompany the Mekong on its journey south, I stood on the river's
northern bank watching the water slide past. Over a period of some 20
million years, geologists suggest, this plateau had been formed as the
Indian landmass pushed against Tibet, a relentless pressure that heaved
and cracked the Earth's crust to create the Himalayas; and as India continued its intense northward thrust, it began burying itself under what is
now the Tibetan plateau, raising it over the millennia to its current altitude of fifteen thousand feet. Ultimately, the collision of these landmasses
produced yawning gorges amid ragged mountain chains, three of which
are now the riverbeds of the Salween, Yangze and Mekong Rivers. The
resulting geology is formidable and forbidding. For me, stretches of the
upper Mekong would prove impossible to reach. But these were also
stretches that were uninhabited, along which no road ran and no settlements were known. For a time, I realized I would have to be content with
a general proximity to the river.

With a thud, Dzatoe's brief swathe of a concrete main street gave
way at the town's edge to packed dirt that meandered across the
plateau grasslands, worn dry and ragged by trucks hauling people or rice or beer to distant settlements. Sudden, looming mountainsides
pushed the dirt track on its course, onto the flatlands or alongside a river
that ran down from still more distant mountains. At times, the road dis-
solved into a crosshatch of eroded runnels and the driver yanked the
wheel hard and set out across the grasslands, toward a gap in the hills that
camped on the horizon. Every couple of hours a truck would jounce by, it,
too, weaving across the plateau far from the road, its driver wrestling with
the huge steering wheel, a cigarette ubiquitously hanging from his lower
lip. No one waved.

Dusk crept over us, and the road arched into a clump of ochre mud
structures, each facing a mud-walled courtyard, a way station for truckers.
We swung through a gate into one of the courtyards, the largest here, a
cloud of fine dust boiling over us in the thin air. A burnished copper streak
of cloud painted the sky. Across the courtyard, like badly fitted dentures, a
row of four blue-plank doors gaped into makeshift adobe rooms, a wood
frame bed against each wall. Opposite the gate, from the door of a larger

mud building, a Tibetan man in well-worn black trousers and a nappy gray wool sweater waved us to a greasy plank table where two Tibetan women set before us pottery bowls brimming with a steaming stew of yak meat and thick noodles—each less than 50 cents. A chicken squawked from a basket hanging from a dowel on the wall, and a stretch of cracked plastic sheeting above our table helped shield us from the wind that had picked up.

Just as we finished our stew, three Khamba, a man and two teenagers, clip-clopped into the courtyard on tiny Tibetan horses. Like most Khamba, the older of the three wore his hair long, wound in a thick red braided cord, or *tashup*. From his belt that cinctured a heavy brown wool sweater hung his *grai*, the elaborately tooled silver-sheathed knife that fathers give their sons when they reach the age of twelve or thirteen. Tall, with high, chiseled cheekbones, an Aquinnah nose and a ruddy, flushed brown complexion, his visage resembled that of some American Indians.

"Come and drink with us," he invited, abruptly and commandingly, in the Tibetan dialect spoken here. He motioned us out through the gate and down the road several hundred yards to another adobe structure. He rode past the gate nodding slightly—a sign of the evening's earlier revelry—dismounted and tossed the reins of his horse to the teenagers, who tied the three horses to the gate. As we entered the courtyard, more a corral, the master of the house was already unfolding small tables and arranging some new blue and white molded plastic chairs for us in the courtyard. From a plastic crate, he pulled liter bottles of Yellow River Beer. Inside his pounded-mud-walled house, an iron-bellied stove stoked with yak dung heated a blackened aluminum kettle.

"You are welcome here," our host, Tashi Tso, said, scurrying about to make sure we were comfortably ensconced. He said he was in the process of opening a truck-stop eatery, a place where the wheelmen of the cargo trucks that rattled through here could stop and relax. There were no women of easy virtue that I could see, a fixture long associated with truck stops across China; no women at all, in fact. The tall Khamba lowered his frame fluidly into a blue bucket chair, his fist clamped around a Yellow River.

"My name is Ngi Mog," he said, his face and hair gleaming with a patina of yak butter, its salty-soury odor raking my nostrils. Edges of a yellow satin jacket peaked from under the stretched collar of his sweater. "I live far up those hills," he said, gesturing into the night. Overhead, a river of light, the Milky Way, washed across the blackness and a three-quarter moon cast its timorous glow over us. "I am thirty-six years old and I have eight children," he went on, raising the bottle to his lips between sentences. I asked him about China's official dictate that families should have no more than one child, although there are dispensations for what the Chinese patronizingly call "national minorities."

"Hah, the Chinese. We never pay attention to them. They do not come here. They are not welcome here. We do things the way we always have, the way our fathers did, the way their fathers did." Ngi Mog uttered these words, it seemed to me, not with arrogance or bravado, but with a matter-of-factness, perhaps tinged only a little with the obvious disdain he felt for Chinese. The Khamba have cultivated a reputation for a ferocious sense of independence and long were the armed defenders of Tibetan civilization. When the Chinese army occupied Tibet, first in 1950, and then in overwhelming force in 1959, thousands of Khamba were slaughtered as they sought with antiquated rifles and muskets to repulse China's far more modern army. China's victory, absolute though it was in military terms, instilled among Tibetans a deep and virulent hatred of both China and the Chinese. Indeed, in the many journeys I have made to Tibet, I have never met a Tibetan who expressed anything other than a fulsome antipathy toward the occupiers.

Ngi Mog took a long and final swig of beer, set the bottle on the table and rose to his feet, swaying like a wind-whipped pine. He clasped his hands together in front of him and, looking unblinkingly into my eyes, announced, "I will sing three songs for you. I will sing a song of welcome. I will sing a song of my people. And I will sing a song of farewell." And then, amid the chilled stillness of that Tibetan night, Ngi Mog's voice pierced the silence, rising and falling in the folk cadence of Tibet, his words stealing across the plateau toward the hills, his song careering through three octaves as he tilted his face to the night.

> Nga tso dhe la zom zom kasang la,
> Ten dhu zom gyu chung na kasang la,
> Ten dhu zom pe mi la kasang la,
> Nyung shi ghue chag maa dang kasang la. . . .

> *We are meeting here today,* kasang la . . .
> *I hope we will meet here often as today,* kasang la . . .
> *Let us always be happy,* kasang la . . .
> *Let us enjoy every moment,* kasang la. . . .

When his last syllable echoed away in steamy breath, he smiled slightly, turned and teetered toward his mount. His teenage companions hoisted him into his saddle, unwrapped the reins of their horses from the gatepost and the three trotted away into the darkness. Ngi Mog's song was one that has been sung here for generations, and it left me tingling.

That night, we slept in the mud-walled rooms on boards softened by a mattress filled with barley husks. A thin candle cast a faint glow on walls gouged by previous guests and a pounded-dirt floor on which a dung-cake brazier offered scant warmth. Morning came early, clean and cold, and the owner of the compound herded us into his faded, whitewashed one-room home for breakfast. We scrunched around a dung-fueled stove, rubbing our hands, sipping from ceramic bowls of tea. I ate my usual breakfast of instant oatmeal, bags of which I had brought in abundance for my voyage. Fixed to one wall was a poster of the Potala Palace, the former residence of the Dalai Lama in Lhasa, and a portrait of the former Panchen Lama, the Tibetan lama regarded as the second most sacred personage in Tibetan Buddhism.

I handed our host a 100-yuan bill, about $12, to cover our meals and board. He fingered it carefully, feeling for the series of anti-counterfeiting bumps along the margin of the bill. "There's so much fake money," he said in a low voice. "Drivers bring fake money here. There's also fake honey and other fake things." He sighed slightly and shook his head as he made change. "The problem isn't with fake things. The problem is with people."

From our way station, the track ran east and north to Jyekundo. We were on the road by eight o'clock, winding up through low mountains, easing away from the river. For several hours we passed no other car or truck, a certain sign that the road was blocked ahead; the truckers leaving eastern Qinghai for Dzatoe should have passed us by now, the driver insisted anxiously. After rounding a hairpin curve high up the side of a mountain, we saw a string of trucks, a few cars and a bus backed up along the road across the ravine. Ahead, the bridge of logs and boulders that spanned a small, tumbling torrent had collapsed. Under the gaze of three maroon-robed Buddhist monks, drivers and passengers labored to reposition the heavy stone and recover some of the logs that had catapulted down the gorge. After two hours of impromptu engineering, a bridge barely half the width of the original had been fashioned and the first truck eased across, directed by a monk with the aplomb of a New York City traffic cop.

Our turn came, and we squeezed as if on tiptoe over the bridge, its beams groaning under the car's carriage. The road, now scarcely wide enough for a single vehicle, laced along a mountainside, fallen rocks littering the dirt surface here and there. After another hour, a landslide of rock from the mountainside blocked most of the road. A few workers with shovels and pickaxes were desultorily gnawing away at the rockfall and a makeshift track had been flattened over the slide, a track that edged the car around the slide at what I deemed a precarious angle. As we surveyed the situation, the driver noticed that our gas tank was leaking; a small puddle of gasoline was forming in just the minute or so we had been stopped. We had to move quickly. The cliff edge to our left allowed little margin of error, or maneuverability, but with tires spinning against the loose gravel, we clawed around the rock pile and made for Jyekundo.

When Dakpa, I and the driver—who piloted the fifteen-year-old tan Mitsubishi with a languor that bespoke life's absence of urgencies— arrived toward noon, heading east, officious policemen in rumpled green uniforms and oversized sunglasses were blocking traffic into the central intersection as workmen struggled to position a cement cast horseman onto a gray-slabbed pedestal. As urban art, there is far worse in China, but the chip in the horse's tail seemed unlikely to receive attention in the near future.

Our car, parched for fuel, squatted at a makeshift gasoline station, a cement blockhouse with two windows and a greasy phalanx of oil drums out front. While Dakpa and I wandered the town, the driver somehow repaired the leaking gas tank without sparking a conflagration. When we returned to the car, a young attendant was sucking on a clear plastic tube poking from the top of a drum until the rush of gasoline ballooned his cheeks. Deftly, and without any noticeable revulsion, he transferred the tube to the gasoline spout on the car and filled its tank, each liter measured by a glass cylinder fixed to the top of the drum.

The streets of Jyekundo were teeming with Khamba who had come into the big city for trading, gawking, arranging horse sales and sampling the high life of restaurants, karaoke bars and electricity. It was the type of town that was springing up all across China, one suddenly filled with consumer goods from coastal factories—boom boxes to blare Tibetan music, televisions, electric thermoses, fake Nike sneakers. Modernish barbershops and massage parlors squeezed between ranks of restaurants, pharmacies and music audiocassette stores; small clothing emporiums displayed the latest clothes from southern China's garment factories. Even here, as remote as this place was, one could sense the power of China's accelerating economy and the force of commerce that is transforming China faster than at any time in its history.

We stopped for lunch in a small place run by Tibetans but serving a mélange of Tibetan and Sichuan food—yak meat fried up in the hot, tingly, somewhat airy and peppery *mala* spices of Sichuan. A young Khamba, his hair elaborately rolled in a red *tashu* with five large silver ornaments and an ivory ring the size of a powdered-sugar doughnut woven into his locks, sat at one of the rickety Formica-topped tables fixedly watching a television showing a Hong Kong–produced kung fu drama, the device wound to what I guessed was maximum volume. As we ordered, an older man wheeled his bicycle through the door, the carcass of half a pig lashed to the rear rack, and rolled into the kitchen. Lunch. Two Khamba women, their robes ragged and their hair matted with leaves, shuffled into the restaurant begging. Dakpa dropped a few coins in their wooden bowl. Then he sighed.

Like many Tibetans, Dakpa's life had been buffeted by China's invasion of his homeland. Born in Belakopi, in southern India, where his parents had fled before the Chinese army in 1959, he returned to his family's hometown of Gyalthang in his late twenties after studying Buddhist scriptures at one of the Tibetan monasteries established in exile in southern India. His father also returned, although his mother and sisters remained in India, and spent his final days wandering the main street of Gyalthang in northern Yunnan, often alone and seemingly lost. Dakpa, though, learned Chinese, which he speaks with a thick Tibetan accent, tinted with the Hindi he also learned along the way. His life, in many respects, mirrors the history of his people, a life of deep belief, exile and return. And yet, though he shares the widespread Tibetan loathing of the Chinese, he somehow manages to rise above the resentments and wounds of Chinese occupation; indeed, his cheeriness in the face of China's policies sometimes infuriated me (irrationally, I know). It was not a cheeriness at the plight of his people, though, but a genuine sense that his identity and faith could never be tainted or erased by China. And that was a determination I saw repeatedly in Tibet.

On the way into Dzatoe and back we regularly queried truckers about road conditions and now were dismayed to learn that the dirt track portentously named Highway 214 that ran south to Chamdo was blocked by landslides. It was not to be the first mountain cave-in to force me off course. The track that ran east from Dzatoe toward Jyekundo eases away from the river, into mountains and new pasturelands. We changed our plans. Our goal now was Sershu, a small town in Sichuan Province, in what used to be part of Tibet before it was sliced away by Chinese administrators. From there I hoped we could go south, and then west to Chamdo. A road of rock and dust rose before us, unyielding and empty, into the crumpled folds of treeless, slate gray mountains. Although Sershu lies scarcely 120 miles from Jyekundo, it took six hours to creep around rock falls, find our way across grasslands and crawl, shudderingly, over a track seemingly raised from a river bottom and baked into a lunar crust.

In 1996, a winter storm of once-in-a-generation intensity here brought temperatures of 40 degrees below zero Centigrade and smothering snow-falls. Yak and sheep herds were decimated, some nomadic herders perished and in small towns like Sershu several townspeople froze to death. As severe as that winter was, government relief efforts were desultory, not in the least because catastrophic flooding along the Yangze River, an increasingly frequent occurrence, had sapped the government's attention, resources and energy. Oxfam, a private relief agency, sent a field-worker to the region three years later to assess needs, but its own resources were modest.

Sershu popped up around a quick bend a bit like a jack-in-the-box. We bumped onto new concrete streets utterly and eerily empty, flanked on both sides by newish, blocky concrete buildings. There were no lights, electricity a convenience evidently not available to many such remote outposts. At the other end of town, an open gate led into a cement-slab courtyard of a government guest house. Again, there was not a soul about. The driver, by now exhausted from the day's work of wrestling the car through the mountains, banged on the horn and yelled out the open window. Several minutes later, a steel door on one of the buildings creaked open and a young Tibetan woman shuffled over to us, apparently startled that anyone could possibly be there. After some negotiations, principally involving descriptions of the earlier rigors of our journey, keys to the wing reserved for senior government officials, whoever they might happen to be, appeared, and we were ushered into rooms with real beds, real mattresses and hefty, clean comforters. I collapsed, senseless, and remained there until a cold shaft of morning sun knifed into the room.

Dakpa accompanied the sun's piercing blindness with a timpanic tattoo on the door, and a steaming cup of instant coffee. Although autumn had not yet begun, already the morning air was frigid. From here in Sershu, my journey would take me south, through the eastern periphery of Tibet and over the next months toward China's border with Laos. Where the river ran there were few Chinese; indeed, my hope was to find echoes of the journey to China's edges described by Gao Xingjian, who was later to win the Nobel Prize for literature, in his magisterial novel *Soul Mountain*. In 1983, Gao, who was hounded by Beijing's literary apparatchiks for his avant-garde plays and writings, set out for China's remotest border regions, a journey that became the biographical foundation for his novel. Wrestling with the central question of what it means to be human, Gao searches among the multiplicity of ethnic groups on China's borders for a sort of primeval wisdom, probing for humanity in the myths spoken by people he encounters, in a forest ranger's hut, in dreams of death, in folk songs—"This is a folk song which hasn't been vandalized by the literati," his novel's narrator is told, a pointed reference to China's intrusion into other cultures.

Though my goal was less ontological than Gao and that of his narrator in *Soul Mountain*, I too sought unvandalized cultures. But because my journey was not a novel, I recognized that what lay ahead—and lay behind in Phon Dza's and Ngi Mog's lives—were not unshadowed by upheaval and change. The Mekong, I hoped, would carry me into the lives of people for whom modernity did not entail the obliteration of traditional culture—as it has for much of Han China—and for whom traditional culture carried meaning and hope.

We intended to make an early start, not sure where the day's end would leave us, but first we decided to stop for breakfast at a small Tibetan eatery just where the town peters out into vast grasslands. When we lifted the thick, felt-backed door flap, an off-white panel quilted with blue and yellow and red triangles, the entire family was snuggled up in two beds under a pile of thick, satin-covered comforters, the beds neatly pushed against the walls of what during waking hours was the dining room. A single bare electric bulb, unlit, hung from the ceiling, and high on the whitewashed walls were plain board shelves piled with ceramic and plastic bowls, a clutter of aluminum pans charred by use and a small number of glasses. A single burner fired by bottled gas was in one corner. An iron stove fired by dried and odorless yak dung and piney scrap wood sat heavily in a makeshift kitchen. As our sleepy hosts padded around, waking up and setting out low stools for us to sit on, the husband, who had slipped into a gray jacket with MARIOGIO ALEXIO emblazoned in crimson on the back, clicked on a battery-powered tape recorder and the sound of Buddhist chants filled the room. A portrait of the Dalai Lama draped in white silk prayer scarves, what the Tibetans call *katta*, was propped on a shelf.

Our host pulled the tea churn from a corner and filled it with hot water, tea leaves, several heaping spoonfuls of salt and dollops of yak butter and then squished the plunger up and down, and remembered that winter of 1996. "We were alone here in Sershu," he said, as Dakpa translated from the Tibetan. "Nothing came here and no one could go out. All the roads were finished. I heard that many yaks died. Some people died also. It seemed like the end of the world." We hurried through breakfast, hoping to find a way into Chamdo this day or soon.

On the highway maps that can be purchased in state-owned bookstores in big cities, China is a mesh of roads and highways in thick blues, reds and yellows. In eastern China, along the coast from Guangzhou to Beijing, the most developed and densely populated part of the country, there is a fair correspondence between the maps and the pavement on the ground. But in the remoter parts of western China, the thick red line numbered 317 we needed to use was a channel of dirt and rough stone that challenged us to exceed twenty-five miles per hour. China's truckers, the ragged men who manhandled rattling, institutional-blue, Liberation-brand open-back trucks over these roads, served as fellow captains of the road, warning of shoals, rapids and blockages ahead. In the days that followed, these truckers were bearers of disappointment, fleeting hopes and reckless encouragement.

Off to the west, shielded by snow-dipped mountains, the Dzachu flowed from Dzatoe toward the ancient Tibetan trading town and way station of Chamdo, the river anonymous, unharried, essing through valleys and around hills, turning southeast toward a mating with the Ngomchu, a small tributary. For more than a millennium, the settlement at Chamdo was at the crossroads of the two principal caravan routes in eastern Tibet: one, Yak Path, which linked the lowlands of Sichuan with Lhasa; and the second, Tea Horse Path, which ran south into what is now Yunnan Province, a land of lush rice fields and tea plantations. After the victory of Mao's Communist armies over Chiang Kai-shek's Nationalist forces in 1949, Chamdo, in the heart of Kham, was on the front line of Tibetan resistance against Chinese rule, principally because of its location on Tibet's eastern rim. This is where the Khamba revolts were bloodily suppressed.

For its part, China cloaked its terror in delusional propaganda. One such screed from 1958 ran like this: "The great Socialist revolution in the pastoral areas has been a very violent class struggle of life and death. At the debate meetings, the masses were so excited that they shouted continuously: Long Live Chairman Mao! Long Live the Communist Party! We Are Liberated!" Hardly. No one knows how many Tibetans have died battling the People's Liberation Army in the half-century since Chinese troops first garrisoned themselves in Chamdo in 1950, but what is manifestly clear is that Chinese control over Tibet has been brutal. In the first decade of its occupation, Chinese cadres winnowed monks from monasteries at a ruthless pace. In 1950, it is estimated that as many as one quarter of the population belonged to a religious order; by 1958, there were 115,600 monks and nuns, a figure that plummeted to 18,100 monks in 1960, and then to only 970 monks by 1976, and these are official Chinese figures. All but a handful of monasteries—thick-walled, packed-mud complexes made up of hundreds of buildings, from monstrous prayer halls to hives of monks' cells—were leveled. Manuscripts, sacred texts and ancient images of Buddha were destroyed.

China's policy toward its colony has, under unrelenting Western criticism, become a bit more nuanced, although, from the perspective of most Tibetans, as stringent and purposeful and equally repressive as before. Lhasa, the Vatican of Tibetan Buddhism, is today surrounded by six army garrisons. Three huge prison camps have been built in the northwest of the city, prisons that are filled with an uncertain number of monks, nuns and laypeople who protested or otherwise opposed Chinese rule. But more worrying to many Tibetans has been Beijing's policy of encouraging the migration of ethnic Chinese, the Han people, onto the Tibetan plateau. During the 1990s, the demography of Tibet was slowly transformed so that now one quarter of Tibet's population is Chinese. This migration, promoted aggressively by Beijing, has been concentrated in urban areas like Lhasa and Chamdo.

Indeed, in Chamdo, where the Chinese established their first military beachhead in Tibet, Chinese is heard more often than Tibetan. Unlike anywhere else in Tibet, Chamdo feels like a Chinese city, a place of Sichuan restaurants, blocky Chinese buildings with blue-glass windows and white-tile facing, and streets filled more with shorter, paler Chinese than the ruddy-complexioned Khamba who used to call this place home. So dramatic has been the influx of Chinese into Tibet that the Dalai Lama has warned that "the very survival of Tibetans as a distinct people is under constant threat" from the tide of Chinese migrants.

It is into this Sinicized ancient Tibetan town that the Dzachu flows, larger and bolder now, as if girding itself for its powerful charge through the mountains and gorges to come. And although until Chamdo the Dzachu runs with an easiness that is almost inviting, there are no river craft here, no boats, none of the coracles, the round, yak-skin canoes that are used on rivers near Lhasa. Here the river is almost ignored. Never once did I see a Tibetan with a fishing rod, far less a net. Perhaps the fish life of the upper Dzachu is minimal, although that is unlikely. I found no Tibetan here who could talk about fish.

For most of the Dzachu's course in Tibet, its passing is seen by few humans; it rushes by few villages and no roads of any description; only the isolated nomad who squires his yaks past the river toward fresh pastures glimpses its waters. We rode south, paralleling the river, plotting our course against the determined obstructionism of nature. The rare road that turned west time and again was washed out, truncated by landslide, caved in. Our dwindling options hemmed us in, as did the mountains. I decided that our only course was to make for the valleys that some believe fired the 1935 imaginings of James Hilton, toward a lost horizon.

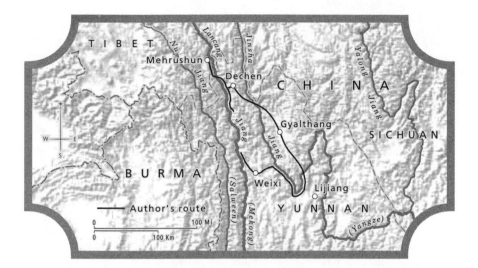

Two

Shangri-la

Marching south like immense armies in granite gray attire and white watch caps, three mountain ranges churn out of eastern Tibet into what is now northern Yunnan, hemming in the Yangze, the Salween and the Mekong, or as it is known by Chinese here, the Lancang Jiang: the Turbulent River. The Yangze, itself known here as the Jinsha, or Golden Sands River, lies over the Ningjing Range to the east, where it heads south for a time, then abruptly U-turns north only to U-turn south again in a sweeping hushed arc. Gradually, though, the Yangze nudges north yet again, and east toward China's major cities, past the industrial megalopolis of Chongqing, past the old capital of Nanjing—known as one of China's "four ovens" because of its furnacelike temperatures in summer—and then spills into the East China Sea just above Shanghai, the largest of China's cities, and one remaking itself into the country's fast, neoned, moneyed and cultural New York City. To the west, cradled between the Taniantawen and the Hengduan Ranges, the Salween, known here as the Nu Jiang, or the Angry River, rushes south. Virtually inaccessible here, it meanders not at all, dashing south almost in desperation through Yunnan and into Burma where it vents itself finally into the Andaman Sea. And while each of these rivers flows scarcely twenty miles from each other as they sprint from Tibet, they journey alone, in their own way, each colored by its own sands and muds and clays, each singing its own song. Even here, the Yangze is wide and mostly quiet, almost stately, but already dangerous in its vastness, while the Salween displays a recklessness, a rage that belies its ultimate placidity.

Between these two rivers, the Lancang Jiang rumbles and roars, stampeding through flat-walled canyons like a herd of bulls through the streets of Pamplona. At times, the canyons yield to the rumpled folds of mountains, some still bearded with virgin forests of towering spruce. From the crannies and nooks of each fold, small streams, young and brash, scuttle down the mountain to join the Lancang, now a complex river of pirouetting whirlpools, white-frothed eddies and rip currents, strange mirror pools and sharp elbows that brush away the mountains' skirts. And etched into the mountains thousands of feet above the river like the

A village nestled in the folds of the Himalayan
Mountains in southern Tibet

faintest tracing are centuries-old ribbon horse paths that climb and wend from one tiny Tibetan village to another and to patches of barley fields carved from sporadic level spots in the mountains, from a solitary, thick-walled, whitewashed mud house to an equally lonely, rejuvenated monastery seemingly velcroed to a mountain precipice.

Our car jolted south from Tibet into Yunnan Province along a rock-and-clay trail that had been hacked into the mountainside. Geologically, climatically and ethnically, Yunnan is the most diverse of China's provinces, ranging from the southern end of the Tibetan plateau to the tropical heat along the Laotian border, a landscape of snow-capped mountains, rubber plantations, rice paddies and plains. I knew that James Hilton's imagination was fueled by photographs of mountains and monasteries here, that the famous Burma Road of World War II had been hacked through Yunnan's mountain jungles, that some of Asia's most ancient music was played here and that where Yunnan bordered Burma, it was said that opium was plentiful. Here ancient and secluded non-Chinese kingdoms thrived into the twentieth century, China funneled armaments through here to Hanoi during the Vietnam War, and for the first time the Mekong was being dammed.

Where I stood now on the southern edge of the Tibetan plateau, the Mekong, now almost five hundred miles long, had already dropped nearly 5,500 feet from one of its sources at 16,441 feet, 9 inches. Evidence of clear-cut logging was apparent in some of the deeper valleys, where primeval forests remained until just a decade or so ago. In that time, loggers from Sichuan Province have penetrated even the most remote ravines in an insatiable quest for lumber; in their wake they have left stubbled mountains and valleys and have precipitated a pattern of erosion that has led to uncontrollable flooding and frequent, and increasingly catastrophic, landslides. At Mehrushun village, the consequences of laying waste to the forests was all around us.

Above the river, on a long platter of land that tilts, not quite steeply, toward the river, a scrabble of heavily seated Tibetan houses edge hanky-sized fields of barley. Between some of the houses, deep gashes cleaved into the cliffside were slowly widening, threatening to swallow a house here or there and spew it into the watery tumult below. Rickety plank walkways were rigged over the fissures between sections of the village, and the road itself, slightly above the houses, was already cracked and crumbling. As the car crunched over the gravel to a stop, we saw a flash of bold pink as a woman scampered down the hill toward one of the larger houses. "A wedding," Dakpa said. "Let's stop and see."

I followed Dakpa as he picked his way toward the house, teetered toward it on a split log thrown across a deep opening in the earth and clambered up another log, this one hatcheted with footholds, to the building's roof. We followed the sound of singing.

On the flat roof of the bride's house she sat cross-legged in front of a low, damask-covered table and a plate of four yellow apples. Her ink black hair was bound in a coil of red-pink-yellow-blue cording, and over a blinding pink shirt she wore a heavily gold-threaded brocade vest and a double string of amber and jade beads. A belt of deeply tooled silver rhomboid plates hung with chains of silver baubles cinched her waist. Her bridesmaid, similarly garbed, sat beside her, both smiling frequently at the fuss. The bride's name was Yongha.

She sat facing a long, rough-wood table of men—her father, uncles, brothers, the elders of the village—all in blue satin robes embroidered and edged in gold thread, and either in formidably tall fur hats (a bit like the bear-skin busbies worn by the guards at Buckingham Palace) or the wide-brimmed bush hats that are now common in Tibet; from each man's belt dangled a silver-handled knife in a tooled sheath. The groom, who had visited his bride in the morning, had retreated to his own family's house and was not permitted to be here for the festivities. A few paces behind Yongha, in single-sleeved, fur-cuffed jackets over high-necked pink shirts whose long tube sleeves brushed the ground, swayed eight Tibetan girls singing to the bride and her family; as they sang, they bowed and glided very slowly back and forth, rippling their sleeves, riverlike, before them.

Under the eaves of a rooftop room was gathered what must have been most of the rest of the village—women old and young in red cloth turbans, down vests and the tri-paneled rainbow-colored aprons so common here, and young children in sneakers and sweatshirts, all comfortably settled on sacks of grain. Small thimbles of a local wine moved around the table among the men, and the women sipped at small cups of tea or beer. And on the far edge of the roof was a small white satellite television dish, apparently for those moments when power found its way here, as it had at the moment.

The wedding of a Tibetan girl, Yongha, on the right,
seated, in the village of Mehrushun, high on a
precipice overlooking the Dzachu

"This is a love marriage," exclaimed Yongha's father between generous
gulps of wine. "The groom"—Little Ma—"came over this morning. He's
from Dechen," a town a few hours to the south. "All the bride's relatives
are here for the party. After five or six days, she will go to his house." As he
talked, uncles and male elders chanted into a microphone bits of Buddhist
scripture, folk sayings and songs; the eight dancers stood quietly and listened, waiting for their turn to sing again.

Then the bride's grandfather was handed the microphone, and he
began to talk, low and calm. "Everything looks so wonderful today," he
spoke, his eyes fixed on Yongha. "You have enough potatoes and rice, and
even a television. But that is not enough. You must be moral and study
hard. You should do good service for your husband. You must take care of
all things in the house and family. And remember, always come and see us.
You are very young. There are so many things to do. You have health and
your future. So make a family and do good things. . . ." His voice trailed
off, and Yongha, tears streaming down her face, wiped her cheek with her
shocking pink sleeve.

After a few sips of local wine—a concoction distilled from barley
grain—and a munch of an apple we edged off the roof and back to the

road. I surveyed the village as it sagged toward the cliff's edge, the tendrils of erosion and cracks creeping among the houses like an insidious, malignant skin disease. And in this case, of course, there was no way the people of Mehrushun could forestall the inevitable cataclysm, or even do much to allay its relentlessness. Below the village, full and loud, the Lancang coursed, indifferent to the small drama above, but certain to consume and pulverize whatever tumbled into its maw.

Mehrushun's impending fate is mirrored across swathes of China, across mountains and river valleys that have been denuded of vegetation by the country's bottomless hunger for lumber. Mountains and hillsides shaved as if by a barber line the country's rivers; their flanks of fragile soil, suddenly unanchored by the roots of the great spruce and fir that once adorned them, begin rapidly shifting, sliding, washing into the rivers. Bluffs crack, roads sliced into mountains collapse, whole villages cling to the lips of thin ridges as if by a single thread.

We pushed south toward Dechen, the northernmost Tibetan town in Yunnan, a town of some twenty thousand people wedged in the crook of a mountain fold. At a broad pass in the mountains, Dakpa, as he always did when reaching the highest point on a road, rolled down the window and bellowed: *"Ohhh, lha gyal lo, Ohhh lha gyal lo"*—roughly, "The victory of God's word"—a shout of spiritual joy and glory at the majesty of passing one of Earth's great divides. A roadside shrine, a latticework of wood draped in thousands of small red, white, yellow and blue prayer flags, like fluttering handkerchiefs in the thin, frigid air, stood beside the road. Many of the flimsy cotton flags were block-printed with the sacred mantra *Om Mani Padme Hum*, "Hail the Jewel in the Lotus," a reference to the Buddha himself. Dakpa, who carries a small stash of flags in his backpack, attached two flags—one for health, one for luck—and stood back to gaze at the range of mountains across the river.

"This is the Khabadkar Range," he said, waving a hand at the steep, snow-drenched peaks that paraded across the horizon. "And that"—he pointed to the highest peak, one scarred with an immense glacier—"is Khabadkar-po, what the Chinese call Meili Snow Mountain. It's a sacred mountain, and that is where I am going." Many Tibetans try once in their lives to visit two sacred places: one is the Jokhang, the St. Peter's Basilica of Tibetan Buddhism, in Lhasa; the other is Khabadkar-po, and many are content only to make a pilgrimage on foot around it. Dakpa, who held fiercely and happily to his Buddhism, was to leave me after Dechen and begin such a pilgrimage, complete with a small team of horses to haul his supplies. He figured it would take between ten and fourteen days to circumnavigate the mountain's girth, following the well-trod trail and camping each evening in the snow. A year later, when we met again in Tibet, he told me that it had taken him nearly a month and that he had seen the bodies of many pilgrims who had frozen to death in the cold. "It was very hard," he said. "Many of the pilgrims only wear their wool robes and boots. They are not dressed well at all. And many pilgrims are old and not healthy enough to walk so far. There are even some people who crawl around the mountain. It's very, very hard."

Near the flapping prayer flags was another shrine, this one in cement, and inscribed on it were the names of Tibetan, Japanese and Chinese climbers who had perished trying to conquer Khabadkar-po—not its circumference like pilgrims, but its summit. Eighty brass prayer drums were fixed in a cement wall; spinning the gleaming drums is thought to send prayers spiraling to heaven.

Behind us, from the north where we had just come, a sign warned travelers: "Beware. No hospitals beyond this point." Dechen was now just a few hours away. Around us, the mountains were a palette of greens, subdued reds, browns and grays, a bit like the sweater collection in a conservative men's store, and the mountain walls plummeted into the river ending in a jumble of boulders and fractured rock. The road, high up from the river, followed the folds of each mountain, swinging us into ravines and then back out to the precipice, all at a courtly twenty miles per hour. At each curve, the driver hammered the horn to warn the improbable oncoming truck, or even more unlikely car. Even after many weeks of being on the road, I still sucked my breath when the driver wrestled the Mitsubishi around sharp curves, several-thousand-foot drops only inches from our wheels.

In 1933, James Hilton, an English writer of modest repute, published a small novel about a sacred utopian kingdom hidden away in the Himalayas, in a place that strongly resembled Tibet. It was a story of a man named Hugh Conway and three companions whose plane crashed in a hermetic kingdom overseen by a Buddhist lamasery—with the rather odd happenstance of a Catholic priest as abbot—which exercised benevolent and mystical rule over a society where people lived two hundred years and, gloriously, possessed modern plumbing. Early on in the book, which Hilton titled *Lost Horizon*, he writes of this magical land:

> To Conway, seeing it first, it might have been a vision fluttering out of that solitary rhythm in which lack of oxygen had encompassed all his faculties. It was indeed a strange and half-incredible sight. A group of colored pavilions clung to the mountainside with the . . . chance delicacy of flower-petals impaled upon a crag. It was superb and exquisite. An austere emotion carried the eye upward from milk-blue roofs to the gray rock bastion above. . . . Beyond that, in a dazzling pyramid, soared the snow slopes of Karakal.

Hilton called the place he conjured up Shangri-la, a word that hurriedly entered the English argot, captivated the imaginations of moviemakers—in particular Frank Capra, who produced a 1937 film by the same name—and, among other appropriations, now lends its name to one of Asia's finest hotel chains. Hilton, whose other principal novel is the schoolboy classic *Goodbye, Mr. Chips*, was not much of a traveler, preferring instead to leaf, in search of inspiration, through the glossy magazines that had become the rage in the thirties. Among the pages he turned were those of *National Geographic*, which had published a series of essays and pictures by the botanist, philologist and explorer Joseph F. Rock, who spent years in northern Yunnan collecting plants and gathering material on the local Tibetan cultures. Rock himself went on to become a major contributor of photographs and manuscripts to the Tibetan collection at the Library of Congress, as well as rare plants to Harvard's Arnold Arboretum. It was Rock's articles that sparked the gleam in Hilton's eye and that provided much of the descriptive garb for his novel.

Indeed, "the snow slopes of Karakal" marveled at by Hilton's Hugh Conway are a scantily disguised reference to the Khabadkar range of mountains we had just driven through. In the twenties and thirties, when Rock was here, the mountains of this region of Tibet were jeweled with Buddhist monasteries, small and grand, the largest and holiest of which, Ganden Sumtsanling, blanketed a hillside overlooking the town of Gyalthang, now a day's drive south of Dechen. For Rock, it would have taken a good week or more to make the journey from Dechen to Gyalthang along mountain mule tracks that villagers traveled and the more durable trails of traditional trading routes. At its height, before the advent of Mao's Communist victory, Sumtsanling, a scholarly center of the dominant *Gelugpa,* or Yellow Hat, sect of Tibetan Buddhism, harbored some two thousand monks, including many of Buddhism's most learned lamas.

In Rock's day, the monastery of hundreds of red tile–roofed buildings with pounded-mud walls painted white, each wall sloping outward slightly from their roofs, faced south overlooking the tiny settlement of Gyalthang. Shorn monks in thick, sleeveless maroon robes—the lack of sleeves because collective debates over logic are a central feature in the Yellow Hat tradition and long sleeves would become tangled amid the vigorous hand gesticulations that are an integral part of each debate— crowded through the narrow alleys between the buildings. The great prayer halls were dark and smoky on the inside, illuminated only by the thousands of yak butter lamps arrayed before the central shrines, tiers of altars overhung with *thankas,* religious paintings on cloth, surrounding immense images of the Buddha. Pilgrims and the locally devout coursed through the monastery seeking guidance on an auspicious day for a marriage, or to find a lama to provide spiritual counseling, to offer prayers and light some lamps, to attend one of the religious ceremonies, or merely to sell yak meat to the monastery's huge kitchens.

Like other great monasteries, Sumtsanling ruled its domain with a measure of autocracy and was its largest landowner, and in the end it was an autocracy of Gyalthang's own making: There was not a family in the valley who had not sent at least one son to the monastery to become a monk. Gyalthang itself, because it is only at ten thousand feet, was a land of farmers who tilled fields of barley and kept small herds of *dzo,* a half-yak, half-cow animal that Tibetans regard as among the stupider creatures on Earth. Gyalthang, the monastery and the valley, was an isolated and, by contemporary standards, a desperately impoverished place.

In the mid-1950s, as resistance to Chinese rule accelerated in eastern Tibet, Chinese political cadres backed by the army swept into Gyalthang to impose what they called "democratic reforms," a euphemism for murder and repression. Monks were forced from the monastery, wealthier Tibetans were summarily executed and fields were collectivized. The Chinese language was decreed the official tongue, and all schools were required to cease holding classes in Tibetan. During the Cultural Revolution, a decade of madness, persecution and murder that swept over China from 1966 to 1976, politically crazed Red Guards, students and workers who outdid one another in violence and destruction in efforts to exhibit their fealty to Mao and his addled notion of a utopian Communist state, together with army troops, vandalized and then completely demolished the Sumtsanling monastery, reducing it to a Dresden-like field of building stumps and rubble. For the Tibetans here, the soul of their culture and civilization had been eviscerated.

In repeated visits to Tibet I am shaken in each instance by the Chinese assault on Tibetan society and culture. China, now riding the big wave of economic free market liberalization and growing amity with the West, explains away the devastations of Tibet in decades gone by as misplaced ideological deviation, or excessive zeal by Mao's Red Guards or the sad consequence of perfidious Tibetan desires for freedom. Driving across Tibet reveals a landscape littered with the shells of thousands of monasteries pulverized by the Chinese, a sight to which I have never become accustomed. Although raised as a Catholic in a solidly Irish family, I am rigorously irreligious, finding the notion of belief in supernatural beings, or if one professes monotheism, a single being, mystifying. But I am riveted by the practice, the rituals, the aura of religious ceremony and belief; I am also compelled by the historical force of religious belief and its institutions, how it has shaped behavior, brought war, pogrom, learning and revolution. Whether it is watching Friday prayers at the Dome of the Rock in Jerusalem, or saffron-robed Hindu priests in Madurai lighting lamps before the tubby elephant god Ganesh, or listening to Mozart's mass in C-minor at Notre Dame in Paris, I find the power of belief moving and the magnificence of ceremony stirring; in many ways, these rituals are windows onto distant histories, their texts the voices of past mythologizers. So the sight of a vandalized religious culture, the decimation visited on Tibet by China, inspires in Tibetans, and in me, deep anger.

In the West, there is a pro forma headshaking, a tut-tutting by governments over the state of affairs in Tibet, followed by a rush to discuss investment, trade and tariff schedules. American presidents shake hands with the Dalai Lama and intone their admiration for the Nobel laureate and his devotion to the Tibetan people. But in Tibet, the grinding away of Tibetan culture continues; police run the monasteries while Communist overseers control the selection of abbots, designate living Buddhas, even kidnap and detain the child who was chosen by the Dalai Lama and his advisers as the reincarnation of the Panchen Lama. For me, the question is how long Tibet can endure.

A monastery of the Red Hat sect of Tibetan Buddhism, near Dechen, in northern Yunnan Province

The road into Dechen squirms through mountains of pine and fir, but more often mountains of clear-cut stubble. Dechen itself is a grotty, gray town that Chinese builders have subdued with sheets of bathroom tile slapped onto the sides of concrete-box structures and plates of blue glass to fill window frames. Though we were just passing through Dechen on the way to Gyalthang, we needed a place for the night, and the only edifice that could be called a hotel claimed it had no rooms available. The police barracks, which we visited next, was unheated, had no water and sported dozens of broken windows, so we settled on a cement meat locker of a place through which we crept, flashlights in hand. Out my window, pigs trotted down the street scavenging through garbage piles, and pilgrims coming or going from distant villages shuffled through the streets gawking at three-story structures and window displays of blue-bladed electric fans. It was not a place to linger.

I had other reasons to hurry to Gyalthang as well. Tashi Kesang, an old friend of mine, a Tibetan from Gyalthang who had studied at the University of Wisconsin in Madison, one of my alma maters, and who ran, among his many ventures, a successful Tibetan carpet shop on Fifth Avenue in Manhattan, had recently opened a Tibetan-style hotel in his hometown. On my map, there was a faint yellow line suggesting a road alongside the Lancang Jiang, the Mekong, running south. That road hobbled down to the village where Dakpa was to pick up his horses for his pilgrimage, but just beyond that the side of a mountain had caved into the river, blocking the road until a bulldozer or two could be found, not a likely proposition any time soon, I figured. I decided to slide away from the river and head straight to Gyalthang and later work my way north along the river to where the blockage was.

I said good-bye to Dakpa, who, after finishing his pilgrimage, flew to Austria to study tour management in a land of mountains not unlike those with which he was familiar. And after Austria, he spent six months in Oklahoma, where he pursued more sophisticated business studies, all to help him establish a tour company to take well-heeled travelers into the wilder reaches of China and Tibet. He seemed positively joyful at the prospect of circumambulating the mountain on foot for a month; I confessed to him that I was glad I was not joining him.

I climbed into the Mitsubishi, waved to Dakpa and headed south. Our car, by now mud-caked and cranky, climbed through the Baimang Pass, the highest pass in the mountains here, at 14,073 feet. The Tibetan driver rolled his window down and cried, "Ohhh, lha gyal lo, Ohhh lha gyal lo." As did I.

Like tens of thousands of other Tibetans, Tashi and his family fled the onslaught of Chinese troops in 1959 and reached India. But unlike many Tibetans, Tashi's talents meant an escape from the subcontinent—to the frigid plains of the American Midwest, where he studied Tibetan literature. He concluded, though, that Tibetan scholarship, however admirable an intellectual pursuit, was unlikely to lead to much of a life. "I decided my skills and interests were more transactional than academic," he explained my first night at his hotel, bundled up next to a roaring fire with a fine beer in my hand. I was now relatively thawed from the weeks up north. "So I wound up in Boulder, Colorado, to rethink life. I taught a little Tibetan, went to Dharmsala and worked for the Dalai Lama. But then I wound up in New York City and did the executive training program at Republic Bank. Ultimately, though, I wound up going back to Lhasa when things were all right there and started a carpet business."

Tashi is a big man with a generous mop of curly black hair, fashionable glasses and a commanding manner about him; he was wearing a brilliantly blue Patagonia down vest when I arrived. His wife, a Tibetan doctor, was in Lhasa having their second child, and he was likely to be late for the birth, as he was for virtually everything else. Before I arrived he was in the process of negotiating the seventy-year lease of a huge parcel of land next to his hotel, primarily to stave off building by competitors that would blemish the view. The negotiations, which were proceeding with the help of a lawyer from the provincial capital, Kunming, were, he told me later, arduous. He did, however, strike the deal.

We resumed our conversation: "Tibetan carpets at the time were a disaster," Tashi said. "So I figured out some designs and got artisans to make them. Then I opened a showroom on Fifth Avenue and Twenty-second Street in Manhattan. But that wasn't really enough. My family is from here, you see, so I was doing some thinking, but more with my heart than my head. You know this was a closed place until pretty recently, but when it opened to visitors I decided to build a hotel here and so I opened it in 1995."

Unlike any hotel I knew of in Tibet or its outlying areas, Tashi's was an architectural reproduction of a large Tibetan monastery hall, although made of more durable cement than the more friable packed-mud commonly used for Tibetan monasteries and dwellings. As is traditional in Tibetan architecture, the hotel's walls were thick at the base, narrowing perceptibly toward the roofline, and the windows were counterpaned in frames broader at the bottom than the top. The whole building was painted orthodox white, and his staff of young Tibetan girls wore traditional garb. As we talked that night, the sounds of Tibetan life echoed faintly in the distance—the drone of monks reciting scripture mingled with the clink-clank of yak bells as the black beasts labored up the mountain behind the hotel to graze.

Morning comes late to Gyalthang and western China—in winter toward ten a.m.—because Beijing, in but one of the blizzard of bureaucratic obduracies that beset the country, insists that the country, as broad as the United States, adhere to a single time zone, Beijing's time zone. It was mid-October and my breath steamed the air in the room when I breathed, but the hotel had its own coal-fired boiler that produced the first hot water I had washed in for some weeks. Gyalthang is in reality two towns, or perhaps three. To the north, against a hill, is the expanse of Ganden Sumtsanling. In the center is a town hammered together from Chinese blueprints, a grid of ferociously straight concrete streets and a parade of white-tiled buildings. A state-run department store tinseled in chrome hulks on one corner of the main street, a dingy place with, remarkably, up and down escalators. But alas, the escalators, the only pair in town, or for that matter the only pair between here and the North Pole, I was sure, were frozen, and the upper floor to which they rose was bathed in blackness. To the south of the Chinese center is the old Tibetan town, a jumble of single-story whitewashed buildings woven together by muddy flagstone paths and alleys. Here, young men clomp through the streets pulling donkeys loaded down with milk cans while children in sweat suits in scalding colors—lemon yellow, pumpkin, raspberry and mustard— tramp to school laden with Mickey Mouse backpacks. Down a muddy alley between tumbledown wood buildings, an ancient man with a single tooth stitched new felt and suede boots in red, white and brown, the tra-ditional footwear for Tibetans here; 150 yuan for the pair, he said, about $18. The old town is the original settlement of Gyalthang. Urban would be too strong a word for it, and today it is little more than an appendage to the newer Chinese town.

Yet this ramshackle town of mismatched Tibetan and Chinese culture has found itself rubbing up against the fussy prose and thinking of James

A shoemaker finishing a
felt Tibetan boot in
Gyalthang, a Tibetan town
in northern Yunnan
Province

Hilton, and at the same time is preparing, just possibly, to be redrawn in the image of Hugh Conway's vision. The instrument of this somewhat fantastical endeavor has proved not to be a Tibetan at all, but a clever Chinese administrator named Sun Jiong, who hails from Kunming. And Sun Jiong has brought with him the finer elements of marketing in all its plasticity and commercialism and wrapped it in the notion that the magical place called Shangri-la is, in fact, here.

In a cold, cutting rain, I trundled into the local government office building, a smaller, dour, gray version of the type seen in every out-of-the-way Chinese town, in search of Sun Jiong. I was directed to his office at the end of a corridor of wooden doors and curtained transoms. He bounded from his chair as I entered, a gesture rare among Chinese officials who, perhaps like petty bureaucrats everywhere, are prone to expect a degree of deference while burnishing an unctuous pomposity; in China, though, the syndrome seems worse than just about anywhere. Sun, a tall, impeccably groomed young man in a sharply pressed white shirt and silk tie, was about as far out of place in Gyalthang, where formality consists of removing one's fur hat indoors, as it is possible to be. He shook hands with a genuine sincerity and bustled around fixing tea, something most officials leave to their lackeys camped in the outer vestibule. His office was an immaculate white with subtle ivory Tibetan hangings over the windows, which were trimmed in red and navy blue. An elegant embroidered *thanka* of the Buddha hung on the wall, and the furniture was simple wood. I could not have been more startled because this was a Han Chinese whose tastes embraced an almost Tibetan asceticism. It was about as unlikely as Jacques Chirac holding a state banquet at McDonald's.

Tashi, who of necessity and habit knew everyone who was anyone in Gyalthang, not that there were many, had urged me to visit Sun because, in Tashi's view, he was the sort of Chinese official who understood and respected Tibetan culture. "He even learned to speak Tibetan," Tashi told me. "How many Chinese do you know who have bothered to do that? He's a good guy. Not so influential, but a good guy."

Sun began by plying me with tea, the Chinese version not the Tibetan, and told me how he managed to wind up in what for him must have been as close to bureaucratic internal exile as one could get. "I used to be just a tour guide," he began. "Then in 1994 I was taking a test that was given to determine who are the best guides in China. One of the questions on this test was 'What is Shangri-la?' And another question was, 'What is the native language of Shangri-la?' Well at the time I didn't know. I assumed it was from English. I let it pass. For the next couple of years, working in Kunming in the government travel office, I didn't think about it anymore. Then in 1996, in the spring, I think, someone from the Indian National Library sent me a copy of the novel *Lost Horizon* and said, 'Why don't you take a look at this?' They told me, 'Maybe you should go to Zhongdian [what the Chinese call Gyalthang] and see what that is like.' People told me that it was a terrible place, that no Han could possibly like it there."

Sun seemed flushed with excitement, bubbling from a memory of discovery and revelation and, I thought to myself, a bit of hallucinatory miasma. "So you see, I came here and I discovered that this place is named in the Shambala [the story of the mystical Buddhist city of perfection], that Zhongdian is in the Shambala. Another name for Shambala is 'Sun and Moon City.' And another name is 'The Heart of the Sun and Moon.' So I thought, Shangri-la, which is the same as Shambala, is not in Tibet at all. Shangri-la is Zhongdian. I talked to the local head of the prefecture and he never heard of Shangri-la. So he said why don't I work on this. So we started to do some research. We went to libraries, including at the American embassy in Beijing. Then we went to a friend of the Dalai Lama. People said that they thought I could be right, that Zhongdian is Shangri-la. So we tried to propagate this, but nobody knew me. What was I to do?" I was not completely following Sun's somewhat convoluted exegesis, but I was certainly taken aback at the sight of a Chinese official who was worrying himself over the site of an earthly fantasia emanating from the imagination of a middling British author. Gyalthang is no utopia.

Ganden Sumtsanling was once one of the greatest monasteries in Tibet, the *ling* in its name indicating that originally it was an independent government; that is, it ran the affairs of its domain independently of Lhasa. It possessed special facilities for study and, like only a few of the most important monasteries in Tibet, it awarded advanced degrees to the most scholarly of the monks. It also owned considerable amounts of land that were tilled by local peasants. That system collapsed with the arrival of communism, but it was not until the Cultural Revolution that the monastery was finally emptied of monks and demolished. For a Tibetan in Gyalthang, the destruction of Sumtsanling was roughly akin to what a Parisian would feel about razing the cathedral of Notre Dame and burning the Bibliothèque Nationale at the same time, with particular attention paid to the immolation of the rare book collection, all done in full view of the citizenry. This is essentially what happened at Sumtsanling, and it went unrecorded, the memory of the devastation preserved only in the telling by old people here. By the onset of the Cultural Revolution, however, all of the most learned monks, the *gyeshi*, had already fled to India as repression by the Chinese increased. When the Cultural Revolution ended in 1976 and a modicum of tolerance of Tibetan Buddhism returned in the 1980s, the first steps were taken by the monks who remained in Gyalthang to rebuild the monastery.

Weathered remains of the old monastery abound. But amid the ruin, a new Sumtsanling is being built. On the days I was there, hundreds of workers were pounding into shape massive mud walls of the new central prayer hall. Women in long skirts and rainbow-striped aprons, stooped under sacks of mud on their backs, climbed wood ladders propped against the plank framing for the walls and dumped their sacks at the feet of men who tamped the mud into shape with long wooden staves. In expansive courtyards, stonecutters chiseled away at refrigerator-sized blocks of granite, fashioning pediments for the prayer hall, while woodworkers planed immense spruce logs into columns that would support the hall's tile roof. Inside smaller prayer halls nearby, young monks in thick maroon robes rocked slightly back and forth as they recited from long, thin texts of Buddhist scripture with the dimensions of a flute case.

I ascended a series of steep plank-runged ladders in a prayer hall to meet one of the monastery's living Buddhas, a designation that theologically applies to those chosen as reincarnations of scholarly and saintly monks. Historically, however, living Buddhas have traditionally come from the larger and wealthier Tibetan families, usually the larger landholding families, and they are part of the monastery's administrative hierarchy. Today, the Chinese government exercises strict control over who can be called a living Buddha, evidenced most dramatically in Beijing's kidnapping and detention of the young Panchen Lama. In his place, Beijing imposed its own young boy as Panchen Lama, and he is being schooled under the guidance of Communist bureaucrats. Still, living Buddhas do have a special place in all the remaining monasteries in Tibet, and that was no less true here.

In what a Parisian would call a garret, tucked into an eave off the edge of a prayer hall, Thuten Kenrinpoche sat cross-legged on a small, carpet-covered platform murmuring softly as he recited scripture from a newish-looking text. Before coming I had bought a *katta*, a white silk prayer scarf, and now presented it to Thuten, a young, tonsured man with surprisingly muscled arms protruding from his deep maroon robe. He had been elected by the monks and approved by the Chinese authorities. He swiftly knotted the middle of the scarf, blew on it and fixed it with a thin red cord. Then he brought it to his forehead and spoke a few words in prayer and draped it around his neck. On the wall of his gloomy chamber was a picture of Beijing's version of the Panchen Lama and a calendar from China's Construction Bank. I thanked him and left him to his prayers.

Sumtsanling is slowly returning to life. In its corridors and the dirt alleys between buildings, young monks scurried about with books tucked into cloth shoulder bags. Other monks hacked away at the hard earth with a hoe, and one balanced a shoulder pole with two baskets piled with potatoes as he padded toward one of the monastery's kitchens. In the prayer halls, the statues of the Buddha are new, the prayer wheels that spin by the door freshly polished and the red support columns newly painted.

Ganden Sumtsanling, one of the great monasteries of the Yellow Hat sect of Tibetan Buddhism, after ten years of reconstruction in Gyalthang

Building the walls of the new
prayer hall at Ganden Sumtsanling
monastery. The original hall was
destroyed by Red Guards during
the Cultural Revolution.

Absent is the deep, viscous scent of votive yak butter lamps that pervades
the old monasteries in Lhasa that avoided complete destruction by the
Chinese. Absent as well is the spirit of scholarship and learning that suf-
fused this place; of all the monks here, there was not a single *gyeshi*.

As the living repositories of Tibetan Buddhism, the *gyeshi* are the foundation of Tibetan intellectual life, the nurturers of succeeding generations
and the embodiment of spiritual accomplishment. Without them,
Tibetan Buddhism dies. So I felt it was essential to talk to one of these
men, to try and get a feel, if only a finger, a touch, of what the future held
for this religious culture. What did these men, these great scholars and
teachers who lived their lives in exile from their society, their homeland,
hope for? Indeed, did they harbor hope at all?

A great part of my quest stemmed from fifteen years of watching a people and a religion—in Tibet, the two are as intertwined as Judaism and the

state of Israel—approaching extinction, extinction in the sense that what makes Tibet Tibet is Buddhism, and Tibetan Buddhism, in the person of the Dalai Lama, is what threatens China's claim over the region. Tibetans suffer as well from their isolation, their distance from Western imagination and experience, the somewhat incomprehensible "exoticism" of their beliefs. I had found a certain strength in the Tibetans I had met so far, but it was the *gyeshi*, I felt, who could provide the insight into a storm-clouded present and an even more nebulously darkened future.

To find a *gyeshi* one has to journey to Yanthang, a few hours south of Gyalthang, one of the small villages secreted over the lower plateau here. I set off for it, past fields purple with primula and red with the small flowers of the euphorbia. Along the road, towering lattices, or perhaps easels, of drying barley edged the fields, while in corrals women beat barley sheaves on logs to husk the seeds. Barley is the principal grain for Tibetans, a grain that is made into a porridge, or a batter for a kind of thick pancake, or distilled into a rather potent arrack. Here, houses are uniform in design: Each is two stories of thick, pounded-mud walls, the ground floor open so that animals can gather there, the main living quarters above that. A central pillar, often a yard or more in diameter, sawed from an old-growth spruce, formed the core support for the house. Windows were few and small, in deference to the frigid winds that jet across the plateau.

Yanthang harbored no more than fifteen or sixteen houses along a muddy street that led from the main road in one direction and toward the mountains in the other. I had come to visit Ngawang Rabgyal, a *gyeshi* who had fled to India with the Dalai Lama in 1959 and now lived there. He and his family were back in Gyalthang temporarily; he was teaching for two years at Sumtsanling. I clomped up the wood-ladder steps to the second floor of the family house and entered the vast living quarters. It was a fiercely cold day, and the family was huddled around a bulging, triple-bellied stove that was being fed constantly from a pile of kindling and hatcheted tree limbs in the corner. Smoke billowed to the peaked roof, charring a hanging grate stacked with mottled cones of yak cheese. The grandmother of the house, swaddled in a capacious blue apron and an embroidered waistcoat fastened at her right shoulder with a single silver button, her hair wrapped in a red turbanlike binding, sat on a low bench churning yak butter tea, which was delivered in large ceramic bowls.

"This house is more than one hundred years old," explained Ngawang, who curled his legs under his maroon robe, a yellow knit cap stretched over his baldness, his long fingers cradling the bowl of steaming tea. "Our family has lived here for a long time. I don't know for sure, but at least for ten generations we have had monks in our family. Before me, there was my uncle. He was very old and he had to choose who would be the next monk in our family. He chose me to be a monk when I was four years old. Now, of course, there are no more monks chosen at four years old. Today it is more often at twenty, although I know of young boys of nine or twelve who become monks.

"I'm fifty-nine now," he continued, pausing as a lacquered wooden bowl of *tsampa* was placed in front of him. The *tsampa* as it is served here was cooked barley grain mixed with yak-milk yogurt and a bit of yak butter tea. A cone of smoked yak cheese was served on the side. "I eat too much *tsampa* and cheese," confessed Ngawang, burping loudly, "more than my stomach can handle."

"As I said, I became a monk at four. Now I'm fifty-nine. I spent eleven years in the monastery here, and then I was sent to Sera monastery in Lhasa. Almost immediately, though, we had to flee because the Chinese army came. I had to flee with the Dalai Lama in 1959. I think there were about fifteen hundred monks who came with us then, but many got sick and died. Most of the monks were from the three big monasteries, Sera, Drepung and Ganden. I think only about nine hundred monks survived on the escape to India. The Dalai Lama went to Dharmsala, but that is a very small place, and the Indian government told us to find a bigger place. We wound up in Belakopi in Karnataka in southern India. In Belakopi, all the three big monasteries were reestablished.

"This is my second time back to Gyalthang. The first time it took two years to get permission to come back. Of course, I will teach at the monastery, but for the most part I will stay here. This is one of the biggest problems for Buddhism, the fact that all the *gyeshi* fled to India. Right now I have six students. But you know, some of the students I have cannot even read. I have to teach them the alphabet. How can you teach logic if the students cannot even read? How can these students become monks? How can they become monks like we did?"

Ngawang stood up and stretched and urged me to join him in the prayer room, a separate chamber that all larger Tibetan houses have. At the end of the prayer hall, about the size of a good-sized living room, a small altar glowed from the flames of half a dozen yak butter lamps and a *thanka* of the Buddha hung from the wall. Tibetan carpets covered the floor of the nearly empty room, although in one corner next to a pile of thick pillows where the *gyeshi* prayed there was a stack of narrow, bound scriptures. "I have been almost forty years in India." He sighed loudly. "There is no way I can live here though. We are not free to practice our lives here. The main thing we need in the world is peace, world peace. If everything is peaceful here we could return here and rebuild. Maybe in ten years we could rebuild everything."

Exile does not rest easily on Ngawang. South India, a sweltering place devoid of yaks, yak butter tea and cheese, *tsampa* and the cold, clear beauty of mountainous Tibet, has become the home to Tibetan learning and, as China persists in exercising complete control over Buddhism, perhaps the ultimate resting place of Tibet's spiritual foundation. "We all try," Ngawang told me, "but it is very difficult. Many monks have given up hope of ever returning to Tibet. They feel lost and alone. Sometimes I do too."

I came away from my visit with Ngawang with a mixture of distress and encouragement. There was, in his words and experience, an intensity and determination to survive and preserve his faith and culture. And yet there were also strands of resignation in him, a sense that he and other senior theologians were fighting a losing battle against overwhelming odds. I cannot help but feel that the transformations being wrought by Chinese officials across Tibet are not ephemeral, that Tibet is being refashioned in a way that will snuff out the spirit of Buddhism as it is known here. An old Communist colleague of Mao's named Chen Yun, a severe and extremely conservative apparatchik who has been dead for some time, used to talk about China's budding market economy as a free market in a birdcage, a market that has well-circumscribed freedoms within a cage of Socialist prescription. Chen, happily for much of China, is daily being proved wrong in his economic prognostications, but the crude cage metaphor seems to apply quite aptly to the condition of Tibetan Buddhism. Most Tibetans hope that the bars of the cage are bending. It is, it seems to me, a distant hope at best.

Even so, here and there, if you look very carefully, the buds of globalization are sprouting ever so slightly. Even this small, insignificant valley of Gyalthang got an airport in 1999, albeit one that manages to field no more than a handful of flights a week from distant Kunming—by the old road two days; by air, scarcely an hour. Red cans of Coca-Cola are available here; the reasonably well-off sport Nokia mobile phones; the Internet has made it. But this was the invasion of globalization. I wanted to see if there were any rays of globalization *spreading from here*, and so when Tashi suggested I visit the isolated Nixi Valley north of Gyalthang, I rented a little van and bumped and clattered for two hours until a deep green harrow appeared between the mountains.

For generations, the village of Tama has been known for producing the perfect pots for yak butter tea, pots shaped from red clay scooped from the hills and fired into a hard iron gray. These pots are irregularly shaped, swollen-bellied, with a bird's beak spout and an off-center handle that somehow seems perfectly balanced, and they nestle comfortably in the palm, flat and secure. Syunno Tsering is the village's master potter. He is also, between work in his cornfield and worrying about his *dzo*, a bit of an international businessman.

His workshop is on the second floor of his three-story house, and to reach it I had to tread across drying ears of corn spread like a blanket over the plank flooring. "I've been making pots for nearly thirty years," said Syunno. His hands were coated with a reddish patina of clay, and his shirt was daubed with bits of red here and there. His tangled black hair hadn't seen a comb in a while. "My grandfather taught me how to make pots. His father before him made pots, and before that too, I suppose." Out a tiny mullioned window flung open to the sunshine mountains rose endlessly, everywhere, most covered now in a scrubby pine that has replaced the clear-cut spruce forests, their peaks cottoned by clouds. Quiltwork patches of newly harvested barley fields carpeted the valley floor, and the bells on his *dzo* clanked faintly.

Syunno creaked open the frame door to his workshop and fired up a kerosene lantern. Wide plank shelves from floor to ceiling were filled with dozens of fired and unfired teapots, braziers, vases and bowls, all thrown with the local clay. As he spoke, he squatted beside his wheel, returning to a tall ewer he had been working on when I arrived. No counterweighted, foot-driven pottery wheel from a fancy California manufacturer this; his was a small board on a swivel base on the floor, a bit like a cut-rate lazy Susan. He spun the pot, pushing it upward smartly with his large hands, then squeezing it until a narrow neck emerged, only to let it widen out to a comfortable rim. Deftly, chattering all the while, he molded a spout, hollowed it and fixed it to the pot, anchoring it with a small flying buttress of clay. Then he daintily chose from a pile of small white stones and pressed them into the surface of the ewer, patterning them as he spun the pot.

"A couple of years ago," he said, "there were some tourists from Taiwan here. Sometimes tourists come up here, and these people from Taiwan were very interested in my pots. One man took down my name and address, and some months later he ordered a huge number of pots. And so

Syunno Tsering, the master potter of the village of
Tama, in northern Yunnan Province. He regularly
ships his pots to Taiwan.

I made them. I made some wooden crates and packed the pots and sent
them to Taiwan. And then he made another order. And I made more pots
for him. It takes one day to make a big pot like this. I do the handle last
because it's the most difficult. You have to know how to roll the clay so
that it is strong and will fix properly to the pot. It can't be too thick or it
looks bad. It can't be too thin or it will break. All these pots here," he said,
putting his most recent creation on the shelf next to a dozen others, "are
for Taiwan. If I can sell pots to Taiwan and make money, I think that's
good. Most people here can't do that. They're only farmers. I'm a farmer,
too. But I also make pots."

In his office in Gyalthang, Sun Jiong had been regaling me with his con-
jectures, and fantasies, about the site of Shangri-la, which he earnestly
believed was here, swirling around us. For the people who live in and
around Gyalthang, whether monk or arrack maker, potter or bride, life
here is arduous, sometimes backbreaking, requiring a daily effort to
endure, far less to improve one's condition. Sun was undeterred, though,
and I must say I admired his enthusiasm.

"This name Shangri-la is very important," he insisted. "This name is very important for business. Foreign businesses don't know about this place. Neither do Chinese. They say they don't know Tibetan customs or traditional customs. But many, many Chinese books talk about a kingdom within sight of a 'snow mountain.' The Tibetans here call it Shambala, or Shangri-la." Even as Sun spun his theories in his office in Gyalthang, officials in other towns in northern Yunnan, particularly in grim Dechen to the north and in the old city of Lijiang to the south, were staking their own claims to be China's Shangri-la, although none with the passion or force Sun exercised. Somehow a frisson of excitement had suddenly attached itself to Hilton's fiction and a bureaucratic skirmish, or at least a battle of words, was well under way.

"These other places," Sun said solemnly, "they don't know what Shangri-la is. And it can't be in those places anyway. Lijiang isn't even in Tibet, and they know nothing about Tibetan culture. Shangri-la is very, very important. You know there is a hotel chain called Shangri-la run by a Malaysian businessman." Yes, I said, Robert Kuok, a man of immense wealth and global business interests. "We tried to get him to come here, but he never came. I hoped he would come but the southeast Asia economic crisis got very bad, so I guess he cannot come."

I asked Sun if his devotion to the idea of Shangri-la was fueled mostly by the business potential it promised. He shook his head vigorously. "No, not at all. Business is important, yes, that's true. But Shangri-la does not belong to business. It belongs to the next century. It belongs to the world. The government of Yunnan sent me here to work on the Shangri-la project. We want to build a lost paradise for the next century." As I left Sun's office that cold, rainy day, the mountains around us were fuzzed with ash gray rain clouds, the street was muddy and my car was broken. I did not feel much like Hugh Conway. It was time to return to the Lancang Jiang.

Early the next morning, the driver, who came with another four-wheel drive I had rented, showed up, and I bundled myself out of Tashi's hotel and headed south on the map's red-colored Route 214. An impenetrable wall of mountains shielded us from the river for the first 150 miles, until the first big bend of the Yangze River, which pulled around the southern flank of the mountain range, giving us an opening to ease back north toward the Lancang Jiang. We left the last of the Tibetan plateau behind us and descended into the western reaches of Yunnan, which historically had been settled by a mélange of ethnic groups, including the Naxi, Lisu, Nu, Pumi and Bai, all of whom have their own languages and cultures and whose presence here long predated Chinese migration and settlement. Rain slicked the mud road. Occasionally I glimpsed the carcass of a truck at the bottom of a ravine where it had failed to negotiate a slick hairpin turn successfully; I remembered Dakpa's nonchalance at such dangers and wondered how his pilgrimage trek was progressing. My driver rounded the lower bulge of the Yangze where it pulled its gigantic U-turn to the north. Rain bashed down hour after hour. Night began to pull its shawl across the sky, so we stopped at the broken-down town of Chudian and found rooms in a dank cement guest house, its halls reeking of stale urine and mold.

Morning brought sunshine, the first for days, and the road toward the river seemed a bit more glorious. Birch trees with blazing yellow leaves and white rhododendrons lined the road. Spanish moss draped from tall firs, and hillsides were dense with gnarl-barked walnut trees. On dried mud walls faint whitewashed Chinese ideographs proclaimed: "We cannot live without socialism. We cannot live without the Communist party." Vegetable fields, great, wonderful fields in dark soil with green vegetables, ran from the edge of villages. The muddy yellow clay of the road dried during the day, transforming it from muck to dust as we drove.

We halted for the day at Weixi, in the heart of the land of the Lisu. Children were scampering home from school as we drove into town, all sporting what must be de rigueur Mickey Mouse backpacks; unlikely, of course, that these packs were those officially licensed by the very remote Disney company executive who worries about such things. A side street was being repaired by a group of women, some of whom were hammering bread loaf–sized rocks into cobbles. Although the area was peopled predominately by the Lisu, native dress seemed a throwback to the years of the Cultural Revolution, women and men in blue or gray Mao jackets and hats; there were, of course, no Mao buttons, but the contrast with the chicness of cosmopolitan centers like Shanghai could not have been greater.

Through Tibet, the quality of cuisine had been fairly basic, and so I was looking forward to a change from yak meat, barley and bad rice. Strolling through the town, not much from one end to the next, I was suddenly startled to find myself gazing at a hole-in-the-wall eatery with a big sign that read: MAMA YANG'S HOME COOKING. It was not discernibly different from its neighbors, just a cement room, open at the front with a rudimentary hibachi of a sort out on the sidewalk under a big red umbrella. I was welcomed by Mama Yang, a big woman in a white apron like a Mama Yang should wear, with a white chef's hat cocked on her head. She showed me to one of the four pink-tablecloth-covered tables; in the center of it was a glass jar of pickled and peppered vegetables, one nicely furred with mold. I sat on a stool and told Mama Yang to bring whatever was fresh.

She barked at her daughter, telling her what to make in a Chinese I could not quite get and sat down at the table with me, pouring both of us a glass of tea. I asked her, naturally, about the sign. She laughed, her head rocking slightly. "I opened this place with my daughter a year ago. There was a *lao-wai*, a foreigner, here like you then, and I said to her, 'What's a good name in English?' My name is Yang Peiying, so she said, 'What do you think of "Mama Yang's Home Cooking?"' Of course she had to explain what it meant to me. Home cooking. Everybody here does home cooking." I asked her what she understood the "mama" in Mama Yang's to mean. "Well," she said, casting an eye toward her daughter's culinary efforts on the grill, "I guess it's something like mother, Mother Yang." I said yes, but a bit less formal than that.

Moments later her daughter brought over a dinner I'd been waiting for for a long, long time—I'd been traveling for nearly two months at this point, and apart from the oatmeal, the food along the road had ranged from the dismal to the deplorable. Now before me was a plate of grilled chicken wings, salted and basted in a spicy pepper; a plate of pork ribs, also peppery; a bowl of sliced beef, not yak, in a vinegary spice sauce, and a plate of the local specialty, *erkuai*, thick-skinned rolls of gelatinous rice flour wrapped around a fiery pepper and oil sauce. (*Erkuai*, rather unappetizingly, literally means "bait bits.") I couldn't stop eating them. And the rice, the rice was not the anemic nubbly bits I'd eaten in Tibet but well-shaped grains, still short, but with some flavor.

"Not too many people like you come here," said Mama Yang, watching with a not unappreciative look as I bulldozed my way through the meal in front of me. "There isn't much here for people to come here for, and young people want to leave." Why then, I asked, was her daughter still here, cooking at a restaurant in a town that most maps ignore? "Ahh," she grunted, "in Chinese families we try to keep our children home. Not like you. You are too far from home." I laughed at that, and that night actually checked my GPS to see how far; the illuminated numbers on the screen told me I was 7,704 miles away. Two days' drive from Gyalthang had only taken me fifty-one miles as the bird flies.

The next day we headed north, driving out of Weixi past the early morning vegetable and spice market where weathered women were camped on tiny, low stools next to rickety, short-legged tables piled with scallions, cabbages, mustard greens, squashes and onions. Burlap sacks of peas, peppers, peanuts, sesame seeds and bundles of rice noodles crowded along the road as life spilled onto the streets, muddy from the night's mist and cold. A young man in knee-high rubber boots and a muddy blue jacket walked by pulling the leads of two black mules, big, empty, woven-reed baskets strapped on their backs. Here the houses were made of gray-brown brick with open second-floor balconies, this time of year stacked with drying ears of corn; doors and window frames everywhere were painted a bright yellow. And from the roofs of some buildings, bright white television satellite dishes blossomed.

Our road wiggled out of Weixi aside the Yongchun River, the muddy dirt track whipping back and forth along the river as it tumbled over rocks, heading toward the Lancang Jiang, the Mekong. I wanted to circle back, heading north along the Mekong and the last edges of Tibet, to see the river as it finished its charge through the envelope of mountain gorges that mark its final descent. In 1913, Francis Kingdon Ward, a British explorer and naturalist of the sort who thrived in the first half of the twentieth century, wrote humorlessly of traveling Yunnan just about where I was: "This was the last we were to see of the great Mekong River. . . . I was scarcely sorry to say goodbye, for the Mekong gorge—one long rent between mountains which grow more and more arid, more and more savage as we travel northwards (yet hardly improve as we travel southwards) is an abnormality, a freak of nature, a thing altogether out of place." Despite his distress and momentary loss of aesthetic judgment that day, Ward went on to write more than twenty volumes on his expeditions, collecting and cataloging the region's plants, flowers and animals.[*] It was

---

[*] Ward, not unlike all self-proclaimed explorers of his time, trumpeted the superiority of the white man whenever possible. In a typical passage from his 1934 volume, *A Plant Hunter in Tibet,* he refers to his baggage carriers as coolies, one of whom "was undoubtedly the missing link. His hairy chest was immense, and he had long ape-like arms; his face, covered with hair, with high cheekbones and projecting muzzle, resembled a gorilla's and indeed he made gorilla noises. He was a good-natured monster."

into this "rent" that we drove, the dirt and gravel road scarcely wide enough for a single car.

Struggling north, we halted on the edge of a precipice where the darker, clearer waters of the Yongchun mated with the red-brown wash of the Mekong. From here, the road was notched on the face of the mountains, once again climbing steadily toward the Tibetan plateau, the Mekong churning below us, its muffled growl the only noise in the mountain stillness. A small village, Xiao Weixi, or Little Weixi, had carved itself into a crook in the hills, and in a grove of walnut trees behind a leaning mud-brick wall we spied the Chinese ideographs *Tianzhutang*, or Catholic church. Earlier in this century, Catholic missionaries had filtered up the Mekong, preaching, baptizing, teaching people to read, building churches.

Although Jesuits first settled in Tibet, principally in Lhasa and Shigatse in the early eighteenth century, missionaries first came to China in force with the British and their opium trade in the 1840s, some missionaries denouncing the drug, others finding their fortunes lay more easily in a quiet, or not so quiet, complicity with Her Majesty's drug dealers. Catholic missionaries were not notably different from their Protestant competitors in their collaborations, but in Yunnan, Catholic missionaries had arrived, not along with British gunboats in the Pearl River Delta, but up from French Indochina and from Burma, a British territory. Along the Mekong here, where non-Chinese ethnic populations predominate, missionaries set about their work much as they had in Africa and elsewhere in Asia, treating the population as heathens in desperate need of salvation. This paternalism, as reprehensible as it is in modern light, was accompanied by a passion for teaching and literacy. But today, what remains are the scattering of churches.

Many of these churches were destroyed after 1949, some converted to warehouses or homes, but some, like the one I stood before, had managed to endure. I pushed open the gate of stained boards and entered a flagstoned courtyard laid before the two-story, tile-roofed church, its upper walls painted white with blue designs common among the Naxi people. As I walked toward the church, a man in a navy double-breasted jacket, a red shirt and brown slacks torn at the knee came from a side building, a cigarette dangling from his hand. He told me his name was Liu Guanghui.

"The priest isn't here," he said, evidently unsurprised at the presence of a foreigner in his little domain. "He's gone to visit relatives. I look after the place. My father used to look after it, but he died two or three years ago so I do now." A chicken clucked across the courtyard, pecking between the stones. "Before this I was a farmer. Of course, I'm still a farmer, but I look after the church as well." He showed me up narrow stairs to the balcony, its balustrade in Chinese crosshatched wooden filigree. From a beam a rusting tire rim hung on a wire, the church bell. Inside, simple wooden pews faced an altar hemmed in by polished red columns. Liu pointed to splintered beam edges. "This is where many carvings were destroyed in the old days. And this is not really good painting," he said, pointing to the rough patchwork paint job. "But we don't have any money. There used to be many, many Catholics here. But now, I think there are only fifty or sixty. After the revolution, people disappeared." A barely legible plaque sunk in a shaded corner of the church announced the date of the church's construction, 1870.

There was only a small stretch of river to the north that I would be able to see. As I traveled, I found myself developing an attachment, an addiction to the sight of the Mekong—and by now I was more often thinking of the river as the Mekong, and less as the Dzachu or the Lancang Jiang; this compulsion to see this river, this great writhing mass of water, became almost as much a driving force for my journey as the desire to see its bounty, the societies that clung to its banks, drawing succor or grief from its passage. And so I pushed on, north toward the village of Badi, just south of the landslide that had blocked our passage from Dechen. Countless streams trickled and gushed from the mountains, and small waterfalls crashed into the Mekong beneath us, the river now a mass of whirlpools and eddies, back ripples and churning counterflows, white-water lace and strange placid pools. Pine forests reappeared as we climbed and Badi sprang from the twilight, lightless and forlorn. For the occasional trucker a three-room roadhouse hammered together from pine boards was home for the night, the window of my room, lit by a solitary candle, opening onto the deafening tumult of the Mekong far below. In the roadhouse's adjoining kitchen, a low brick room with stoves fed by log splits, two women, a Tibetan and a Naxi, fixed a simple meal and told of their town.

"This is a place where many stories are told," the Tibetan woman began. "There was a time long ago, my mother told me of this, when everything here had white stars with five points. One day, a flying machine fell from the sky. It had painted on it this five-point white star. From the place of the crash, three big noses with blond hair came out. Everyone was very surprised, my mother told me. So people took pieces of the flying machine and put them away. The big noses went away. We don't know where." From this I gathered that a helicopter or plane from the U.S. Army must have crashed here during World War II and somehow its pilots had survived. I was told it would take a day to walk to the old crash site, but the young people were no longer too certain where it was. The Tibetan cook told us that her mother, who was a font of local tales and legends, had died nearly two months ago and that the following day was the forty-ninth-day ceremony, an auspicious and sacred day to honor her mother's memory and pray for her soul. She invited us to her house, still farther up the hill. I said that I would come.

In the morning, we drove gingerly north to the landslide that had added nearly two weeks to my own journey but, more important, had severed trade and travel along the river for local villagers. Below where the road had been, the wall of the mountain had collapsed completely, cascading mud and boulders into the river several hundred feet beneath us. And that collapse had in turn undermined the mountain slope above the road, launching still more rock into the river. The road itself had vanished into the newly formed mountainside. On the other side of the landslide, a small group of people from a village to the north precariously picked their way single file over the slide, bits of gravel shifting and slithering under their feet and sending smaller slides over the precipice into the river below. I turned around and returned to Badi, and to the funeral ceremony.

Climbing a path shaped from worn boulders and flat stones, I was pulled toward the house of the Tibetan cook by the screech of horns and the light thud of a drum. Other villagers scrambled up the hill ahead of me. Inside, across the gated courtyard, a group of monks from the smaller Red Hat sect of Tibetan Buddhism sat cross-legged on flat pillows around a low wood table, two blowing on reedy wood and brass horns that reminded me of an Indian snake charmer's horn, while a young boy whacked a hide-skin drum hanging from a rafter. Unlike the monks of Tibet's dominant Yellow Hat sect, the six monks here, four elderly men and two boys, were in everyday clothes—dark blue sweaters, shearling vests, shiny coffee-colored sports jackets; two of the men wore wool snap-brim caps. A tiered, white-clothed altar laden with brass candle lamps, flowers and Buddhist icons was pushed under three dark *thankas*. When the drumming and horns stopped, three of the monks began chanting from a slim-leaved volume of scripture, the life of the Buddha, a finely worked silver knife weighing down the pages. Incense seeped from brass bowls.

As the monks chanted, and then resumed their dirge on the horns and drums, villagers moved in and out of the room, some gathering in the courtyard to drink arrack or tea, or to nibble on sweets that emerged from the kitchen. "This is a very important day for my mother's soul," the Tibetan cook from the roadhouse told me. "All the village will come to honor her. The monks come to pray for her. We pay them thirty yuan"— about $3.65 — "and give them food. We will pray all day for her. This is our way." One of the monks wandered outside and squatted in the courtyard, extracted a curved, long-stemmed pipe from his jacket pocket and lit up. His head wreathed in smoke, he smiled.

I left the funerary ceremony, struck in part by the absence of real griev-ing. It had, of course, been forty-nine days since the death, but there was a mood of confirmation, a sureness about the rhythms of life and death, in a way just as the marriage ceremony some one hundred miles to the north had been—a sense of depth that comes from embedded and preserved cul-ture and belief, a sturdiness of a sort.

In 1968, David Snellgrove and Hugh Richardson, in their important book A Cultural History of Tibet, wrote of their reasons for their work: ". . . because the civilization of the Tibetan people is disappearing before our eyes, and apart from a few gentle protests here and there the rest of the world lets it go without comment and without regret." This is true even more so today, three decades after they expressed their anguish over the assault on Tibetan civilization. Yet for me, as I prepared to leave Tibet behind and head south, I was torn with a mix of emotions: a sense of despair, it is true, over the devastation China has visited on these people and their land; and yet a somewhat surprising sense of confidence that somehow Tibet would endure. Civilizations are not so easily erased. No more than the Holocaust failed to end Jewish culture and exterminate the Jewish people has China been successful in obliterating what it calls "this invidious splittist superstition"—Tibetan Buddhism. The people I had met know very well who they are, what it means to be Tibetan and, equally important, what it means not to be Chinese. I knew, as I prepared to turn south, that China itself was changing rapidly, that the repressions of the past were facing new and substantial challenges, that a Chinese civil society that demanded a voice and rights was forming under the nose of the Communist party and there was nothing that could be done to stop it. And I know that those changes will inevitably loosen the noose Chi-nese communism has thrown around Tibet.

I clomped down the pathway, leaving the shrill of *gyalin* horns and the low thump-thump of the *nga* drum, back to the car that would take me south, toward Lijiang and Tibet's border. Tibetans, a people with an immense lode of oral folktales, have many sayings about journeys, with one of which I am passingly familiar. It ordains that before embarking on a journey on foot one should first take seven steps in an auspicious direction as dictated by an astrological calendar. If that should prove impossible, one should then walk seven steps toward the entry of a magpie's nest. And if on horseback, one should first ride the distance of an arrow's flight upright and steady. With no almanac and no horse, and bereft of magpies, I marched seven steps south from the roadhouse, the Mekong lashing the rocks beneath me and Shangri-la, if that is what it was, behind me. It was time to go on.

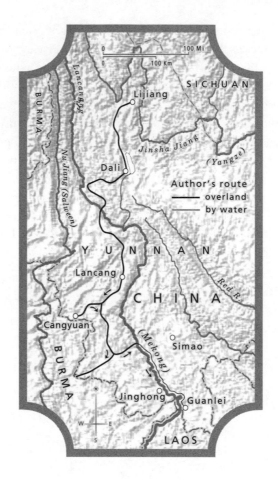

Three

Brigands, Headhunters and Banana Pancakes

I n 1925, scarcely a decade after the last pretensions of the Qing dynasty—a reign of Manchu emperors that began in 1644 and expired under pressure from the West, restive Chinese intellectuals endeavoring to modernize their country and grotesque corruptions of the imperial court—had evaporated in a maelstrom of warlordism, intrigue and the machinations of Western powers, a band of Tibetan marauders, fierce horseborne warriors who plundered and killed at will as they ravaged caravans and villages in search of loot, swept down on the town of Lijiang, a remote settlement of Naxi people in the northwestern mountains of Yunnan Province. A garrison of ragtag, badly armed Chinese soldiers attempted to resist the onslaught and were wiped out with relish and efficiency by the Tibetans. The skirmish, one of countless that raged up and down the gorges of the Mekong and the Yangze, was recounted by Joseph Rock. For Rock, there was a picaresque quality to life amid such dangers. Accustomed to traveling in considerable style in the course of his work, he himself moved in caravans made up of twenty-five or more mules, several dozen soldiers, cooks, batmen, muleteers, cargo handlers, assorted aides and a wind-up Victrola phonograph while repeatedly fending off, or fleeing, bands of "brigands" in his quest for new species of primula or an unknown shamanistic healing ceremony.*

A not untypical encounter took place that same year as Rock was heading north, to the place approximately where I was preparing to head into Lijiang. He wrote,

> We had not gone very far when my head muleteer reported that robbers were behind the caravan. . . . I rode on, but not for long, as my boys yelled in Chinese, 'Robbers are coming,' and at that moment the bandits began to shoot. My soldiers behaved admirably, climbing to the ridge and opening fire on the brigands, but we soon found that we were considerably outnumbered. . . . The shooting continued all afternoon, but, thanks to the bad marksmanship of the brigands, we lost only one soldier killed.

---

* It was not only local brigands who bedeviled Rock. Invading Japanese troops, Japanese submarines and the arrival of Mao's armies all conspired against him, although not always successfully. His seminal dictionary of the Nakhi language—spoken by Naxi—survived a Japanese torpedo attack on his ship off Calcutta in 1944 only because he had photostated a working copy of it while in the United States earlier. Even as he was completing it after the war in Lijiang, Communist troops finally arrived in town, but, as he put it, "Fortunately I lost nothing and was permitted to depart with all my material, for the Reds were local Reds, and the real Reds from the North had not yet taken over."

The bandits are gone now, replaced by the new dangers of hell-bent-for-leather Chinese truckers in rattling, Wedgwood-blue, open-bed Liberation trucks, and Swedish buses filled with Japanese or American tourists. Because the Mekong charges south into largely empty fir-clad hills and canyons that are utterly without roads, I had to detour parallel to the river's course, a detour that carried me onto ancient trade routes that crisscrossed this part of western China. From here to the border of Laos, I intended to stop and linger often, in towns or villages where non-Han societies dwelled, where old kingdoms flourished, where the edges of Chinese control were fraying. I could not be sure of everything I would find as I journeyed south, but there were thick brushstrokes of history I sought: Heading to Lijiang I intended to find the last remnants of ninth- and tenth-century Tang dynasty music; farther south I would poke about for signs of the opium trade—illegal and punishable by death in China but very much part of the lifeblood of Burma's corrupt military regime. Then I would go to the last edges of China before plunging into southeast Asia.

Lijiang itself, once a circular town of gabled and tiled mud-walled houses woven together by a briar of crooked flagstone streets and a network of microcanals, today preserves much of its original character in what is now called the Old Town; outside of it, the straight-razor streets and

Lijiang, an ancient town originally inhabited by the Nakhi, and a haunt of the botanist, ethnologist and linguist Joseph F. Rock, from the 1920s to the 1940s

bathroom-tile buildings of small Chinese towns reign. For centuries, it was a stopover and market town on the tea route that brought the luxurious leaves of *puer* tea from the southern reaches of Yunnan, from a kingdom once known as Sipsongpanna. *Puer* tea leaves produce a dark, deeply fragrant, almost pungent tea with an earthiness and power that is absent from other, more delicate Chinese teas, and was prized across western China; Tibetans, however, traditionally were shipped not the luxurious *puer* leaves, but an inferior version called *guzong*, which was fermented and shipped north to Tibet on mule caravans from Lijiang. In and around Lijiang, an area that historically had been mostly ignored by the Chinese—Beijing was very far away—the Naxi people settled, a Tibeto-Burman people who retained strong cultural and religious links to pre-Buddhist Tibet and developed an archaic written language of pictographs that was known only by *Dongba*, the priests of the shamanistic *Bon* religion that had pervaded pre-Buddhist Tibet.

The road to Lijiang was paved, smooth and terrifying. There is something about the presence of asphalt that encourages drivers in China, of cars, trucks and buses all, to don imaginary goggles and calf-skin gloves and hurtle down these two-lane macadam ribbons at what seem Formula One speeds. Over the previous week, at growing volume and frequency, the driver of the four-by-four I had hired voiced his unhappiness at my preference for out-of-the-way villages, bad accommodations and what he took to be inferior food. Declaring that he had had enough, he suddenly decided to abandon me and return to Gyalthang. On a deserted road north of Lijiang, I realized that traveling had by this point become more a matter of luck than planning, and I found myself making a bit of a fool of myself frantically semaphoring my arms in the hopes that the infrequent car or truck would take pity. Finally something on four wheels stopped, a contraption—a car I was told—that had been cobbled together in Anhui Province according to its badge. My new transport, this sad machine—various shades of red tin sheets had been hammered and folded into shape forming its carapace—beetled about the highway, shuddering as trucks rumbled by, gasping up hills and swaying alarmingly on the gentlest curves. China boasts hundreds of car factories that produce vehicles such as this, all handmade, and all the reflection of vain bureaucrats in obscure provinces who contend that anyone can make a car.

Entering Lijiang today is no longer broaching the portals of a remote kingdom as it was in Rock's day. Rather, it is more akin to landing in an admixture of an Asian colonial Williamsburg and a rural Chinese community. Instead of Naxi, who themselves romanize their language and ethnicity as Nakhi, the language heard on the streets is a mélange of Chinese dialects, the hard gutturals of north China, the elisions and fricatives of Hunan and Sichuan, and the clipped, blocks-falling-downstairs staccato of Guangdong. An earthquake in 1996 leveled parts of the old city, killing more than two hundred people and injuring nearly four thousand, but a civic prescience, rare for China, required that all buildings reconstructed on the ruins of old structures be in traditional Naxi style. The result is a mix of the classic mud-walled, courtyarded houses, their walls painted white with delicate brown frame tracings, and more sturdy houses in cement or cinder block painted in the classic Naxi manner with gray brick frames. Ancient worn flagstone streets bend and weave, squeezing among houses and shops, leaping across finger-thin canals on hump-backed stone bridges and scuttling out to the town's edge, toward fields of spinach, onions, cabbages and beans. Brooding, upturned eves of tiled roofs shadow the flagstones glistening from the early morning scrubbings by ladies in sea blue hats and sea blue aprons with stiff twig brooms. Small restaurants banged together from weathered boards list warily over canals as their cooks nonchalantly fling vegetable peelings into the sprinting waters beneath the kitchen window. Along broader main streets, still of flagstone, are the Kodak photo shops, the knickknack storefronts hawking scrolls, plastic Buddha figurines, Coca-Cola, T-shirts, Naxi basketware and wood carvings. Domestic Chinese and foreign tourists prowl these boulevards, seemingly oblivious to the daily life of Lijiang two or three streets away.

Although Lijiang was simply a short stop on my dash south to rejoin the river, I was in search of a scholar, musician and ethnomusicologist named Xuan Ke, who almost singlehandedly has resuscitated the musical culture of the Naxi after having endured the brutalities of Mao Zedong's savage attacks on the country's intelligentsia, its musicians, artists, poets, writers, indeed, attacks on the Chinese nation itself. I found Xuan Ke at home in a classic *siheyuan*, a courtyard house, just a few paces from the main tourist area. He was tucked into a capacious, pillowed armchair in his third-floor study. Against the far wall from the steep, wood staircase, a wall-to-ceiling bookshelf was crammed with tomes on music, language, anthropology, history and classic literature, dictionaries of classical Chinese and the only extant dictionary of the *Dongba* pictographic script of the Naxi, a dictionary compiled, of course, by Joseph Rock.

"You see this desk," said Xuan Ke, laying his volume atop a stack to the right of his armchair, gesturing to a large black wooden table, "and these two chairs. These were made by Joseph Rock and used by him in his study when he was here for *National Geographic* in the 1920s. For some reason, I don't know why, this study was left alone during the Cultural Revolution. I don't know why, really, all the books survived." Tumbling down a scroll hung on the wall, bold ideographs chalked an elusive Taoist sentiment:

> *There is an essence that precedes heaven and earth,*
> *It is formless, empty and blank,*
> *It is the master of myriad things,*
> *And it does not bend with the seasons.*

A slight man with large glasses, a thatch of tangled and only slightly graying hair—"I'm seventy now. Can you believe it?"—and a rapid gait, Xuan Ke was now hurrying through Lijiang's maze of streets until the flag-stones guided him to another old Naxi house, this one converted into a small concert hall. In front of the building one of the town's many canals gurgles by, clear and quick, and two fig trees frame the doorway. In a small room off the theater, Xuan unhooked a royal blue Chinese robe from a peg, a Sinitic cassock, slipped it on and moved on to chat with an assembling group of ancient, bearded men, many well into their eighties or nineties, he tells me. And then, from suede skin wraps and scarred wood boxes, the old men extracted flutes and gongs and delicate, long-necked lutes. "We play ancient Naxi music," explained Xuan. "This music, even though we say it is Naxi, originally comes from the Tang and Song dynasties"—from the seventh to the thirteenth centuries. "But it has been lost in China, and only here can you hear this music. You see the musicians, though. They are very old. Every year now we lose one or two."

On the walls of the cramped stage were hung black-ribboned portraits of musicians who played here and who had died in the last decade. As the hall fills quickly with tourists, both Chinese and foreign, who settled onto wooden benches, the elderly musicians, now garbed in brocaded satin robes, some peering through Coke-bottle-bottom spectacles and many with chest-length straggly white beards, shuffled out to chairs onstage, their instruments cradled in gnarled hands. And then Xuan Ke himself entered, standing before the audience to explain the night's performance. The music started abruptly, to a Western ear a somewhat dissonant melody of high-pitched flutes and unfamiliarly tuned stringed instruments—one a *sugudu*, an ancient Persian lute now played only in Naxi music, and another a four-stringed, curve-necked *pipa*—in a presentation of dynastic court music from the Tang and Song. A piece called "Waves Washing the Sands" was originally performed in the Tang court to accompany the offering of incense in Taoist rituals, the lyrics for the piece written later, by the last Song emperor during his imprisonment. This, like the other pieces, "Song of the Bound Feet," "Clear Stream and Old Man" and "Sheep on the Hill," all would have been lost had not Xuan lured these old men together in the years following the Cultural Revolution.

Raised the son of a scholar, his father Naxi, his mother a Tibetan singer, Xuan lived a childhood of comparative privilege, including the almost unheard-of luxury in a place like Lijiang of a German nanny. His father was close to Rock and worked with him regularly. Xuan himself grew up immersed in music, not the music of China or the Naxi, but the classical oeuvre of Mozart, Beethoven, Handel and Schubert, music inculcated at the Roman Catholic mission school where he was educated. Like many educated Chinese, Xuan welcomed the victory of Mao's armies over the corrupt, rampaging armies of Chiang Kai-shek's Nationalist government. Indeed, on the wall of his study hangs a faded brown-and-white photo of the young Xuan, his arms raised slightly as he conducts an orchestra and chorus of singers in welcoming the arrival of Communist troops to Kunming in 1950; he played Schubert's *Marche Militaire*. "We were all overjoyed," he says, gazing at the photo, memories of that time a half-century ago washing over him. "It was like being born again. Everyone was happy. There was peace. The Nationalists were gone. It seemed like everything was possible."

Quickly, however, the pleasures of that moment soured as the reality of Communist rule became apparent. Political campaign after political campaign inundated the country, gathering victims in each wave. Then, in 1956, another ray of light appeared. "We were told to come out and criticize the government, to criticize the Communist party itself. We were told bad things had been done and we, the intellectuals, could make things right. But it was a trap." Yet another political pogrom crashed upon China, this the so-called Anti-Rightist Campaign, and Xuan was swept away in its currents. "I was sent to prison for four years," he said. "There was nothing I could do. I was denounced as an enemy of China. I was denounced as a bourgeois remnant because I loved Beethoven." Almost casually now, Xuan rolls his sleeves back, revealing two glistening scars wrapped around his wrists where his jailers hung him from the walls of his cell. "This was a terrible time" is all he says of the torture.

"It is better to speak with humor of those days. Many people suffered. After I was released from prison I was sent to the tin mines near Vietnam. I was in prison altogether twenty-one years. But I never forgot the music. I used to whistle compositions to myself in jail, Mozart, Beethoven. I also whistled Naxi tunes. I think this is how I remained sane. I came out of the mines and the Cultural Revolution was over. Mao was dead. The campaigns were over. I came back to Lijiang and it was like death. It was very quiet. People were very poor. All over China lots of construction began, investments. But here, we were too poor so no new buildings came up. Now, of course, we know that was good because the town was saved. Of course some Communist bureaucrats wanted to make a new city. They wanted to tear down the old city, which they said was decrepit and dirty. They said it wasn't representative of the 'New China.' But politics and the lack of money stopped the destruction of the old city. You look around China now. Look at Beijing, or Kunming. All the old buildings are gone. Only our town has been saved."

I asked Xuan about his musicians, about how he managed to revive Naxi culture. He sighed and shook his head slightly.

"The Chinese, they want to wipe out these cultures as living cultures. They just want things for tourists, not as culture. You know, there are no Naxi schools. All the children are taught in Chinese. And I know only two priests who can read the *Dongba* texts. After the Cultural Revolution, I came back here and met some of the old people my father knew, and I knew, who played traditional music. Little by little I got them together. Many of these musicians, they suffered a lot, too. They hid their instruments. They buried them in their gardens. They hid them in the rafters of their houses. So they went and found their instruments. Some of these were very ancient, four hundred years old. And we began to practice. One day when we were in a schoolyard playing, I saw that there were villagers standing around listening to us. Then we began to have small concerts for the people in town. Of course, when Lijiang became an open city [that is, a city that was open for visits by foreigners] in 1986, we wanted to play for the tourists who started to come. There were foreigners who came who were interested in classical things. But the local government here was very backward. They told us, 'How can you play such music? These musicians are old and ugly. Some of them don't even have teeth.' But in the end we were able to play. I suppose it's because there is money to be made and all these bureaucrats are interested in getting money now."

For Xuan, the future of Naxi culture now rests largely on the preserva-

tion of its ancient music and his hopes to spread it to a younger generation. "We have a school now," he told me, "but it is not easy to get young
people to want to learn this music. They want loud music, karaoke." He
leaned back in his chair. "I want to tell you this poem of mine."

> I walk into the narrow streets of Lijiang,
> I enjoy and watch the world.
> The feeling from these strangers as they travel on these cobbled paths,
> Never having been here,
> Breathing the scent of pine needles from all the forests at once.
> Now I give up all human desires,
> Wine, women and karaoke.
> I want nothing but to step into this world.
> A place which cleans my heart always.
> You may drink one thousand cups of wine,
> But here you may drink one thousand cups of history.
> I hear the songs of the ancient universe,
> the tunes of the Song and Tang. . . .

As I eased open the heavy wood door on Xuan's house, I wondered
whether Xuan could keep his music alive, or whether, as had been the
case for much of China's culture, it and the other facets of Naxi culture
would become little more than petrified artifacts, carefully nurtured, fragile fragments of a past tended under glass, something no longer alive.

In these old walled towns like Lijiang, where the Naxi live, the tide of
Han assimilation has proven irresistible. Local languages, marriage rituals,
fashions of dress and coiffure have given way to Han practices. And yes,
there are people here who mourn the loss of their way of life, not out of a
febrile nostalgia for the past, as the Chinese so often insist, but from a
sense that their identity has been effaced, their histories neatly tucked
away in museums of fading memory, unthreatening, lifeless. Frederick
Wakeman, one of the finest historians of China in the last century, tells of
his experience visiting the Library of Congress to view a collection of
Naxi *Dongba* scriptures, the fifty-foot rolls of Naxi pictographic script
recounting creation myths or funeral rituals or healing ceremonies. "It
was like looking at an illuminated manuscript," he said, "like a medieval
illuminated Bible." The Middle Ages were alive and well until 1949, until
Mao Zedong came to power; there is but one reason the Naxi have lost

their culture, and it is the deliberate Sinicization of China's ethnic groups, a conscious, systematic effort to scrub away languages and habits and beliefs that "offend" Chinese culture, that "are not in accord" with Socialist practices, that are, in the end, not Chinese. But as if to demonstrate that they are not complete barbarians, once a year, in the spring, China's rubber stamp parliament allows a few delegates decked out in the colorful costumes of near-extinct ethnic peoples into the Great Hall of the People. Smiles are bountiful, Chinese television cameras hover lovingly over this panoply of diversity, and when the parliament ends its theater, the museum doors, so to speak, close for another year.

Yet glimmers of ethnic revival—or is it resistance?—appear here and there. Walking down Lijiang's cobblestones, I saw women in traditional Naxi dress—a loose tunic with a black and white cape, symbolizing heaven and earth, decorated with an array of seven embroidered circles representing the stars—carrying their evening's shopping home. Dashing by them were determined young people in bright parkas who ducked into Lijiang's newest phenomenon, an Internet café. There, with cups of coffee flowing and slabs of carrot cake served up by eager staff, Chinese and foreigners hunched over computer screens, reading e-mail, playing complex Internet games, searching for information. To me, these computers in a rustic building seemed an appropriate bookend to my stay in Lijiang, the edges of modernity filtering down cobbled streets smoothed by the slippered feet of Naxi women, the last strands of Xuan Ke's music faintly in my ears.

The next morning I resumed my journey, still distanced from the Mekong by impenetrable mountain ranges. I bargained aggressively, and not altogether successfully, with a local taxi driver to take me five hours south to Dali, a town that not only was once along the traditional trade routes through western Yunnan, but had also been a way station on the Burma Road during World War II. It was along that mud-and-rock track that allied armies resupplied Chiang Kai-shek's armies in western China, with American Lend-Lease trucks lumbering through the mountains from the railhead in the remote frontier town of Lashio in northeastern Burma, across the Salween and Mekong Rivers, past Dali and on to Kunming. That Chiang spent as much of his new weaponry battling Communist troops as invading Japanese armies was largely unknown to the allies, and even when they knew, it did not matter. Even the fact that some generals in Chiang's army were selling these same allied weapons to Communist forces—purportedly while fighting them—in routine black market deals ruffled few feathers, except those of the resolute American general Joseph "Vinegar Joe" Stilwell, who struggled to shape the Chinese into a fighting force while slowly going mad under the barrage of Chiang's corrupt duplicities.

Dali itself, wedged between the Cang Mountains to the west—mountains that form the gorges through which the Mekong, the Salween and the Jinsha, or upper Yangze, flow—and Erhai Lake to the east, first entered Chinese historical records in 109 B.C., when the Han dynasty emperor Wudi organized a prefecture here. Eight hundred years later, as China's influence in the West dissipated, a prince of a tribe called the Mengshe established the Nanzhao kingdom, a state made up predominately of the Baiman people, the ancestors of the Bai people who inhabit the region today. When the Mongols under Kublai Khan overran the last remnants of the Song dynasty in 1253, they incorporated Yunnan into their empire as a province, and though the Nanzhao empire was supplanted, the Bai themselves remained largely undisturbed by the Chinese.

Like many towns in China, Dali was once surrounded by a stout stone wall some ten yards thick at the base, pierced at intervals by towering gates. That wall is largely gone now, though some original fragments remain, but much like the Great Wall north of Beijing, sections of Dali's city wall have been reconstructed with a crispness, a just-off-the-shelf newness that lends it a discordant, ersatz quality. And unlike Lijiang, where much of the old town remains, inside the wall virtually none of the older buildings from pre-Communist days survive in Dali, displaced by Chinese sardine boxes of white-tile facades and blue glass. Even more, in a celebration of local resources, the local government has installed in Dali lampposts made of marble; in Chinese, marble is called *dalishi,* or "Dali stone."

Descending into the Dali Valley, some six thousand feet above sea level, the two-lane asphalt road beelines for the old town, past traditional Bai houses, two-story, U-shaped structures around courtyards, with intricately carved balconies, and balustrades and doors, and whitewashed walls painted with delicate landscapes, or images of birds, fish or flowers. On some walls of storehouses, newly painted slogans, garish and hectoring, instruct: PROTECT THE EARTH AND WATER SUPPLY. IT'S EVERY-ONE'S RESPONSIBILITY. Or, STRENGTHEN KNOWLEDGE OF THE

LAW. EARLY MARRIAGE AND EARLY BIRTHS ARE FORBIDDEN. Or, IF SOMEONE JOINS THE ARMY, IT GIVES GLORY TO HIS FAMILY. Not the slogans of the Cultural Revolution, to be sure, but testimony to the admonitory political culture that endures here.

I had two goals in Dali, one to locate He Liyi, the author of a book called *Mr. China's Son,* an account of his persecution during the Cultural Revolution that was published in the United States in the early 1990s. I wanted to spend some time talking with him about his life in Dali, the Cultural Revolution and a passage from his book in which he had written, "We agreed to throw away many of our Bai people's local customs." And the second task I had was to organize my trip south to China's border with Laos.

Dali is a small place; it takes no more than twenty minutes to walk from the south gate to the north gate down the main thoroughfare, inelegantly called Revival Street. Easier to reach than Lijiang, Dali has emerged as a major tourist destination for Chinese vacationers, who now arrive in fleets of buses and parade through the town trailing a young woman guide garbed in traditional Bai dress—an embroidered red or blue vest over a white blouse, a white apron and on the head an embroidered white chaplet—brandishing a blue, yellow or orange pennant. Revival Street has been transformed into a gantlet of tchotchke shops selling everything from marble sailing vessels to Bai costumes for children.

Off Revival Street, one block to the west, I walked by a café, its signboard in English announcing MR. CHINA'S SON CAFÉ, before realizing that the similarity with He Liyi's book title was too great to be accidental. Inside, a gray-haired man in a rumpled, navy blue Mao jacket sat at a corner table. He looked tired, worn out. I explained who I was and what my intentions were. He told me to return the following day.

At ten o'clock the next morning I appeared at the café. The man I had met the previous day seemed nervous, his hands wrestling with each other. He coughed repeatedly. "I gave your name to the police," he said hastily. "There has to be someone here when I talk to you. I have suffered too much." I was stunned, both because it *was* He Liyi, and because of what he had done.

China in some measure is still a police state, although far less so than when I first lived here in the 1980s. All foreigners who live in China have Chinese friends, feel no impediment in meeting and talking to new people and, except in Tibet, feel no constraints on where they go and who they see. He Liyi's reaction was utterly unexpected, at odds with the current climate. Yet clearly he was afraid to talk with a foreign writer. "I cannot talk with you unless someone from the police is here," he insisted. It was clear that any effort to talk to He would be so constrained and artificial that it would be pointless. I thanked him and left, reverberating with the image of a man clearly still terrorized by the power of the Chinese state, by the memory of his experiences as a victim of China's political warfare.

His written observation that Bai customs had been shed by much of the population in the Dali region was apparent not only in the widespread use of the Chinese language but in the systematic destruction of traditional Bai homes in the city and the creation of a Disneyesque version of old Dali. I spent some time discussing this with a woman named Ma Wei, who ran a local furniture carving shop, a business that churned out handmade chairs and tables in a ponderous Chinese style that hotels and state companies relish. Cherub-cheeked, with long black plaited hair, an unnerving frankness and an occasional habit of wearing Bai clothing, Ma was a single, thirty-something Chinese mom with attitude. "The government is terrible. It's corrupt. It pays no attention to what people want. The officials come and go and could care less about anything except filling their pockets," she told me within an hour of our meeting. We sat drinking coffee at an outdoor café that catered more to foreign backpackers than Chinese tourists, serving among its fare banana pancakes. "They're going to tear down all the old buildings. My father's house, down there"—she wagged a finger toward the eastern periphery of town—"cost two hundred thousand yuan to build," about $24,700, "and the city is going to rip it down because it's old and doesn't look like this shit." She pointed across the street to a garish, beige-tiled building with the ubiquitous blue-glass windows, gold plastic Chinese ideographs declaring it a dance hall and a string of malfunctioning decorative string lights. "And what are they going to pay him, twenty-five hundred yuan [about $304]?"

"There's nothing you can do," she continued. "The police, the government, the army, they're all in this. They know they're all going to get red envelopes," the expression used for bribes throughout China. "If you complain or write a letter, they will surely make trouble for you. You know these government people, these leaders. They're only here for three years and they get their cut and then they leave. They know the tourists only want to see old things, not this new shit, but they don't care. Unless you build new shit how can they get red envelopes?"

As we talked, hawkers with shoulder poles dangling with jars of wine, or baskets of vegetables, or bins of coal loped by. *"Maiiii de jyyoouuu,"* one cried. "Seelllinng wiiinne." Ma Wei sipped her second cup of coffee and scrutinized a passing gaggle of Chinese tourists, their heads pivoting like owls, cigarettes dangling from the fingers of the sunglass-wearing men. She snorted. *"Hanzu,"* Han Chinese, "they're pigs. They spit. They throw cigarette butts on the ground. What can you do with these people?" Ma, the daughter of a Hui, or ethnic Muslim, father and a Bai mother, had little taste for Han Chinese, an attitude I was becoming aware of that seemed spread through non-Han regions of China.

To a great extent, Beijing's policy has been to assimilate non-Han people into the maw of Chinese culture. In 1999, Jiang Zemin, China's president, complained to French president Jacques Chirac about the global popularity of the Dalai Lama and the cause of Tibetan independence. "These people are so backward and dirty," he told Chirac, according to a French diplomat who was present during the exchange. "They are uncivilized. Why shouldn't we try and help them?" This obtuseness runs rampant among Han Chinese. It is an attitude I have heard throughout China, expressed unapologetically, consistently, rigidly, a view I have heard even in Europe and the United States among educated Chinese. Ma Wei said that the Bai had no real future. "The Chinese slowly are taking away our culture," she said. "Children only speak Bai at home. There are no schools for the Bai." I suggested that to prosper in China, learning Chinese, both to speak and to read and write, were essential. "Yes, that's true. But we are Bai. We are Bai."

Before I began my voyage, I had met a Chinese painter, an artist named Luo Jianhua, in Kunming. We met for dinner in an out-of-the-way restaurant, uncapping bottles of Lancangjiang Beer (i.e., Mekong River brand beer, which in my unnuanced outlook I construed as an auspicious sign) as we ate. Luo's paintings, moody, earthy, sometimes vaguely impressionistic, portray the life and landscapes of western and northern Yunnan, the lives of people who are decidely non-Han, in a style that evokes, but never mimics, the work of Vincent van Gogh or Paul Gauguin. It is also a style far removed from the school of modern painters in Beijing and Shanghai who have achieved some fame abroad. Luo is a man of passions, a vigorous violinist and a connoisseur of obscure single malt Scotches. He is a collector of everything, his studio spilling over with bounty: framed and unframed paintings, a couple of violins, a Chinese stringed *erhu*, odd dolls in papier-mâché and china with outlandish dresses, baskets, Chinese hats, an old coal-fired clothes iron, an abacus, strings of amber and ivory necklaces from remote parts of Yunnan, a model of a Spanish galleon, a jar of marbles, revolutionary armbands from the Red Guard era, a blood-red model airplane, a bow and arrow, a brass Tibetan prayer wheel, a Morse code key, a white porcelain bust of Mao Zedong.

"I paint people. The way they live, where they live," Luo told me, lighting another in a ceaseless chain of harsh, filterless Chinese cigarettes. "I spend a lot of time traveling in distant parts of the province, taking photos to use later. The Cultural Revolution had a terrible impact on the minorities," the term used in China for non-Han people. "Now I would say things are quite a bit better. But minorities have no political voice at all. The government likes to dress minorities up in their costumes and show them on television for the National People's Congress," China's parliament, "but it's not real culture. Here in Kunming, this used to be a beautiful old city. Now look at it. There are no old buildings or streets left. There are lots of skyscrapers, lots of new apartment buildings. This is good for the people, of course, but everything that was old China, that was our culture, was destroyed here. So it is not just minorities who are losing their past. We Chinese are, too."

Luo's subjects range, in geographical terms, through much of the territory I passed through so far on my journey, from a stark painting of a solitary Tibetan house silhouetted against a mountain peak near Dechen in the north of the province to a sensuous portrayal of three nudes of the Dai nationality in the far south. His palette of oils favors browns and golds, oranges and grays and purples; light is shadowed, clouded, distant. Traditional Chinese painting, pen and ink, or watercolors on scrolls, holds no allure for Luo; neither does the wave of abstraction that dominates new Chinese art today. Indeed, Luo is fond of quoting the German expressionist Max Beckmann, a painter who was hounded from his homeland by Hitler and who thrived in exile as a great artist. Beckmann, in a 1938 lecture, addressed precisely this question of why he never succumbed to the stylistic conventions of abstract painting: "I hardly need to paint abstract things, for each object is unreal enough already, so unreal that I can only make it real by means of painting. . . ." For Luo as well, the scenes of a thatched hut in a Jin village, of fishing boats, of a woman in a sarong leaning over a simmering pot in her hut, of three Mosuo women in pleated skirts and shoulder baskets chatting, these are the substance of his art, the substance of the world he, like Beckmann, makes real by painting.

·   ·   ·

For nearly fifteen years of my life I have lived in Asia, some in China, some in India, five years of it in Hong Kong, and as frustrating and disturbing as life is on the day-to-day level, as deeply disturbing as the grotesque abuses of human rights are, and as unsettling as the creeping social and cultural homogenization of much of this continent is, there is an irresistibleness to it. Perhaps because I spent so many years immersed in the study of early Chinese history, its society, literature, poetry, economic formation, I found myself on this trip gravitating toward China's remotest regions, those that still echoed of the past. Most of China, particularly the coast and the major cities, are unrecognizable as especially Chinese; for the most part they are undifferentiated replicas of what a modern city must seem to be—glass-walled towers, apartment blocks, well-paved boulevards. Beijing is the worst of these, with virtually every ancient neighborhood inside what used to be the boundaries of the old city wall (itself leveled by China's premier vandal, Mao Zedong) bulldozed to make room for office complexes, Lego-like apartment parks and eight-lane thoroughfares. Even historical treasures like the courtyard house where one of China's greatest novelists, Cao Xueqin, the author of the eighteenth-century saga *The Dream of the Red Chamber*, once lived have succumbed to the wrecking ball.

Romantic or uncritical mourning of some historical past is not particularly profitable intellectually or aesthetically, but the imperatives of modernity are not necessarily incompatible with a reverence for, or at least a simple appreciation of, historical beauty and accomplishment. Most troubling for me in China—as opposed to India, where there is an enduring sense of culture, religion and the past—is what seems to be among most Han Chinese an indifference to their history, to what it is that makes China China. To be sure, traditional festivals are celebrated, but more often than not these are celebrations without memory. For Gao Xingjian, the Chinese Nobel laureate novelist, this obliviousness to the past is precisely what is stripping China of its identity.

In a passage from *Soul Mountain*, he writes of a small village:

On the river-bank there used to be a round carved stone with seventeen barely discernible tadpole-like ancient ideograms on it. However, as no-one was able to decipher them, when stone was needed to build a bridge they dynamited it. Then they couldn't raise enough

money and the bridge wasn't even built. . . . The generations of villagers who have lived here since don't know the history of the place,
don't know about themselves.

Meant as a metaphor for China, this indifference to, indeed this inability to, recover the meaning of being Chinese ripples across the country.
Out by the Mekong though, I felt some sense of something larger, larger
not by design but from a mix of inadvertence and neglect. Never the
same threat as Tibet, China could easily ignore, for the most part, the
welter of ethnic groups that spread through the mountains and down
along the Mekong. China's hand was present, but under its shadow, there
were visible and tantalizing threads to a pre-Communist past.

Nearly a day's drive to the west from Dali, the Mekong, still the Lancang Jiang to Chinese, cascades from the gorges of the Yunling
Mountains in furious torrents, glorious white water for hardy
rafters, were there any, but unnavigable for the more placid boats and
river transport I was seeking. In Dali I arranged for a four-wheel-drive
Toyota with a new driver, a hard-charging half-Tibetan, half-Han wheel-
man of infinite resourcefulness named Song Putong, to take me to the first
reaches of the river that could be navigated, with several side trips thrown
in. Heading south meant descending instead into a welter of mud tracks
and stone byways.

China's population is shifting inexorably from villages, from tending
vegetable plots and tilling paddies, to towns big and small. Statistics in
China are murky, skewed by interests local and not, but broadly a population that was 83 percent rural in 1980 was by the end of the century 34 percent urban. But most of this urbanization is not so much the result of the
migration of rural jobless into huge metropolises like Shanghai,
Guangzhou and Beijing, but the filtering of people from the land into what
were once smaller rural outposts and are now boomtowns or even cities of
a million or more people. Like dandelions on a rolling hillside, these fast-
growing towns and cities are spread across China, indistinguishable in
their newly laid streets, the glazed-tile buildings mingling with the older
gray blocks from the 1950s, strips of new cement storefronts selling Japanese televisions, refrigerators, hip shoes and stylish dresses from Shanghai,
Colgate toothpaste and Johnson & Johnson shampoo, motorcycles and

The Lancang Jiang, as the Chinese
call the Mekong River, early in the
morning in Yunnan Province

Rototillers. The road from Dali slithered through towns such as these, immemorable places, characterless, unwelcoming, but the inevitable commercial and industrial centers of a nation undergoing a breathtaking economic modernization.

Late in the afternoon, we reached a concrete arch bridge spanning the Mekong tucked in the cusp of two mountains, my first sighting of the river in some time. Since the Tibetan plateau, I had found myself more absorbed by the river itself than I had expected. There was something about this seemingly endless roughened ribbon of water, its boundless vagaries, its evasiveness and relentlessness, the way it plunged through geologic time and the small present of my journey, how it rampaged loudly and sashayed mutely across Asia's vastness. Here, as I had in Tibet, I tossed a couple of bottles into the river, bottles with a small note asking the finder to contact me with the story of where and how he or she recovered the message. Dusk was descending and we made off along a farm track beside the river, winding up in Shanyangcun, or Fir and Poplar Village, composed of a main street in robust concrete lined by decaying one-

and two-story cement buildings. For reasons that eluded both me and the driver, the town had erected barricades at the bottom of the main street barring access, so we parked in the mud and hauled our packs up the virgin concrete to a rooming house where itinerant truckers bunked down for the night. Spartan rooms on the second floor were served by an outside stairwell, the doors of each room opening onto a balustrade overlooking the main street. Downstairs, the inn's proprietor and his wife toiled over woks heated on gas-bottle-fueled burners in a kitchen black with soot; at the room's other end, a square wood table with four low stools served as the dining room.

Before eating, I headed down the main drag, toward the harrowed vegetable fields that enveloped the village center. Quickly, Pied Piper–like, I had attracted a small pod of children, amused and curious about what they must have decided was a new species. As our troupe shambled toward the vegetable fields, I began asking them about the sprouts of green leaves, the bulbous tubers, the bits of orange that peeked from the black soil. "Cauliflower," they chimed. "Ginger. Turnips. Sweet potatoes," at each of my inquisitive gestures. I presumed they took me for a complete idiot, the notion that someone could not know a sweet potato from a turnip being simply unimaginable to them. And, of course, they were right. Then one

Terraced paddy fields in southern Yunnan Province,
near the Mekong River

little girl, in pigtails and a yellow sweatshirt with the visage of a gleeful Mickey Mouse on it, tugged on my sleeve. "Sweet potatoes," she began, struggling to keep her high voice serious and sufficiently stern, "you can stir fry them with beans. You can bake them in coals. You can steam them. You can fry them in slices. There are lots of ways to cook sweet potatoes."

Fir and Poplar Village was a settlement of ethnic Yi, once a slave-owning and warlike people who battled incursions by Han Chinese well into the twentieth century. The water buffalo in distant fields fringed by coconut palms signaled that this was also the edge of southeast Asia, culturally, linguistically, agriculturally and climatically. Although once the Yi delighted in their defeat of Han invaders and their enslavement as serfs on Yi farms, in this village there was little now to distinguish the people here from Han Chinese up the road. Ethnographic maps show a swathe of Yi all along the Mekong watershed here, but apart from the distinctive two-story adobe houses with flat roofs, there was little to suggest a distinct or vibrant cultural identity; in the 1920s, when Rock encountered the Yi, he described the headdresses of Yi women as "hats, with broad, flopping brims, resembling the heads of antediluvian ichthyosaurs." Alas, such haberdashery has gone out of fashion.

The children spoke to me and each other in Chinese, and the meal I had that night was typically western Chinese, a plate of lip-numbing *doufu*, chicken chunks under a mound of fried chili peppers, with some salted longbeans. As I ate, the owner of the inn invited two men in tattered sweaters and gray slacks into the kitchen and brought them over to my table. "Can we see your passport?" one of the men asked, explaining that he was some sort of town official, what sort I could not quite make out. For some travelers, particularly for journalists, passport checks in China are often moments of suspension, of doubt about what will happen next, whether their voyage will be cut short, whether some obscure regulation, unwritten, unknown, will be summoned from the air, resulting in that nebulous Chinese state of *mafan*, or trouble. But I have never worried excessively about such checks, particularly in remote parts of the country; I also was traveling on my maroon Irish passport emblazoned with a harp, a passport from a country almost no one in China has heard of.

I handed over to one of the sweatered men the passport, which he paged through unfamiliarly, his brow caricaturely knitted. Then he produced a folded piece of lined paper of the kind that schoolchildren use and, helped by me to find the correct page, laboriously wrote down the information about me. When he couldn't quite manage, I invited him to share a beer and then copied out the information for him. "Thank you," he replied. "*Ganbei*" (Bottoms up). It was a toast he took with utter seriousness.

When I finished, I asked him what he wanted the information for. Although in major cities in China, in five-star hotels, it is customary to take the passport details of guests, in China's far west, such formalities are generally ignored, even when they are required by police regulations. "You are the first foreigner ever to stay in our village," solemnly replied one of the men. "We want to have a record of your visit. You are our honored guest." And with that he refilled our beer glasses, toasted our eternal friendship, insisted I must return to the village and slugged down his beer. The two men then got up, ceremoniously folded the paper with my data on it and lumbered out.

Among the subjects in China that one finds the most distasteful, and best avoided, is that of toilets. When I decided to avail myself of the facilities after dinner, the proprietor directed me across a paved schoolyard to a public outhouse. Approaching it proved impossible. A tsunami of stench washed toward me, physically repelling me and sending me scurrying for a remote corner of the schoolyard at the edge of a cabbage field. I was not particularly surprised at this, for almost all toilets in China reflect a conspicuous aversion to hygiene. But what happened next reeked of the clash of civilizations. When I was back in the restaurant to have a final cup of tea—and to watch the proprietor and some friends sit down to their water pipes, his a gigantic blue plastic tube the size of a bazooka—one of the smokers asked me if I wanted to watch television. "I have five satellite dishes," he boasted. "Do you want to watch CNN?" I thanked him and declined, but I did wonder about the paradox, a paradox only an intruding foreigner would conjure, of medieval toilets across the street from a late-twentieth-century television complex.

China is a land of such disjunctions. The arrival of the car in China is another case of old habits shadowing modern conveniences. There are, for anyone who has driven in China, no discernible rules of the road; right-of-way is accorded to each driver in every circumstance, a practice that leads frequently to horrendous accidents. In the pre-automotive era, which was not that long ago, horse riders or cart drivers (of whom plenty are still to be seen) could largely go where they pleased at a pace that brooked few dangers. Today, drivers in China pilot their cars, trucks or buses as if they are the only ones on the road and other cars are merely obstacles to be avoided, maneuvered around, pushed aside. Although

China has built hundreds of new freeways, drivers will blithely proceed up off-ramps and down on-ramps if they feel it will hasten their trip. A rough-and-ready driving etiquette emerges from this motoring bedlam, of course, but it is an etiquette that collapses more frequently than it is observed. Indeed, pedestrians who are hit by cars are often held liable under the country's laws for the accident, even if they are killed; there are no rights-of-way for pedestrians in China. The point, of course, is that the appurtenances of modernity come more easily than do the cultural, or behavioral, transformations one has seen in the West. In remoter regions of China, Western suits and sport jackets are the rage for men, but they are invariably worn with index-card-sized labels prominently sewn on the outside sleeve cuff, just to let the public see the suit's brand. Televisions are rampant, and in restaurants, even in fancier places, waitresses will bustle over to turn the device on at full volume as soon as you are seated; conversation becomes impossible. I construe such practices as an invitation to celebrate all that's new and wonderful, but there is at the same time a self-defeating undercurrent to such efforts. There is a certain clichéd vérité to the French adage *Plus ça change, plus c'est la même chose.*

As we headed south the next morning on little more than farm roads, the mountains of previous weeks slowly subsided into endless swells of pine-covered hills. Towns and villages with names like Dog Street (a village made of a single street through patchwork fields), New Factory and Reservoir came and went. We were, I determined, now nearly ten thousand feet lower than the source of the Mekong, but still well over a mile above sea level. Song, the driver, adjusted his dog-fur kneepads every hour or so, all the time grieving aloud over the beating his Toyota was taking. A compact man who treasured his Toyota, Song nonetheless drove relentlessly, sipping tea from a screw-top jar, frowning regularly at the rustic scene that seemed to offend his sense of his own urbanity, a trait acquired in Kunming. As we drove, terraced rice paddies began to appear, like great green felt and mirrored staircases in some extravagant Busby Berkley musical, the new rice shoots a phosphorescent green in the midday sun.

I was heading for Manwan, where, in 1986, the Chinese opened the first dam on the Mekong River, one of hundreds of dams China has built or is in the process of constructing across the country. I have always retained an ambivalence toward dams: on the one hand, they provide the power that enhances living standards; but on the other, they disrupt and scar the beauty of the rivers they bar. Now widely seen as environmentally destructive in the United States, dams are being built with a frenzy in China, from the immense and internationally controversial behemoth on the Yangze River at the Three Gorges, to smaller dams on a myriad of middle-sized rivers in northern and western China. At Manwan a great dam sundered the Mekong, and I wanted to pause there, if only for an hour, to contemplate this wound.

Suddenly, we jounced onto an immaculate highway, yellow-lined, race-course smooth and bounded by comfortable shoulders dappled by sunlight sifted through swaying fronds of banana trees. We whisked along it in silence toward the dam. But just before Manwan, we paused at a yawning hole that had been blasted into the side of a hill. On a hefty bronze plaque outside the mouth of the cave, I read: MAИ GHUAI DAZHUAИWAИ TUИИEL: THE RUIИS OF YUИИAИ-BURMA RAILWAY, a sign erected on October 1, 1998 (China's national day) by the local Communist party and tourism office. Here, during World War II, Chiang Kai-shek's army began but never completed a railroad to link up with the rail line in Burma.

Just beyond the remains of the aborted railway, the road banked left and the massive arc of concrete that is the Manwan Dam loomed into view. On the far side of this immense curved wall, soaring 416 feet from the water below, the Mekong, which only a day ago I had seen eager and frantic in its gallop through the hills, lay flat and still, a lake, not a river, extending more than forty miles into what was once a deep valley. Across the lake, a scattering of thatched adobe houses nestled among terraced paddies. Two gaping jaws on the dam's face spewed the lake into a new, infant river, indelibly rainbowing the sky in a vast cloud of mist. Regroup-ing, the Mekong grabs the valley, building itself anew from small streams and lesser rivers as it continues south. But its efforts are once more chal-lenged, for only a half-day's drive away yet another dam is being built, only fractionally smaller than the Manwan.

We headed toward the new dam site, struggling along a mud track through hills and paddies. The previous night's rain had stirred the mud into a gloppy, oozing channel apparently intent on capturing and swal-lowing our panting Toyota. After thrashing through the mud for an hour, all four wheels grinding, slipping, clawing for some patch of traction, we rounded a bend to find a small truck, a Chinese microvan, the sort with doughnut-sized wheels and an engine scarcely lawn-mower size, sunk to its undercarriage in the mud. Four men, shin-deep in the muck, were assessing the fate of their vehicle, smoking and chatting with a remarkable nonchalance. Somehow my driver managed to edge by the mired truck by creeping up the hillside on our right. And then, charitably, he uncoiled a chain from the back of the Toyota, attached it to the microvan and with a shriek from the engine managed to haul the stranded van from the road's clutches.

Another few hours down the road, the mud road gave way to a broad new concrete highway sturdy and wide enough, it seemed, to support jumbo jet landings. This runway led down to the new dam, its gray concave wall falling more than 350 feet to a pan of concrete. I stared.

The Mekong was gone. Below the dam, dozens of immense concrete mixers and red-cabbed dump trucks, buses, cars and cranes were parked on the flattened and bone-dry river bottom. For geologic eras the Mekong had flowed here, gouging its passage through these hills, shaping the landscape even as the crush of the Indian and southeast Asian landmass crumpled the Earth's crust around it. Now it was gone. I am not an engineer, far less a student of dam building, and so the technical marvel of it all escaped me, but the sudden sight of an empty river bottom, the vanishing of this river I had been tracking now for more than two months, was somehow unsettling. On the far side of the paved river bottom a hill of coniferous trees rose steeply, and then I noticed that far to the south, to the right of where I stood, the Mekong was being reconstituted; in building the dam, engineers had drilled three tunnels through the mountain I was looking at and had diverted its waters through the tunnels so that the dam could be constructed on dry ground. Altogether, the Manwan Dam and this, the Dachaoshan Dam, would supply China with 2,850 megawatts of electricity. Already, the 1,500-megawatt Manwan Dam—about three-quarters the output of the Hoover Dam—was sending power eight hundred miles away to the new industrial heartland of Guangdong Province. China's need for power has been rapacious as its economy has grown for two decades at more than 10 percent annually; as big as these dams are, they are dwarfed by the Three Gorges Dam Project on the Yangze, which at an ultimate cost of $30 billion is the largest infrastructure project on Earth, but which also has displaced millions of poor farmers, and will inundate dozens of small towns and hundreds of villages. Dam building will be in China's future for decades to come.

I was headed toward the small border town of Cangyuan, a town that had sprung up on a narrow road that squirreled its way into Burma past villages and hills peopled by the Wa, a place I sought as a fabled crossroads in World War II as well as once a well-trod opium caravan route. Among the most ancient ethnic groups in western Yunnan, the Wa were widely feared well into the twentieth century for their skills as headhunters, a practice that scared off Chinese migrants and titillated the imaginations of American and European adventurers who described the Wa, whom they, of course, never met, in terms of chromatic celluloid. One of these characters was Nicol Smith, who managed to maneuver a 1937 Ford over the Burma Road just as it was opening for arms shipments in 1939, a trip he did in high style, including, of course, a steamer trunk packed with the requisite black tie evening wear. Herb Caen, for decades a revered columnist at the *San Francisco Chronicle*, eulogized Smith on his death in 1995 at the age of eighty-five:

> Nicol, whose parents were trés social but impecunious, paid his way through Stanford by playing terrific poker. Later he was recruited for the OSS, precursor of the CIA, by "Wild Bill" Donovan, who gave him a couple of million bucks and sent him deep into the jungles of Burma, where he read children's stories over a transmitter: "It was a cold and rainy day, but the tiger went out anyway." Or, "It was so hot the rhino sank in the mud," etc. He was giving weather information to Allied flyers. There was always something Evelyn Waugh-ish about Nicol.

In his jaunty account of his Burma Road rally, *Burma Road: The Story of the World's Most Romantic Highway*, Smith did his best to perpetuate this fierce image of the Wa.

"The Wa people surpass in ferocity those of the 'Triangle' and the Naga Hills tribesmen, on the border of Assam," Smith said in quoting a lonely but hospitable British colonial official stationed near the Chinese border.

> They are headhunters, without doubt. No young Wa is considered to have reached his majority until he has produced a human head lopped from its body by his own hand. They have avenues of trees leading into their villages. These trees have been stripped of their branches, but they bear strange fruit—fruit which is not of Nature's making. Niches have been carved in these trees, and in these niches are placed human heads. The flesh is still on the bones, but it has been treated with preservatives known to the old men of the tribe

and the head will grin there pleasantly for many years—perhaps longer than the man who put it there.

In fact, the Wa *were* headhunters, believing that skulls kept in a household were auspicious, totems that augured well for new crops and talismans to ward off sickness. But the fanciful descriptions of such dilettante travelers as Smith were aimed more at reinforcing clichés of the inscrutable, mysterious Orient than explaining or understanding the societies through which they journeyed. Indeed, Smith's travel accounts are capsules of jolly meetings with the French governors of Indo-China, American consuls and British colonial officials who amusingly found themselves in Asia. Chin up, old boy.

The glossiness of those adventures, enormously readable yet utterly uninformative, was not unlike the stylishness of films from that era, cinematographic displays of style and glamour and wit, and not many doses of reality. That chipper worldview, of course, has long since dissipated, and the Asia of the Mekong I sought was one of how people saw their own world, how they pursued their future. In a sense as well, my journey was a quest for genuineness, for the unadorned, for the unbrushed. Much of journalism, particularly that practiced in global capitals, is consumed with sifting through clouded language, feints, misdirection, lies and outright lies. Along the Mekong, for the most part, nobody lied. Nobody had to.

As we rolled into Cangyuan, we drove past outlying Wa villages, no longer settlements of ferocious headhunters but collections of rickety huts of woven bamboo walls and thatched roofs surrounded by low dirt walls or bamboo-splint fencing. There were no paddies here; the Wa engage in the most primitive of farming techniques—slash and burn. Hillsides were charred and eroded. Cangyuan scraggles from the valley, a jumble of low, boxy buildings, a border town crawling with fancy dark-windowed, four-wheel-drive Mitsubishis bearing Burmese license plates, sunglass-wearing Chinese traders talking deals at sidewalk restaurants shrouded in clouds of cigarette smoke and platoons of hookers in stack-soled shoes and tight, short, neon minidresses. A mood of fast money, secret bargains and arrangements, unfettered businesses of shadowy purpose, permeated the town; Cangyuan existed to service trade with Burma, trade I would chase the next day.

Shortly after the sun peeked over the eastern hills the following morning, my driver and I made for Burma, just a handful of miles over the mountains. Near the border, we stopped at a Wa village, a desperate place

of worn huts and garbage-strewn lanes. A villager told me the place was
called Yunluek. On one side of the road, an old woman, her face cracked
and weathered, sat on a low stool a scant six inches high in front of a
primitive loom, its frame fashioned from tree branches, the warp a narrow
breadth of vermilion wool, the woof a succession of yellow, blue, orange,
baby blue and pink streaks, the makings of a *mban,* or sash, that all women
seemed to wear here. The young man who offered the village's name
invited me to his home, and we wended our way between huts, all of
woven bamboo walls and thatch roofs on log stilts about four feet off the
ground. A few piglets and a couple of scrawny chickens rooted in a pile of
garbage next to his house.

He gave his name as Nisae Anup and said he was twenty years old.
"This is a very old village," he told me as we settled in the large room that
was his house, a room without tables, stools, a bed or a stove. A single
lightbulb dangled from a rafter. "We trade with other villages across the
valley and bring things into Cangyuan. Mostly rice. The problem is that
the land is not good for growing here, so we can't grow very much to sell.
Many people work on the roads. They break rocks or dig ditches. Nobody
has very much money." Unlike people in other villages I visited, Nisae did
not offer me tea or even water; perhaps it was because he was young, perhaps he was too poor to offer tea. It didn't matter, but it hinted at the village's desperation.

"Let me take you to the church," Nisae offered after a while. Burma, as
a former British colony, had been a hunting ground for flocks of Protestant
missionaries earlier in the twentieth century. And because most of the Wa
people lived on the Burmese side of the border, many of them were subject
to the efforts of missionaries, efforts that were evaluated by the home
office in terms of the number of baptisms. The border means little to the
Wa, who regularly move back and forth into Burma to trade and to visit
relatives, and so it is not surprising that Protestant missionaries had made
converts here as well. At the northern end of the village stood a small
chapel made of brick walls and a corrugated asbestos roof, two twigs on the
apex of its roof making a cross. Inside, a handful of benches were aligned
before a plain wood altar. A sign in the Wa language read YAOK YAW SIYEH
PA TAW BWAN U-IK, Praise God from Whom All Blessings Flow.

Nisae picked up a worn hymnal from a bench and told me that the pas-
tor came to the village once or twice a year. I opened its ragged cover to
learn that the hymns had been translated and compiled by the Reverend
M. Vincent Young and was published in Rangoon, Burma's capital, in

1985. On the flyleaf, the names of the hymnal's owners were laboriously written: Sai Meung, Sau Rehong, Maw Pa. I turned to a Wa hymn and asked Nisae if he would read it for me. "I can't," he murmured. "I can't read." I was not shocked, but I wondered what use hymnals were for an illiterate people. I asked him whether there were others in the village who could read. "Most people here cannot read. There are some young people who can read a little Chinese. But most people cannot read hymnals."

Song and I left the village, heading toward Burma. We passed a Chinese customs post and waved at a green-uniformed soldier slumped on a folding chair under a flagpole dangling China's five-starred red flag. The rutted dirt road wound past roughly plowed fields. As we rounded a bend, a mule train appeared, plodding toward us and China, bulging sacks flung over the flanks of each mule.

"Opium," whispered my driver.

Opium? We were far from the Golden Triangle, although I could see poppies growing on a hillside. The mule train moved steadily through the no-man's-land between border posts, its handlers, armed only with tree-limb walking sticks, padding along in rubber flip-flops. Apparently the lethargic Chinese border guards behind us were of no concern; this was a border where passports, much less import documentation stamped and in triplicate, were superfluous. I wanted to talk to the mule drivers, but the driver suggested that these particular men were not eager conversationalists. Where the mule train was going I never determined, although several Western officials familiar with Asia's opium trade told me later that there were, in remote parts of Yunnan, processing laboratories for Burmese opium, labs under the protection of local police and army. "On this kind of thing, China is a very delicate problem," explained one official, who was scornful of his government's reluctance to press Beijing on this issue. "China is very tough on drugs in general, but out in the wilds, a lot goes on that Beijing doesn't know about and doesn't seem ready to control. There's a lot of money to be made."* This was the first opium I was to see; it would not be the last.

Asia was changing under my feet as I traveled, geographically, climatically, aesthetically, historically. Tibet seemed a long time ago, its arid,

---

* Fully 80 percent of all the opium and heroin seizures in China occur in Yunnan Province, which, according to some estimates, also is home to half of all of China's drug addicts. The Yunnan government has made some efforts to cooperate with Burma in helping farmers switch from growing opium to more benign cash crops like fruit and coffee.

chilly heights, its yaks and monasteries, and these first ruffled hems of southeast Asia suggested promise and surprise. Except for an occasional chat with Song, who was not an accomplished conversationalist, I was often left wallowing in my own thoughts, the novels tucked in my backpack and my single conduit to the larger world, a tiny shortwave radio that brought the BBC to my ear. Yet, even the travails of Bill Clinton creeping scratchily over the airwaves had little resonance. I felt a solitude of sorts, not the solitude of a recluse, but of time and distance and culture. Watching the muleteers urge their burdened charges forward, oblivious to me and the border, was tingling. Here was the raw material that fueled crime and human devastation in the West, but on this dusty road it was just another mule load. If I felt loneliness, it was scrubbed away by these sights and the meanings they implied.

   We drove on. The precise border between China and Burma here is demarcated by a stubby obelisk of cement incised with the date, 1994, in Chinese on the north face and Burmese on the south. Beyond the marker, a patchwork of charred acres mixed with roughly plowed fields and raggedy villages of Wa spread across this border region. I did not intend to spend time here; we had wandered at least two days' drive from the Mekong and I wanted to get back, closer to the river's flow.

Mountains in a sea of clouds in Yunnan Province,
beside the Mekong River

. . .

Just two hours out of Cangyuan, the Toyota's aches and pains, which had been accumulating at a worrying rate—an electrical problem, a punctured radiator, a flat tire and then an oil leak—finally gave way to engine wheezing, plummeting oil pressure and steering problems. These ills occurred as we were climbing through a vista of pine- and oak-covered hills boaed in gauzy clouds; rounded hilltops peeked above the clouds like islands in a vast milky sea.

By dint of luck, prayer and the lack of any alternative, we managed to gasp our way into a place called Twin Rivers—the rivers being the Black River and the Mekong—a typical small rural town that as best Song could determine boasted a single repair shop, this an open yard with a cement ditch used to examine the underside of a car, a shack with a few odd tools, piles of old tires, a stack of discarded engines and two other Chinese-made taxis that appeared ready for intensive care. There was no computerized diagnostic machine, the type of thing a Toyota really needs, no spare parts, oil filters or, indeed, any cans of oil for our engine. Song dashed across the street and returned with a plastic pitcher of oil that he emptied into the crankcase. Unhappily, it began leaking from somewhere in the engine after he started the car. By this time the repair yard's own mechanics, if that is what they were, had gathered around the open hood to scrutinize the engine, more than one of them casually tugging on cigarettes. Opinions were offered, rejected, offered again at enhanced volume and rejected again. Song, by now acquiring a fine coat of oil on his hands and face, spotted what he thought was the leak and with a wrench produced from somewhere unhooked a length of metal tube, its greasy surface revealing a long split. There were no Toyota dealers within five hundred miles, so Song went off to find a local welder to try to suture the tube's wound. Miraculously, he succeeded. Reattached, the car seemed to run acceptably, although the steering problems remained for the rest of the journey. It was, I realized, an exercise in automotive self-reliance that has fallen out of fashion in the West, but without which transport would seize up in much of Asia.

That evening we reached a town called Lancang (Turbulence). I was desperately hungry, and though there seemed to be few restaurants open after dark, I found one and, as is customary in rural areas, wandered back into the kitchen, actually just a couple of gas-fired burners behind a glass counter in an open shopfront, to see what was fresh, or at least available.

The owner, excited at the prospect of a late customer, offered up a couple of house specialties. "How about some *zhuchong?*" he asked. I looked at him, puzzled. I knew, or thought I knew, each word he had said, *zhu* meaning bamboo and *chong* meaning worm or insect. Together the words did not make much sense to me. Flustered by my confusion, the owner, clearly the chef, grabbed a length of bamboo about three inches in diameter and banged its hollow onto his palm. A heap of squirming white worms tumbled out: bamboo worms. Of course. He suggested preparing them with garlic, fermented beans and chili peppers. I declined. In that case, he asked whether I'd prefer the *feng 'er*, a term I did know—bee larvae. I told the chef that alas I would pass on the bee larvae as well. We settled on a bit of fatty pork with chilis, some *doufu* (tofu to Western eyes) and a plate of peppered long beans. I do not regard myself as excessively squeamish, having eaten scorpions, ants, grasshoppers and all variety of obscure sea life, but I could not quite wrap my palate around those wiggling worms.

Morning came and with it, for the first time in my journey, a welcome warmth in the air, the gentle edges of the torpid, humid coverlet that blankets southeast Asia. I changed into shorts for the first time, and did not put on long pants again for nearly a year. At midday, we rolled gently to a rise just over the Mekong, broad and powerful again, shushing between hills with authority and purpose. A bridge crossed the river here, a long graceful arch supporting the two-lane roadway that ran west. Broadleaf banana plants and the first palm trees we had seen lined the river, the sun casting a green opalescent light through their leaves onto the shoreline. Here, the rounded hills were corduroyed with dark green, bushy-leaved rubber trees, the northernmost reaches of the rubber plantations that roll south to the border with Laos. On the Mekong's west bank, downriver from the bridge, two rusted, two-deck river boats—passenger or cargo vessels, it was difficult to tell—were tied up at a dock; another was heaved onto the shore, listing crazily on its broad V-shaped hull, its propellers paralyzed on encrusted shafts. It was here I intended to find a boat to take me south, down the river, and off the backwater roads I had traveled for nearly two months.

A handful of seventy-foot, steel-bellied barges with flipped-up prows and squat steering cabins on the stern chugged back and forth across the river and up a feeder riverlet ferrying villagers with sacks of rice, chickens bound at the feet and plastic jugs of cooking oil. Two more barges were tied up against a crumbling pier. My small computerized navigation device told me that I had dropped 14,393 feet below the heights of the

Mekong's source, and that I was still 2,048 feet above the river's goal, the South China Sea. None of the big boats seemed river worthy or ready, so I waited until one of the small ferries returned from its rounds. When its driver, should I say captain, clambered onto the concrete dock, I explained that I wanted to head down to Jinghong, the next big town downriver, and the place where I hoped to find a boat to take me to Laos.

He looked at me, then looked at his boat as it tugged at its mooring line, and then back at me. "Jinghong," he said. "Very far. Very far. I don't go to Jinghong." I told him that it was only forty miles or so and that I would pay him better than if he spent the day running passengers back and forth across the river. "Jinghong, Jinghong," he repeated, an internal calculator working to determine precisely how exorbitantly this foreigner could be scalped. "Okay, thirteen hundred kuai," or nearly $160, he demanded; kuai means "piece," and is shorthand for a unit of money. I told him that was extortionate, that I'd pay him 700. "Thirteen hundred," he reiterated. This back and forth went on for some time. But as I looked around I realized bleakly that there was no alternative short of swimming, so I handed over thirteen grubby one-hundred yuan bills.

"I've been driving a boat for three years," said the barge captain, who introduced himself as Yang Youhua, "so everything is fine. I've been to Jinghong a few times, so no problem." As he talked, he tapped and wrenched tight various parts of the engine, which sat under the aft wheel-house. His ensign, or boat boy, polished a patch of the steel-plate barge deck to throw my pack on, and then cast off. We backed into the current, charcoal-black smoke coughing from a tin stack. It was 1:15 in the afternoon and I was elated by not being on terrible roads, and more so by finally being on the Mekong itself. No longer, I told myself, would I have to contemplate the colored tracings on road maps to find a passable road, or any road for that matter. Now my road would be the river.

The barge's engine thudded in rapid pulses—*chugg, chugg, chugg*—a timpani remarkably redolent of Humphrey Bogart's *African Queen*. In a moment we were around a bend, and the dock, and signs of humanity, had vanished. Fawn-colored sandbanks rose from the river's edges toward forests of palms and teak and oak, a mosaic of greens mottling the shoreline. Above, or between, the engine's clatters, the call of birds echoed from the trees. The river itself, a tawny current perhaps a quarter of a mile wide, ran easy, here and there wrapping itself into spiraling whirlpools.

Washed by a wave of reverie, I failed to notice that the engine behind me had begun belching smoke. Yang spun the wheel to starboard and we swerved toward the right bank and then ran up onto the sand. The boat boy leaped from the prow and sank a sand anchor to hold the barge. I stood at the wheelhouse and watched Yang fiddle with various tubings. "The line is leaking," he muttered. "This oil line has a hole in it." I asked if there was, by any chance, a spare line on board. He shook his head. "Downstream I can fix it," he said. Then he tore a strip of toweling with his teeth and cinched it around the ruptured tube, cranked the engine and with the boat boy clutching the retrieved anchor, backed once more into the river.

We putt-putted on. For more than an hour we saw no other boats, not a hut, no sign of human habitation. After a time, on a far bank, we saw that a wooden motor pirogue had been hauled up on shore and Yang made for it. We anchored into the sandbank again, and he pilfered the pirogue for a bit of tubing; I never determined whether this was convention, theft or a boat that somehow belonged to Yang, and he did not say. In a matter of minutes he had replaced the leaky tube and the engine was restored to health. Yang tipped some soap flakes from a plastic bag of Tide detergent onto his greasy hands and washed them in the river. "This is an old boat," he explained. "I think it's more than thirty years old. I've had it for three years. It breaks a lot." Yang was thin, muscled and, beneath a wild hedge of black hair, smiled continuously, baring his cigarette-stained teeth. He leaned on the wheel like a trucker.

"My parents are farmers," he said, "from Simao," the prefecture near the bridge. "Here there isn't any work besides farming, so I thought I would try this. You have to get a license to drive a boat. That costs three hundred sixty kuai every year," about $44. And what about the boat? I asked. "A boat like this is about sixty thousand kuai," or $7,300, a fortune in rural China. "I borrowed the money. Nobody has that kind of money. I pay five hundred kuai each month." I was juggling these sums and asked him what he earned. "Passengers pay three kuai for each trip, usually just to a nearby village. Every month, I earn about two thousand kuai," or $244, far more than the average farmer, and a plausible figure. And then, to confirm my computations, he added, "a lot more money than being a farmer." The river textured around us, from washboard ripples to great glassine pools, from spurts of white water around half-hidden boulders to stocking-run currents. Two yellow butterflies bobbed and darted over the water.

"I'm thirty years old now," Yang went on, "and this is good work for now. I have two children." And what would they do? I asked. A village appeared around a bend, and we turned toward it. "My kids are too young.

I haven't decided what they should do. But you know, children don't always do what their parents want these days." Yang's life, and his musings on his children's future, reflect the tumultuous changes in China proper. Where at one time state mandate had dictated employment, housing and lifestyle, the collapse of the Socialist economy at once freed people from controls and opened before them the uncertainties of economic freedom. No more the security blanket of the past, but no more as well the impoverishment it entailed. Even here on the Mekong, or perhaps especially here on the Mekong, life is changing.

At the village, we beached the barge again and Yang, a ten-gallon plastic jug in each hand, strode up the hill in search of diesel. He returned and filled the barge's tank, and once again we turned into the river. As we pulled into midstream, a villager splashed into the water with an inner tube folded in half into a black sausage and began paddling furiously. We watched as he drifted downstream, gradually managing to cross the river; finally, just as we chugged out of sight, he made shore.

Suddenly, ahead of us, the river turned white and gnarled as it was squeezed between towering walls of granite and gneiss, and forced through and over a jumbled boulder field. River spray drenched us as we nosed into the rapids, the flat-bottomed barge skittling across the tumultuous surface. And then, just as suddenly, the water stilled, as if the river had finished its rodeo for the time being. Further on, we passed a bamboo raft with two fishermen in straw hats, one guiding it on its clumsy meander with a long bamboo pole. "They have fish on that," Yang said. "They drift down to Jinghong and sell the fish. Then they take a bus back to their village and build a new raft and start all over." I waved as we went by, and the fishermen did, too. I asked Yang what he thought about the river, whether there were songs or tales that boatmen told. He shrugged. "Songs? No. No, I never heard a song about the river. It's just a river. What's the big deal?" So much for romance.

History provides a similarly meager bounty. Traditionally, Chinese poets brushstroked their poems about what they saw and felt, and few ever saw the Lancang Jiang. By the time Mao Zedong had conquered China, the cultural czars of the new Communist state had revved up poetic paeans to the great man, including an obscure and by now utterly forgotten bit of doggerel celebrating the helmsman's glorious achievements along the river. Purportedly written by an anonymous Lisu in the early 1950s, it is particularly insidious because it praises Mao as the salvation of non-Han peoples, when, in fact, Mao and the Communist party were systematically pulverizing non-Chinese cultures and forcibly assimilating non-Hans into the motherland. The poem, typical of the era, is one of few that even mention the river.

> *Biloh Shan, the snowy mountain,*
> *is so high, the Lan Cang River*
> *so deep;*
> *you*
> *the Communist party*
> *i-yao!*
> *you are the light of the poor peoples*
> *on all our borders*
> *you,*
> *Chairman Mao*
> *i-yao!*
> *you are the saving star*
> *of all our minority peoples.*

Four hours after we left the bridge, the outskirts of Jinghong appeared, at first simply settlements of bamboo huts on stilts with the elaborate thatched roofs of the Dai people, roofs that are tucked in sharply at the ends before spreading out again into the classic southeast Asian roof, a design that ensures regular air circulation and a surprising coolness in the damp heat. Banana trees were planted in neat rows along the bank, their leaves fanning in the breeze; a grove of orange trees nestled in the low right bank. Slowly, more substantial buildings of cement appeared, some with corrugated roofs, others in red tile. And then a road swung along the river filled with trucks, buses and cars. Before us, an old steel cantilever and concrete bridge spanned the Mekong's half-mile girth. Yang piloted us onto a mud bank under the bridge. What had been forty miles on the map had taken just over four hours.

I jumped from the prow of the barge and promptly sank up to my ankles in gooey mud. Yang tossed me my pack and waved good-bye. He had to find a place to moor for the night before setting off early the next morning for home; he said it would probably take more than eight hours for the return journey. And I had to find a place to stay before searching for another boat to take me through the last miles of China before reaching Laos. Jinghong itself swirls with dust from unpaved streets and construction sites, a river town that is the capital of the Xishuangbanna administrative region, a place where China's usual strictures are less vigorously observed. Chief among those activities that thrive here and are prohibited elsewhere in China is gambling: Jinghong sported casinos in most of the bigger hotels and dozens of smaller gambling parlors scattered around the town. Beijing is far away, and its tentacles of control are more flaccid here. Not being a gambler though, I found a small hotel and prepared for the next morning.

After breakfast in a little café that catered to Western tastes, in my case that meant orange juice—which I had not had in months—oatmeal, banana pancakes and coffee, I hailed a taxi, a white Volkswagen Santana, and told the driver I would pay him by the hour. I had no idea where I would find a boat, and someone at the hotel had told me there were no such things as passenger cruises downriver. I set off over the bridge toward what looked like a dock on the riverbank opposite Jinghong where two cargo barges piled with logs were tied up, each of them flying the flags of China, Burma, Laos and Thailand. Here, the Mekong first flashed its commercial skirts. I chatted with some of the men straggling around the pier, but none knew of any boats headed south. I climbed aboard one of the cargo barges and talked to a deckhand, but he said the boat was not heading back downriver for a week. Too long.

Frustrated, I told the taxi driver to take me back across the bridge to where I had landed yesterday at the foot of a support column. There, a barge was grounded; next to it was another of the rusting two-deck riverboats I had seen upriver. On the upper deck around a table, four people were eating lunch. Behind the riverboat was a mud-spackled white speedboat. Sliding down the mud hill, I glopped over to a plank that led to the barge's deck, and then, teetering clumsily, scooted across another plank to the riverboat. Up steel stairs to the second deck, I began my pitch by telling the diners that I was trying to find a boat that was heading to Guanlei, the last town in China on the border with Laos, and the town from where I hoped to plunge into southeast Asia. "No boats from here," said one of the men, returning to his bowl of rice. No passenger boats? No cargo boats? I asked again. "No boats," he shot back. I persisted: Well what about hiring a boat to take me by myself downriver? Chopsticks lowered from the four bowls and the three men and one woman looked at one another. "How much would you pay?" asked the man. How much do you want? I answered. The table went into a huddle, and the man turned to me. "Six hundred kuai," or about $73, less than half of what I had paid for yesterday's boat. Too eagerly, I agreed. "When do you want to go?" he asked. Now. "Okay."

I told him I had to get my pack from the car and would be right back. Sliding down the hill once again, this time with my pack, I felt even more ungainly and steadily muddier. I was looking forward to a classy ride down the river, the white prow of the speedboat slicing through the river, a wake of frothy troughs spinning out behind us. I clomped back up the steel gangway to the upper deck of the riverboat with my pack to find one of the men leaning into a bicycle pump, its hose snaking over to a rubber zodiac. A rubber boat? I assumed we would pull it behind us as our safety boat. The rubber boat was heaved over the side. And then, from the back cabin, one of the men emerged lugging a forty-horsepower Johnson outboard engine that he brought down to the lower deck and clamped onto the back of the zodiac. "This is the boat?" I asked. "This is the boat," was the answer.

With an utter lack of ceremony, we shoved off, the driver yanking the starter cord sparking the engine to life. In a few seconds we shimmied out into the current, under the bridge, and Jinghong was gone. For a time, a road paralleled us to the left, but it dropped away and we plunged into forests rising from banks of shattered and foliated shale, great blocks of basalt like massive axe blades sunk into the shoreline. Then, slowly, we moved through expansive sandbanks and sandbars dotted with still pools in which long-necked black cormorants waded. An eagle rode air currents above us, circling lazily. Now the rubber boat moved swiftly down the river, shuddering through shallow rapids, bounding off humpbacked rocks like submerged hippos.

Some three hours after setting out, the forests on our right became Burma—deep, dark forests with no signs of habitation, unlike the last fragments of China on our left, where crisp rows of rubber trees revealed human hands, and sprinklings of Dai thatch-roofed huts emerged in forest clearings. As we wound south, river traffic, boat by boat, increased. Needle-thin wooden pirogues with lawn-mower engines chuttered upriver with a dozen passengers; in the front of one stood two monks in the brilliant saffron cotton robes of southeast Asian Theravada Buddhism. A pair of fishermen in a pirogue stood easily in their boat, one flinging a circle net like a disc of poetry into the gentle swirling current glittering in the late afternoon sun. And suddenly the driver announced, *"Daole."* "We've arrived."

Guanlei burst into view, its concrete-pan dock crowded with barges, double-decker cargo vessels, a line of canvas-covered trucks stretching up a ramp to the town carrying apples from Shanxi, I later discovered. Stevedores pouring sweat heaved boxes from one to another, and into the hold of the largest boats I had yet seen on the Mekong. The driver wheeled our tiny rubber boat around the congestion and sped up onto a mud bank. A path had been worn up the riverbank to the crest, where a couple of men with walkie-talkies were attempting to orchestrate the loading of the boats, the arrival of another cargo vessel, its whistle echoing, that was arcing toward the wharf, and the collection of sheaves of documents that were being passed from captains to runners. Here, for the first time, I saw the Mekong in full flower, the river broad and sure, the dense jungle of Burma across the water, all the jostling cargo boats flying the four flags of the region's countries.

Behind me stretched Guanlei, like a frontier town in the American West, two spartan ranks of shops, eateries and little hotels lining a dusty main street three hundred yards long. Beyond it were hills and forests. It took only a few minutes to tour the town, a place so new the cement of the shop rows hardly seemed dry. A couple of men in white short-sleeved shirts walked down the street, pistols tucked in the waistbands of their baggy gray trousers. There was no bank, no post office, no government office. A border control office staffed by police in informal uniforms serviced the shuttle of import and export documents and sheaves of passports for the crews, rubber stamps whacking down like punch presses. A limpid Chinese flag dangled from a pole. Guanlei had that border-town feel, the atmosphere of a place that lived by its own rules, that belonged to no one in particular.

I plopped into a plastic chair at an open-air restaurant and ordered a beer. The owner emerged from the back with a frosted bottle of Huanghe (Yellow River) Beer and sat down with his bamboo tube water pipe, introducing himself as Lei Xiayu. He spoke Chinese with a southern accent, so I asked him where he was from. "I'm from Guangdong"— eight hundred miles to the east—he laughed, breaking into Cantonese, only some of which I got. He took a deep draw on his bong. "I've been here five years. You should have seen it five years ago. Nothing. Just a couple of buildings. I built this place last year." Why, I wondered, would anyone leave booming Guangdong, the province that abuts Hong Kong and has prospered more than any other province in China in the last two decades? "I got divorced," he said, "and wanted to do something

A small steel barge heading south on the Mekong
River in southern Yunnan Province

new, go somewhere else. Some friends told me about Guanlei. I was
never here before. But I like the weather. Nobody bothers us here. Now
I married a local girl and have a daughter." His head swiveled toward a
pigtailed girl bent over a notebook, pencil in hand, who sat at a table in
the back of the restaurant. "I started over, a new life." That is something
that never before had been possible in China. He had gone west, young
man.

I had begun my journey down the Mekong nearly four months earlier, in
Tibet, on a hilltop with a nomadic yak herder who was trying to cling to
old ways, to the life of his ancestors, and I was ending this stage of my
voyage at the China-Laos border with a restaurant owner starting over in
a wild west town. While much of that time was spent traveling, there were
quiet moments as well, time reading in towns like Lijiang, or sitting in
cafés in Dali, or paying my bills over the Internet, where I could find it.
Still, for the most part, the Mekong I had seen slices through lands whose
people were searching for handholds in the past—in a forgotten written
tongue, in a neglected music, in a faith under seige, in well-preserved ceremonies. In China none of this is easy. Whether Tibetan or Lisu, Bai or

Naxi, or one of the dozens of ethnicities that inhabit the far reaches of China's empire, the overwhelming force of the Chinese is difficult, and often impossible, to withstand. It is not just China's political dominance, exercised ferociously at times, that rides rough over non-Chinese, but China's economic power—seen in the profusion of consumer goods, the pervasiveness of Chinese-controlled economic life—and, most important, the government's discouragement of local languages and the compulsory use of Chinese in schools almost everywhere.

For many of these people, the forced use of the Chinese language is particularly galling. The Chinese, not they, are the immigrants to their land. Their ancestors lived along the Mekong long before the first Han Chinese set foot here. Indeed, the decimation of the Native American populations in North and South America is an apt analogy with the fate of remote ethnic groups in Yunnan. But I took heart from the efforts of men like Xuan Ke who sought to rescue their cultures from extinction. One man cannot, of course, stem tides, but without him there would be no Naxi music today, a loss not just to his own culture but to China's as well.

What seemed apparent as well was that the plethora of societies along the Mekong, whether celebrating a marriage, mourning the dead, herding yaks or struggling with hymnals on the Burma border, were often turning inward, away from the wider world, a world that had brought nothing but persecution, destruction and death for decades. Of course, isolation is never absolute. The world, and more China, intrude in the guise of television, radio, tourists and commerce. Youngsters in Lijiang, as preserved an ancient city as there is in China, revel in the town's newborn access to the Internet, and the language in which they surf is Chinese; but if they glance out the window of the Internet café, they see flagstone streets laid centuries ago between stone buildings of equal age.

In the last two decades, ripples of China's increasing prosperity have spread here. As much as life is hardscrabble, there are buses to distant metropolises, telephone lines being strung, Chicago Bulls caps being worn, pots being sold from the Tibetan plateau to Taiwanese merchants. But as much as livelihoods are improving, as much as gel-filled sneakers are creeping into shoe markets and Mickey Mouse adorns schoolkids' backpacks, there is the unmistakable scent of civilizations dying—some quietly, like the Lisu or the Bai; others brutally, like Tibet's.

When I mention to Chinese friends how troubling I find this cultural erosion, this creeping homogenization, they accuse me of wanting to stifle modernization. There is as well, I find, a need to avoid falling for a notion of a romantic nobility in untinged cultures. But modernization does not preclude cultural integrity and meaning, and the imposition of Chinese values and practices is hardly synonymous with modernization; for me, it is just another form of cultural domination. In the United States there is an ongoing debate over the virtues of bilingual education, with one school of thought insisting that a uniform language, English, should be the language of instruction; only with English, it is argued, will students eventually succeed in further education and in the workforce. Such arguments always struck me as characteristically American and provincial. European students, whether in Scandinavia or Switzerland, for example, manage well in two or three languages, and do more than succeed. Here along the Mekong, at the simplest level, I delighted in the mélange of languages, dress, food and habits. And I mourned signs of their fragility.

To the south lay what was once French Indochina, where for more than a decade Americans battled Nationalist and Communist armies, and lost, and what now was emerging, if haltingly, into sunshine. I had been to Vietnam several times, and looked forward to returning there, but Laos and Cambodia were unknown to me apart from histories and the diaries of French explorers I had read before setting out. Sitting in Guanlei, I wondered what lay ahead.

A fat copper sun slunk away into the Burmese jungle, dragging dusk behind it. Two Burmese girls in long white skirts slit provocatively to their thighs sashayed down the sidewalk on black platform shoes. From somewhere, an old Nissan car with Burmese license plates appeared, its steering wheel on the right, motoring slowly in great ellipses up and down the broad main street. A card game started up at another table at Lei's place, one of the players a policeman from the border post, his green jacket slung over the back of his chair. I wandered toward the town's edge overlooking the Mekong, the glow of bare bulbs from the shops casting dim shadows. Below me, in the dark, I could hear the river whispering by.

Author's route
— overland
— by water

0 ——— 100 Mi
0 ——— 100 Km

CHINA

Guanlei
Mohan
CHINA
Meung Sing
BURMA
Xieng Kok
Takhilek
W—E
S
Houay Xay
LAOS
Mae
Nam Sai
Chiang Khong
Mekong
Luang Prabang
THAILAND

Four

The Golden Triangle

I n the thirteenth century, Kublai Khan, the Mongol warrior and the first emperor of the Yuan dynasty, rolled over China with startling ease and stumbled onto the Mekong River, down which he sent his armies. In their wake they absorbed swathes of what is today Thailand and Laos, coming to a halt at Angkor, where the Khan left an ambassador to keep an eye on things. For the next six hundred or so years, virtually no foreigners, neither explorers nor armies, penetrated into the jungles, forests and grasslands of the Mekong Basin in southeast Asia. That ended in the mid-nineteenth century, culminating three centuries of European global exploration and colonization, when the French dispatched an expedition of naval officers, geographers and botanists to make their way from Saigon as far up the Mekong as they could manage.

As chronicled by a mutton-chopped, hollow-eyed and pompadoured French naval lieutenant named Francis Garnier, the explorers proceeded in grand style up the river for two years from 1866, first on gunboats, then on barges, elephants, horses and palanquins, accompanied at various times by dozens of porters and armed escorts, and laden with a considerable cargo of tents, mattresses, gold and silver ingots, the latest Lefaucheux rifles, brass compasses and a holosteric barometer. As Garnier said of the members of his expedition: "They were charged with ascending this great river, the fertile delta of which they and those that surrounded them had so often traversed, dreaming of its unknown origins. They were leaving for the unknown. . . ."

For Garnier and his colleagues, the real task was to determine how the river could be used for commerce and for speeding French colonization and, in his view, France's destiny of civilizing the world. So wedded to Gallic notions of chivalry and propriety was Garnier that he felt compelled in his journal to apologize profusely to any French lady who should read it that he did, in fact, find Lao women "pretty." His two years of travels took him and his team through Cambodia and Laos and up into Yunnan as far as Dali, all conducted in the nineteenth-century, matter-of-fact conviction of the cultural and intellectual superiority of the *colons*; Garnier studied "racial types" and never hesitated at the sweeping judgment. China, he wrote, was a "sick civilization," and "when the Chinese are better informed about the West, they will understand its superior power."

When deserted by porters, he dragooned peasant farmers, their buffaloes and their carts to haul his caravan's supplies. When offended, he felt no compunction about caning a presumptuous local. And when his pirogue rowers, fighting relentless currents, exhibited fatigue, Garnier spurred them on by threatening them with his revolver. His expedition was, in today's lights, a rather grotesque exercise in arrogance, ignorance and power; but in his day, Garnier was fêted, festooned with honors (including the first award to a geographer of a knighthood of the *Légion d'Honneur*) and sent forth on further conquests. To the everlasting mystification of the French, the Vietnamese continued to resist their colonizing efforts and battled French troops up and down the country. Garnier, who had declared, "nations without colonies are dead," was ordered to suppress these intemperate rebellions, but found the going a bit less easy than his triumphal trek up the Mekong. On December 21, 1873, he and his soldiers were ambushed by a guerrilla force of Black Flag fighters. The Black Flag hacked off his head and took it away in triumph. It would take France another decade before it properly subdued Vietnam and still more years before the French erected a statue to Garnier, which now stands in a distant corner of the Jardin du Luxembourg in Paris.

Garnier's legacy, in the broadest sense, was more than a century of conflict in southeast Asia. Already by the time of his death the French were referring to the Mekong as "our river," and the colonial war drums were thumping in the National Assembly for the expansion of Indochina to include Thailand. Accomplishing that goal meant first laying claim to all the land east of the Mekong, a task that essentially delineated the existing borders of a land the French called "Laos," but which also sundered the traditional cultural and linguistic lands of the Lao in half, leaving the region west of the Mekong under the kingdom of Siam, as Thailand was then called. What France got in Laos was a land of subsistence farmers, few resources and a barter economy, what ultimately was an appendage to its principal colony, Vietnam. But the resistance to French rule, which simmered continuously until the final defeat of the colonialists in 1954, bubbled in Laos as well, a resistance fueled later by the Communist ideologies that would entangle the United States in more than a decade of war across southeast Asia. Eventually, Vietnam, Laos and Cambodia were pulverized by American forces, horrors that have been documented in vast and wrenching detail. It is, though, the aftermath of those wars that is still unfolding, and it was into that emerging history I was headed.

My intention, roughly sketched in my mind, was to cross into Laos and work my way back toward the Mekong, and then try to find boat transportation south, to the old royal capital of Luang Prabang, to Vientiane and then south to the Cambodian border, a trip that I assumed would take two months or more. It was a journey that would carry me across the discarded shards of French colonialism and the more recent scars of the American war in southeast Asia, offering, I hoped, some sense of how Laos, a quarter of a century later, was surmounting its past and, more important, whether it was in any sense settling into the larger landscape of Asia. The Mekong marked its border with Thailand, but was it a barrier or a bridge, a thoroughfare of commerce or a defensive moat?

First, however, my goal was to wander through the territories of what is still called the Golden Triangle, the lands and trade routes that funneled, and still do to a lesser extent, opium and its processed product, heroin, into the veins of addicts in Europe and America. I never shared the exuberance for drugs, hard and soft, that swept the hippie movement of the sixties and seventies, and even less so the addictions of heroin or cocaine (I've always preferred a gently aged Paulliac), but still I subscribe to the view that people should be free to consume what they want. Holland's rather sensibly permissive policies on drugs do not seem to have led that affluent and thriving society into perdition; in the United States, by contrast, billions of dollars have been spent fighting drug smuggling and distribution, to no discernible effect other than to fill prisons. For me, however, it was important to see who lived there, what they did and what opium meant to them.

A fine paved road bullets south in Yunnan toward the border with Laos, a road built originally by the Chinese to ship weapons to North Vietnam during its war with the United States. The military trucks are gone now, displaced by sporadic cargo trucks lugging cases of beer or sacks of rice. I was traveling the final few miles to Laos by road, and not by river, because border formalities, the requisite red passport stamps, were not available in Guanlei, though they were in the border town of Mohan.

Mohan sparkles like a bathroom in a television commercial—a two-story hotel, an open-air restaurant, a few open shopfronts piled with boxes of Sony and Hitachi televisions, all lathered in gleaming white tile. My taxi, a red box manufactured in Shanghai by Volkswagen, idled outside the border post where a young policeman stamped my passport and asked me, rhetorically, why anyone would want to go to Laos; he didn't wait for an answer. I set off, the taxi puttering past the elevated red-and-white-striped border pole toward Laos. Precisely at the border itself, a stumpy black marble marker, Chinese macadam gave way to Laotian dirt, and a thousand yards farther on was a small, decaying, corrugated, asbestos-sheet-roofed building baking in the midmorning sun. In a room of bare cement and only a rough wooden desk, a Lao border official fingered my passport before stamping it. Then he ripped a slice of paper from a notebook and stamped and signed that as well, the first of what would become a hefty sheaf of stamped paper scraps documenting my comings and goings, all part of the Laos government's efforts to control movements within its borders rigorously, and the first glimmers I had of its all-consuming paranoia.

Beyond the border station, a bus of ancient vintage, its window frames glassless, canted slightly to the left, and a posse of dust-filmed pickup trucks with bench seats in the back were surrounded by drivers dangling cigarettes from their fingers and day traders wearied with sacks of rice, or plastic bowls, or boxes of tea, all jawing over the price to the next town. Dirt tracks wiggled away into a forest, and a nearby string of earthen-walled huts hemmed a stretch of dry clay the color of rust. Heat and dust and languor washed over me as I trudged toward the pickups, a sense sinking in already that I had stepped into a land scythed from modernity. I approached one of the pickup drivers, wary that my command of Lao at that point did not extend even to numerals. I tried Chinese and we managed, though his was essentially confined to negotiating prices, and I hired him to take me to a town called Meung Sing, a town on the way back toward the Mekong, a distance measured by a fingernail on a map, but in his pickup a voyage of five hours.

As we drove over a road that had been part of the Vietnam War–era Chinese military highway, discernible now only by odd scraps of asphalt, the driver halted regularly to pick up passengers who wagged their hands at him, mostly rural women in long saronglike skirts, their hair bundled in black cotton scarves, traders all. Onto the truckbed they slid sacks of potatoes, cardboard cartons of Beer Lao, small nylon bags of clothes and cans of cooking oil before crowding onto the parallel benches in back. We jolted along the rutted track through forests that showed signs of being nipped at by loggers, past lonely villages of bamboo and thatched huts on three-foot-high stilts, serenaded by the chat and laughter of the women in back, a melodious "Wwwooooo" erupting at particularly hilarious, teasing moments. No other trucks or cars passed us.

We rolled into Meung Sing in a cumulus of dust that had shadowed our passage from the outset. A rake of low, whitewashed buildings edged a central road that ran out to fields of sugarcane and coconut stands and poppies, along which two open-front restaurants stood cheek by jowl, each with half a dozen rectangular tables, all filled with foreigners. I was surprised to see so many Western faces in this obscure settlement near the Chinese border, in a part of Laos peopled principally by the Akha, a tribal hill people numbering scarcely one hundred thousand, who are sprinkled across northern Laos and Thailand. These travelers were not the tourists who swan through Asia from fancy hotel to tropical beach to storied monuments. Instead, in tie-dyed T-shirts, baggy cotton pants, hair often in luxuriantly beaded dreadlocks, these were participants in a river of their own, a hard-traveling stream of Europeans, some Americans and some young Israelis who had just finished their military service, who rippled down the Mekong seeking cheap eats, cheap beds and remoteness from the world they had escaped; some came as well to smoke the opium that was plentiful here. As I entered one of the restaurants for dinner, one of these travelers rose and announced, "Well, I guess I'm off to the den," in the weary tones of a middle-aged office worker off to catch the morning train. A few of his comrades shambled to their feet to follow. The "den," it was apparent, was Meung Sing's hangout for smoking opium.

Laos remains the world's third-largest producer of opium, surpassed only by Afghanistan and Burma, just on the other side of the Mekong. And although huge areas of northern Laos are cultivated with opium poppies, the poverty of Laotian farmers and their rudimentary farming techniques consistently depresses the yields of their poppy crops compared to their Burmese neighbors, who are far more firmly woven into the fabric of international drug production, refining and transport. During the 1990s, opium production in Laos rose and fell depending mostly on the weather and, if the U.S. State Department's reports are to be believed, fell sometimes because of eradication and alternative cropping programs. Since most of Laos is largely inaccessible by road, the successes touted by the State Department are open to some skepticism, skepticism perhaps even more warranted by the department's own Bureau for International Narcotics and Law Enforcement Affairs, which in 1999 noted dryly that "given Laos's poverty and the very low salaries of Lao government employees, it is assumed that there are officials and military personnel who receive bribes from illicit drug trafficking. These possibly include some officials at relatively senior levels." Indeed, a senior-level army officer was then earning about 100,000 kip each month, which was worth less than $12.

Darkness shuttered Meung Sing with a tropical finality, and bare bulbs hanging from ceilings flickered to light like so many fireflies. A few strands of power lines ran out of town, fragile signs of some distant possibilities. There were no telephones in this town of perhaps eight thousand people. The restaurant owners moved among their tables setting out candles, murmuring that the power would remain on for only an hour or so. And indeed, little more than sixty minutes later, the harsh glare of the bulbs suddenly dimmed, and then expired. I finished a cup of thick, dark *café Lao*, a version of *café filtre* that Laotians often mix with hefty dollops of sweet condensed milk, and wandered into the ink black streets, flashlight in hand. I strolled toward the town's edge, listening to the sounds of crickets and the bass drones of conversations seeping from open windows.

A lambent glow emanated from an open doorway off to my left. As I neared the low-eaved building, the sounds of deep inhalations came from the doorway; then I saw some of the foreigners from dinner, men and women both, lolling against a wall, cupping long-stemmed pipes in their palms. Slowly, as if they were underwater, they waved me in, their eyes wide but only vaguely, distantly focused. A silver-haired Lao man squatted on the dirt floor and doled out the opium with stained, gnarled fingers as the smokers ignited the black pellets with disposable lighters. "Smoke, smoke?" he asked me, tubing his fist before his lips. I shook my head. A sweet, thick, charry aroma perfumed the room, heavy and tangy. No one talked, the opium seemingly molding spheres of individual contentment and sufficiency. I moved on.

That same month I was in Meung Sing, I later learned, a heroin-processing laboratory on the Mekong, a bit west of the town, in the heart of the Golden Triangle, was raided and destroyed by a team of police and army troops. In 1998, the same year that the first American Drug Enforcement agent was posted to Laos, Lao police announced the arrest of 361 people for various drug offenses; of those seized, seventeen were foreigners. Still, in Meung Sing, the lure of cheap opium—$2 or $3 would cover an evening's smoking, and a kilogram of pure heroin could be had for $100—was the magnet for these late-twentieth-century travelers to this obscure corner of one of the world's poorest countries.

For Lao farmers, though, opium growing is the only chance they see of improving their lives. The morning after my nocturnal promenade, I bicycled into the countryside for some hours, a land of flat valleys rimmed with hills a bit like doughy edges in a pie pan. My companion was a young man named Amphay, who spoke some English and whose father owned one of the pocket restaurants in town. "I was at the university in Vientiane," Amphay had told me, "but I had to come back here because I couldn't pay the fees." How much were they? I asked him. "Every month was one hundred thousand kip," he replied, which at that moment was about $24; two months later, with the value of the kip in free fall, it was less than $16 and a year later less than $12. In early 1998, 4,220 Lao kip were worth $1: by the end of 1999 it took 8,550 kip to buy that same greenback. The Laotian economy, if it can be called that, hardly functions at a measurable level, although there is, as I soon learned, a brisk smugglers' market across the Mekong from Thailand. Amphay worked now in his father's restaurant, where the travelers paid in dollars, and said he was hoping to go back to the university the following year.

As I churned past a field edged by cane stalks on a clanky and leaden Chinese-made bicycle of some age, a farmer poked his head out of the stalks, his fist tubed before his mouth, an invitation to yet more opium. Amphay asked me if I wanted a smoke. I said I did not, but I did want to talk to the farmer, a request he relayed. We retreated into the field and hunched down on two dirt mounds, the farmer rearranging a cloth sack that contained his opium, pipes and other paraphernalia. I asked him to tell me about growing opium. "This isn't my field," he said, waving his hand a bit eastward. "This is a good place by the road to sell some opium." But why not rice or coffee? I suggested. "The soil is not very good here," Amphay translated, "and we cannot make money growing rice or vegetables." The farmer paused and fished a lone cigarette from the side pocket of his blue jacket and lit it with an inch-long match he plucked from a small box. Then he fished another cigarette from his pocket and offered it to me. I shook my head.

"Opium is hard work," he said, "but every year there is opium and every year we can sell it for dollars. Who would buy potatoes along this road? Would you buy potatoes from me? I sell opium for American dollars." How much, I wondered, could he earn in a year? "Some hundreds," he said. I pressed him, but he repeated, "Some hundreds." What did he do with his dollars? Squatting, his arms dangling over his kneecaps, his fingers thick, knotted with calluses, he glanced at me appraisingly. For a time he was silent, sucking on his cigarette, contemplating the horizon. "In China there are many things to buy," he replied eventually. "I have a bicycle. I have a generator. I have a television and a satellite dish." A satellite dish? He laughed. "We watch Thai television. If I did not grow opium, I could not afford a television." He rose to his feet, his knees cracking slightly, gathered his sack and lifted his bicycle from the ground. Without a word, he pushed it to the road and pedaled away.

Back in Meung Sing, I biked over to the parking area near the morning market to find some way to get to Xieng Kok, a village on the Mekong just south of the Chinese border, a way station and small river trading depot that led farther into the Golden Triangle. Because Meung Sing is just a few miles from the border, some of the drivers spoke a bit of Chinese. I found myself talking to a well-groomed thirty-something man in a new, almost elegant nylon jacket standing next to a polished green four-door Toyota pickup with chrome roll bars. I told him where I wanted to go, but he just shook his head. A friend lounging on the truck's polished fender interrupted, "Okay, I can go." Did he have a four-wheel drive? I asked. He gestured across the street at a two-story stucco house, a dirt-encrusted pickup tucked behind the gate. Once again, I found my bargaining position weak and I agreed to pay 350,000 kip for the trip, at that moment about $80, to set off shortly after dawn the next day.

But that evening, I was curious about the travelers who assembled each evening at the two restaurants, almost all of them stirring images of Haight-Ashbury or Woodstock, late-twentieth-century explorers. Sandals were de rigueur, as were balloon-baggy cotton drawstring trousers. T-shirts, tie-dyed or imprinted with the monikers of rock bands (Megadeth) or political messages ("Save the Earth") dominated. The travelers sported multiple earrings, nose studs, tattoos, silver pendant necklaces, beaded bracelets, all the accessories of what once was called hippie culture. I joined a table of three young men because they were the odd table out—no tie-dyes. One of the men, Björn, turned out to be an electrical engineering graduate student from Stockholm who was taking time off between semesters. Ed, who was missing a front tooth, the visible consequence of a motorcycle accident, was a former drug addict from San Francisco who was trying to turn his life around. And Edgar was an eighteen-year-old Dutchman who was bicycling across Asia by himself during a sabbatical year between high school and college.

Edgar favored a Chinese brown felt fedora, the sort that Humphrey Bogart would have approved of, a hat that shadowed his peachlike teenage face and mirthful and mischievous green eyes. I asked him how, and why, he was in Laos. Like most Dutch, he spoke perfect, colloquial English (and French and German, and read Greek and Latin). "Most of my friends think I'm crazy." He laughed. "I didn't want to go straight to university. I've been in school for a long time. I wanted time to do something else, so I flew to Hong Kong and took a train to Guangzhou. None of my friends would come with me. They really thought I was crazy. In Guangzhou, I found a store that sold pretty good bikes, but the problem was most of them weren't big enough. I got one that fit and got a good seat with it. I brought my own panniers to hold my stuff. Then I just bicycled out west. So far it's been four months."

I ordered an omelette, the best the menu had to offer, and coffee. The others ordered another round of coffee. Björn, almost a cliché of a Swede—tall, blond, angular—told a similar tale of taking some time off between years of schooling. Immensely knowledgeable about European politics and the quickening pace of the European Monetary Union, over the next days of our travels he would bemoan each announcement by the

BBC of gravity's tug on the value of the Euro against the dollar. And Ed, who sported a fresco of tattoos—a devil on one arm and an angel on the other, and on his back a reproduction of Michelangelo's *Finger of God* from the Sistine Chapel—though less schooled than the other two, brought a sobriety and solidity to the trio. "I had three choices in my life," he told me later, after having described being jailed for drug dealing at the age of fifteen, "death, jail or going sober. I've been sober for seven years." The threesome had banded together in part because of a common disinterest in opium smoking and more by a desire to search out obscure locales, a desire I shared as well.

Laos had become not a place to discover, as it had been for foreign explorers in the nineteenth century, but rather a place where you could discover yourself. And it was not really Laos itself that was the lure—it could have been anywhere, as long as it was remote, unlinked by the copper wires that bring the Internet and e-mail to life and with nothing recognizable to impinge on the journey from the familiar. The multiplicity of Lao cultures—although the Lao government recognizes forty-seven ethnic groups, there are, scholars insist, roughly two hundred languages spoken in Laos by an equal number of ethnic peoples—does not lure many of these foreign travelers. And, of course, Laos has also become a magnet because, as one of the world's poorest countries, it is also among the least expensive to visit. The gold and silver ingots of Garnier's time have given way to belly pouches of dollar bills, only four or five of them necessary each day.

I told my trio of friends that I was heading to Xieng Kok the following morning and that they were welcome to join me. At dawn, I shouldered my backpack and made for the parking area and my ride. From the thick fog, Edgar emerged, fedora cocked, his small pack slung on one shoulder. And then came Björn, followed by Ed, his head wrapped against the chill in a thick, woven cotton scarf. The driver grumbled around as we heaved our stuff in the back of his truck, and then burst out, "Four hundred thousand kip," a $12 price jump. Extortion, I thought. I refused to pay it. He refused to go. Beyond the trucks, the morning market was bustling, with women wearing long skirts and Chinese nylon-padded jackets flip-flopping past piles of vegetables and bamboo baskets of squawking chickens, and tin tables piled with boxes of Colgate toothpaste and Jergens face soap. He had all day, and I wanted to get to the Mekong. I tried to explain to the driver that we had reached an agreement the day before and a deal was a deal. He told me that he needed more money. Fortunately, our increasingly animated haggling drew a crowd of other drivers, one of whom was the nattily attired owner of the new green Toyota. I asked him if he remembered the previous day's negotiations. He shrugged. Then reluctantly said, "Three hundred fifty thousand." For reasons I could not fathom, his declaration settled the price. Still unhappy, our driver climbed into the truck, and we were soon in a jungle cottoned by a deep mist.

A rutted track, bouldered and muddy, scraped through the dense foliage, dipping into shallow streams and weaving up low hills. Our truck yawed back and forth like a badly balanced rowboat, slamming off rocks and pawing through pools of muck. After two hours, a scattering of thatched huts on six-foot stilts appeared in a clearing, patches of field hacked from the forest nearby, evidence of the slash-and-burn agriculture practiced in much of the Lao highlands. Another hour on the track and we slunk into Xieng Kok, little more than a procession of thatched huts leading toward a clay bluff overlooking a sandy beach, and the Mekong River. Across the caramel waters rose the jungles of Burma.

We halted outside the village's only durable structure, a cement-faced building fixed with a sign reading, SINGSAVANUBKED GUETHOUSE WELLCOME. Four chambers of the guest house faced onto a central room that served as the home for the proprietor's family, a restaurant of sorts and, when there was beer, a tavern. A few reddish-gold chickens pecked at the edges of a dirt path that ran toward the hills, and a pair of black piglets snuffled in a heap of leaves and garbage. I stood on the bluff's edge, overlooking Laos's northernmost river outpost. A small herd of lumbering wooden cargo boats, veritable arks, big-bellied craft with thimble-sized wheelhouses, were nosed up to the beach. Around them, a small swarm of wasplike speedboats, long, needle-nosed machines with monstrous automobile engines fixed to their sterns, bobbed lazily, tethered to the beach by frayed lines.

Our driver was hustling around the village trying to find passengers for the slog back to Meung Sing, and I rejoined my trio of traveling companions. We padded around the village paths, parched and hungry. It was a village desolate in its isolation and impoverishment. A clot of children in torn shirts and muddy shorts surveyed our progress, children in a country where four out of every ten children under five are malnourished, and where 20 percent die before the age of five.* Here in Xieng Kok, a place

---

* The harshness of poverty and underdevelopment in Laos is starkly and clinically exposed by data from the World Bank and the United Nations. One hundred seventy-nine

with no electricity, no school, linked to the world by the erratic arrivals of cargo boats and commuter speedboats, agricultural seasons are life's metronome. I assumed that some opium moved through here, although I could not be sure; I could concoct no other explanation for the spanking-new green Toyota pickup in Meung Sing. And as we were touring the village, its sudden arrival in Xieng Kok, a tarpaulin spread across the cargo in the rear, did little to erase my assumptions; obviously, the owner did not need our money to make the trip through the jungle.

A shack banged together with scrap planking, propped over the edge of a gully and supported by lashed bamboo poles, served as the local diner— as opposed to our guest house's facility. The four of us took the only empty table, sliding past the tables of villagers well into a case of homemade liquor. One of them fiddled with the knobs on a karaoke machine, and I heard the sound of a generator being fired up beneath us. There was no menu and none of us spoke Lao, so we pointed at dishes on our neighbors' table; what arrived were two plates of fried vegetables, cabbage and a green leaf of some sort, and an enameled bowl of tasteless round-grained rice, the meagerness of our dinner mitigated by six bottles of warm Beer Lao that the owner excavated from somewhere. We ate with tin soup spoons while a villager at the next table began singing into the microphone, his words pillowed by pulses of static and tempoed by one man bongoing a drum and another keeping pace on a wooden flute. Eyes were bloodshot and merriment abounded.

Again, morning's early gray light filtered through long cloudy boas, feathering hilltops and smudging the forest. Roosters chain-called—one half-choked cock-a-doodle brought another, then another, until nobody could sleep. After a tumbler of *café Lao*, Björn and I trudged down to the sandy beach to determine how the four of us would get to Houay Xay, the first major Laotian town on the Mekong and an outpost for the Central Intelligence Agency during the Vietnam War. Houay Xay was also the

----

countries have higher per capita GNPs than Laos's $330, and that includes such desperately poor nations as Bangladesh, Ghana and Haiti. Between 1990 and 1997, the percentage of paved roads in Laos declined from 24 percent to 14 percent. It has five telephones per thousand people, fewer than Eritrea, and with four televisions per thousand people, fewer per capita than the Central African Republic. Laos has no scientists or engineers in research and development and has never filed a patent application, which cannot even be said of the devastatingly poor country of Burundi.

major Lao commercial center in the heart of the Golden Triangle, across the Mekong from the small Thai town of Chiang Khong.

Xieng Kok's riverfront was a hive of activity as cargo boat workers unloaded sacks of rice and refined sugar from Thailand and stacked them on the sand. Under a thatched canopy, a woman in black trousers and a flowered nylon shirt leaned on a three-pane glass counter piled with packs of Lucky Strike cigarettes; cans of Coke, Fanta and Sprite; plastic bags of coconut crackers; and hip flasks of eighty-proof, five-year-old Sang Thip whiskey from Thailand. An unplugged white, chest-high refrigerator stood behind the counter, and the woman made change from wads of kip stashed in the egg tray.

A speedboat driver clambered to his feet from the sand and swaggered over to us, adjusting his baseball cap over gold-framed sunglasses. "You want boat to Houay Xay?" he asked, in English. I told him yes but I was looking for one of the slow boats, a cargo boat perhaps. "No slow boat," he replied, "just fast boat." I told him I wanted to talk to the drivers of the big boats. He shrugged. We buttonholed some boat workers and the driver of one boat, each time pointing downstream, mouthing "Houay Xay." They all shook their heads. One said, "Meung Meung," referring to a small village about halfway to Houay Xay.

Björn and I sat down on the sand to contemplate our options. Deep brown in the morning light, the Mekong swept past, spinning off rebellious, dimpled eddies and coy whirlpools. Four Akha women in elaborate conical headdresses of silver bands and bangles of coins, trinkets and mirrors came down the bank, each carrying a woven basket on her back hanging from a wooden collar board. They set their baskets down near the pile of rice sacks, and one woman came over to us. She touched a coin on her headdress and extended her hand; I fished a stray aluminum Chinese coin from my shorts, the only coin I had, and handed it over. She seemed unimpressed. The speedboat driver reappeared and asked us what we wanted to do. I asked him how much it would cost to rent his speedboat. He stooped down and with his index finger wrote in the sand, "2,500 baht," a sum of Thai currency worth about $62; that would cover the four of us. I bent over and fingered "1,500" in the sand. He erased it and rewrote his original price. Our choices were apparent; remain in Xieng Kok another day, hope to cadge a ride to Meung Meung without any certainty of getting out of there, or the speedboat. Once more, my resolve to bargain more ardently collapsed under the rubble of my position: I was stranded. Okay, I said, fast boat.

We went up the sandbank to the hotel, rounded up our two colleagues, paid our room bill ($2 for the night), and returned to the riverbank laden with backpacks, while Edgar, jaunty in his fedora, wheeled his bike next to him. Our boat driver pulled his craft to the sand, a fragile fiberglass shell painted brilliant yellow with a bold British Union Jack plastered on its flank; on the stern, an eight-foot shaft protruded from a four-cylinder Japanese car engine, ending in a two-blade propeller. Four bench seats faced forward, toward the boat's beak. Our driver pulled a motorcycle helmet from a side locker, tied our packs and the bicycle into a recess in the prow, and we tumbled in. He keyed the engine, which then thundered to life, and in an instant we were screaming down the river like demented drag-car racers, a soaring rooster tail of white water chasing our every move. I checked my GPS; we were doing forty-five miles per hour.

On our right, the forest of Burma was dense and unyielding, while on our left, the forest thinned and thickened, giving way at times to villages perched over the river. We flashed by one village where an old woman in a straw hat bent over the shallow waters near the riverbank panning for gold. An orange Chinese river barge chugged upriver, its cargo strapped down under sheets of black plastic. But mostly we traveled between walls of impenetrable jungle, towering stands of hairy-leafed apitong and broad-

Cargo and passenger boats along the shore of the
Mekong River in northern Laos

leafed mahogany fringed by bamboo, the boat's engine howling like an enraged beast, our driver leaning forward, plotting his timing on the river's curves and veering away from the sandbars that fingered out from the shoreline.

It was in these jungles during the Vietnam War that the freelancing Central Intelligence Agency warrior Anthony Poshepny, known more by the alias Tony Poe, ran his own guerrilla war against North Vietnamese troops, made raids into China and Burma, and collected gruesome trophies of war, including strings of enemy ears—"chitlings," one fellow agent called them—as well as a head in a jar of whiskey, or so it was rumored. Heralded by CIA colleagues for his fearlessness and audacity, not to mention his prodigious drinking, he played a role in smuggling the Dalai Lama to safety in 1959 to avoid invading Chinese troops, had his fingers in an aborted rising against President Sukarno in Indonesia and worked with doomed paramilitary efforts by Taiwan's government to infiltrate mainland China.

But it was his exploits in northern Laos that brought him unacknowledged fame in the persona of Marlon Brando, who played Colonel Kurtz in the 1979 film *Apocalypse Now,* Francis Ford Coppola's Asian adaptation of the Joseph Conrad masterpiece, *Heart of Darkness,* set on the Congo River. Coppola's Kurtz, fashioned after Poshepny, or perhaps his legend, also ran a kingdom of warriors up the Mekong, though his was rather more gruesomely festooned with heads on bamboo spikes. "The horror. The horror," whispered Brando's Kurtz before he was executed by an army assassin for having gone native, or as the CIA said of Poshepny, of "having gone bamboo"; he, and Poshepny, were in some senses very much in and of the heart of darkness. In the movie, Brando's Kurtz has his throat slit. In the real world, Poshepny got a handshake at CIA headquarters in Langley, Virginia, and eventually retired to live in northern California.

Nearly three hours later, we skidded around a bend and slowed as a floating dock appeared on our left. A dozen or so other speedboats were tied up, some taking on fuel from upright steel drums. "Okay," the driver said, "Meung Meung. Here you take new boat." Another surprise, but what could we do? He unloaded our bags and dropped them in another speedboat. Apparently, the river was commuted in stages, with drivers sticking to the stretches they knew best. Without a word, the new driver cranked his engine and we growled out into mid-stream before he slammed the throttle forward, snapping my head back and almost deafening me. Meung Meung vanished, and the jungle enveloped us again. Then two hours later, in an eye blink, the riverbank jungle on our right gave way to stretches of modern buildings, power poles, telecommunication dishes, the flash of cars and trucks on slick roads—Thailand.

Before the arrival of French colonialism, as I've said, there was no country of Laos but a kingdom of Lan Xang, known fully as the Kingdom of a Million Elephants and the White Parasol, whose boundaries extended well into what is now Thailand. Ethnically and linguistically, northern Thailand and modern Laos overlap, and Thai trading women have no difficulty hawking their wares on their daily excursions across the Mekong. Laos's modern boundaries were carved out by France in agreements with Siam between 1893 and 1907, and only in 1953, as its colonial regime in Vietnam was collapsing, did the French yield independence to Laos. By then, however, deep and ultimately irresolvable chasms had grown between the traditional Lao royalty and its notions of noble and hereditary legitimacy, and the populist and communist Pathet Lao.

When France capitulated to the Vietnamese resistance army, the Vietminh, at Dien Bien Phu on May 7, 1954, the seeds of the conflict that drew in the United States were sown. From that war, the Pathet Lao, secretive, paranoid, rigidly authoritarian, emerged victorious over a land that had been as relentlessly pounded by American bombers—a total of 2,092,900 tons of bombs—as all of Europe and Japan in World War II.[*] Moreover, across the Mekong Laos faced Thailand, a country that had been a major staging point for air raids into Vietnam, Cambodia and Laos, a country whose military was hostile to communism and whose economic

---

[*] The Geneva Accords of 1962 forbade any foreign troops in Laos, which was supposed to be a neutral country; both North Vietnam and the United States blithely disregarded them. North Vietnam used Laos as a highway for supplying its troops in South Vietnam along the Ho Chi Minh trail. The United States not only bombed the Ho Chi Minh trail, it had hundreds of military and CIA advisers in Laos, some of whom were actively involved in fighting the Pathet Lao, and later in the war bombed in support of the CIA-sponsored "secret war" waged by the Hmong general Vang Pao. Vang, often depicted as a hero of the Hmong, had a lot of pokers in the fire; U.S. drug officials long believed that he ran a heroin-refining operation out of the secret CIA base at Long Tieng in northern Laos.

chieftains embraced the capitalist model of the West. The Mekong, a river that sings of promise—as an artery for regional trade, a tourist waterfront, an adventurer's highway—became southeast Asia's watery Berlin Wall.

Laotian leaders, a reclusive and secretive cabal, now stare nervously across the Mekong's rust-colored waters toward glitzy Thailand. What they see, though, is not opportunity but danger, not hope but peril, not a representative of any broader truths but a sinkhole of corruption. Despite the ethnic bonds between Thais and Laos, the ideological shackles of a peasant communism under seige hobble the imagination and the will of Laos's rulers. They struggle to preserve a bankrupt system, bankrupt in all senses, and their people gaze across the river at what could be. Further south, Cambodia struggles to reconstitute itself two decades after committing auto-genocide and, even farther on, Vietnam treads timidly toward an uncertain future. Only Thailand soars, and stuck with neighbors such as these, largely ignores them.

As we rocketed down the Mekong, glazing the surface of the river like a well-struck hockey puck, I found the contrast between Laos and Thailand so stark that it was jarring. Every mile of Thailand was hung with power lines, modern Japanese-made trucks glided over roads that were yet to see a pothole, a huge golf ball–like weather radar station perched on a bluff, lights blazed from riverfront restaurants. On our left, Laos was rugged, untamed, roadless, without power. Scraggles of bamboo huts on stilts hunkered along the river, and their occupants stared hopelessly at the bright lights just a quarter of a mile away. As dusk eased over us, the Thai shoreline swelled up with tile-roofed houses and low-rise office blocks, and our driver pivoted the boat toward the left shore. For a moment I felt like bribing him to drop me in Thailand, but we rumbled into a tree-shrouded, mud-bank dock just north of Houay Xay, my ears still whining with the roar of the engine.

During the mid-1960s, Houay Xay was a major heroin-processing center—owned and run by the Lao army—for Burmese opium that was lugged in on mule caravans run by the Chinese Nationalist Fifth Army, a remnant of Chiang Kai-shek's defeated forces that had settled in northern Thailand and northeastern Burma. The Mekong was easily crossed, and Lao opium farmers, who found that the opium poppies grew most productively in the alkaline soils that formed on the limestone extrusions that are typical of the northern Lao Mekong watershed, discovered it was easy to ship raw opium downriver to the refineries in Houay Xay.

That night, after a quick meal, Björn and I wandered down the town's main street, a street that paralleled the Mekong and was lined with small shops and offices—among them the Golden Triangle Sapphire Mining Company and something called the National Organization Board—and dimly lit hotels, toward the river. There were hills rising to the east, one seamed with a cement staircase that climbed toward a Buddhist temple. Farther on, though, we heard music drifting down from a hill we could not see and, for a time, could not find. Winding our way around the back of a black hill, we could hear that we were closing in, but we could see nothing. Abandoning the road, we hit out through the dark up the face of the hill itself, my flashlight providing paltry illumination. Scrambling over tree roots and managing to avoid tumbling into a ravine to our left, we finally reached the summit.

Before us, a huge circle of fifty or sixty dancers, women on the outside of the rim, men on the inside, revolved slowly, languorously, counterclockwise, women silently weaving their arms together, angling their palms slowly up and down, finger and thumb forming an O, turning rhythmically in their long silk *pha sin*, or sarongs, as a four-piece band played while a singer crooned an Isan tune. Isan culture, the music and folktales of northeastern Thailand and this part of Laos, is shared on both sides of the Mekong; its music is often a steady beat with high-pitched, but very melodious, singing and is powerfully infectious. As we stood there watching, a short, ebullient man in a short-sleeved blue shirt bounded over to us and shook our hands endlessly. "Come in, come in," he repeated. What was going on? I asked.

"I am Dr. Kham On," he said, "and this is a party for the Bokeo Army Hospital. Twentieth anniversary." He shepherded us over to a long table littered with the remains of a feast and bottles, in various states of emptiness, of a homemade rice liquor he called *lao-lao*. "Here," he said, half filling two tumblers for us, "toast." I nearly died as a blowtorch seared my esophagus. In a blur of activity, Kham bustled around introducing us to people at the party, finally stopping to have us shake hands with a dour, disapproving man. "This is the lieutenant colonel," we were told. "He's in charge of the hospital." Then he whispered to us, "He's not a doctor, but he's the boss."

At once we were swept into the circle dance, the *lam-vong*, a traditional dance that I found enormously sensual. Women moved gracefully, unhurried, almost alone but somehow in concert, in slow swirls and with gentle gesticulations, as the men moved with equal ease inside their great

circle. I felt a bit like the hippo at the ballet, but the laughter of my neighboring dancers at my efforts seemed not cruel but happily amused. Then,
of course, we were urged to sing for the party. I demurred, my singing a
wretched thing, but Björn managed a Swedish drinking song that went
down well. For party crashers at an army fête, we were treated well,
although the colonel glowered at us foreigners from time to time; all foreigners are regarded with suspicion by the Lao military. After too many
tumblers of lao-lao, we started to leave, but Kham insisted we visit him at
the hospital the next day. How I got down the hill in one piece I am still
unsure.

The next afternoon, Björn and I, on rented motor scooters, found our
way to the Bokeo Army Hospital, Camp 10. Down the road were the pastel yellow buildings of the old French colonial military garrison, now used
by the Lao army as its provincial headquarters. A decrepit jumble of
unpainted, single-story clapboard buildings stood on a rise, a flagless pole
in front. We found Kham in a spartan room with a blackboard and a few
hardback chairs.

"I'm originally from Vientiane," he told us. "I studied in Vietnam,
where most of our doctors study. I've been here five years so far. These
buildings—" he spread his hands almost in supplication "—these buildings were built by the Americans in the war," which made them at least
three decades old. He guided us around the small complex, opening
creaky wood doors onto unlit wards and what passed for clinics. Ageless
wooden frame beds with thin mattresses were lined up against a wall.
Three patients lay under thin cotton sheets in the gloom; no charts hung
from the foot of the beds. There was no privacy, much less any medical
machines. "Our biggest problem is malaria," he said quietly. "We get our
drugs from a pharmaceutical factory near Vientiane, or from Vietnam."

I pointed to a newly painted cement structure next to the hospital and
asked Kham whether it was a special clinic. "Oh no," he replied. "That's
the building we use for political studies."

With roots deep in the culture of guerrilla warfare and a ferocious rural
Communist ideology, the Laotian army is an integral part of state control,
functioning primarily as an instrument of internal policing. For several
years after the defeat of the United States in Vietnam and the victory of
Pathet Lao forces in Laos, former CIA-backed tribal insurgents, mostly
the Hmong, attempted to wage war against the Communist government.
By then, though, America's interests had shifted from southeast Asia, and
the Hmong lost their benefactors, and their war. In the last decade, the

Lao military has emulated their Chinese colleagues by intruding into and dominating significant segments of the country's meager economy. Much of the logging operations in the north of Laos, operations that the government itself has declared illegal, are run by the Lao army in collaboration with Chinese companies. And the wholesale opium operations, transport and refining, are now controlled by the army. With no external enemies, the army has decided to make money rather than to make war.

Houay Xay anchors the southeastern corner of the Golden Triangle, a place from where sapphires from Laotian mines and opium from inland poppy fields are smuggled. Upriver, there are endless places to land small boats, away from the desultory Lao and Thai customs offices. Even market ladies from Thailand, big women in floppy straw hats and girth-girdling sarongs trundling bags of chili peppers, five-liter cans of cooking oil, bolts of cotton cloth and sacks of rice across the river, do so routinely, without formalities, a major pillar of an unregulated but buoyant commerce that keeps Laos from sinking into a tar pit of economic paralysis.

Before continuing south to Luang Prabang, the old royal and religious capital of Laos, where I wanted to explore the state of Laotian Buddhism, I said good-bye to my traveling companions, exchanged e-mail addresses and headed back toward the heart of the Golden Triangle, which is still one of the major opium-producing and heroin-manufacturing areas on Earth, second only to Afghanistan in total output. A wooden ferry boat chugs back and forth across the Mekong from Houay Xay to the Thai river town of Chiang Khong, and my ferry mates were a couple from middle America who seemed to have somehow gotten lost. I had noticed them carefully walking down the main street of Houay Xay earlier in the day, she in a beautifully matched peach pantsuit, her hair coiffed like a lovely meringue, he in pressed khakis and a starched blue shirt. As they stepped onto the ferry, she bent down to flick a splat of mud from her leather pumps, distress flooding her eyes. She told me that they were driving around Thailand and wanted "to step into Laos for the day." She examined her manicure. "It's so awful," she said. "It's so dirty. There's nothing to buy. And there's nothing to do." I sat in the back of the ferry, my pack nicely floured with dust, in torn shorts and a shirt that hadn't been washed in some time. I just nodded.

I'm all for luxurious travel and have managed to bunk down in some of the globe's most exquisite resorts. But in traveling down the Mekong, I never seemed to miss such comforts, propelled by both the intellectual and physical challenge of the journey. Even so, I marvel at people who arrive in the underdeveloped world immaculately tailored with a procession of porters bearing luggage emblazoned with one chic logo or another. My rule was keep it light and simple and be prepared for everything to go wrong.

When I landed in Chiang Khong I saw what she meant. This old Thai town had been transformed into a tourist haven, ranks of cute, tile-roofed guest houses along the Mekong, open-air cafés offering frothy cappuccino, ice-cold beer and brownies, and knickknack shops piled on top of one another selling teak coasters, carvings of water buffaloes, straw hats, bracelets, bamboo mobiles, weavings, everything to gratify the tourist—and not an opium pipe in sight. Thai road workers were busily installing a new concrete main street eighteen inches thick, a street that not only was perfectly fashioned but was sturdier than any road I would see in Laos. Indeed, roads are perhaps one of the most accurate indexes of a country's economic health. In Zaire, Mobutu Sese Seko pilfered the treasury, and the roads, built by the Belgians with slave labor, vanished into jungle tracks. In India, barely a scrap of internationally standard highway exists, while China is laced with superhighways; and not coincidentally, China's economy is booming and India's trudges along like an overworked camel. And in Thailand, a country that has developed rapidly in the last decade or so, pristine macadam roads web the country from north to south.

I headed north, along the river, in a Nissan pickup truck I rented in town. Thailand, I was somewhat startled to learn, has more pickup trucks per capita than any country on Earth, and the state of Texas. As I meandered along the river, virtually every vehicle I passed was a pickup. As I drove, fields freshly plowed by Ford tractors climbed easily into the hills. Occasionally a small town, which had been an agricultural village when I visited Thailand a decade before, straddled the crisp, two-lane blacktop highway. Now the village was a clutter of businesses selling tractors and motorcycles and pickups, CD shops, furniture stores, supermarkets and restaurants, all the stuff of a country that has become very middle class. Power lines guided me along the river, but to the east, in Laos, only the occasional clatch of bamboo-thatched huts was visible. A few hours later, rising from the easy hump of hills, the groves of bamboo and the elephant grass, I saw a pristine, rambling white building with an overhung wood-beamed roof and sheets of smoked glass crouched over the river, the Golden Triangle Meridien Hotel. There, at the geographical site where

Thailand abuts Burma and Laos, the intersection of three very different nations, where the Mekong bends slowly south and east, I had a cold Singha Beer on the deck of a first-world hotel and contemplated the placidity that masked an economy as cutthroat and vigorous as any on Wall Street; thirty years ago it had been even worse.

In July 1967, just below the deck where I was standing, a two-day war erupted when the Burmese opium warlord Khun Sa tried to ship sixteen tons of opium on a three-hundred-mule caravan to the tiny Lao village of Ban Khwan, just across the Mekong from where I was standing. Hot on his heels were troops of the Chinese Nationalist Fifth Army, based in Thailand, who wanted to hijack the opium. And from the south and east, troops of the Laotian army stormed in, determined to reassert Lao sovereignty over their occupied village and, more important, grab the heroin for General Ouane Rattikone, who spent part of his time as commander of the Lao army, and more of his time controlling Laos's opium trade. Khun Sa's troops fought off the Chinese with machine guns and carbines from a palisade they erected around a lumber mill. But General Ouane won the day with hundreds of paratroopers and dive-bombing T-38 propeller planes, driving off Khun Sa and the last straggling Chinese troops and capturing the opium that he then sent downriver to his refinery in Houay Xay. He became very rich, and his victory went into history as the 1967 Opium War.

Ronald D. Renard, one of the more knowledgeable writers on the opium trade, suggests that the appellation Golden Triangle was coined on July 12, 1971, by a U.S. assistant secretary of state named Marshall Green, who used it not merely to denote this area of rampant opium production, but to indicate that the United States recognized that only three countries were involved in the growth and refining of opium—Thailand, Burma and Laos—and, more precisely, that China was not. Timing is everything, and it was not unnoted that the term, and its implications, became common parlance just as Richard M. Nixon was preparing to be the first American president to visit China, a trip he took in February of the following year.

Unlike across the border to the north in Burma, or across the Mekong in Laos, Thailand has worked aggressively to crack down on opium production. Now there are virtually no productive fields in the entire country, and drug possession here is a serious crime. Opium still exists, of course, and I was to see the stark evidence of it in a few days, in the hills to the west, which had been settled by Chinese Nationalist troops who fled Mao Zedong's Communist armies in 1949. But in the 1990s Thailand successfully severed the major opium shipment routes across its territory, forcing the Burmese opium lords to find other routes up through China and from Burmese and Thai ports to the south.

Of course, it was not Burmese farmers on their own initiative who suddenly began growing opium in commercial quantities. Only with the rigorous encouragement of British officials, whose colonizing efforts in India and Burma included decrees monopolizing the opium trade, did large areas of northern Burma become covered with red- and pink-flowered opium poppy fields. (Britain has had a long and sordid colonial and imperial history of pushing opium; Hong Kong was ceded to Britain by the Qing dynasty as reparation for losing a battle to prevent Britain from selling opium to the Chinese.) And to ensure that the opium trade made economic sense, Britain employed the strongest of strong-arm marketing techniques in China, over the objection of the impotent Qing dynasty, to force the sale of opium in Chinese cities. Only after several forays by gunboats and the capture of Hong Kong by British forces did the Chinese acquiesce and legalize opium trading in 1858. In Burma itself, the British summarily exiled the king in 1886, revoked his royal decrees against opium production and began awarding prizes to farmers who produced record opium crops; by 1942 the British government had licensed 154 opium dens in Burma.

A small stream hidden by fields of shore reeds, the Mae Nam Sai, marks the border with Burma, the stream emptying into the Mekong, or as it is called in Thailand, the Mae Nam Khong. Hugging the Mae Nam Sai is a blacktop road, snaking toward Mae Sai, the official border crossing with Burma. At Mae Sai, the Thai border town, a four-lane highway pouring from the south abruptly halts at a one-lane concrete bridge across the desultory stream into Burma. I had no intention of tracking down Khun Sa or other opium traffickers in Burma; my goal, slight as it was, was merely to sense briefly Burma's contrast with Thailand, the clash of rising affluence with dire, entrenched poverty.

Mae Sai is much like the border towns of any rich country hard against an impoverished one—whether the border of Estonia with Russia, South Korea and North Korea, or Thailand's other land border with Laos—the richer neighbor weighing down its border posts with the fruits of economic abundance, to tempt, to boast and most of all to make some money. Here the road to the border is a gantlet of raw commerce, a dense thicket of shops whose owners hawk pots and pans, towels, small farm implements and, for the tourist, a hefty supply of trinkets. Border formalities are minimal leading to Takhilek, the Burmese town on the other side of the bridge. Local Burmese and Thais seemed to flow back and forth across the bridge with ease, and if there were difficulties, one could wade the muddy stream below without much hindrance.

Stepping into Takhilek, I noticed that the clock at the border was set thirty minutes behind Thailand time, but it struck me, looking quickly at the rutted streets and crumbling buildings, that Burma was more like thirty years behind Thailand. I turned around and looked back at Thailand, at the glitter of Mae Sai, and then back to survey Takhilek. A pair of dusty roads ran east and west around a central hill topped by a Buddhist stupa. A warren of dirt streets spread on either side of the hill, worming into shanty neighborhoods of low, rattan-walled shacks set off from one another by fences of corrugated steel sheets hammered into the earth. In truth, the streets were more paths than roadways, with boulders jutting from the ground as the paths struggled up the hill. In one yard, a bare-breasted woman with a purple sarong loosely wrapped around her waist bathed by scooping water from a steel drum with a red plastic basin. There was no running water, no electricity. Chickens pecked in yards, and children in bare feet and dirt-stained shirts played in the road. Many women who padded through the neighborhoods had gray-white mud rubbed on their faces, a practice used by some ethnic groups here as a cosmetic.

At one shop, an old woman sat on a low stool eating rice from a white ceramic bowl with her fingers. Behind her, the shop walls were hung with the skins of tigers and leopards—animals virtually extinct here—the skull and antlers of forest deer, glass cases littered with bones and scraps of fur, bowls of beetles, small worked silver boxes and brass opium pipes. Next door, a woman sat behind a card table on which sat a blue plastic telephone, a cardboard sign propped at her feet announcing the prices for calls to various Burmese cities; private phones are just about unknown here. And the faces that passed in the street were not as ethnically uniform as elsewhere in southeast Asia. Burma is the bridge between people of the Indian subcontinent and those of east Asia, where skin colors shade from the darkest brown to the palest gold, where the double-fold eyelids of south Asia mix with the single-fold eyelids of the east. A Buddhist stupa on a hill, a whitewashed Christian church with a stubby bell tower, a gold-domed mosque crowned with a silver crescent moon—it is a mélange of

traditions that reflect Burma's past, as do the languages spoken here, not
Thai, but Burmese, Hindi, Bengali, Chinese, a bit of English, the lan-
guages of history and conquest and trade. In the mid-nineteenth century,
Britain annexed Burma as a province of British India, ruling until the
Japanese occupied the country in 1942, creating their own puppet state.
In 1945, Burma returned to British rule and three years later was granted
independence. Since then, Burma has been ruled by a succession of military dictatorships; a momentary glimmer of hope in 1990 when Aung San
Suu Kyi's National League for Democracy overwhelmingly won national
elections was extinguished by the military, which has ruled with a thick
mix of brutality and corruption ever since.

There were no shiny, chrome-studded pickups here, just gaggles of
dented and creaky fifteen-year-old Toyotas. Economic activity, such as it
was, seemed to employ more Thai baht, a hard currency, than the ephemeral and largely useless Burmese kyat. At a tiny samosa eatery tucked below
street level, a garrulous Burmese chef plopped three immense puffy triangles stuffed with spicy potato and cabbage on a plastic plate. "These are the
best in Takhilek," he insisted, in perfect English, about which I asked. "I
went to missionary school," he continued. "In the old days there were lots
of missionaries here, brought by the British. So we all learned English and
English manners. But we never learned English food." He laughed out
loud. "No. No English food." In the 1960s and 1970s, Takhilek was another
of the biggest opium-refining centers in the Golden Triangle, so I asked
him whether the refineries were still operating. He shrugged. "I don't think
so." I paid him in baht and headed back to Thailand in search of the Chinese villages in the mountains, villages that were once both the former
headquarters of a renegade army and home to a major heroin-producing
operation.

As I strolled back into Thailand, it seemed so obvious that the decrepi-
tude of Takhilek was visibly emblematic of the economic buffoonery,
incompetence and corruption of Burma's ruling military council, rather
ominously dubbed SLORC, for State Law and Order Restoration Council. Only the faintest of rivulets sundered rising wealth from entrenched
poverty, democracy from dictatorship and terror. It was madness.

A few days later, I wound through hills of staggering beauty, great
groves of eucalyptus, tropical pines and pincushions of bamboo, valleys
flat and glistening with the green irridescent shoots of newly planted rice
in manicured paddies. I was headed to Mae Salong, the hilltop town near

the Burmese border where the Chinese Nationalist general Tuan Shi-wen
had run his drug operations with his Fifth Army of eighteen hundred
troops in the 1960s and 1970s, an army that was funded entirely by the
proceeds of the opium trade after the Taiwan government cut him off from
the national treasury in 1961. From here, Tuan sent mule caravans, sometimes as many as six hundred mules at a time, into the poppy regions of
the Shan state in Burma to collect raw opium for processing. So extensive
were the Chinese general's operations that he also performed border surveillance duties for the Thai government, levying duties on other opium
caravans that moved through Thai territory.

A velvety ribbon of blacktop now courses up into Mae Salong, the
opium caravan mule tracks nothing more than romantic memory. Immediately, I was in a different world; everywhere, signs were in Chinese and
the language on the streets was Chinese. A three-story pagoda-shaped
restaurant in white-and-red tiles and roofed in orange tiles with upturned
eaves hulked near the summit of the hill. But the town itself, which was
draped over the pate of a small hill, was little more than a gnarl of small
byways that wrapped around tidy whitewashed cement houses. Except for
an occasional clot of older people huddled by doorways chatting, Mae
Salong was deserted. I climbed a small rise to a plywood-walled building
papered on the outside walls with dozens of handwritten sheets of Taoist
obscurantism and prognostications, rambling texts about rabbits and the
moon and turtles, about forces of yin and yang. Inside, a gray-haired man
in a blue cotton Chinese jacket with knot buttons and green slacks
crouched on a wood stool peering through thick glasses at a newspaper,
surrounded by towers of Chinese newspapers yellowed with age. A long
glass counter was filled with jars of deep brown tea leaves, expensive and
rare teas from China and Taiwan.

There are few trails one can take that trace so fully the history and flavor of tea as the Mekong. Drunk across Asia in dizzying varieties, tea is the
stuff of legend, passion and art; it is not the stuff found in tea bags sold in
groceries in the United States or Europe. The most ancient of legends
describing the discovery of tea in China recounts the moment at which
the mythical emperor Shen Nung, who is deemed by legend if not fact to
have ruled in 2737 B.C., sat under a tea tree and a leaf fell into a cup of
boiled water, an act of gravity that triggered the first tea infusion. It was
not until the eighth century, however, that tea drinking became widespread in China; it was at that time that the profusion of varieties and
preparation of tea were described in *The Classic of Tea,* by the scholar Lu

Yu. "The effect of tea," he wrote, "is its cooling flavor. As a drink, it is well suited to persons of self-restraint and good conduct."

The Tang, a dynasty that endured from the seventh to the early years of the tenth century, was the great age of poetry in China, and tea, like love, wine and song, was a frequent subject for the scholar-poets of that era. Lu Tung, a poet of occasional bombast and occasional delicacy, brushed an ode he called "Drinking Tea":

> *The first cup moistens my lips and throat;*
> *The second cup breaks my loneliness;*
> *The third cup searches my barren entrail but to find therein some five*
> *   thousand volumes of odd ideographs;*
> *The fourth cup raises a slight perspiration—all the wrongs of life pass*
> *   out through my pores;*
> *At the fifth cup I am purified;*
> *The sixth cup calls me to the realms of the immortals.*
> *The seventh cup—ah, but I could take no more! I only feel the breath of*
> *   the cool wind that rises in my sleeves.*
> *Where is Elysium? Let me rise on this sweet breeze and waft away. . . .*

There are, of course, other legends surrounding the first cuppa, as the British would put it, and poems celebrating tea's elixir-like properties. Although most Chinese regard their country as the world's foremost producer of tea, India produces more and tiny Sri Lanka leads the world in tea exports. In India and Sri Lanka, however, tea is drunk with milk and sugar, an abomination to the east Asian palate.

Of more than fifteen hundred types of tea grown worldwide, six major varieties are produced in China, their taxonomy set by color rather than botanical designation: green, black, yellow, white, dark-green and gray. Rarest among them is white tea, which, in fact, is a kind of green tea and is found only in China. By tradition, white tea is picked only at daybreak in northeastern Fujian Province and the principal distinguishing characteristic of the leaf are tiny white hairs on the tea bud. An infusion of this rare tea is the lightest of greens, an almost clear liquid. Less rare but prized no less is "dragon well," or *longjing,* tea, the green tea that was regarded as sufficiently good to present to the emperor. Grown in Zhejiang Province, it is picked in late April, around the time of the festival of Qing Ming, a day on which Chinese sweep the graves of their ancestors, and processed not by machine but by craftsmen. Today, the best dragon well tea is not sold to the public in China but is kept by the central government for banquets and gifts to worthy foreign visitors.

None of these teas, though, is much consumed in Yunnan, along the Mekong. Instead, the tea of choice is *puer*, a green-black tea that is heralded for its medicinal qualities as a digestive and nerve stimulant; in slang, one would say it gives the imbiber a nice buzz. Processed into compressed circular cakes, *puer* is still wrapped in bamboo for shipping, a practice that was first described in the eighth century.

Tea is also produced in abundance in southeast Asia, sometimes with an incomprehensible fastidiousness. In Thai Binh, Vietnam, tea specialists paddle into lotus ponds at night and place pinches of tea into lotus blossoms, bind them with ribbons and then return in the morning to collect the leaves infused with the scent of the lotus flower. In general, though, Vietnamese drink green tea steeped in small pots; often guests are asked to *uong nuoc*, literally to drink water, but which really means to drink tea.

In what is now northern Thailand, tea was eaten more than it was drunk. William H. Ukers, whose two-volume opus on the plant and its uses remains the definitive work, described the Shans of northern Siam boiling *miang*, or the leaves of wild tea trees. "In Siam," he wrote, "people consume enormous quantities of native *miang*, which they chew with salt and other condiments." The Burmese go even further, further in the sense of preparation, producing an edible tea concoction called *letpet*, which involves boiling and kneading jungle tea leaves, then wrapping them in papers or stuffing them into the internodes of bamboo stalks and then burying them in underground silos to ferment. Eventually the bamboo is dug up and the fermented tea eaten as a delicacy at marriage feasts and other festivals.

And so, as I looked at the teas along the counter in this shack, a wave of historical reminiscence swept over me, a mood of contentment that certain things in life remain. The old man welcomed me into the shack and gave his name as Mr. Chen. I pulled up one of a dozen or so short-legged stools that lined a wall papered with old newsprint, and he bustled around pouring boiling water from pot to pot, preparing tea the proper, careful way, ensuring the cups are adequately warmed, that the tea is steeped correctly and and that it is poured gently but crisply. I asked him to tell me about his town.

"Ah, in the year of the Republic 38, when the Communists took over China, fifty thousand Kuomintang came here," he said, using the Chinese

Nationalist calendrical notation for 1949. "We had our own army then and no one was living on this hill. I was in the Kuomintang army and we just had to leave China. Maybe someday we can go back." I asked him about China, a country not so far from his hill. "I hate the Communists," he said. "Look at what they did to that country. It is so poor. During the Cultural Revolution they killed so many people." He rubbed his hand over his steely brushcut.

Two bare bulbs, unfrosted, dangled from a rickety rafter that supported a corrugated roof, casting a low, harsh glare. I wondered about the town's reputation for opium. "Opium is evil," he declared. "Yes, there was lots of opium here. But it was wrong. Now there is no opium." The old war-lord of Mae Salong, General Tuan, used to defend his opium business here in practical terms: "Necessity knows no law. That is why we deal with opium. We have to continue to fight the evil of communism, and to fight you must have an army, and an army must have guns, and to buy guns you must have money. In these mountains the only money is opium."

Chen savored his tea with quick, precise sips. I asked him about the young people here, those who had no memory of China. "Many young people have jobs and have gone off to the city. There is no work here, only farming." Out his door, the hill dropped steeply toward one of the mirror-flat paddy fields. And what of the fortune-telling? I asked. "Many Taiwan tourists come here," he replied. "They come here and want to know the future, and I help them. There is still a good deal of trade now with Tai-wan. All this tea—" he waved to his canisters of dark-green leaves "—this all comes from Taiwan." He made another pot of tea and went on. "I think now this is really Thailand here. We are all Chinese, but this is not China. Things change."

His fatalism, if that is what it was, did not seem to me so dire. Thai-land's booming economy, an economy that weathered the financial crisis of the late 1990s far better than many people believe, had brought power and communications, satellite dishes and bevies of done-up pickup trucks to this remote region. As I began to drive down the hill, a shiny white Volvo tour bus pulled into the town disgorging a horde of camera-festooned Taiwanese tourists smartly turned out in khaki photographer's vests and yellow baseball hats provided by the tour company. They headed straight for the pagoda restaurant.

I took the back way out of Mae Salong, skimming the edge of the Burmese border, before twisting into a ragged village, the rattan on the huts broken and badly patched, the roof thatch disordered and pocked with holes. An Akha woman shambled across a dusty square, pushing her tubed fist to her mouth. Smoke, smoke, she was telling me. Her face was green as a lima bean. And for the first time I had known in a Thai, or even a Lao village, the place gave off the stench of garbage and human waste. It was a village that had reached the end of the line, a village consumed by the beast of opium. Squatting on the wood steps that led inside a tumble-down hut, a man in filthy torn clothes stared into a distant nothingness, his eyes glazed, his skin green as well. A scramble of children dashed toward me dangling small swatches of weaving from their hands, trinkets for the visitor. It saddened me, this scene of devastation, nothing by the hand of God, this. No, this was the hand of man.

If anything challenges arguments urging the relaxation of draconian drug laws, it is the emotional impact of seeing a village scourged by opium. Yet, a short drive away, there are villages equally embedded in the geographical maw of the Golden Triangle but which are healthy, whose fields are lush, whose children traipse to school in clean blue uniforms and matching red backpacks. The opium village, a human tragedy, was, however, not a sign of a flourishing opium industry in this tiny wedge of Thailand, but a relic from a past of warlords, battles and mule trains of opium, a past that has almost been eradicated here.

I had wandered far from the Mekong's waters, and from Laos. But this route into the Golden Triangle helped stir tales of history—a bit like going to Gettysburg and imagining the battle that transpired there—and lay plain the changes that have swept the region. What overlooks the conjunction of Laos, Burma and Thailand is a luxury hotel, not the operations center for warlord opium shipments. Still, the poverty of Burma and Laos, as in Afghanistan, continues to spur the cultivation of opium poppies, as do the eager appetites of junkies in Europe and the United States. I could see no end in sight to this agricultural practice and its trade, although Thailand's economic growth, as much as the efforts of police, had done much to banish opium from its swathe of the triangle. Reassured in some measure, I made for Laos.

Five

Boats, Buddha and a Million Elephants

I left Thailand and returned to Houay Xay to begin the trip into the historical heartland of Laos, to the ancient royal capital at Luang Prabang with its multitude of Buddhist temples, or *wats,* and the preserved royal palace, and then on to Vientiane, the capital of Laos today. Historically, Communist regimes have savaged religious practice, and I knew that in its early years, the particularly rigorous form of authoritarianism here had shattered Buddhist practice. Although Buddhism had recovered in recent years, I wanted, especially in Luang Prabang, to sample the life of Buddhist monks. The road to Luang Prabang is the river.

The Mekong ran low in its banks past Houay Xay, a broad café au lait current moving silently, inevitably. In Laos, where oral folktales are an artery of culture, the birth of the Mekong is recounted in a tale of two great dragon kings, Souttoranark and Souvanranark, who both lived in a

vast lake called Nong Kasae, a lake in the distant north. Though neighbors and friends, the kings fell out over a misunderstanding about the
nature of porcupines and elephants. One king who had never seen a porcupine, but who was presented porcupine meat and its spines as a gift by
the other king, could not understand how an animal with such lengthy
spines could be so meager of meat. An elephant, he insisted, had much
smaller hairs and so much meat; thus this porcupine meat offered as a gift
was only a small portion of a much bigger beast—an insult. And so the
dragon kings went to war over the supposed slight in gift giving, churning
the waters of Nong Kasae until they were dark and muddy. As the battle
went on, driving animals away and unsettling the gods, the king of the
gods ordered the war to stop and ordered the kings, in compensation and
repentance, to build two rivers to restore the land. One is the Nan, the
other the Mekong.

Muddy indeed was the Mekong as I skittered down the riverbank
toward a swollen-sided wooden cargo boat, a white 179 painted on its
peeling, sky blue prow, the craft I would take for part of my journey. The
captain, his shirt unbuttoned to a Buddha belly, sat in the wheelhouse in
front of a blackened brass, six-spoke wheel, staring through a sheet of
narrow plate glass framed in curious gingerbread. Two wood planks
served as the gangway from the soggy shore to the front deck, some one
hundred feet from the stern. The whole boat was bowed, like a banana,
its prow and stern rising gently from a tubby cargo hold. Sacks of rice,
some barrels of who knows what and a pile of corrugated asbestos sheeting were packed into the stomach of the boat, and some fifty passengers,
Lao and hard-traveling foreigners, squeezed into the gloomy interior,
propping themselves against rice sacks and backpacks. A few windows
pierced the hull, offering panes of daylight. I picked a patch on the tiny
triangular front deck, just under the wheelhouse. A red beam bow sprit
was sandwiched between two flowerpots blooming with delicate crimson
poppies.

A customs officer, or at least an official-looking fellow in a grubby uniform, came aboard, and the captain pushed a wad of bills into his hands. A
swarm of boat boys clambered over the roof grabbing long bamboo poles
with which they prodded the blue boat from the shore, straining under
the bending poles like a team of pole vaulters warming up. Grudgingly,
the mud bank relinquished boat number 179 to the gentle clutches of the
Mekong. The captain yanked a cord, and the engine, far in the stern,

began to rumble. My location computer told me I was now nearly three miles below the trickle in Tibet that gave birth to the river beneath me.

Thailand gleamed off to starboard for a short time before the river ducked east, into the hills and forests of Laos, and then south. From time to time, a village would materialize from the forest, a villager waving a shirt or a towel, and the captain would edge his vessel toward shore, close enough for additional passengers to wade to the waiting arms of the boat boys who hauled them aboard with their gunny sacks of rice or rattan baskets filled with squawking chickens. Gliding downstream, the detritus of civilization marred stretches of the river, bits of orange-white foam, discarded plastic bottles, archipelagos of Styrofoam pellets.

Over the year I spent on the Mekong, its waters at times bore the scars of civilization. In the far north, on the Tibetan plateau, the crystalline waters that tumble from mountain crevices are touched only by the plateau's rusty silt. But farther on, in Yunnan, the river moves away from the remote geologies that shield it from exploitation and abuse—it is dammed and controlled, and the lakes those concrete walls create are still relatively clean. Almost no industry abuts the Mekong's passage, and the absence of large towns and cities on its banks spares it the discharge of sewage that has blighted most of China's other great rivers. In southeast Asia, too, there is little in the way of concentrated industry along the river, but as the Mekong wanders south, through Laos and Thailand into Cambodia and Vietnam, urban areas crowd up against its waters. Sewage is pumped directly into the river from these many towns, but it is washed inexorably toward the sea. Still, boatmen drink from the river, village dwellers along riverbanks wash their clothes in it and children splash in the silty waters. A virtue of underdevelopment, which is the economic blanket that as yet covers the Mekong watershed, is an absence of the horrendous pollution that is, more often than not, the partner of industrial prowess.

For seven hours we steamed south, and then east again, the sky darkening by the hour as steel-wool clouds scrubbed away the sun and the blue. A tough, fast wind began sprinting from the north, whipping the river into white-edged shards. I turned to look at the captain and saw him scan the angry sky; he yanked the string over his head and the engine got louder, pushing the lumbering boat a bit quicker downriver.

We rounded an elbow of the Mekong, and in the sinking blackness the village of Pakbeng appeared, flickering for a moment in a blinding slash of lightning. Then the sky opened and walls of water rushed over us, rocking the boat as sheets of rain pummeled the tarred roof beams. Under the front deck awning, I strained my eyes through the rain and lightning, searching the shoreline vainly for signs of life or light. I had no idea what to expect here, Pakbeng being just a village along the Mekong, the tiniest of dots on a map. Our captain rushed toward shore, the lightning his only spotlight as he searched for a place to run up on the bank. Suddenly I heard the scrape of rock and sand under the boat. Rain, not in drops, but in fat, hurtling dollops, slammed down and spun sideways, liquefying the air in drenching whirlpools. I stumbled from the boat, soaked in an eye blink, leaped to the gooey sand and struggled half-blind toward the clay bluff that led to the village. A ribbon of a path and footholds pick-axed into the bluff face were slick with rain, but I somehow managed to reach the top without tumbling into the river. Then, from the flapping curtains of rain, a faint pinprick of a flashlight squirted over the bluff. I trudged toward the light, head down, my pack shedding water like a new aluminum gutter.

"Here, here," a voice in the dark said. "You want to stay here?"

I looked up, my glasses fogged and blurred by rain. A two-story bamboo structure loomed in the dark. "Yes, yes," I said. I would have said yes to anything by then. A young man, his white T-shirt and tan pants soaked, pulled me through a door into a wide hall bathed in the cottony glow of kerosene lanterns. He pushed open a door into a rattan-walled room with two rough beds on wooden frames under mosquito netting. "Fine, fine," I said, and asked how much. "One night, ten thousand kip," he replied, less than $2.

Outside, the wind shunted around like loose freight cars in a railyard, and the wood frame of the building groaned, stilettos of wind razoring through the braided rattan walls. I dried myself as best I could and poked my head out the door of the building in time to see the corrugated steel roof fly off a nearby building, butterflying through the storm like a scrap of paper on a New York street. With no hope of fighting through the rain in search of food, I hunkered down in my room over a meal of Thai crackers and bottled water. Weary and wet, I decided that the morning would be time enough to see Pakbeng and dozed off.

The wind must have died down because when I awoke in the pitch blackness I heard only a shuffling and scraping at the foot of the bed. In my grogginess I groped for my flashlight and managed to twist it on to see what had woken me and found myself staring at a rat the size of a house cat enjoying a late-night meal of my remaining crackers. I waved the light around and flashed it in its eyes. The rat just stared, as if to say, So what are you going to do about it? In truth there was nothing I could do. I fell back into the bed; the rat presumably finished its meal and moved on. And then it was morning, blue, hot and sticky.

A frayed cord of asphalt curled from the edge of the clay bluff into Pakbeng, between a shabby procession of bamboo houses and shops, and a few restaurants on stilts that had sprung up, evidently to cater to the foreigners who filtered through on the daily cargo vessel. Most of the foreigners who were on my boat were down on the shore early, ready for another day's travel downriver. I decided to stay in Pakbeng to explore the village a little. There was no reason to hurry; the river would be there tomorrow or the next day, and there would always be another boat. Two ranks of bamboo buildings followed the road around the base of a hill and then toward the dense woodlands that rose on low drumlins. Outside a thatched, low-eaved house, two women in sarongs jackhammered a smooth, thick tree limb into a wooden tub of unhusked rice. From time to time, another woman would scoop the rice from the bucket into a winnowing basket and then add more unhusked rice to the bucket. It was a laborious process that went on through the day. Here, as in much of Laos, the rice grown is glutinous and served in cylindrical, woven bamboo baskets with tight-fitting covers. I was surprised to see sprouting here maybe a dozen television satellite dishes pointed toward the Thai satellite, Pakbeng being a place without electricity. In the evening, the mosquito drone of generators explained how the televisions worked.

I wandered toward the woodlands, a ragged quilt of fields spreading toward the hills. The asphalt expired into a track of ocher mud. Off in a field, a farmer labored behind a wooden plow pulled by a plodding water buffalo, its head swaying from side to side with each step, the farmer barking encouragement, or threats, as he tromped in the new furrow. I was struck by the absence of bird life; I saw none, and only occasionally did a bird's cry filter from the forest above me to the left. Indeed, until now along the river, there had been a few birds—an eagle in Tibet, scatterings of cormorants in southern Yunnan—and little other wildlife. I am not a birder by any stretch, but I do carry a field guide and binoculars with me and find the passion of wildlife enthusiasts infectious. When I lived in Africa, I used to ride a motorcycle with friends into wildlife parks, crashing along next to loping giraffes and cruising ostriches, an experience exhilarating and invigorating. Nineteenth-century accounts of China and southeast Asia invariably wallow in the lushness of flora and fauna, both winnowed in recent decades by war, development, hunger (birds in China have been relentlessly hunted) and environmental degradation. It was eerie that one hears more birdcalls in New York's Central Park than outside a distant Laotian village.

I returned to the village center. Below the bluff overlooking the Mekong, smaller cargo craft than the one I had come in scuttled in to shore to load sacks of rice and disgorge crates of beer, boxes of Thai-manufactured food products like crackers, cooking oil and soy sauce, and drums of gasoline for the village generators. Narrow wooden pirogues needled up and down the river on chirping two-stroke engines, local water taxis for villagers in a panoply of hill-tribe attire. An immense pile of mahogany logs, each one's dimensions daubed on the end in silver paint by Chinese loggers, waited for a barge to come down from Jinghong. Here, villages like Pakbeng lived off the river. It was its road and fishery; women washed clothing in it, drying sarongs and shirts on the sands of the shoreline. The river was the bush telegraph, bringing news from the big town downriver, Luang Prabang, and from Thailand upriver. And the bluff above the river was a stoop for watching the world go by. Men, more than women, squatted in clumps above the Mekong, smoking, swapping gossip, observing the river life below—the darting of the pirogues, the waddling of the jumbo freight boats, the trotting of the smaller, low-riding wooden cargo vessels.

The following morning I trundled down to the shore to catch a boat east to Luang Prabang. Pandemonium reigned. As best I could determine, two boatmen were locked in a ferocious argument over the allocation of passengers and cargo for the day's journey. At a thatched shack on the bluff's edge, I bought a ticket downriver for 19,000 kip, less than $4. An official in the shack hovered over a ledger filled with photographs of local people, marking down their comings and goings. He issued foreigners scraps of paper he stamped with an illegible smudge and a scribble from a blue ballpoint pen. Judging which boat would actually depart was impossible, so I simply climbed the plank that rose from the shore to the deck of the nearest boat, a shovel-browed, unnumbered, smaller craft than the one in which I had arrived. Inside, the boatman's family, his wife and daughter, sat cross-legged on grass mats beside the wheel. The boatman sat on a wood crate, tugged a rope line above his head three times, a bell clinking in the back on each yank, and the boat boy hunched by the engine in the stern cranked it to life. Another boat boy stood on the bow and shoved us from shore with a bamboo pole.

I stretched out below the wheelhouse under tufts of clouds and a rising sun, white and warm. Broad and rumpled, the Mekong flowed before us in lazy, curving arcs. On the sand and clay shoreline laid dry by the low river, villagers tended plots of vegetables, crops made seasonal by the rise and fall of the Mekong. Inside the boat, under a roof that was barely four feet from the deck's planking, the Lao passengers sat on rice sacks in the back, toward the engine, chatting and laughing. Toward the front, a handful of Europeans who looked as if they had stepped out of Woodstock sucked on cigar-sized marijuana joints as one hammered tunelessly on an acoustic guitar. A young woman was curled up with a paperback book; I spied one passage—"I will be instantaneously born in a heavenly realm by means of transference. . . ."—and wondered whether smoking pot was necessary.

Nearly nine hours later, the remains of the day just a magenta glow in the west, our vessel crept up against a shore fireflied with light—Luang Prabang. For those hours that slipped by effortlessly, at times I was mesmerized by the passing jungle, at times I dozed on the foredeck in the fat, hot sun. At times as well I felt a touch of timelessness, a sense that here, wrapped on both sides by jungle, sometimes dense, sometimes stubbled by slash-and-burn agriculture, the wagon trains of globalization had yet to venture. I jumped from the boat and set out through the town's streets, paved and lighted by hazy fluorescent bulbs, past rows of two-story, pastel yellow houses, their glowing windows mascaraed by mauve or aqua shutters, the architectural leavings of French colonialism. Violet bougainvillea tumbled over gated walls. In the deepening dusk, I could see the faint glow of the white walls of Buddhist *wats* settled along the finger peninsula of old Luang Prabang, barely discerning the fuzzy silhouettes of their soaring, tiered roofs as I trooped by. I was tired and dirty and headed for a hotel that I had heard about somewhere, the Douang Champa, Lao for frangipani. Winding my way toward the Nam Khan, the river that forms the southern rim of the Luang Prabang finger, I plodded up the street, checking buildings. Suddenly, I was standing before two large, polished wood-and-glass doors. I bounced up the cement steps, pulled open a door and stepped into a whitewashed room of low-slung arches hung with dim lights in bloodred shades, a long wooden bar and tables covered with ironed red tablecloths. I felt as if I had walked into Rick's Café Américain, straight out of *Casablanca*.

. . .

Dawn trickled into Luang Prabang in cobalt blues and mauves flecked with gold and coddled in a cocoon of mist. Before six o'clock, thuds of drums echoed in the distance, and from my balcony I watched silent processions of saffron-swaddled monks, wooden bowls cradled in their palms, pad toward the town center on their morning alms rounds. Women were waiting there with kettles of sticky rice that they scooped into the monks' bowls in exchange for heavenly merit. Buddhism lies at the center of lowland Lao culture and identity—the Lao Loum, as opposed to the highland Lao, or Lao Theung, who are predominately animist—and there are at least thirty wats in Luang Prabang, the oldest dating to 1513. Here, Buddhism and royalty were inextricably intertwined for centuries, a bond sundered in 1975 by Laos's new Communist rulers. Yet despite a government that at the beginning viewed Buddhism with hostility and now with a strained tolerance, the place of Buddhism in Lao life has remained and continues to grow in importance.

Luang Prabang's origins are veiled in the swirl of myth and folklore, a consequence of migrating peoples and an early nonliterate culture. Still, the dominant legend tells, as recounted by the leading historian of Laos, Martin Stuart-Fox, of two hermit brothers who joined their kingdoms under the protective wrath of snake spirits, and that after time they offered their kingdom, or as Stuart-Fox prefers, the mandala, or circle of power, to a sandalwood merchant from Vientiane. At some point, the region, known as Moung Swa, was overrun by a new warrior, Khun Lo, who became the first Lao king, ruling over the area now known as Luang Prabang. More rigorously, we know that from 1353, the kingdom of Lan Xang—the Land of a Million Elephants—was established here, and that during the next two centuries Theravada Buddhism, the version of the Indian religion that settled and evolved in southeast Asia, flowered. The final act that symbolically united Buddhism and kingship occurred during the reign of Vixun in the early sixteenth century, when he brought the Phra Bang, a sacred image of Buddha, to his capital; it is that Buddhist image, which still exists, that lent its name to this town—Luang, or Great, Prabang.*

---

* An historian of temple architecture in Laos, Charles F. B. Wilding-White, renders Luang Prabang as "Important Place of the Noble Thin One," the Buddha.

At its apogee from the mid-sixteenth to the early-nineteenth century, the kingdom of Lan Xang stretched from the Chinese to the Cambodian border, and from the edges of Vietnam well into what today is Thailand; the Mekong River was the kingdom's central axis. When the French colonialists arrived in the latter half of the nineteenth century, Lan Xang had been pulverized by the Kingdom of Siam, and large areas of the decimated kingdom were under Siamese occupation. Only a major effort by the French won back occupied swathes of Laos, and the Mekong River, which once ran through the core of the Laotian civilization, became its border.

Under the French, Luang Prabang remained the royal and religious capital and the king was permitted to exercise a measure of rule over his domain. After independence from France in 1949, the town continued to be the locus of royal life, although Vientiane had long since emerged as the country's administrative capital. Royal politics—murky, necessarily incestuous and unpredictable—patterned national life for nearly three decades until the last king, Sisavang Vatthana, and Queen Khamponi were imprisoned by the Communist government in 1975. The royal couple died, probably after starvation and the lack of medical care, around 1980, somewhere in remote, northern Laos. To this day the obsessively secretive Lao government refuses to provide an account of the royal couple's fate.

That morning, as the early sun chased wisps of fog from damp streets, I shadowed a column of monks on their rounds, struck by the devotion of the women who ladled balls of rice into alms bowls, by the certainty of the monks that they would be provided for by a devout people, by a ritual that has endured for centuries—simple, direct, a bond between belief and daily life. I wanted to feel Luang Prabang's rhythms, to begin unfolding the day with the monks who greet the dawn, and the almsgivers who share it. Wandering through Luang Prabang's streets, only four of which manage to squeeze into the tiny finger of the old town, which is washed on either edge by the Mekong and the Nam Khan, I saw more clearly the decay that had eaten away at the old French buildings. On many, the pale colonial yellow was cancerous with black mold; the louvered shutters that framed mullioned windows were cracked, peeling and askew. Yet other buildings were being restored, and looked crisp in newly painted walls and red-tiled roofs behind gardens of white-gold frangipani and cornucopia of bougainvillea.

I wanted first to visit the Royal Palace where the Phra Bang, the golden Buddhist statue, was officially on display, a statue whose fate charted Buddhism's own in Laos. The palace itself was built during French rule in 1904, a muddle of traditional Lao and French beaux arts design and motifs, under a series of tiered roofs topped by a golden spire. Set back from the road by a well-trimmed lawn and the king's private prayer hall, on which gold leaf was being applied as I passed, the palace is a single story built roughly in a cruciform shape. I climbed a series of broad marble steps—Italian marble, word has it—to the main entryway and proceeded down an arcade to my right, to the first room on the regular tour. There, amid a jumble of immense, yellowing elephant tusks, clutters of teak carvings, piles of brocaded cushions, all on a floor patchworked by Persian carpets, stood the gold, slightly jeweled Buddha, the Phra Bang. The museum leaflet described the icon as made of gold, silver and bronze and tipping the scales at fifty-four kilograms, about 119 pounds. But whether this was the genuine Phra Bang, the image of Buddha cast in India nearly two millennia ago and presented to the legendary king of Lan Xang, Fa Ngum, in 1356, is another of Laos's shadowy mysteries.

The Phra Bang, a standing Buddha a fraction over thirty-two inches tall, projects at once a sense of serenity and insight. But the original Phra Bang, historical accounts agree, was not an admixture of gold, silver and bronze, but solid gold. And many people I met in Luang Prabang, older people in particular, insist that the statue at the palace is but a fine copy. So where is the original Phra Bang, the Buddha that embodies the spirit of both royalty and Buddhism, and is hence an object of devotion for many Lao? The leading rumor is that the Phra Bang stands in the dark vaults of the state Central Bank, followed by a fading rumor that somehow the statue was spirited to Moscow after the victory of the Communist Pathet Lao in 1975. I asked a guide at the palace whether the Phra Bang I was observing was the real Phra Bang. "Of course," she replied gently, and smiled. "It must be." And she pointed to the placard on the wall describing the Phra Bang. She went on, "It says here this is the Phra Bang." In much of what I was to hear in Laos in the weeks to come, there was a pervasive and disturbing ambiguity to statements and answers, a sense that much lurked beneath the surface. I felt a deep uneasiness about this, a disquiet primed by a government cloistered in secrecy and a people—I had been told, and would soon learn—who shielded their fears by silence or dissimulation.

For the government of Laos, the Phra Bang and royalty represented the dilemma confronted by all Communist governments in their own societies: how to maintain its authority and legitimacy as truly Lao, while at the same time eviscerating or marginalizing central features of Lao culture. Rule by gun is, of course, a powerful persuader and the ultimate arbiter of legitimacy, but sheer power has done little to transform the thinking and beliefs of average Lao. Nothing exemplifies this more than the government's approach to Buddhism. At first, in the years following 1975, the government shipped monks to reeducation camps, attempted to force them to strip away elements of Buddhist belief the government regarded as superstitious and banned Buddhist festivals. In the years that followed, reports emerged from refugees who told of monks being arrested and others being shot for protesting against government policies. In 1979, the country's senior monk, the Venerable Thammayano, at the age of eighty-seven floated across the Mekong to freedom in Thailand on a raft of inner tubes. That same year, it was reported that only seventeen hundred monks remained in the country; twenty thousand had lived in Laos's *wats* just four years before.

A decade later, communism was collapsing across Europe; the Soviet Union, the largest subsidizer of the Laotian economy, fractured into a dozen pieces. There was little the Lao government could do to retain its hold on its people, and the shackles on Buddhist practice were greatly loosened. By the time I arrived in Luang Prabang, the *wats* were being rebuilt and monastic life was thriving. Indeed, so little has the government done to improve people's lives that the revival of the *wats* as the most important institution in Lao life seems inescapable; party offices are empty and the *wats* are teeming.

I left the palace and walked east, down the main thoroughfare, Thanon Phonthisalat, toward the tip of Luang Prabang's finger, toward the oldest *wats*. Rarely, a car would pass, although tiny Honda and Suzuki scooters whined up and down, most driven by young men and women in blue jeans, T-shirts and baseball hats with the Nike swoosh. Occasional squalls of saffron washed down the street as groups of novice monks migrated to or from their classes. A Scandinavian bakery catering to foreigners sold baguette sandwiches and carrot cake and boasted the town's first Internet connection; it had opened only a month before. On many houses, the Lao flag of blue and red stripes with a central white disk flew, and sometimes next to it, a red banner emblazoned with a yellow hammer and sickle. I bought a copy of the official English-language paper, the *Vientiane Times*. The headline news was that the post office, after reorganization, had sold

$1 million in stamps in 1998. Another front-page article exhorted the Lao people "to honor the achievements of the armed forces during the thirty-year-long struggle full of difficulties and sacrifices for national liberation and the past twenty-three years of struggle to protect and build the country."

At the end of the main street, under the voluminous leafiness of thick-trunked ficus trees, Wat Pakkhan, an undistinguished duckling among the great swans of Luang Prabang, sat quietly at the confluence of the Nam Khan and the Mekong. The *vihan*, or prayer hall, was simple yet characteristic of the region—huge sweeping roofs, layered one on the other, dipping toward the ground and overhanging the outside walls painted white. A flight of cement steps led to the hall itself, a long room illuminated only by the light filtering through half-closed carved window shutters, at the end of which sat a huge, seated, golden Buddha. Elsewhere on the grounds of the *wat*, smaller bamboo buildings served as cells for the monks and novices. On the steps to the *vihan*, a young novice wrapped in loose cotton saffron and brown robes fingered a copy of the *Oxford Elementary English Dictionary*, with translations in Thai; there is no Lao edition. I sat down and joined him. He smiled broadly.

"I am Novice Somchit," he said, working my arm like a well pump han-

Novice Somchit, on left, with other novice monks at Wat Pakkhan, one of dozens of Buddhist *wats* in the old royal town of Luang Prabang in northern Laos

dle. "How do you do." I was charmed—by his careful English, by his awk-ward hand pump, by this boy drowning in saffron robes. He rummaged around in the cloth sack that all monks carry and extracted a bundle of schoolbooks to show me. I pulled a can of Sprite from my shoulder bag and passed it to him. "Thank you," he said with careful deliberation. Somchit was quite dark, and his hair was shorn as is customary for monks and novices. Well-muscled arms poked from his robes, and his hands were large, his fingers roughened with calluses. He had surprisingly large ears and drooping earlobes, often seen by Buddhists as auspicious. I asked him how he came to be at Wat Pakkhan; the practice of families sending sons to the *wat* is something that has been deeply embedded in Lao culture. Even today there are few schools in Laos, and the *wats* have become the principal educational institution for boys; girls more often than not go uneducated.

"Now I am nineteen," he began, rubbing his hand across his fuzzy pate. "When I was fourteen I came here from my village, which is near Luang Prabang. My parents were killed in a *tuk-tuk* accident when I was eight years old," *tuk-tuks* being rural three-wheel motor taxis. "I lived with step-parents in the village. Of course, everyone in my village is a farmer." And why, I asked, did he leave the village? "My stepparents are very poor," he said. "I could not stay with them anymore. They said I could learn to read and write if I went to Luang Prabang. Here we do not have to pay money to go to school." We rose from the steps and walked around the prayer hall. "Come tomorrow," he said, "we can talk more then." I asked him what time he left for alms collection. "Six o'clock," he answered, "but we first start meditation at four o'clock."

I rise early, but four o'clock is normally beyond my abilities. I have never been much of a meditator, probably to my psychic detriment, and have found late nights more amenable to writing than the early hours of dawn when struggling with consciousness is difficult enough. Asia, how-ever, particularly its more remote corners, does not abide by the time-pieces and schedules of the urban world, far less those of the Western urban world. For farmers and fishermen and monks, there is little reason to be up late. Often there is no electricity; in Laos there were few if any books, the day's work has been done and nightfall is a time to sleep. And so inevitably I changed my habits, rising before dawn—the first smear of violet or crimson often accompanied by the throttled croak of roosters—and moved to the rhythms of the lands I traveled.

At six the next day I waited outside Wat Pakkhan, across the street, to

Monks and novices eating their noon meal
at Wat Pakkhan

follow Somchit as he went for alms, and to sturdy the bond we had created
between us the day before. I also wanted to see Somchit as a novice, not as
a young boy struggling to speak English, and for him to see me seeing him.
A drum was beaten and four monks and ten novices, in order of seniority,
though not height, flip-flopped out of the gate and turned toward town
into a talcum fog, each bearing a begging bowl. Somchit smiled as he
passed me, and I followed. Along the main street, women bundled in
sweaters kneeled on the pavement, scooping lumps of glutinous rice from
big aluminum pots with wooden spoons and carefully dropping them in
begging bowls. Longer columns of monks from other *wats* flowed past,
linked up and cut across the small line from Wat Pakkhan, the streets a
river of saffron currents. By seven, Somchit and the others had filled their
bowls and returned to the *wat* where the monks and novices sat in a circle
on cushions in the prayer hall for a simple breakfast; a golden morning sun
poured light through the open doors of the prayer hall haloing the monks

as they ate. At eight, his bowl cleaned and his books retrieved from his cell, Somchit scampered up the street to school at another, larger *wat*.

Later that afternoon, I rejoined him on the steps of the *vihan*. "Today we studied English and physics," he explained, delighted that I produced yet another can of Sprite. "We do not have books. The teacher writes on the blackboard. Then I write in my notebooks." Once again he pulled his well-worn notebooks from his sack, leafing through them as if to demonstrate the diligence of his studies. I asked him why he studied English and not French, Laos being a former French colony. "Nobody wants to know French," he said. "It is not useful. Only English is important. Everybody in the world speaks English so the Lao should, too."

Other novices tripped up the steps and crouched down as we talked, more to listen to English being spoken, since Somchit's was quite good, than to talk themselves. I asked him whether he would become ordained as a monk. "No, I don't want to be a monk," he answered. "I like the *wat* because I can go to school. We do study Buddhism, but I want to go to Vientiane. I want to go to university there, but I have no sponsor or money. In Laos if you don't have a sponsor or money, it is impossible." Somchit gazed through the trees at the collision of the Nam Khan with the broad Mekong. "You know," he said, "in the summer I swim in the river every day. It is very nice to be here."

Like all monks and novices, Somchit adhered to the monastic precepts common in a *wat*, including prohibitions on killing, lying and stealing. Monks also are not allowed to wear perfume or jewelry, must not sleep on high beds and may not eat after noon. In addition, monks are not to engage in sex, dance or play games. Despite the austerity, there was little sense of rebellion or resentment among the novices I met, and a broadly flexible view of the rules seemed to hold sway. At some *wats* I saw very young novices, six or seven years old, playing like mad in blurs of saffron robing, like children anywhere. "Yes, there are rules," Somchit told me. "But they are good for us. We must do these things to learn and to be good Buddhists. For me it is fine." It was difficult to tell how many young boys and men were novices at Luang Prabang's many *wats*, but it could have been well over a thousand, and this in a town that has fewer than twenty thousand people.

At nineteen, Somchit is too young to remember pre-Communist Laos, but at the same time as a novice he has no contact with the mechanisms of state control. His world is circumscribed by his school and the community of monks and novices, the predawn meditation, late-afternoon strolls

A door in a Buddhist *wat* in
Luang Prabang

along the riverbank and the elaborate New Year ceremonies that are
staged by each *wat*. He is part of what Buddhism is becoming in Laos, part
of the emerging soul of this country, part of the mosaic of this country I
sought to piece together as I wandered from *wat* to *wat*; the fate of Buddhism, in a very real sense, is the fate of Laos. There are other young men
in Luang Prabang whose lives have been deeply affected by the triumph of
Communist rule in Laos. One of these young men I met while sitting
along the waterfront doing some sketches of temple architecture, an irreg-
ular habit I maintain. I will call him Sak. He strolled up the path and sat
down next to me, silent for a time before introducing himself. His English
was remarkably fluent, and he asked if we could chat so that he could
practice it.

"Before I was born, my parents lived in Houay Xay," he began. He was
young, twenty-one he told me later, with a hip, center-parted flop of hair
and somewhat anxious eyes. "My father was a doctor. He studied medicine
in Thailand and came back to Laos to work. After the war, he was sent to

Luang Nam Tha to a reeducation camp. Here in Laos they say he was at seminar. Everybody was at seminar. They sent him there to change his thinking. He used to tell stories about his life there. He had to work very hard, hard labor every day, and listen to political studies all the time. He was there for twenty years."

Sak rubbed his hands together, glancing behind him a little nervously. I asked him if he was worried about talking to me. "No, not really," he said. "But the government wants to control everything. Nobody can say anything against the government. If you do, you will go to prison. The government is very worried about Luang Prabang because the king lived here. The government has tried to take away anything that would remind people of the king." I said that I found that odd since great care was being taken to restore the palace and its grounds. "Yes, that's true," he said. "But that is for tourists, not for the Lao people. We used to honor the king, but we cannot say anything about the king now. Nobody knows how the king died. The government never said anything. Everything is a big secret." Much of Laos's recent history is cloaked in official secrecy, evasion, obfuscation; it is a subject I will return to.

"You know what?" he continued. "The government says here in Luang Prabang we are not supposed to listen to foreign music. Not American music. Not Thai music. But people do. Some people have a satellite dish. My parents have a satellite dish. That is legal, but we have to pay ten thousand kip for a license every three months," about $2. "There is government television, but nobody watches it. All they do is political talk. All the time, just political talk. Nobody cares."

And what, I asked, happened to his father. "My father is here now," Sak said. "But he is not allowed to be a doctor. All he can do is sell some things at a small shop we have. If this had not happened, maybe he would be the head of a hospital now." Scholars of the recent history of Laos have argued that while as much as 90 percent of Laos's educated elite fled the country after the Pathet Lao took control, those who remained, including military officers under the old, American-supported regime, agreed to go to "seminars" with surprising equanimity. There was, most scholars agree, none of the wholesale slaughter of members of the ancien régime that occurred in Russia and China after the victory of communism. Even so, Laos was stripped of its educated, scientific and technical elite, a gaping wound that has done much to hobble the country's economic development and has continued to foster a distrust of the outside world by a government led by a handful of men schooled as guerrilla fighters and little else.

"I'm the oldest in my family," Sak continued, "so my parents rely on me. I have a sister who is in school, too, but my parents want me to finish so that I can become a teacher." Sak shook his head, his hair bouncing. "When I get a job as a teacher my salary will be eighty thousand kip each month. Do you know how much that is?" I said I did; on that day, it was worth about $16, a year later, scarcely $10. "And you know what, the government just changed the salary. Until now it was fifty thousand kip." I asked Sak how he could expect to live on so little. "This is Laos." He sighed. "Nobody makes money at jobs like this. So we do other work. Some people grow vegetables. Some sell things. I hope I can be a tour guide part-time. If you want to have a business, you have to pay bribes. The government and the army all take bribes because they earn no money, but they have the power. Many people have no work. I think most people are poor."

That night, I took Sak to Luang Prabang's Rama disco to check out the royal capital's nightlife. We scootered through barren streets, save for the occasional tourist on a nocturnal promenade, and parked in front of a dark, glass-fronted building a few minutes out of the old city. Inside, young people sat at tables drinking Beer Lao, all in tight blue or black jeans and rip-off DKNY T-shirts, the richer kids sporting cell phones ostentatiously clipped to their belts. A mirrored disco ball rotated grudgingly from the ceiling. Sak and I grabbed a couple of chairs, and the house music died and a band started up. In sunglasses, a blue satin shirt and baggy black pants, a Lao crooner launched into Joe Cocker's moldy classic "Unchain Your Heart," recognizable, barely. People danced desultorily. Swiftly, the singer switched to a Lao Isan tune, and the dance floor filled, not with hip club dancing, but the traditional Lao circle dance, the *lam-vong*. "You see," Sak shouted in my ear, "the police don't want too much Western music. But anyway, Lao people like Lao music."

The next morning at my hotel I had my usual breakfast of a baguette, the culinary remains of colonialism, jam and coffee in the high-ceilinged restaurant sectioned by lovely, long arches. A Madame Vine presided over the Douang Champa, a striking woman born in Laos but educated in Italy and France before the war and exiled until 1989, when the government began encouraging educated exiles to return. "I first came back in 1989 when my father died," said Madame Vine, who graced the morning in crisp slacks, a silk blouse from Paris and exquisite French. "At that time people didn't have enough to eat. Laos had been closed and people really knew nothing of the outside world. Everything was strictly controlled. People had to have passes to travel anywhere. I came back in 1995 to open this hotel. This used to be our family's business, but the government took it over. In 1995 they gave it back to us. When we started, there was no electricity and no telephones. Only in the last two years have we had steady electricity. In those first years it was very difficult. We had no customers. Now, it's a little better."

I was curious, I asked Madame Vine, about how she stocked her wine cellar (a spirited collection of Beaujolais and Bordeaux), where she bought lightbulbs and how she managed to have brasserie cutlery. "Nothing is available in Laos," she explained. "Every two or three months I go to Thailand with empty suitcases and come back with things I need." She pointed to two sconces at the foot of the stairwell that led to the four huge rooms over the restaurant. "I cannot even get bulbs for those—next month, when I am in Thailand."

Virtually nothing is manufactured in Laos. Luang Prabang's main mar-

An old woman palm reader on a
street in Luang Prabang

ket, the Dara market, a loud, disorderly square block of hundreds of merchants' stalls under a tin roof, sold everything from Dove hand soap to
motorcycles, electric fans, leather shoes, paint, steel axes, all of which
were imported, or rather smuggled, from Thailand. The Lao kip was
accepted, but merchants smiled at the sight of Thai bhat or American
dollars, a nationwide practice that threw the government-run Lao-
language newspaper *Mitthila* into paroxysms of despair: "While the country has suffered from the financial crisis in recent years, traders should not
be too selfish and help the country fight the crisis," the paper wailed one
day. Unfortunately for the government, the value of the kip was falling
like Newton's apple, and Laotian merchants, hardly an eleemosynary lot,
were shedding kip and demanding harder currencies. I visited the market
that morning after breakfast to change some dollars with the ladies in
sarongs and bulging shoulder bags who served as the backbone of foreign
currency dealing in Laos. Two hundred dollars produced bricks of kip
bound up with rubber bands; I didn't even count it. Then I puttered down
to the Mekong and tried to figure out how I would manage to get a boat to
Vientiane, a two- or three-day journey away.

A sign on the desk announced that M. Anoulom Soulivong was the
harbor master at the navigation office, a whitewashed colonial building
that also housed a local office of the police. His chair was empty, but a colleague pointed him out among the crowd along the shore—stevedores
lugging rice sacks and jerry cans of cooking oil from the morning's boat
arrivals, villagers arriving in the big city with chickens or bound piglets or
heading home with new bicycles. Arriving cargo boats nuzzled toward
shore, pushing for room among the craft sand-anchored to the riverbank.
Pirogue taxis flitted back and forth across the Mekong, and to nearby villages, leaving shallow wakes in the caramel current. After sorting out
problems with some cargo, the harbor master strode panting up the hill,
and I buttonholed him before he could attend to the crowd waiting in his
office. I told him I wanted to get a boat to the capital and that the sign
above his desk was offering a price of 16,000 kip, a shade more than $3.
"No boats," he retorted, aggravated and gruff. There have to be boats, I
insisted. He had the rates in his office. "No boats," he repeated. "The river
is too low. No passenger boats this time of year." The Mekong's seasonal
fall and rise not only created temporary farmland upriver, but sharply
restricted long-distance transport during the winter and early spring. I
refused to be defeated, however, by such niggling problems as navigability.
What if I rented an entire boat, I suggested, a proposition that would

surely prove more pricey than I anticipated. "Eight hundred thousand kip," he replied instantly. "You can rent a boat for eight hundred thousand kip," at that moment about $160 and precisely fifty times the cost of one-way passage on a scheduled boat. Done, I told him. He asked an assistant to shepherd me down to the riverbank to assay the boat that would take me to Vientiane. Bobbing gently in the lap of Mekong wavelets was a green bean of a boat, long and narrow, low in the water on its anchor line. "Okay?" the assistant asked. Okay, I said.

Fog furred the morning light like a Giverny idyll of greens and grays and browns, softening edges and smudging the soaring roofs of the prayer halls against the dense, leafy ficus trees. A deceptive early chill hurried me along, a clutch of baguettes under my arm and my pack seeming heavier on my back than usual, although I had thrown away some of the warmer clothes I had worn farther north. Some of the weight, I reflected, represented a bit of weariness, a desire to slow down even more, a hope to spend a week wiggling my toes in a swimming pool some-where. That sense of fatigue passed, but I dreamed of swimming pools for days.

I caught sight of Somchit as he wound his way back from his morning alms round and waved. The vegetable street market above the quay was bustling with morning shoppers as I trooped down to my boat. Inside the wheelhouse, a portable radio was quietly playing Lao folk music, and the captain, who introduced himself as Pheng, seemed less than overjoyed to have me on board. A plank bench ran down the starboard and port gun-nels, and a mountain of a diesel engine sat like an immense Buddha in the stern, a maze of steel pipes and copper tubes knitting the machine together in a Rube Goldberg confabulation. Astride a stool, nursing the engine, sat the engine boy, a young blind man whose fingers walked over the blackened engine with a magician's deftness. I slung my pack on the grass mat behind the wheel while a second boat boy stood on the roof and bamboo-poled the craft from shore, backing it into the Mekong's lazy stir.

Pheng jerked the cord above his head, clanking a bell back over the engine, and with a jolt and a cough of black diesel smoke the propeller bit into the river, pushing us forward and away from shore. Even as the mist began to sizzle away under the climbing sun, Luang Prabang slipped away and we were alone. I drew some encouragement from the vitality of monastic life I had witnessed there, at the resilience of belief and the durability of religious culture. But Sak's near despair and the desert of educated professionals offered little near-term hope. Governments can slice their own appendages off in displays of ideological or religious fervor, but it tends to end in a bloody mess. Buddhism's revival in Luang Prabang was helping to stitch the culture back together, but the broader health of the society seemed to me hardly assured. I could not decide whether I should be happy or morose.

Clattering along, the engine wheezing and coughing, a steady vent of smoke from a stack fashioned from tin cans trailing us, the boat eased downriver. In back, the blind boat boy worked a bilge pump to keep ahead of the river that leaked steadily into the hold. Pheng sat on a plank, leaning over the red steel wheel, sipping tea from a glass jar. His left hand lay loosely on the throttle, an aluminum door handle fixed to a big-toothed bronze gear jerry-rigged to a wire cable that stretched back to the engine.

Panning for gold on the Mekong
River south of Luang Prabang

Suddenly, ahead of us, the placidity of the Mekong was wrenched apart; fields of black boulders heaved from the surface like angry hippos, and the river was gnarled and twisted. "*Wooowww, wooowww,*" hollered Pheng, hammering the wheel to starboard and then sharply to port to try to keep the boat intact and moving. The hull sheared a boulder and Pheng's tea jar tumbled to the deck. A rip current surged through the boulders, pitching the boat uncontrollably. And then, just as suddenly, we were in calm water, the river stippled like the surface of a newly painted canvas. On the far right bank, spindles of bamboo poles restrained fishing nets ballooning into the current, and fishermen in wooden pirogues paddled out to their catch.

After some four hours, Pheng nosed his vessel toward a floating service station, one of the riverside truck stops for cargo captains where food, diesel, engine parts and dalliances of a more erotic sort were available. Pheng nudged the floating wooden dock, and a boat boy secured a line to a wood beam supporting the dock's corrugated tin roof. A cadaverous man with sunken cheeks and rivet eyes, Pheng climbed through the narrow window of the wheelhouse onto the dock. I followed. "Engine broken," he announced, lighting up a cigarette next to a pair of oil drums filled with diesel fuel. I urged him to fix it, especially because we had days of travel ahead of us. "Broken," is all he said. He climbed back into the boat and frog-walked under the low ceiling to the engine in back where he and the engine boy talked about the mechanics of the breakdown. Returning to the dock he told me, "You take fast boat. No problem." I told Pheng that I had paid for his boat and it was his boat that was taking me to Vientiane. Our argument continued, my voice rising in volume uncharitably as my frustration over the situation got the better of me. An hour went by as Pheng scooted off to the village on shore, his rubber flip-flops slapping the plank gangway in anger, and then returned with a piece of tubing. The engine repaired, if indeed it had been truly broken, and the diesel tank replenished, we chugged back into the river and slowly made our way downstream.

Some hours later, and by my GPS only thirty-seven miles from Luang Prabang, Pheng again swung the boat toward shore, approaching a sizable village of thatched bamboo huts and a scattering of cement structures that spread along the riverfront. A gaggle of pirogues and cargo vessels were huddled up against the shoreline as our boat boy jumped onto the sandbank and rammed the anchor into the shoreline. Pheng slithered through the wheelhouse window—there was no proper hatchway to enter the boat—and scurried up the riverbank. Where, I asked the boat boy, had Pheng gone now. "New captain," he replied. "You want fast boat?" he asked. No, I sighed, no fast boat. This boat. An hour went by, and Pheng returned with an older man, at least his graying hair suggested he was older than Pheng's forty years. Pheng was in a foul mood. "One hundred thousand kip more," he demanded. I asked him what he was talking about. "One hundred thousand kip more," he repeated. I told him that there was no way he was getting another kip, that I'd paid 800,000 already and that the harbor master in Luang Prabang had fixed the deal. Then Pheng tried another tack. "Engine broken," he claimed. Frustrated, I did not even bother to reply but left the wheelhouse, grabbed a book, Saul Bellow's *The Adventures of Augie March* (a novel that at one level is a story of discovering the new horizons of growing up, a book I found somehow apt for my journey) and slumped down on the grass mat to wait things out. After a while and a long conversation between Pheng and the older man, I heard the bell over the engine clang, and then we were back on the Mekong.

I peered into the wheelhouse to find the older man at the wheel and Pheng squatting on a plank sipping from a new jar of tea. In the distance, the pale gray-blue silhouettes of mountains stenciled the horizon and pocket villages sprang from clearings seemingly higgledy-piggledy. Amid the litter of basalt outcroppings that studded the river, fishermen balanced precariously on rock faces, stringing fishing nets into the pulsing water with delicate lengths of bamboo. On the shorelines of fine sand, women in sarongs, their hair bundled in bagel-sized buns, washed clothes.

With its shallow draft, the boat heeled easily in the slightest turbulence of the river, a small rapids enough to fling the boat about like a twig. Every mile south brought a greater profusion of black-gray shale protrusions and sandstones with periodic swellings of deep, black basalt. Here the Mekong coursed through what geologists call the Paklay-Luang Prabang Indosinian folding, a great geologic crumpling of the Earth's crust that occurred about 220 million years ago during the Middle Triassic period. A few tens of millions of years later, there was considerable volcanic activity along the folding, the evidence stark in the huge bulging pectorals of igneous rock formations, pitted and twined columns of rock squeezing the river into a frenzy of anxiety and brief sprints of anger.

Dusk ambushed us as our boat heaved and saddled in the whipsaw currents, and Pheng started to worry aloud to the older man who wrestled with the wheel. A desolate shoreline both port and starboard greeted our scrutinies, just fading forests rising from the rocky cliffs. The boat had no spotlight, so it was impossible to travel at night; Pheng, who evidently possessed no knowledge of the river this far south, was increasingly nervous. Then, almost miraculously, although I suspect truly not uncommonly along the well-traveled Mekong, a tubby wooden cargo vessel manacled to the shoreline appeared before us and our captain wheeled to the riverbank just as night's blackness clammed shut on us. An irritable Pheng shouted up to the boatman on the cargo vessel and left me in the hands of the boat boy who began cooking a stew of fish and tubers on a small burner set on the grass mat behind the wheelhouse. He washed a few bowls in the river and scooped some glutinous rice from a bamboo basket into them before spooning some stew on top. I ate it with an aluminum soup spoon while Pheng laughed over storytelling on the boat next to us.

As rice went, it was not the worst I'd eaten, nor by far the best. Most non-Asian Americans, and Europeans for that matter, see rice through a monocular lens, as a pile of white grains on the corner of a plate, not terribly tasty but an occasionally interesting accompaniment to a slice of beef, a leg of chicken, a rack of lamb. In Asia, though, rice comes in multitudinous varieties, and I'd eaten most of them. In Tibet, a dumping ground for China's worst commodities and its worst food products, the rice *was* tasteless, stubby-grained kernels, specky white spheres that were devoid of flavor and character. Indeed, for all the rice consumed in China, much of it is undistinguished, of such shadowy and shallow flavor that it is seen as the food of peasants; indeed, at banquets in fancy restaurants rice is almost never served.

But it is in southeast Asia that rice achieves its full flower. In Thailand, legend holds that each rice grain possesses a spirit and is to be planted in the rainy season to become "pregnant." But before planting, the rice goddess is to be honored; in Bangkok, the Royal Plowing Ceremony is a public holiday, and ceremonial oxen are garlanded with flowers before they begin pulling a sacred gold plow, an act marking the onset of the planting season. At its best, Thai rice is to my palate the most subtle and exquisite in the world, a faintly perfumed, long-grained wonder that is addictive and utterly distinctive. In northern Thailand, though, and in Laos, it is glutinous, as opposed to loose-grained, rice that is normally eaten, a flavorful, sticky concoction that is consumed with a spoon, or one's fingers. It is very filling. In Vietnam, where typical markets offer anywhere from ten to twenty different varieties of rice, it is eaten from ceramic bowls as in China, although it is often longer grained and more flavorful than its Chinese cousin. Vietnam boasts a profusion of rice cakes and buns, my favorite called *banh tet,* which is filled with mung bean paste, pork and lard wrapped in two square layers of sticky rice; it is a treat usually eaten only at New Year's, and has a bit of the association attached to it that fruitcakes in the United States do—nobody professes to like them, but somehow they get eaten. And for a truly tasty roadside snack in rural Cambodia, it is often possible to find sticky coconut rice baked in bamboo tubes. Sweet and succulent, there is hardly a better afternoon snack on Earth.

As the boat boy cleaned up after dinner, I spread my sleeping bag on the grass mat and lay down to read a little, clipping my pocket reading light onto the book. In the back of the boat, the boat boy and the engine boy talked quietly before falling asleep on the deck planking. The boat lolled gently in Mekong ripples, thunking against the larger vessel from time to time. I switched off the light and reflected on the contrasts between the isolation and beauty of the river, the loneliness of solitary villages, the heft of geologic time over the landscape, the balletic elegance of fishermen perched on shale outcroppings, and the surliness of Pheng and his endless attempts to maneuver out from under the trip he had signed up for. It had not spoiled the journey, but it did tang the day somewhat sourly. Then, as I lazily mused about what the next day would bring, that familiar melody of the 1960s seeped from the belly of the boat next door. . . .

> I took my troubles down to Madame Rue
> You know that gypsy with the gold-capped tooth
> She's got a pad down on 34th and Vine
> Sellin' little bottles of Love Potion Number 9. . . .

I woke to the sound of the boat boys leaping into the Mekong for a scrub-down, a bath I decided to forgo. Scraps of light fluttered through the hills bearing dawn and the prospects of another day's travel. Pheng, across the grass mat from my sleeping bag, rustled under a blanket in his brown shirt and camouflage pants, before rousing himself for river ablutions. I doused my face with water from one of my diminishing supplies of bottles and breakfasted on a stale baguette and bananas. Pheng and the engine boy examined the diesel block, checking each other's diagnoses. Fat cushions of fog pillowed the boat.

Not to miss a chance, Pheng began the day preemptorily. "You take big boat," he told me, jerking his head toward the large vessel against our starboard side. "It goes to Vientiane." I waved my hand and told him no, repeating my worn mantra about having already paid him to take me all the way. The older man, who had gotten us this far, stood on the shore as we poled back into the current and the fog. Grumbling, Pheng yanked the bell cord and the engine gears clanked into forward. A man in a pirogue piled with sacks of nuts slipped by us, his paddle plopping in the river as Pheng pushed the aluminum door handle throttle forward, propelling us slowly into the fog as he sipped from a glass jar of tea brewed from Mekong waters.

Pheng steered us carefully, swaddled in a foggy embrace, the shorelines at times lost beyond gray-white walls of mist. A climbing sun fought the brume, poking tunnels and chasms and then vanquishing our morning swaddlings. Fields hacked from woods and brush flattened the shore sporadically, huts on storklike bamboo stilts lining the river in linear villages. On sand flats to port, three plumed egrets, snow white on their spindly black legs, watched our passing. Then Pheng, his unhappiness brewing, decided to top off his earnings and yanked the wheel to starboard, toward a huddle of villagers whirling white towels above their heads, the Mekong flag down. We ran to shore and sand-anchored as the boat boy helped pull the villagers into the hold, one with two baskets of shoats on a shoulder pole, another with a nice-sized black pig, snorting and kicking its tethered rear hooves. The pig's owner slipped easily through the window frame into the boat, sliding gracefully onto the plank seating, dressed in a khaki zip-up jacket and jeans with a blue Chicago Bulls porkpie hat clamped firmly on his head.

A bit farther downriver, Pheng again wheeled to shore, gathering more villagers and more pigs, these wrapped in old rice sacks with only their snouts protruding from an end hole. Bamboo baskets of chickens and bags of vegetables were heaved aboard, the produce of villagers heading to markets downriver. And farther still, we rumbled to shore and disgorged our passengers; the big pig was tossed from the boat into the river and nearly drowned before his owner hauled it ashore. Back on the river, a hot-chocolate brown, Pheng fingered his takings, a small stash of kip. Our craft moved easily, past great masses of rock breaching like whales in waters laced with foam. Along the shore, wooden canoes were bundled on the sand beneath villages and silent riverine pools were stalked by fishermen with looping nets.

Toward noon, the town of Paklay rose on our starboard side, the south-ern reach of the Indosinian fold belt that shaped the topography through which we traveled. Pheng ran the boat up onto the shore, poured himself through the wheelhouse window, trotted up the riverbank to town and vanished. The blind engine boy rubbed a rough rag over the engine, sway-ing slightly from side to side as he worked, while the boat boy lay down on the vessel's roof and went to sleep. No explanation was offered for our stop, so I disembarked and wandered into the town, wading through a wash of sweltering humidity. A scattering of cement buildings was strung along a strip of asphalt that ran into dirt and denser clusters of bamboo huts. But there were almost no people. Two schoolboys in shorts pedaled by me, book satchels slung over their backs, but a low row of roadside mar-ket tables, plywood sheets on beer crates, was empty. I returned to the river and the boat. The engine boy and boat boy were gone.

Two hours ticked by. Two thick-browed water buffaloes stood dumbly in the mud next to the boat, cooling themselves from a griddling sun. Slumped against my pack, I mopped my face and struggled to lose myself in Bellow's prose, my perspiration soaking into the book's pages. At the third hour of idleness, I began to worry about whether I would be in Pak-lay for the night, and if so where I would stay, and whether Pheng intended to reclaim his vessel.

Here, the river widens dramatically and begins an abrupt swerve east-ward, a radical diversion from its apparently natural course toward Bangkok and the Gulf of Thailand, and even apparently toward the great lake of Tonle Sap in northwestern Cambodia. Instead, massive earth-quakes and faulting wrenched and twisted the course of the Mekong dur-ing the late Cenozoic period, perhaps 10 or 20 million years ago, shoving it far to the east, and then south into its present watershed. I was trapped in a late Cenozoic fault, crewless, near the end of my drinking water, drenched in sweat and increasingly hungry. Bellow provided scant com-fort, and I weighed my options: stay on the boat until Pheng decided to return or find lodgings in Paklay. A pair of large-motored river rockets bobbed off a jetty behind my boat, but I grated at the idea of spending more money to go the rest of the way. By Pheng's boat, the trip was at least eight hours, I figured, which meant that by mid-afternoon there was no possibility of reaching Vientiane that day.

As I reflected on my situation, there was a knocking on the roof of the boat. "Hello, hello," a disembodied voice announced. I stuck my head out the side of the vessel to see a well-dressed man in tan slacks and a white shirt standing in the sand at the prow of the boat. I scrambled outside, shook his hand and asked if I could help him. "Me?" he asked. "I think maybe I can help you.

"I am Savay," he said in halting, although serviceable, English. "I think boatman has gone. He is not coming back today." I asked him why not. "I don't know. He is just not coming back. I think he does not want to go anymore." I explained to Savay, whom I was beginning to see as an emissary from the absconding Pheng, that I had already paid 800,000 kip for Pheng and his boat to take me to Vientiane. Savay nodded his head and sat down on the sand. I joined him. "Yes, I know that. But he will not go." I let that go by for the moment and asked Savay how he, obviously educated and English-speaking, came to be in Paklay. "Oh, I am an engineer," he replied. "I studied in Czechoslovakia for seven years. I lived in Prague. A very beautiful city. I used to work in Vientiane, but now I moved here because my wife is from Paklay." I told him that Paklay seemed very quiet. "Yes, very quiet. Nothing happens here." He said it with a hint of relief. Perhaps, given Laos's history, it was best nothing happened here. Savay sat in the sand, his arms wrapped around his knees. "I think now you must take fast boat," he said finally. "I think there is no other way." I explained again, too pedantically perhaps, that I had paid Pheng and that I expected him to take me downriver.

"I know," Savay said. "But boatman is finished." Then he got to his feet, as did I, and pointed at one of the yellow speedboats tied to the jetty. "You take fast boat. No problem. No money needed." It seemed pointless to argue. A deal had been struck somewhere with Pheng having paid off Savay to get me off his boat. I had no choice. Okay, I told Savay, fast boat. Clearly delighted at his diplomatic triumph, Savay jumped on the boat to grab my pack. I followed him to a fast boat, a fragile needle of wood clamped to a prodigious car engine that no doubt gobbled the Mekong's miles in a frenzy of sound and water. The boat driver appeared from nowhere, two helmets dangling from his arm. Savay shook my hand. "This is best," he said. "Tonight, Vientiane." I thanked him, stuffed the helmet on my head and settled onto the red vinyl seat cushions.

In a moment we were thundering down the river, a towering tail of spray tacked to our stern. Weaving through basking boulders, the driver skimmed the river surface, flinging the boat into wide turns as the Mekong serpentined between forested hills rumpling the landscape. More than a century earlier, Francis Garnier, the nineteenth-century French explorer, labored up the Mekong here, scarcely managing six or seven miles a day; now the miles were vanishing at a rate of almost one every two minutes. Garnier also described a Laos that has long since disappeared, a land of huge herds of deer and stalking tigers, and, in what gave Laos its classical appellation, vast herds of elephants that lived in deep forests, visiting the Mekong to drink and bathe. In the months I traveled in Laos, I saw not one elephant.

And as it had before, in a flash, Thailand appeared on our right—glistening power lines; a prim ribbon of blacktop that mirrored the river's meander; Buddhist *wats* with gleaming gold spires; solid, rambling cement houses. Trim, perfectly proportioned cement steps marched down from Thai towns to the river. Gradually the steep-sided canyons and rugged hillsides mellowed, as if they had been filed down by a Zeus-like woodworker, and the river broadened, baring its heft and muscle. More fast boats whizzed by, hurtling upriver toward Paklay and intermediate villages before nightfall. Just as darkness draped the river anew, my driver spun the boat toward shore where a flotilla of yellow river rockets bucked in the collision of waves and currents. We were north of Vientiane, but this was the boat station for town. I toiled up a steep clay bank to a dusty parking lot lit only by the lamps of an open-front police station, where I picked up another in my growing stack of stamped paper scraps marking my progress through Laos.

Outside, to my surprise, my boat driver waited on an idling motor scooter. "I take you to city," he told me, in what must have been the final part of Pheng's deal. I hopped on the pillion and we whined into Vientiane, the streets a whirl of dust under faint streetlights. For the first time in weeks, I was in car traffic, instinctively shying away from what I saw as reckless drivers doing twenty miles an hour. My driver banked into a darkened town square, a dessicated fountain silent in its center. "Okay?" he asked. Okay, I said. Through the haze and dust of the square, a lighted sign announced: L'OPERA, RISTORANTE ITALIANO.

That evening I ate the first Western food I had had for some time, a menu I remember vividly: *insalata mixte, spaghetti aglio e olio, pollo cacciatore* and chocolate mousse. I drank an entire bottle of Chianti. It was glorious.

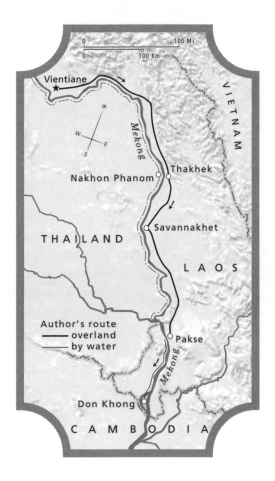

Six

Baguettes to Marx

L ao civilization, its culture, patterns of kingship and indeed its very
existence as a distinct society, approached extinction in the nineteenth century, only to be plucked from oblivion by, of all people,

the French. Lao historians, particularly those of a Communist bent, would not put it that way, concerned as they are with trumpeting the heroic struggles fought by courageous Lao peasants against feudal occupiers, but the devastation suffered by the Lao at the hands of an imperious and merciless Siam kingdom leads to few other conclusions.

Troubles for the Lao began soon after a prince named Anouvong assumed the throne in Vientiane in 1804, a separate kingdom from that in Luang Prabang, but a kingdom nonetheless. Like his predecessors, Anouvong paid tribute to Siam and exercised rather limited control over trading practices in his realm. The Siamese, unfamiliar with the precepts of free trade that would sweep the globe 150 years later and generally rapacious in appetite, imposed all sorts of fees, charges and taxes on commerce and generally made life difficult for Anouvong. Unsurprisingly, he bridled under Siamese restraints and set out to liberate his kingdom from the Siamese yoke. In 1826, after having raised armies and plotted strategies, he captured swathes of the land of the Lao on both sides of the Mekong, driving the Siamese back from the borders of his kingdom. Unfortunately for him, the Siamese were wealthier, had solved their foreign policy problems with the British in Burma and had a bigger army. They swept down on Anouvong, decimated his forces and captured the rebellious monarch, whom they shipped to Bangkok where, imprisoned, he died in excruciating conditions. And then, to cement their victory and ensure the utter evisceration of Anouvong's kingdom, Siamese troops sacked and razed Vientiane. Four decades later, Garnier stumbled onto the ruined royal capital. This is what he saw:

> The palace of the kings of Vienchan, in spite of its fallen roofs and burned colonnades, was the only dwelling of which the remaining vestiges were still recognizable. . . . Everywhere else only shapeless pieces of brick under the bushes indicated where the other important dwellings were located. No other edifices remained standing but the pagodas. However, the fragile splendors of these, abandoned by their priests and constructed in the same materials as the palace, forty rainy seasons have tarnished. The ever vigorous tropical vegetation, which fortunately softened the appearance of these barbarous devastations and covered them with greenery and flowers, gave these ruined sanctuaries a deceptive appearance of decay. Tall grasses grew everywhere on the sacred porches, climbing plants

already clasped the columns and vigorous trees made their way across the roofs. . . .

By the end of the century, after bullying the Siamese into relinquishing everything east of the Mekong with a flotilla of gunboats outside the royal palace in Bangkok, the French were busily rebuilding Vientiane as capital of their new colony, a place they named "Laos." The Mekong, no longer the sinew of Laotian civilization, became the epidermis between Siam and Laos, while in France it was simply known as "our river."

A century of Vientiane's travails wears heavily on the capital's visage, travails visited mostly by foreigners, although twenty-five years of Communist rule has brought depredations as well. The French left behind streets shaded by plane trees and blocks of provincial colonial homes in pastels of lemon, robin's egg blue or ivory, two-story structures under tiled mansard roofs, discreet behind louvered shutters and prim cast-iron fences. The Americans, who fought part of the Vietnam War from here, left ranch-style homes in what would be near-in suburbs in the West; here, these low-slung houses are camped behind high walls off dusty dirt and stone alleyways, now the residences of foreign diplomats and flocks of international aid workers. And the Soviets, who did not linger long here, are best remembered at the decrepit Vieng Samay Theater, a place shuttered by a corroded steel gate under a cracked and sagging marquee dangling a serif of neon tubing, plywood-boarded windows and a charcoal patina of mold/ fungus that blotches the facade; in the *"aujourd'hui"* window, a torn and water-stained poster announces UN DÉPASSEMENT DANGEREUX, that well-known drama by Nikolai Ivanov and Alexandre Boulganine. There are no active movie theaters in Vientiane anymore.

A riverfront road and esplanade of sorts, sweeping along the northern arcuate of the Mekong, passes several restored *wats*, as well as the recent vintage presidential palace, a strangely deserted compound in the middle of which sits a miniature pinkish Buckingham Palace watched by a few indifferent, dozing guards. There is also a string of restaurants newly opened in anticipation of a hoped-for tourist boom. A grid of ruptured asphalt and raw dirt streets spreads from the river past shallow boulevards of commerce, into checkerboards of shanty towns and neighborhoods of shabby opulence, wedding-cake mansions for a new elite. Shreds of economic life are scattered on the ground of international assistance: Vietnamese road workers, molasses-like in their exertions, lay brick sidewalks by hand and struggle to blacktop the riverfront road with antiquated and erratic Russian machinery; Australian and Japanese engineers battle to build the country's first and only national paved highway, Route 13, two lanes of macadam that is to run from the Cambodian border to north of Luang Prabang; the capital's garbage is picked up in spanking new navy blue garbage trucks, courtesy of the Japanese government. And the government of Laos? It does little but cling ferociously to the reins of power.

Compulsively secretive, the Laotian government from its inception in 1975 has revealed little about its inner workings to its own people, far less to the outside world.* Wedded initially to a soup of Marxist-Leninist and peasant-revolutionary ideologies, the government, which is indistinguishable from the ruling Lao People's Revolutionary Party, headed resolutely down all the blind alleys Communist states had taken before them. When it announced a five-year plan for the economic development of the country in 1980, not only did it never publish details of the plan, it never made it available to the United Nations Development Program, an agency that was called on to help alleviate some of the country's worst poverty. And only in 1991, sixteen years after it took over, did the government finally get around to writing a constitution for the country, not that any of the document's high-blown rhetoric about democracy and freedom had any actual meaning.

For most Lao, none of this matters greatly; subsistence farmers have enough problems surviving year to year without worrying about ideological rectitude, Socialist planning and constitutional quibbles. But in Vientiane and in the other large towns along the Mekong there is among most Laotians a palpable air of indifference and ignorance about their own country and, indeed, their future. "Did you ever notice," one Laotian who has spent considerable time abroad asked me, "that there are no newspa-

---

* As an exercise, I visited a diplomat at the American embassy in Vientiane to get a sense of how much was known about the workings of the Laotian government. Apart from a familiarity with the sorts of economic and social data provided by United Nations and international multilateral organizations, there was a great, shadowy eclipse when it came to an understanding of how government decisions were made, how people were promoted or demoted, and what went on in the corridors of power on a week-to-week basis. "We know decision making is taken in a tightly knit group of people," this diplomat told me. "Beyond that, we don't really know very much."

per stands? There are no newspapers. There are no bookstores. This is what I call a nonliterate country. There is absolutely nothing to read in Laos. There is no way people can learn about their own country, much less the rest of the world."

To be perfectly fair, there are newspapers, all state-run, but distributed only at government offices, as well as an English- and a French-language paper, both twice-weeklies, and both occasionally available in Vientiane and Luang Prabang. And there is a government bookshop here, a corner building with dirty windows and dusty glass cases scantily littered mostly with English-language textbooks and curling posters of Marx, Lenin and other luminaries of the Communist pantheon; in one corner, however, a revolving wire magazine rack sported a clutch of foreign fare—months-old copies of *Newsweek*, *Time* and *Motor Trend* magazines. And most inexplicable of all for a government that rigorously controls the expression of ideas, satellite dishes capable of sucking down Thailand's no-holds-barred television programs are permitted, if taxed.

Across from the strangled fountain that welcomed me my first evening in Vientiane are the offices of the *Vientiane Times*, the state-run English-language paper, tucked into a cramped, two-story white 1960s building. I opened the glass-paned wooden door and told a receptionist that I had an appointment to meet Michel Somsanouk Mixay, the editor of the paper. I wanted to see Mixay because he had a reputation for reasonable candor leavened by an embedded faith in the Communist regime.

An open doorway led to a room of desks and typewriters, eerily silent for a newspaper newsroom. After a few minutes of browsing through a bound volume of the year's papers, I was ushered into Mixay's office, a simple room with a desk, a table and a few plain chairs. Mixay, less than six feet tall, with clear, powerful eyes and graceful hands, waved me to a chair. Immediately I asked him about the wreckage of the Laotian economy I saw around me.* "There is difficulty," he began, picking his words as if he were stepping from stone to stone across a stream. "There is crisis. We

---

* While I was in Vientiane, the prime minister, four ministers, four deputy ministers and the governor of the Central Bank jetted off to Beijing to pay ideological fealty to the largest remaining Communist state and to beg for help for the collapsing economy. As a Western academic in Laos put it to me, "The government is broke and scared. Their only hope is China. They're taking guidance from China in everything in the hope that China will bail them out."

thought we would be outside the economic crisis in Asia but we are not. Five years ago, the kip was seven hundred to the dollar. Today on the black market a dollar is fifty-five hundred kip. The government tries to curb this, but it is impossible." I asked Mixay if the country's current problems could be traced to the Socialist planning in the early years of Communist rule. "There was collectivization after the Pathet Lao took over," he said. "It turned out that collectivization is not in the mentality of the Lao people. The Lao farmer is a very hard worker, and then overnight he had to put his land and rice and feed and cattle in common. Production declined. There were no markets. Yes, it was terrible. In 1986, Kaysone Phomvihane"—the man who led the Pathet Lao to victory in 1975 and ruled until his death in 1992 — "reversed all that. We decided to shift to a market economy. Things started to improve."

I asked Mixay why the government allowed no room for the public discussion of its policies, particularly since Laos remained mired in a backwardness shared by few other countries on Earth. Without flinching, he replied, "I don't think anybody thinks about changing the regime or having a multiparty system. We can see all these nonconfidence debates in Thailand's parliament. Fortunately we don't have that here." He paused and adjusted a small sheaf of papers on the table. "There is no famine here," he continued. "Everybody eats. The big issues are health, education. There are, of course, no telephones, no electricity, no railroad, terrible roads. . . ." His voice trailed off.

For some seconds we sat in silence, he perhaps deciding where to go, and I uncertain whether to break his train of thought. Then he resumed. "We used to say that the Soviet Union was the rampart of socialism, but then it collapsed. There was anxiety for a time, but then we began to count who's left—Vietnam, China." I wondered aloud how he, who had obviously spent time abroad, could seek solace from countries so poor, so corrupt and so politically rigid. "I was educated in France," he replied, somewhat stiffly. "I came back to Laos in 1971, during the war. It was very American here. The Lao-American Association was right next door to this building. There were a lot of bars here, lots of girlie shows that you don't even find in Bangkok. It was not a very good place. Everything was imported. Laos didn't even grow vegetables; we imported them. In 1975 the Pathet Lao took over, and things changed completely overnight. Thailand closed the border overnight. Thailand put out a list of what they called strategic goods that could not be exported to Laos—medicines, construction goods, even bicycles. It was a very hard time. I had been working at a radio station and decided to stay." Unspoken was the fact that Mixay had ties to the Communist movement, ties that propelled him to a visible and occasionally influential position in the capital. "Then, in 1995, the government started this newspaper as a weekly. Now we are twice a week. Maybe someday it will be a daily."

And what of the future? I asked Mixay. Where could Laos hope to go in an Asia welded to fast-track capitalism and insurgent political democracy? He sighed, clearly unhappy at my focus on the country's political system, and finally said, "I hope Laos will improve. I think the economic situation will improve over the next five years. The government is encouraging people to produce. We started this year with a good dry-season rice production. There will be more next year. I think little by little things will get better." I wondered.

Outside the paper's offices, the sun scorched the pavement and dust boiled from under the tires of scooters and cars, filming the air with billowing ocher clouds. On foot, I found Vientiane sweltering and grubby. I strolled over to a Vietnamese noodle shop that rented scooters on the side and motored over to the central market, a cacophony of shop stalls cheek by jowl in acres of cavernous cement warehouses and, on the peripheries, under layerings of corrugated tin roofing. My camera had died a meek death at the hands of Mekong boat travel, and I was hoping I could find a serviceable replacement in Vientiane.

Sectioned by trade, the sarong merchants hawked their silk and cotton garments from behind polychromed towers of handwoven fabric; hardware merchants sat amid buckets of nails, hammers, piping, wrenches, paints and wheelbarrows; jewelers camped behind glass counters of broaches, gold necklaces and velvet pads furrowed with rings, and electronics salesmen scrutinized shoppers gawking at the boxes of radios, televisions and cameras, all smuggled from Thailand. There was even a wine merchant offering a weekly special on a South African 1994 Bersig Estate Briotage. Indeed, as in markets elsewhere in Laos, virtually everything in Vientiane's central market has been brought in from Thailand, just a short boat ride across the muddy Mekong. At one counter I asked to examine a quick-and-easy 35-millimeter camera, not quite aim-and-shoot but nothing a professional photographer would want either. I bargained hard, my position sustained by a plenitude of other camera dealers, and marched off with a Nikon camera for $300, certainly more than I should have paid, but far less than was first asked, a very minor triumph.

Unshackling the thick-link chain from my scooter, theft being an

enduring feature of Vientiane life, I kick-started the little machine and
headed north, toward Dong Dok and Vientiane University, a little more
than six miles from the city center, in an effort to assay the state of the
country's educated elite. Laos has only one university, an institution that
began its life under Communist rule as a reeducation camp and prison.
There was no signboard for the university, or if there was I never found it,
and passed the turn-off twice before I stumbled onto the correct road. I
swung off the main road and putted onto the campus under scanty shade
trees, past concrete-box classrooms and rows of barracks that served as
dormitories. Schools of students, all in white shirts with the university
seal affixed to their sleeves, male students in black slacks and female students in black sarongs, flowed from building to building clutching texts
and notebooks. A young woman student in a sparkling white Honda
drove up, parked under a tree and emerged with a tennis racquet under
her arm. It was the first tennis racquet I had seen in Laos, an implement
not widely employed in a country where most people daily wrestled with
buffalo-drawn plows and hand-pounding rice huskers. So I rushed over to
talk to her, or try to. Do you speak English? I asked, after reaching her. "A
little," she answered, clearly uncertain about this gawky foreigner button-
holing her on the way to the tennis courts. I explained a bit of who I was
and that I was interested in talking about the university.

"I am a third-year student," she told me, a bit impatiently. I asked her to
backtrack and tell me how she was admitted to the university, an obviously difficult accomplishment in a country with one institution of higher
education. Before we sat under a tree, she carefully tucked her sarong
under her so it would not wrinkle. "My father is a businessman. He
imports and exports things. When I was younger, I went to a private
school. So when I took the examination for university, it was not so difficult." And what, I asked her, was her education like here. "I study English," she replied. "Many students here want to get a government job. I
think I will work with my father in business. If you do not speak English,
you cannot make business. I think the government is not a good place to
work. What does the government do? Nothing. Look at this university.
The library has no books. We only have our first copy machine two weeks
ago. Some foreign person gave us this copier. And you know, the teachers
here are not good. They really don't know very much. Look at universities
in Thailand. They have laboratories and libraries. Laos is a poor country.
Here we don't have anything like that."

She rose to leave, and I asked if I could walk her to the tennis court. She agreed, and I asked her whether she felt that her classmates envied her obvious affluence. "I think some students do," she said, shrugging her shoulders. "But now everyone can make business in Laos. It is not a crime. I don't care about politics. My parents don't care about politics. We only make business." Surely, I pressed her, there were students who were the children of the country's government leaders, students who might regard her as the sort of person communism was trying to get rid of. "I don't care," she said. "They say what they want. Politics is for people with no brains." And then, whacking her tennis racquet on her palm, she turned to me. "Okay, enough?" I thanked her and then watched her stroll off toward the courts, which I could not see.

As I walked back to my scooter, I felt vaguely depressed, perhaps at the utter utilitarianism the tennis-playing student displayed, perhaps at her evident indifference to her country. Yet, as I thought about it more, it seemed clear that her attitude, and her father's, was perhaps the best survival strategy in a land with few opportunities and many risks. There are no open political discussions in Laos; in 1990, when the Communist party was drafting the country's first constitution, a small group of what could be called social democrats, encouraged by the collapse of the Soviet bloc, began agitating for a multiparty system in Laos. Three of the most prominent members of the group were rounded up and have not been heard from since.

Though China, the latest palladium of communism for the Laotian party, seethes with intellectual and artistic ferment and creativity despite desultory official appeals to an increasingly ambiguous orthodoxy, Laos exhibits few intellectual life signs. "We are intellectually stunted," a Lao writer who lives in Paris told me. Occasionally he returns to Vientiane to visit his relatives, but mostly, he said, he cannot bear being here. "This government is frantically paranoid about information on Laos seeping out or comprehensive news and ideas of the real world filtering in. As a result, there is an intellectual indolence, a social indolence, a passivity that pervades this society at the urban level. And the financial crisis in southeast Asia has provided a convenient excuse for doing nothing." Dressed in a blue work shirt and khaki slacks, the writer carried a cloth sling bag with a notebook and an issue of *Le Nouvel Observateur*; I suspected there was a beret in there, too. I met him on his last day in the capital, a day before he was to return to Paris, a city that has become a refuge for many educated

Lao in the years after the Vietnam War. We drank espresso at a new bakery down the street from the *Vientiane Times* and he chain-smoked Gitanes from a blue packet.

"The hardest thing for someone like me," he continued, his voice sandpapery from the parade of stubby cigarettes, "is that nobody here has ever read a book. Imagine a city at the end of the twentieth century where nobody, not one person, has read a book from the first page to the last page. People only talk about their family, about prices going up and up, about sending their son to the *wat*. No one ever talks about their country. No one *knows* anything about their country. When I come here I feel like I'm walking around with a bag on my head. It seems that everybody is walking around with a bag on their head. Sometimes I don't even feel like a Lao." He sucked deeply on his cigarette, and then let go a tensile jet of blue-gray smoke. "Maybe now I'm just another Frenchman."

National identities are tricky things. Americans, I learn on my occasional visits home, increasingly see themselves—or is it that they always have—in regionally crafted mirrors. San Franciscans, to choose an example, are quite content in the belief that they are superior in all ways to the country that lies to the east, across the bay; the poet John Ashbery described San Francisco as a city "where everybody is congratulating themselves on what a wonderful place they're in." How they fit into a larger national consciousness is uncertain, both to them and in many ways to the rest of the country as well. In India, where I lived for many years, a sense of nationhood exists mostly at the rhetorical level of the chattering classes. In truth, Tamils feel little affinity for cow-belt Uttar Pradeshis; they look different, speak different languages, worship different gods, eat different food and see the world of caste very differently. Mention Pakistan or cricket, and one and all are Indians, but that is about as far as things go. And in Europe, where the web of the European Union and a common currency is woven ever tighter, many people are coming to think of themselves as generically European as much as they regard themselves as Irish or Danish or Italian.

Invariably, however, societies create edifices that bit by bit and in their collectivity provide a description of who they are, why they are, what they think and imagine and what, in some cases, they hope to be. These edifices are the museums, theaters and libraries that display a society's art, its crafts, its written words, the panoply of its cultural expressions; these edifices also document the choices societies make about how they define who their people are. I see museums in some way as mirrors of civilization, reflections on identity and purpose. And so, one afternoon I motored a few blocks to the Revolutionary Museum, built in 1925 as the French governor's residence and, after a series of permutations as a royal abode and government offices, designated as the national museum in 1985, a decade after the Pathet Lao's victory. The day I was there it was empty, my shoes kicking up lazy tufts of dust as I moved from one hollow room to the next.

Bits of Laos's past in glass cases—a handful of stone tools, a reliquary of bronze Buddhas—and a few oil paintings of early kings in Leninist poses sum up the history of the Lao people until the arrival of the French.* Heroes (King Xayasethathirath, "leading the people in the fight against the Burmese feudalist") and traitors (King Ounkham, "the king who handed the country to the French colonialists") are the unnuanced protagonists in Communist historiography. I was delighted, though, to see a copy of the agreement between France and Siam establishing the Mekong as the border between the Thai kingdom and the new French colony; the originals, I presumed, were in Bangkok and Paris. But most rooms of the colonial governor's home are devoted to the guerrilla wars of the Pathet Lao and the heroism of the Communist party in defeating "the American imperialists who killed the Lao people." A sign next to a reverently displayed coconut half-shell informed me that "this coconut bowl was used by Comrade Kaysone Phomvihane for drinking during the fighting against the French colonialists." Further on, there were glass cases containing the comrade's briefcase, gun, kettle and canteen. And on the walls, there was a procession of framed pictures of the comrade "delivering

---

*The paucity of historical artifacts in Laos can be attributed almost entirely to foreigners who have looted the country. The roots of this can be traced to Francis Garnier, who writes almost unselfconsciously of his exploration of the ancient Wat Sisaket: ". . . a few sacred books were lying around here and there: they consisted of long, narrow strips cut from leaves of a particular species of palm, gilded on the edges and joined to form books . . . each of us wanted to take a specimen of it, which we carefully hid at the bottoms of our small suitcases, to conceal a theft from the locals which they would have considered a sacrilege." And which, of course, Garnier did not. It is revealing to visit the homes of longtime diplomats or foreign correspondents to admire their extensive collections of Asian art objects, much of which has been smuggled out of Asian countries under diplomatic cover.

political reports" to gatherings of Lao. And for the history after 1975, still more photographs of party leaders, always smiling, addressing Lao people, always smiling, about some unstated issue.

There is no question that Laos endured extraordinary death and destruction from American bombers during the Vietnam War. But a quarter of a century later, it is that war that continues to define and shape the tunnel vision of Laos's leadership. Even Vietnam, which lays genuine claim to defeating "American imperialism," has largely let the war slip into the past. Here, not an issue of the *Vientiane Times* is published without a ritual panegyric to the triumphs of the Laotian army twenty-five years ago. Yet, when Lao party leaders survey their nation, even the most rigid among them cannot point to substantive achievements their rule has brought. Laos remains impoverished, isolated and afraid of the world around it. Even when the United States offered to open an office of the Peace Corps in Laos and send volunteers around the country to teach farming, machine repair, forestry management and literacy, the Lao government could not manage to sign the agreement. "They were afraid," an American diplomat told me. "No one wanted to take responsibility."

Despite a rampant xenophobia, a secretiveness that casts a penumbra of uncertainty and anxiety over urban life here, Laos exudes a magnetic quality, a lure that cannot easily be explained. I was interested in finding a woman I had heard about for some time, a weaver by training who had been living in Laos for a decade and who was probably the most well known foreigner in the country. One afternoon, on yet another searing day, well over ninety degrees, I bounced my scooter over rutted roads and pulled through the gate of a white picket fence that hemmed in a hanky-sized lawn outside a restored French colonial home. Behind the house, from an open-sided workshop, a clacking of wooden looms timpanied with the clatter of walnuts falling on a wooden floor. Inside the house, loosely draped over teak racks or in folded sheaves, there were hand-loomed textiles in blacks and greens and blues, with abstract designs that resonated distantly with more traditional motifs, particularly that of the *siho*, a mythological half-lion, half-elephant. I was welcomed by Carol Cassidy, the woman I had been seeking, a weaver and businesswoman originally from Connecticut, but now a demi-Lao in her devotion to this country. Almost singlehandedly this slight, moon-faced woman with piercing eyes and an efficient black ponytail has resuscitated Lao hand-loom weaving and has brought it into the modern world.

"My grandmother was a tailor," Cassidy said as we sat in her office, away from the well-heeled visitors in the showroom who were prepared to shell out hundreds or thousands of dollars for a one-of-a-kind wall hanging, "and that gave me an appreciation of a uniquely made product." After high school, she hitchhiked across Alaska before heading to Norway to study weaving at the National Academy of Art and then, for a time, living in Finland. "Seeing people in Finland making a living doing weaving was very important for me," she continued. "As a result of this I had all this art stuff but no idea how to use it. I applied to the University of Michigan and I had a portfolio of my weaving but none of the requirements. Anyway, they let me in. Eventually the dean gave me a bachelor of fine arts." Then, in what would ultimately point her toward her life in Laos, her sister told her about a job in Lesotho with CARE working with women weavers. "I was working with miners' wives who had mohair goats to see if there was a way of creating income possibilities. My counterpart was the African National Congress representative who wound up getting murdered in a raid by the South African army in 1982. I stayed on until 1986, eventually working for the United Nations, but at one point was asked to leave for my own safety. I went on to Zimbabwe and then later was in Mozambique." During this time, she met her future husband, an Ethiopian agricultural economist.

"In 1988, the International Labor Organization asked me to come to Laos. They said they needed a weaving expert, someone who had worked with women and who had technical expertise. As it turned out they had a different idea than I did. I did go, though. They had two hundred village women weavers with Swedish looms in a sort of import substitution project, weaving cloth for shirts, bedclothes, really industrial hand weaving. I got here in 1989 and almost nobody was allowed into Laos, only Russians, Bulgarians, Cubans, those sorts of people. Of course, when I got to Laos I'd never seen a piece of Lao weaving. I'd never heard of Lao weaving. I went to work for the U.N. although I was not very happy about what they were trying to do. We had no phones, but we did have some electricity. There were no *tuk-tuks*, no elevators. It was very rustic. I could sit in my garden without any noise pollution. There just weren't any private cars in Laos, no scooters either."

Cassidy paused in her account and strolled into the workshop behind the house. At some forty looms, women in white T-shirts and cotton sarongs flicked wood shuttles between warps of silk or cotton, some in the delicate colors of lettuce leaves and fruit salad, others in charcoal and chalk. "Now we have I think forty-four weavers here," she said, as we stood and watched a woman working on a taffeta-like stretch of fabric. "This is a special order for a customer in England to cover some sofas at their country house." I fingered the luxuriant, shining fabric, and clumsily asked her what it was costing the country squire. She laughed. "A lot. It is very, very expensive." Her fabrics, exported principally to Europe because of American tariff barriers, are regularly seen in the homes of the glitterati displayed in glossy fashion magazines, and she has exhibited her weavings at the Fashion Institute of Technology in New York.

We walked back to her office, gently applauded by the clapping of treadles. "I was thirty-two when I came here for the U.N. I looked at their weaving program and did an analysis of where the project was going. They didn't expect this sort of analysis. I realized that this was just not going to work out, and I said I didn't want my name on this. As I was doing all this, old Lao pieces of weaving were beginning to show up in Vientiane and I thought, These are wonderful. But I realized that the skills of these weavers was not so high. The older pieces were all natural fiber, vegetable dyes, with tremendous creative expression. But the new pieces had a very different feel, garish colors, non-natural; they had become simpler in design and technique. So I decided to apply for the first wholly owned American foreign investment license. My idea was that there was clearly talent. I could encourage farmers to raise silk. I wanted to have an impact on the product. I know how to weave, and I knew I could work with Lao weavers. My proposal to the Council of Ministers was to revive traditional skills, to have farmers raise silkworms, to develop new skills and to export fabric." As her contract with the U.N. ended and the government sat on her application, Cassidy had little choice but to sell her car, close her bank account and return to her family's home in Connecticut. "I had no idea what to do," she said, remembering her departure with lament. "Then one day I got a call that the Lao government had approved everything—visas, the right for me to hire and fire, tax exemption. I got on a plane immediately.

"I knew how big a job this was. I felt strongly I had the possibility to impact history. How many weavers got visas to do this, the cultural preservation of weaving? That's what I asked myself. This was an opportunity to do what I'd been working at all along." I asked her about the house we were in, a pristine French colonial masterpiece with a sweeping teak-banistered staircase curving to the upper floor. "I had to go to Paris for this house," she said. "This house was in the Souphanouvong family," the family of Laos's "Red Prince," one of two royal brothers who supported the

Pathet Lao's guerrilla campaigns. "I had to go to every part of the country to where I thought people might be raising silk. Originally I thought it would be easy, that we would have satellite weavers. Then I realized that would be impossible, I had to have my own workshop. So I began building big, heavy looms out of rosewood. I hired my first weaver in 1990 and then another and then we were ten, fifteen, thirty. Most are still with me."

I asked her about Laos, how her life had changed over the decade of her work. She sat, her head on her chest for a moment. "Laos has changed," she began. "There's the Laos I put my life savings into—no phones, no faxes, no satellite television. It was very isolated, but it had a certain charm. Charm is not the word, but a rhythm, a rhythm when you're not dictated to by phones and faxes. I struggle now between the tempo of a client base and my production here. It's that gulf I stand between. As expatriates we're pretty lucky. It's a very pleasant and comfortable life. There are no barriers between people. Because it's a small society, like my hometown in Connecticut—the town's called Woodbury—there is an intimacy. You earn respect by how hard you work. There were a few years gaining that trust. But Laos is going into a new and different period. Businesspeople tell me it's the hardest year ever with the bureaucracy. The government people are afraid to put their signatures on things."

Cassidy has thrived in Laos, not least because she has a passion for woven artistry, a conviction that she can reinstill a traditional craft in a culture that was losing some of its rootings; her work, everyone recognizes, enhances Lao civilization. That cannot, however, be said of other foreigners who have tried to work in Laos. In 1997, a longtime resident named Claude Vincent, who ran a thriving travel business here, was ambushed on the road north of Vientiane and machine-gunned to death, a killing that sent chills through the community of foreign investors. One such investor, a Frenchman who exhibited the caution of many foreigners in discussing Laos by asking me to withhold mention of his name, said he was particularly alarmed by Vincent's murder. "You must understand," he told me, "the army here is very corrupt and virulent. It is moving into all sorts of businesses, travel, the new gambling casino at Ang Nam Ngum," a glossy hotel casino on an island in an artificial lake created by the country's only hydroelectric dam, which the army runs with a Malaysian company. "The army controls the Internet. You know yesterday the Net went down because the army was trying to put blocks on sites they don't want people to see. One argument has it that [Vincent] was killed by the army because he was seen as being too profitable, which probably wasn't the case anyway. Nobody was really making very much money. But the army wants to run everything here, and they're getting pretty aggressive. I tell you, it scared the hell out of everybody here."

My last night in Vientiane, I sat in a red plastic molded chair nursing a liter bottle of Beer Lao at one of the small impromptu riverside cafés overlooking the Mekong, shallow now in its course, languid in its sashay south. Rivers have a gravity about them, a seriousness and drawing power that demands attention and presence. Shrouded by its jungled shores, the Congo speaks, as Conrad wrote, of darkness, even today, while the short and stubby Hudson suggests not so much majesty as an alluring evening cocktail. Cities grow up beside rivers, commerce and conversation and conquest follow them; they are the fishing hole and the waste receptical. And they flash a beauty that shifts with seasons and weather, at times placid, at others vengeful. Watching the river below me, dappled by the voluminous saffron sun gliding into the Thai horizon, I tried to summon up a poem by John Ashbery, a poem called "Into the Dusk-Charged Air" that runs for 150 lines, each of which contains the name of a river. I couldn't remember it well, so later I looked it up and it begins:

> Far from the Rappahannock, the silent
> Danube moves along toward the sea.
> The brown and green Nile rolls slowly
> Like the Niagara's welling descent.
> Tractors stood on the green banks of the Loire
> Near where it joined the Cher.
> The St. Lawrence prods among black stones
> And mud. But the Arno is all stone.

Later in the poem, Ashbery comes to my river:

> The Weser is frozen, like liquid air.
> And so is the Kama. And the beige, thickly flowing
> Tocantins. The rivers bask in the cold.
> The stern Uruguay chafes its banks,
> A mass of ice. The Hooghly is solid

Ice. The Adour is silent, motionless.
The lovely Tigris is nothing but scratch ice
Like the Yellowstone, with its osier-clustered banks.
The Mekong is beginning to thaw out a little
And the Donets gurgles beneath the
Huge blocks of ice. The Manzanares gushes free.

Only the surface of Vientiane has really thawed, the deep ground of public life still frozen, and the Mekong walls the country from the world. Winking at Vientiane across the river, the small Thai town of Sri Chiang-mai, not much of a town really, mocks the Laotian capital with the airs of a city girl to her country cousin. Laos looks, in part enviously, and turns away. But the Mekong, so vital to the daily life of the villagers who live along its watershed, still lures the urbanite. Along the esplanade, a bit concreted, more of it dirt path, lovers walked arm in arm; a flock of young monks, their robes flapping winglike in the dusky breeze, spirited by, and young boys spun fist-sized wooden tops in earnest combat. The sun bedded down, leaving behind a smudged palette of magenta and bronze.

I woke the next morning at my small hotel, what Asians sometimes call a bungalow, to the slow bang of a *wat* drum, the call to alms, and found a *tuk-tuk* to take me to the bus station. Downriver transport had stopped for the season, the river's shoals too frequent and dangerous to allow safe passage. I was unhappy about leaving the river, but there was no other way of travel; the bus had become the new river ferry. Night still clung restlessly when I hauled my pack from the *tuk-tuk*, a gleeful disk of moon dangling above me. Across from the dirt-pan bus yard, a file of monks moved past a line of kneeling women who ladled scoops of sticky rice into alms baskets. As the last monk passed, a little boy of perhaps eight, the women bowed three times, and then on his short legs the boy scampered after his elders, his tangerine skirts flying. On the edge of the bus yard, vendors with wheeled carts sold airy, flavorless baguettes and bottled water to passengers. I bought my breakfast.

My plan was to head south toward the border with Cambodia, but first I wanted to explore several of the decaying old French colonial river towns, towns where obscure officials and traders estranged from their homeland served out their careers trying to infuse something of French civilization into distant possessions. They also came to make money, but here in Laos they failed. Still today, France continues to try to build on its legacy of colonial paternalism by incorporating Laos (as well as Cambodia and Vietnam) into the Francophone universe; the fact that nobody here wants to learn the French language anymore, English for better or worse having won the champion's belt as the global language, seems to have escaped the French. Yet, the French have erected a grandiose château as their embassy in Vientiane, an architectural relic intended to impress but that somehow reminds one only of faded glory.

Road transport in Laos runs an eclectic gamut from *tuk-tuks*, for short hops, to open-back pickup trucks, Thai discards all, and a range of buses, some of which have glass in the window frames, some of which have actual padded seats and some of which offer wooden benches. That morning, I found bus transport with windows and cushioned seats and felt blessed. Route 13 follows the Mekong south, a yellow clay roadway, furrowed and rutted, hugging the river for much of the way. Out the rightside window, I watched the Mekong, unhurried but empty, save for scattered fishing pirogues being paddled into untroubled currents. My fellow passengers dozed, women with their children curled up against them, men from roadside towns heading home with bulging parcels of city-bought goods, a pair of monks up front. I sat toward the back, an empty seat beside me. Five hours later we creaked to a halt outside the town of Thakhek.

Once a minor French trading post, Thakhek is now a virtual ghost town of eroding French buildings edging a silent town square, in the middle a mute fountain sclerotic with rust. An empty four-story hotel overlooks the Mekong, and across the river is the bustling Thai provincial capital of Nakhon Phanom, the burial ground for waves of French missionaries to Laos and once a major operational center for American forces waging war on Vietnam. Later in my voyage, I visited Nakhon Phanom and went to the graveyard behind a solitary Catholic church. On a tiled tombstone atop a cement mound, I read of one of seven missionaries buried there: ICI RÉPOSE AIMÉ-MARIE SALLIO, MISSION, APOSTOL DU LAOS, NÉ LE 14 AOUT 1860, DÉCEDÉ LE 20 MARS 1890. They died young here, swatted down by the scourge of tropical diseases, the heat, the unbearable heaviness of a life depicted elsewhere by George Orwell in *Burmese Days*.

At the ramshackle River Inn in Nakhon Phanom, once a watering hole and hot-pillow hotel for American troops, Air America pilots and CIA agents who lived out at the airbase outside town, Surachart Arkanit—"call me Lek"—the owner, lamented the loneliness of peace and the abrading of prosperity's finer flourishes. The floor's blue-and-white linoleum was stained and peeling. The nightclub hadn't seen a shimmy in years, and the restaurant's menu was down to a handful of dishes.

"My grandfather built this place in 1952," Lek told me, cupping a tumbler of brandy in his palm, a tumbler I suspected lurked there most of the day. In a washed-out floral shirt that hung loosely over his spreading belly, Lek, who was pushing fifty, wore the air of an over-the-hill surfer fond of talking about the big wave he once rode. "My grandfather used to run a steamboat up and down the river to Nong Khai," the next big town upriver on the Thai side near Vientiane. "During the war this was *the* place. Soldiers used to stay here and eat here. One of those soldiers took my sister off to Seattle. She runs a restaurant there." I asked him whether Laos affected life in Nakhon Phanom at all. "There used to be forty thousand refugees from Laos here in camps," he said, "but they're all gone now, probably most to the United States. The camps are all closed. I used to have a lot of Lao working for me, but they all ran off to Bangkok to get jobs. Now I'm just holding on." He sipped at his brandy and sucked on a cigarette. On the southern end of town—Lek's is on the northern tip—a couple of glitzy hotels have sprung up in recent years, decimating Lek's business. A few locals come in to drink with him, but the tourist trade, now mostly Thais on upcountry vacations, prefer the swankier pleasures of a fancy hotel, not the scuffed-heel shabbiness of Lek's River Inn.

But even Lek's hotel was sharp compared to Thakhek's rudimentary offerings. I wandered along the river there and back to the town square. Not even a dog scratching itself lingered in the square, a place where I guessed Frenchmen and their wives had strolled under fringed parasols in the evening's lessening heat. Town squares as gathering spots work only in temperate climates, but the French brought everything with them, including the uncompromising orthodoxy of provincial town planning. At a staging wharf for commercial ferries across the river, here more than half a mile wide, a line of twenty-three trucks waited, each laden with immense teak logs thirty feet in length and two or three feet in diameter. Laos's hardwood forests were being clear-cut by army companies to feed the insatiable lumber industry across the river, Thailand having long ago depleted its own forests.

On a corner of a square, as I sat at a table having a *café Lao* and watching the sun ending its day's travels, a gentleman in neat slacks and a pressed white shirt walked over and sat down. Very formally, in difficult English, he introduced himself; I had found that if I sat somewhere in

Laos, sketching, sipping coffee, reading, or just watching the river run, someone invariably would sidle up to me and strike up a conversation. "I am Khamphay Sonepho. How do you do," he said. I shook his hand and told him my name. "Nice to meet you," he replied, a schoolbook cadence to his reply. Then, from a plastic clutch briefcase, he extracted an English text and began to read questions at me:

"Where are you from?

"How do you find the food here?

"How do you like the weather here?

"Where are you staying?

"How long are you staying in Laos?"

I replied slowly in English to each question, his head nodding at my replies. But whether he understood me, I never knew. Then he gestured for me to follow him. I paid for the coffee and we walked around the corner to a government office, a Lao flag limp on its pole, a sign in English above the open front announcing LAND AND HOUSING MANAGE- MENT OFFICE. He squired me to his desk, importantly placed against the back wall facing out to the street, his colleagues arranged against both walls facing one another. Then, with few words, he pulled housing dia- grams from his desk drawer, renderings of traditional huts on stilts. "My work," he beamed. "House for Lao people." I asked him how much it cost, and he wrote down the figure of 15 million kip, about $3,000, a sum that struck me as staggeringly high in a country as impoverished as Laos. Then he handed me a rendering. "For you," he said. "For your house." I laughed gently and shook his hand and thanked him. I tried briefly other avenues of conversation but gave up when it was clear his English, though far bet- ter than the rudimentary Lao I was acquiring, could not sustain a real dia- logue. Leaving his office, I was moved by his desperate urge, a genuine thirst, for contact with the outside world, a desire to conquer his isolation by grappling with an unfamiliar language. Yes, there was a thaw.

I doubled back to the ferry dock to ask about the possibility of a boat down to Savannakhet, yet another French river town, although one, I was told, a bit grander in its original pretensions and its current incarnation than Thakhek, and a town where the French had settled in force. I had heard that some people even still wore berets there and for that alone I thought it was worth the trip. A customs official penciling logging-truck departures into a ledger shook his head. "No boats. No more." I had no choice but to find a pickup truck.

The next morning I found a *tuk-tuk* to take me to the bus and pickup truck marshaling compound on the edge of town. There, on a dust-churned lot, rattletrap buses, most canting to one side or another, waited for upcountry passengers along with dozens of pickup trucks scattered about in no discernible order. I wandered around mouthing the word Savannakhet over and over until a driver lounging on his front fender waved me over to his truck. I heaved my pack up onto the tin-sheet roof shading the truck bed and squeezed onto a bench that ran along one side. Other passengers, all Lao, clambered in, more elegantly than I had, tucking bags under the bench and, on the roof, sacks of rice. One young man cantilevered an electric guitar and speaker-amplifier onto the roof, and his companion, gripping a clear plastic bag filled with fish, eased himself onto the open tailgate.

As we waited for the truck to overfill, a young Vietnamese man in a green pith helmet pedaled an oversized black bicycle next to our truck. Strapped to the back of his cycle like immense pontoons were two white sacks that he showed one passenger were filled with red and blue plastic basins, the sort of basic houseware that Vietnam churns out by the millions and Laos is yet to learn to fabricate.

Route 12—one would be reckless to call it a road—winds east to Vietnam, and it is along that route that basic Vietnamese manufactured goods are trundled into Laos. One of our passengers, a woman of commodious proportions swaddled in a flowered sarong and sporting a rakish purple straw fedora, extracted herself from the back of the truck. Examining a basin with the jaundiced eye of a jeweler, she opened the bidding on a bulk order of one hundred basins. The Vietnamese peddler laughed and began to rewrap his wares. She countered. He stopped wrapping and recountered. After a time, the inevitable deal was clinched and one hundred of the basins were hoisted to the roof of the truck. When nineteen people had managed to stuff themselves into the rear of the small Toyota pickup and the driver seemed satisfied at his profit margin for the trip, we sagged out onto Route 13, heading south in a cyclone of dust through a scrubland of stunted trees and desiccated bushes.

At a place called Xaibouli, just outside Savannakhet, we whirlwinded to a stop and the guitar player and his fishmonger friend hopped out. Waiting for them was a man with a pistol tucked into his pants who helped carry the amplifier. The life of a Lao rock star, I thought. From roadside food stalls, women waving bouquets of skewered chicken and roasted corn swarmed around the pickup offering lunch. I demurred, but my fellow passengers dove in. I think one of the passengers was still waiting for change when the driver pulled away. We were in Savannakhet soon after that.

Unlike Thakhek's lifeless pallor, there was a frisson of activity in Savannakhet—a hubbub of traders at the cross-river ferry dock, a buzz of motor scooters piloted by willowy girls with saucy ponytails, the hum of monks reciting their lessons at Wat Sayaphoum. Under French colonial rule, there was an effort to build Savannakhet up as a trading center, but those grand intentions collapsed, despite efforts to encourage Vietnamese, whom the French regarded as more entrepreneurial than the Lao, to immigrate to the region; alas, for the French, Savannakhet—and Laos in general—remained a huge drain on the French treasury throughout its colonial history. From 1960 on, the CIA manned a station here from which they ran surveillance of North Vietnamese transport routes south through the eastern Lao mountains; from its base the agency also sponsored guerrilla units to harass and ambush North Vietnamese troops. Today, there is little evidence of the American presence here, apart from the fences around many people's gardens, fences fashioned from the perforated steel panels the Americans used for quick-build runways.

Savannakhet's ferry operations were the busiest I had seen in Laos, with regular ferries and smaller wooden cargo carriers scuttling back and forth across the Mekong from the Thai town of Mokdahan, the river itself some forty feet below the high-water mark painted on the highest of the tiered jetties. On the Lao side, a small posse of customs officials attempted to keep track of the flood of goods being lugged up the riverbank to waiting *tuk-tuks* and pickup trucks. For a while I sat by the river watching the maelstrom of trade, trying to inventory the range of goods coming across the river, a fair indication of what Laos could not produce itself. The variety was startling. The Thai trading ladies, for some reason all heftily built women in floppy straw hats, oversaw the commerce; I watched them order Lao stevedores in numbered green jerseys to haul fifty-kilogram sacks of rice up the bank with the imperiousness of plantation owners. Behind them were crates of Heineken and Singha beer, galvanized steel gutters and pipes, stacks of grass mats, garish piles of polyester blankets, bags of dried Chinese noodles, cartons of Sony and Hitachi televisions, electric rice cookers, white porcelain toilets, scooter tires, boxes of Breeze detergent and black plastic bags of dried chilies.

As I watched this slice of international trade, a young man sauntered up and sat down next to me. He gave his name as Thasan, but, in good French, said to call him Alain; he wore a red T-shirt with a big Nike swoosh on it, gray pants and rubber flip-flops. We watched the activity on the dock, and I asked him what he did here. "I used to work in a bank," he said. "I worked in three banks here, but I quit." I asked him why. "In a bank you cannot earn very much. Every month, I only earned one hundred thousand kip," a sum on that day worth about $17.70 (all the banks are run by the government). "So I want to try to find some better work." I inquired about his family, something one is always expected to do in Asia. "My father was a colonel in the old army. He was in prison camps for many years after the Communists took over. He was forced to study politics, things like Marx and Lenin. Totally useless. He was released in 1981 and escaped across the river. Now he's in Louisiana, in America. I have a brother and sister in the United States, too, and a sister in Sydney who works in a telephone factory." So, I asked the obvious question: Why did he remain here if his entire family was out of Laos?

"I want to stay in Laos," he replied. "It's my country. I like living here. My father sends me money so I can live. But I hate the Communists. I think most people hate the Communists, but there's nothing we can do. It's dangerous to talk about politics here. There are spies who watch you. It used to be worse, but you can still go to prison for talking."

We shared a Beer Lao and continued to survey the maritime commerce before us. I asked Alain what he thought the future held for Laos. "Laos is very poor," he said, shaking his head slightly. "We produce nothing. What do we export? Electricity and trees. That's all. Farmers here don't even grow chilies. Some don't want to, but most don't even know how. I grow chilies in my own garden."

I told Alain that I was surprised that he spoke French, since most younger Lao seemed to me so intent on learning English. "That's true," he said. "Once we studied French here, but no more. Nobody studies French. Only English." Suddenly, a scooter horn squawked behind us, and a young woman called his name. "Okay," he said, "my friend is here." And with that, he hopped on the scooter pillion and was off.

That evening, at a simple corner restaurant just off the riverfront, I treated myself to *steak frites*, sopping up the juice from the meat with a crusty baguette. The bill came to less than $2.

For several days I walked the streets and alleys of Savannakhet, immensely pleased with the town's core of French architecture, stolid pink or blue or yellow houses and commercial buildings, all with tall windows framed by purple or gray louvered shutters. At one intersection, in a small patch of ground next to a café, teams of men, some in navy wool berets, heaved steel balls about, endeavoring to roll their balls near a small wooden marker ball while skittering their opponents' balls away; it was the old French game of *boules* on a homemade *pétanque,* or court. I also stumbled onto a dinosaur museum opened by the French in 1991 and staffed by an eager geologist who showed me around. "There are only two geologists in Laos," he rued. "Nobody wants to study geology. It's too much work, and nobody can earn a living doing this." I left him a tip for showing me about. I also began spending some time at Wat Sayaphoum, a late-nineteenth-century *wat* of minor architectural interest, but a place teeming with life. It is where I met Thong Souk, a novice of twenty-one, older than other novices I had met on a day when I watched young

A *boules* player, complete with beret, tossing a steel ball on a rough *pétanque* in Savannakhet in southern Laos—a remnant of French colonialism

novices of six or seven charge up the steps of the drum tower to launch a homemade parachute of a plastic bag, string and a rock amid explosions of laughter and noise. I was sitting on a bench watching the young boys when Thong Souk joined me, wrestling, unfamiliarly, I thought, with his saffron robes.

"My name is Novice Thong Souk," he began. "Can you speak English?" I nodded, and he instantly whipped out an English learner's text from a cloth sack hung from his shoulder. He opened it and pointed to a passage of dialogue accompanied by cartoon drawings. His finger pointed to a line: "Wife: Darling, how do you like my hair? Husband: It looks like a bee-hive." I burst out laughing, trying to envision the arrival of the beehive bouffant as a fashion must in Laos. Thong Souk was distressed, his finger going back over the line. Patiently, I tried to explain the absurdity of the sentence and how it was of dubious relevance in Laos or to well-spoken English. "Oh, I see," he said after a while, although I don't think he really did. Then he told me about himself.

"I am a policeman," he said slowly, before rephrasing: "No, I was a policeman. In Pakse," a town to the south of Savannakhet. "Now I want to be a monk. I came to this *wat* three months ago. When I was a police-man I earned fifty-five thousand kip every month," then about $10, "but I do not want to be a policeman anymore."

In the days that followed, I would come and read English with Thong Souk, both to get to know him and to linger at the *wat* (I spent some time trying to explain a lesson that involved a traffic warden giving a parking ticket to a motorist who parked on a double white line, violating a British road convention, Laos has no double white lines, parking wardens or parking tickets), watch the child novices play king of the hill with bam-boo swords and talk about his life. Then one day, very solemnly, he said to me, "Tomorrow I will be ordained as a monk. I want you to come please. My family will come. It is a very important day for me." Many young Lao men come and spend time in *wats* during their twenties, although as a rule they return to their secular lives after a year or so. For Thong Souk to abandon the laity was uncommon.

Tall and awkward, Thong Souk was still adjusting to his vocation, fid-dling with his robes, half absentmindedly flicking ends of the voluminous saffron wrapping about, searching for a suitable arrangement. I told him that I thought it rare that someone would leave a job in something like the police to join the monkhood. He laughed lightly. "The police are not so good," he said. "The police take money from people. I think that is not so good. Also, I need to learn English and other subjects. And I want to be a good Buddhist. So I decide to come here. This is a good *wat*, and it has a good school." I guessed that there were upward of two hundred monks and novices at Wat Sayaphoum and the classrooms, rudimentary cement-walled rooms with thatched roofing, buzzed with the recitation of lessons in arithmetic, history and English.

I rose early the next day and found a clean if unpressed shirt in my pack. Already the morning drum for alms had been struck, and the sun was hurrying from the horizon, smiting the morning mist that lathered the riverfront. I had my usual breakfast, a baguette and black coffee, and gave small thanks to the French for leaving, if nothing else, a taste for bread and coffee in Laos. Then I walked down the small alleyway to Wat Sayaphoum, past tidy two-story cement homes fronted by meticulously arranged gardens brimming with five-petaled orange jasmine, the protuberant yellow-tipped pink blossoms of the lotus banana, the purple-pink petals of bauhinia, and some gardens fringed with waterfalls of violet bougainvillea that scented the air like a passing woman.

Ordinations are conducted in a special hall inside the walls of the *wat*, a building called a *sim*, after the sacred stones that surround it. At Wat Sayaphoum, the *sim* bordered on the garish gold columns twining to an ornate sweeping roof with bold filigree borders. The staircase to the ordination hall was flanked by cement-cast nagas, mythical dragon snakes that figure prominently in the creation myths of southeast Asia, each with a red gaping mouth and white fangs. Thong Souk's women relatives were outside, kneeling on cotton blankets; women are not permitted into the *sim*.

I climbed the stairs trailing the elderly monk who would conduct the rite and twenty other monks who were to witness Thong Souk's acceptance into the monkhood. Four of the male members of his family joined me; we shed our shoes and kneeled at the rear of the hall. The elderly monk sat down on a cushion on a raised platform facing the door and the other, younger monks formed two kneeling ranks to his left and right. Then Thong Souk, draped in new saffron robes, his head freshly shaved, entered and kneeled facing the senior abbot. A series of prayers were chanted from memory, followed by a period of silence, broken suddenly by the abbot, who began reciting stories of the Buddha's life, weaving accounts of the Buddha's enlightenment with admonitions on the requisite asceticism of a Buddhist monk, all the while his eyes focused on the kneeling novice. Then he started questioning Thong Souk about the

Buddha's life, questions intended to instill the purpose of the monkhood firmly in the candidate's being.

Thong Souk stammered, his hands shaking with nervousness, his voice failing. Gently, one of the monks near him whispered the answer and Thong Souk managed to blurt out a response. Then came another question, and again Thong Souk was stymied, more I hoped from the drama and significance of the occasion than true ignorance, although I knew he had been at the *wat* for only three months. And once again the answer was whispered. Somehow, he made it through and, with a chanted prayer, Thong Souk passed from novice to monk.

Outside the *sim* his relatives gathered, presenting him with a plate-shaped fan painted with an image of the Buddha and mounted on a staff (the symbol of monkhood), new flip-flops, a new alms bowl wrapped in white cotton, some new towels and a bit of money. On this day, everything Thong Souk had was new, a sign of his passage into the order of monks. I stood apart from the relatives, watching him hug his parents, but then he came up to me. "Thank you for coming." He grinned. "I couldn't remember anything. I was supposed to study, but I forgot everything." He sighed, and then, looking at me carefully, said, "Yesterday I was a novice. Today I am a monk."

I was moved by the ceremony—by Thong Souk's earnestness, by the innocence he seemed to bring to his new life and by the durability of a faith and ritual that survived assaults by an obtuse and corrupt political order. I do not mean to romanticize Buddhism—across the Mekong in Thailand the Buddhist monkhood has been shaken by a continuing series of financial scandals, not to mention a handful of murders committed by deranged monks—but there was a comforting sense of a cultural continuance, a hardiness of belief and practice that has been flexible enough to absorb the batterings of Marxist ignorance and emerge intact as a central element in the lives of people.

As I left Thong Souk with his family, the other monks who had witnessed the ordination broke out cans of Pepsi, and child novices played with bamboo swords, a whirligig of boisterous saffron.

Back at the ferry pier, I searched for a freelance boatman, trying to find one who could float me downriver to my next stop, Pakse, a necessary way station on the river south to Cambodia. Stevedores drenched in sweat in the blinding heat grunted around me as they trotted up the riverbank with hundred-pound rice sacks, and the Thai market ladies hollered for things to be moved here or there. I hailed the captain of one boat snug to the shore and yelled "Pakse" several times. He came down off the boat's roof where he was stashing bamboo poles and shrugged. "No Pakse, no Pakse," he said. I waved at some of the other boats roped to the shore. "No boats," he said. The Mekong was low, its tan waters fended off by impetuous sandbanks and angry gatherings of rocky outcroppings. Even if I could persuade a boatman to take me, I reasoned, it was not clear the vessel would make it over shoals so bold. So once again I was faced with the prospect of a long bus ride. It was eight hours of chewing through the cocoon of dust that enveloped the bus on the dirt road to Pakse, dust that clogged every orifice, muddied my tongue, talcumed my body and clothes, and turned my hair red; the only humor I derived from my state was that something like my appearance must have inspired Charles Schulz's Pigpen, the character in the Snoopy comic strip that moves forever in a cloud of dust. I was shaking dust from my clothes for more than a week.

Pakse did not hold me long, for from here cargo boats were running south to Si Phan Don, the so-called Four Thousand Islands sequinned

A passenger minitruck in Pakse, in southern Laos

across the broad belly of the Mekong as it enters Cambodia, a girth of nearly nine miles. Nineteenth-century travelers had written of the area's majesty and isolation, a place of some mystery, a place I wanted to see for this alone. Recovering from the bus journey over black coffee and a baguette at a small eatery on the periphery of the central market, I observed a Westerner amble in, not tall but toughly built with cropped black hair and acute eyes, a young Lao woman on his arm. They had emerged from a white Land Rover parked out front, a rare enough occurrence, so I introduced myself and offered to buy them a cup of coffee. "I work for MAG," he told me, shaking my hand and taking a chair across the wood table from me. MAG is the acronym for the Mine Advisory Group, a British aid organization attempting to clear unexploded mines and bombs from Laos, a truly Sisyphean task. During the Vietnam War, the Americans dropped bombs on Laos for nine years, part of what has become known as the Secret War. It is unclear precisely how much tonnage fell on this country, more, certainly, than on Germany in all of World War II, more, perhaps, than was dropped by the Americans altogether during that war. "We estimate that there are eight million devices in Saravan and Xekong Provinces," the man from MAG said, referring to the two provinces through which the North Vietnamese hacked and bulldozed the Ho Chi Minh trail. I asked him how long he had worked in Laos.

"I've been here three and a half years," he replied. "I was with the British air force, bomb disposal, for twenty-three years." He sipped his coffee and worked on a cigarette. "When people ask how long it will take to demine Laos, we say that they're still finding bombs in Europe." Why, I asked him, did the Americans seem to play no role in demining southeast Asia, to help remedy a catastrophe they created in the first place? "I don't know," he answered. "I can tell you that only in the last few weeks did the United States provide us with CD-ROMs of the bombing runs in Laos. And this is more than twenty-five years after the war. There are now some American special forces doing some bomb disposal and demining training. But let me tell you this, you look at the CD-ROM for Xekong, and the ground is completely black with only a few white dots. The black is the bomb drops. When American bombers were coming back to Thailand from runs over Vietnam and they couldn't hit their targets, they would drop their bombs on Laos, anywhere. They weren't allowed to land in Thailand with their bombs. This is one of the most heavily bombed countries in the world." MAG has reported that over four years of working in Xekong, a province roughly the size of Wales, it managed to clear fully only 114 hectares (almost 250 acres). I expressed surprise at seeing so few amputees in Laos compared to those I had seen in places like Afghanistan and Cambodia, usually one of the tragic consequences that follows in the wake of a long period of war waged by bombing and mining.

"In Xekong it's one casualty a week," he explained. "But there really aren't many amputees in Laos. This ordnance, and we've identified eighteen different kinds, is designed to kill people, not to maim them. But nobody knows where Laos is. If you show somebody a picture of a double amputee, it has an effect. But when you show a grave—" he shrugged, and his voice trailed off "—it just doesn't have the same effect." Was he worried about his own safety? I asked. "No, not here. The villagers know where the bombs are. I go out with a team of six, including a medic. There's lots of ways to defuse bombs. We can either blow the fuse off with something like a shotgun shell or we use a device that unscrews the fuse very, very rapidly. But I will tell you this, I think Cambodia is too dangerous. Two and a half years ago one of my colleagues was kidnapped by the Khmer Rouge. He was executed. They've only just identified his remains."

Although eastern Laos was not part of my journey, the thought that just a day's drive from where we were lazily drinking coffee a lunar landscape of menace and death remained, largely forgotten or ignored, was deeply depressing. For its part, the Laotian government has done nothing to burnish its international reputation, something that might induce a smidgeon more sympathy for its plight. Instead, the bombed and mined wastelands provide a handy cudgel for the government in its ideological armory: The Americans were murderous imperialists and we defeated them, and here's the evidence. What a price the Lao people pay.

Morning's shadows still stretched away from the villagers who were staggering down broken concrete steps to beached cargo boats under sacks of sugar, rice and salt when I arrived at the dockside shortly after dawn. A cargo boat heading downriver was pointed out to me, and I slithered down the riverbank to grab a space on deck. Already the hold was filling up with supplies villagers had bought in town and were taking back with them. Apart from the sacks of grain and sugar, mattresses piled like sliced bread were stacked back by the engine; cartons of televisions and a huge plaster statue of the Buddha were jimmied into the hold. Passengers piled in, camping down on bulging plastic bags and rolled grass mats. Once again,

Selling baguettes in the market in
Pakse

the Mekong beckoned boats, exerting itself as the artery of commerce for
southern Laos. I handed 10,000 kip, less than $2, to a boat boy who
wormed his way through the tumult collecting fares while the captain
clanged the engine to life. Boat boys poled us from shore, and slowly we
wheeled about, nosing into the Mekong's broad current, the engine muffled by the mounds of cargo and the din of conversation.

No express, this tubby boat, more a milk run, a wallow from shore to
shore dropping passengers and their sacks and boxes at scarcely visible villages perched on banana tree–fringed banks high above a low-water river.
Just a holler from the hold would send us toward the shoreline, a holler
prompted by an island landmark, a sculpted rocky outcropping, a curve in
the river that signaled home. Hours passed under a baking sun that batted
away intruding clouds and steaming fists of spray that brushed the deck on
romping turns. Nine hours later, our vessel shaved the western shore at
Don Khong island, one of the "four thousand" islands embedded in the
river, and a boat boy made us fast. By then, most of the passengers had

alighted upriver, and there were only a few of us who stumbled out into the day's skulking light. On the shore, a couple of *tuk-tuks* waited for the run to the island's eastern edge where a handful of guest houses were located. One of the *tuk-tuk* drivers addressed me in Russian, a language I barely speak, but I managed to communicate my destination, a teak house on stilts overlooking a filament of the Mekong.

My days in Laos were nearing a close, the islands here just a few miles from the boundary with Cambodia. Although the Khmer Rouge, the atavistic and genocidal movement that gripped Cambodia for four murderous years, had surrendered there, robbery and murder—what was euphemistically called banditry—was prevalent just over the border, and I remained apprehensive about the cross-border journey. But that would wait, for first I wanted to visit Khon Falls, the ferocious cataracts that for a time bedeviled French efforts to transform the Mekong into a commercial thoroughfare. There, I hoped also to find boat transport into Cambodia.

Don Khong's few thousand people necklace the island's rim, living amid thick groves of bamboo, columns of coconut palms and erratic vegetable plots. Fishing nets dangle over the river, suspended by bamboo architectonics, and peak-roofed wooden houses on stilts are bathed in colors worthy of Mexico City, papaya and grape, marmalade and banana. In the shade under the raised houses, women rocked children in hammocks slung from floor beams. Gaggles of ducks waddled down paths, sending chickens scurrying, and water buffaloes were tied up to house support posts; fresh buffalo dung perfumed the air as I cycled by on a bike lent by the guest house at which I was staying. A disused grass airstrip in the center of the island is overgrown behind strands of rusted and collapsing barbed wire. Here, the Mekong is clearer, a silty broth entangled in a geologic maze of islets. At dusk, the river glinting slyly, I saw a fisherman in a pirogue spin as he hurled a circle net into the current, a solitary balletic pirouette, an unstained ritual.

With the rising sun I was on an island boat, a hefty pirogue powered by a dinky outboard engine. I headed down to Don Khon, an island perched on the summit of the falls. We maneuvered among islands, following watery passages, winding among barren dollop islands before pushing into a clutch of reeds toward shore. I leaped from the boat and told the driver I would meet him on Don Det, an island spit linked to Don Khon, where I would finish my trek. On foot, down beaten paths, I trudged toward the southern edge of the island under the fanning leaves of coconut palms.

Here, houses were simpler, less ornate than on Don Khong, though there were also, tucked deep in the trees, a smattering of moldering French bungalows, the decaying remnants of colonialism. My objective was a village on the island's tip, where I hoped a boat could be found for the run to Cambodia. Instead, I found myself standing before a signboard announcing that no boats went to Cambodia. Never. Defeated, I determined to deal with my transport problems later and struck out to locate the remains of France's colossal engineering project to surmount the Khon Falls, a fourteen-kilometer, narrow-gauge railroad that hauled cargo from beneath the falls, up Dhon Khon island and across to a wharf on Don Det.

The railbed appeared in the woods, a linear mound I climbed and followed out of the trees past paddy fields dry in the winter heat. The steel rails were long gone and only occasionally did bits of the wooden ties surface from the eroding railbed. It was a walk in complete silence, remarkable for the absence of people; only at odd moments was there the faint whistle of a bird. As I walked, I tried to imagine the Frenchmen overseeing crews of Lao laborers, the Frenchmen sweaty in their colonial attire, haranguing and threatening the Lao workers to greater effort, driving them onward to complete a railroad that would benefit not the Lao but

The train engine used by the French to ferry cargo around the Khon Falls on Dhon Khon island in southern Laos, just over the border from Cambodia

the French. The flour that would make baguettes and *tartes* for French administrators in towns like Savannakhet and Vientiane, the wine for dinner and the summer frocks for the ladies—all was to travel by this railroad.

And then, in the jungle, off to the side of the railbed as if on a siding, hulked a black rail engine, not much more than a great riveted boiler on steel wheels, a skinny platform on one end where coal was shoveled into its fiery maw, certainly not by a Frenchman. Frozen in place and time, the engine rested on rails slowly being consumed by the ground beneath them. For the French, Indochina was the end of their Asian colonial road and, standing beside this small blackened beast of an engine, there was a small sense of symbolic finality, a train that died here, and with it the hopes and dreams of France. There are no railroads in Laos today.

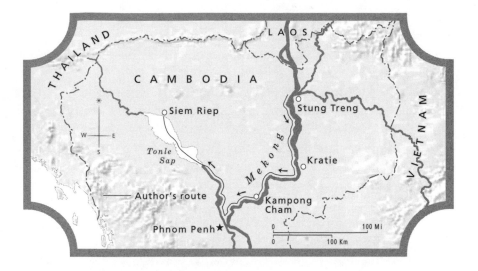

Seven

Dolphins, Smiles and Murder

Among Cambodia's dwindling repository of folktales, most lost during the years of the Khmer Rouge, there is a particularly chilling fable, one of the lamb and the jackal. It goes something like this: A lamb and a jackal lived near a stream, and the jackal, being a jackal, wanted to eat the lamb, but also being a jackal, wanted to demonstrate his cleverness to the lamb before eating it. So, while the lamb was drinking at the river, the jackal began harassing the lamb, accusing it of sullying the waters where he was drinking, but the lamb retorted that being upstream, the jackal could not be drinking dirty water. Enraged at the lamb's insolence, the jackal screamed at the lamb, accusing it of having spoken ill of him the previous year. But, the lamb replied, I was not even alive last year. Fury rose in the jackal, who then accused the lamb's brothers and sisters of slurring him. But once again the lamb threw the accusation back, insisting it had no brothers or sisters. Then it must be your parents who said evil things about me, the jackal said, his teeth showing. There was nothing the lamb could say, no way to escape, and so the smirking jackal devoured it.

Here, a tale of irrationality and innocence, a triumph of obsessive rage and violence can, without much difficulty, be seen as an allegory for the Cambodian nation, for the pivotal three years, eight months and twenty-one days in the twentieth century, the nearly half-decade of madness and murder, when a society consumed itself. I was heading into Cambodia twenty years after the slaughter, genocide that left perhaps 2 million people dead—one of every five Cambodians—and another half million as refugees and was so painfully documented in the 1984 film *The Killing Fields*, about the young Cambodian photographer Dith Pran. I was seeking some explanation of mass murder on such a scale, and some understanding of how a society reconstitutes itself.* It was not to be an easy journey.

My failure to persuade any Lao boatman to take me downriver into Cambodia meant taking a lengthy, circuitous route by boat, bus, truck and plane to Stung Treng, the northernmost settlement in Cambodia on the Mekong. I flew to Stung Treng in an old Fokker belonging to something called President Airlines, landing on a frayed macadam strip hemmed by scraggly forest after swooping low over the fat, brown Mekong. A swarm of motor scooters idled just beyond a wire fence, their drivers yelling at the eight passengers like taxi touts at New York City's airports. I picked one driver from the scrum, one I hoped was the least reckless of the lot, and we darted down a dust track barely ahead of the tunnel of dust spewing behind us. He dumped me at a single-story riverfront hotel called the Sekong, eerily empty. After some time, the woman who owned the hotel emerged

---

* More than folktales have disappeared. Three scholars of Cambodian society, Judy Ledgerwood, May M. Ebihara and Carol A. Mortland, have described the devastation in blunt terms. "Not only dancers, but monks who knew how to chant certain religious texts properly, craftsmen who knew how to construct distinct kinds of ox carts, and women who knew how to weave specific designs perished with their knowledge. Much of the written documentation on Khmer culture was similarly lost . . . the loss of cultural artifacts, such as musical instruments, masks for the dance, and Buddhist images, was also tragically high. . . . The changes in Khmer society during the years of Khmer Rouge rule are sometimes interpreted by Khmer to have been the end of a Buddhist era, the extinction of the world as they knew it."

from the back into the reception area, barefoot on its polished wood floor, and handed me a key to a dark room that lacked electricity. It was clean, and she said there would be power for a couple of hours in the evening.

As the Mekong runs, looping, twisting, squirming through gorges and mountains, I was now 2,610 miles from the source—as the bird flies, I calculated, 1,583 miles—and just 117 feet above sea level, or more than 3 miles lower than where the river takes its first breath. I was tired, not drained, but I did feel in my bones the months of travel and the miles that had passed under me. I was also torn by the pace I traveled—should I have stayed longer in Lijiang? should I have spent more time in the *wats* of Luang Prabang?—although there was the realization as well that I could never stay long enough anywhere. I was also by this point longing for regular companionship, for some time lounging on a couch, going to the theater and dinner with friends, seeing some familiar faces. I manage alone quite well for periods of time, but now it had been months, and snatched phone calls and scattered e-mails were inadequate emotional solace.

At the same time, however, I let my memory run back over the miles I had journeyed, the people I had met, the moments of delight and despair, of courage and resignation. China, for me, has always been a troubling place, a country that inspires a mix of love and loathing. On the one hand, I had seen the consequences of institutionalized barbarism in Tibet, while on the other I relished the triumph of survival and culture in the Naxi orchestra, a quiet testimony as well, I thought, to Joseph Rock. I was moved by the tears of the rooftop bride in northern Yunnan and still haunted by the penetrating song of the Khampa horseman on the high Tibetan plateau. Unlike the Yangze River, China's greatest, which washes through the heart of a modernizing nation, the Mekong clips China's western flank, washing against peoples trying to preserve a way of life, a music, a language. So much of each of these cultures has been lost at the hand of Chinese Communist cultural imperiousness that I had the sense of visiting vanishing civilizations, a distinctly depressing feeling. And in Laos, too, I had seen what Communist rule had wrought, what ideological righteousness backed by force yields. Traveling in and observing a society that is hostage to fear and paranoia is deeply unsettling, an experience that tends to undermine all optimism. But Buddhism's flowering in such hostile terrain did offer some hope, some expectation that change could come even there.

Ahead of me, though, lay the most emotionally harrowing leg of my journey. Of all the countries through which I was to travel, the hardest for me to anticipate was Cambodia—its nap of social fabric. Like anyone who has lived in Asia for a long time, I had followed the Vietnamese invasion and rule, the unveiling of the true extent of the Khmer Rouge holocaust, efforts to reconstruct a society and nation, the death of Pol Pot. But what all that implied for the resurrection of the human spirit, I knew not. During my early years in college, apart from studying Chinese language and history, I also spent considerable time exploring the roots of the Jewish Holocaust, both the intellectual transformation of German society and the political and economic underpinnings of National Socialism. Even before that, I can recall long discussions with my parents about the Holocaust when I was still in primary school, because it was an event that exerted a powerful influence over my father, whose principal scholarship focused on modern France, and his conception of history; for his generation of scholars, the Holocaust was the seminal moment of crisis in Western society, a horror that did not lend itself to easy explanation and that influenced the political sensibilities of a generation. Entering Cambodia was, for me, very much a return to those agonies.

From the Khon Falls just twenty-five miles to the north, the river meanders south, untrammeled and free, toward its destiny with the South China Sea. It runs as well through some of the most tortured lands of recent history, less the merciful and powerful presence of popular spiritual belief than unwitting collaborator and unforgiving landscape of death. Around Stung Treng, the Khmer Rouge, the nativist, ruthless movement that had been headed by Pol Pot, had been absorbed into the Cambodian army, or melted back into the jungle. I was told it was safe to travel here, although renegade Khmers Rouges were said to be roaming the countryside. I decided to take my chances.

Stung Treng is a desolate place, once little more than a Lao village, but today a hollow town peppered by dust devils and scraps of windblown palm fronds in a pulverizing heat. What was earlier in the century a central green laid out by French planners has devolved into a vast dirt carpet, unrolling for three or four blocks before expiring into dirt tracks running north and south into isolated villages. Restless young men on scooters buzzed by like angry horseflies before whining down side alleys, stirring flimsy plastic bags discarded throughout the town into sudden blue-green squalls. Other young men squatted in the shade of dilapidated colonial buildings, many just cement shells with punctured roofs and bullet-scarred walls. I struggled to find a place to eat, pacing the green and the alleys, but found nothing but shuttered doorways or meager stalls hawking plastic buckets, brushes and withered oranges. Then, finally, I stumbled onto an open-front box of a building half filled with diners hunched over linoleum-topped tables. I found a space in the back and, after a time, a bowl of soury fish soup, *samla machou banle*, rice and a surprisingly cold Angkor beer were set in front of me. Most diners simply spit the fish bones on the table or the floor; in the relentless grip of Western etiquette I deposited them in a spare plastic bowl.

That night, over a cup of tea at the hotel, the proprietress told me a bit about her town and her life, versions of which I would hear for weeks to come. "Originally we were from Battambang," she said in flawless French, referring to the country's second city in western Cambodia. "We owned a hotel there. My husband was a pilot in the old government, but then he was assassinated by Pol Pot. I managed to escape to Thailand. During the war, there was nobody in Stung Treng." Even today, the best guess is that there are only thirteen thousand people in the district, an area that includes the town, and only perhaps eighty thousand in the entire province. "I came here later, but it was still almost empty, just a few Khmer Rouge," she said. I asked her about life in Stung Treng today. "The Khmer Rouge are gone now," she replied, "but sometimes the trucks get shot at on the way south. Here, it is very quiet. Nobody comes here. There is nothing to do really." As we spoke, two pickup trucks pulled up in front of the hotel and a group of young men and women emerged, faintly hip in black jeans and open-necked satin shirts. My eyebrows went up, and the proprietress laughed. "Oh, they're a music group that will play here tomorrow. You should go." She hurried to welcome the musicians and their entourage, showing them to rooms next to mine.

Morning came steaming, a herculean sun burnishing the river and drill-pressing Stung Treng with a shuddering heat, ridding the dusty green and alleys of people and sending stray dogs panting to deep shade. The proprietress of the hotel had told me that a foreign woman working as a nurse in the area lived up the road a bit, so I decided to seek her out to get her sense of the area; it is often the case that foreign workers in NGOs (non-governmental organizations) have very accurate and broad assessments of the places they work, the sort of analysis that local residents do not make or, perhaps, make differently. I headed up the river road, a path pounded into the high riverbank, toward the house of a Swiss woman who was living and working here for Médecins Sans Frontières, not the private French relief agency, but the Swiss-based group that, like its French counterpart, works around the world, primarily in poor and often dangerous

conditions. I was met on a second-floor veranda of an airy cement-walled
house—of the sort that one sees throughout tropical Asia—by Claire
Fieffé, a short, garrulous woman with fine, big hands and acute eyes. She
was finishing a letter when I arrived, a task she said she never had time
enough for, and brought out some tea after fiddling with a burner fired by
gas from a metal bottle.

"I'm here to train secondary midwives," she told me, settling into a rattan chair, her face capturing a trace of a breeze. "I'm a midwife and my
area is three villages, two along the river and one in the bush. I'm trying to
set up a mobile midwife and infant care team, but there are many problems. Women with children don't know what their mothers or grand-
mothers knew. And all the knowledge of traditional medicine seems to be
wiped out. There aren't a lot of old people left in the villages, very few.*
And there aren't any traditional doctors left anymore. There aren't many
doctors trained in Western medicine either. And these are paid only
twenty dollars a month. But they haven't been paid for three months, so
their motivation is not so good, as you can imagine." I asked her if she was
the only foreigner working here in Stung Treng. She shook her head. "No,
there's another NGO, a group called Youth with a Mission. They do some
medical work, yes, but first they preach the Bible. They do health care,
but it isn't free; there's all this preaching people have to listen to."

There is in Asia a disturbing proliferation of fundamentalist Western
Christians who disguise their central purpose of proselytizing in the garb
of good works. While on the surface, opening hospitals, teaching English
and providing agricultural technology is laudable, when such work is
accompanied by the drone of preaching it becomes little better than the
bait-and-switch salesmanship of used-car dealers. To my mind, and that of
many Asians, such relentless missionary zealotry is simply part of a traditional Western colonial paternalism, a notion that somehow these poor
Asian savages need to be redeemed. It is, in its deepest and most abusive
form, an assault on the foundation of Asian cultures and religions. I did,

---

*The ravages of the Khmer Rouge genocide are apparent from the demographic struc-
ture of the Cambodian population. In 1999, 42.5 percent of the country's 11,627,000
people were under the age of fifteen; by comparison, only 21 percent of the population of
the United States were under fifteen the same year, what demographers call a "mature"
population. Only 4.6 percent of Cambodians were over sixty years of age while 16.5 percent of Americans were over sixty.

though, breathe easier when I heard a Jesuit working with amputees tell me simply that he abhorred such preaching. "We want people to be good Buddhists," he said.

I asked Claire if she felt safe as she made her village rounds. "It's difficult," she answered. "Eight months ago there was a big ceremony here where all the Khmer Rouge assembled and everyone turned out and the Khmer Rouge took off their uniforms and put on government uniforms. That was supposed to be the end of the Khmer Rouge here, but who knows. The road south to Kratie hasn't been safe. There've been a lot of robberies. Bandits. Last month the government met with us and said the security situation is better. But who knows?" I was headed to Kratie, the next town south on the Mekong and one of the towns I wanted to visit that had a substantial Chinese population, and I did, in fact, want to know. And what of the people in and around Stung Treng? I asked her. "It's not good," she began, "not very good. This year the rains were too long, and people lost half their rice crop. People eat mostly rice and salt. There are almost no vegetables because they don't grow them. Or they don't know how to grow vegetables anymore. Let me tell you this, mothers almost always stop feeding breast milk to infants after one week. The mothers put rice in their mouth, chew it and then put it in their infant's mouth. It's just not nutritious at all. I try to get them to keep breastfeeding, but they simply will not." Claire said she had to go off to a meeting with her team, and so we shook hands and I stood to leave. "It will take many years, ten, twenty, to change people's thinking. It won't happen while I'm here."

I was not utterly comforted by Claire's offhand remarks about the dodgy security situation on the road to Kratie, especially because I had seen no boats tied up in Stung Treng. More disturbing was her observation that the entire collective knowledge of a society, the people who lived here, had been obliterated. The ragged life of Stung Treng, the absence of any civil organizations, garbage collection, routine medical care, a public system of schooling, reflected a society struggling for its footing, a society still far from the coherence bred of confidence in the past and any sense of optimism about the future.

That night, on the urging of the hotel proprietress, I found my way by flashlight toward the open field past the town green, pulled by the echo of loudspeakers powered by the clatter of generators. In the blackness of the night, the sky spread wide and glittering—Venus intense, the vivid hour-glass of Orion, both Ursa Major and Minor tacked against a sequinned sky, the Milky Way whitewashed above me. At the open field, candles and flashlights and lanterns flickered, and on a makeshift stage my hotel neighbors hammered guitars and pounded a drum set, singing into cranky microphones; still, the crowd, mostly young, watched and cheered. Others gathered around lantern-lit card games or fortune-tellers. It was a scene that gave me a glint of hope, a sense that all was not lost and that there was some way forward, although the path would not be serenaded in the most melodious manner.

Stung Treng had barely enough glue to hold itself fragilely, together, and none extra to bind me. At dawn, I heaved my sack onto the back of a pickup and having paid fifty cents more for the privilege of sitting in the cab instead of in back on the truck bed—the entire fare was a bit more than $2—I tried to determine whether the hole in the door panel was caused by a bullet or something more innocuous. In back, villagers heading home or those heading for Kratie, the next town of any description on the Mekong, slung sacks on the truck bed and climbed in. The driver, a young kid with a Nike cap, scooted out of the hotel courtyard, and we turned east and south, heading into spare forests that suddenly thickened into deep and lightless jungle. Isolated villages were slung from the roadside at distant intervals, villages of scrap-made huts, salvaged boards or tin sheets, huts made of lengths of blue plastic wrap, all fronted by tiny garden patches. A thick, choking red dust billowed from our passing, enveloping us in heavy powder every time we stopped. On the maps the track is called Route 7, but no signs gave any hint where we were. From time to time, a lone figure in olive army fatigue pants, usually shirtless, would watch us pass, an AK-47 or an M-16 propped against a log by his encampment. If this was the army that made this route safe, I was not terribly comforted. Five hours later, though, we made Kratie, a town larger than Stung Treng, smack against the east bank of the Mekong.

In the mid-nineteenth century, Kratie was hardly more than a large village, a place on no trader's route, just another settlement along the river. Francis Garnier, who made it here in grand style on gunboats flying the French tricolor, described what he saw:

> . . . well-built huts are spread over a great distance along the bank, surrounded by some fruit trees and some gardens. Behind the narrow ribbon they occupy at the top of the riverbank, the land falls quickly and beyond this there are only some poor, scattered rice-fields in the

plains. Nothing provides a sadder idea of the carelessness and indolence of the Cambodians than the sight of these small squares of rice, lost amidst the fertile land left fallow . . . enough to feed themselves, but nothing more, that is the limit which the Cambodians set to their efforts almost everywhere.

French administration would put an end to that soon enough, and by the early part of the twentieth century, a core of colonial architecture had sprung up around a thriving central market. Taxes were being extracted and indolence was, if not banned, at least made more difficult by the demands of colonial officials. Now the town has the wary look of a beaten dog; the town market is anemic in produce and activity, but it functions, and a few restaurants and a café have opened their doors. I found as I walked the ancient, crumbling paved streets that most of the commerce was run by Cambodians of Chinese descent, a phenomenon found throughout southeast Asia, in Vietnam, Cambodia, Thailand, Malaysia and Indonesia.* The Chinese, as the commercial engines of Southeast Asia in the twentieth century, did much to invigorate economic life, but a perception and distrust among non-Chinese about cabalistic Sinitic monopolies has also sparked ethnic unrest; Indonesia has witnessed the worst spasms of ethnic slaughter in recent decades, while Malaysia has enacted legislation restraining ethnic Chinese influence over the economy. In Cambodia, ethnic Chinese were slaughtered as easily as were ethnic Khmer by the Khmer Rouge, an equal opportunity murderer.

That afternoon I found myself in a small shop-front restaurant—appropriately monikered The Mekong—tucked under a double-deck rathole calling itself the 3 December Hotel, the name commemorating the day in 1978 on which the Vietnamese established their puppet government for Cambodia. The restaurant owner bustled out and quickly determined that our mutual language was Chinese. He gave his name as Chen Shuangmei, but it was his thin, ponytailed fourteen-year-old daughter, Lizhen, who wrote it in Chinese ideographs in my notebook. "I can't write Chinese," he confessed, after delivering a warm can of Victoria Bitter, an Australian beer, to the table. In the back of the restaurant—little more than a dozen tables pushed up against either wall—stacks of Belgian Stella Artois beer and Schweppes soda water crowded the passageway to the small kitchen.

---

* David Chandler, a leading scholar on Cambodia, notes that "the bulk of the population of [Cambodia's] main urban centers is of at least partly Chinese descent."

Chen sat down and worked on a cup of tea. A gregarious man with a hefty shock of black hair and an eager smile, he seemed amused by a foreigner who could manage Chinese, although he spoke to his wife in Cambodian. "My parents are from Shantou," he said, referring to a southern Chinese coastal city, "but they came here before I was born. I'm forty-three now, but I never learned to write Chinese. My daughter goes to a Chinese school. There's a Chinese association here now, and we've bought a place to build a school, but we still don't have enough money." I asked him about the merchants in town—who they were and where they came from. "There's quite a lot of Chinese who have businesses in town," he said. "That's to say, everybody is Cambodian, but their parents or grandparents were Chinese. But you know, we Chinese are good at business." I asked him if the Chinese had been singled out by the Khmer Rouge, a period he certainly remembered.

"It was a terrible time," he replied. "I'm not sure how many people from here were killed. My father's cousin was killed because he refused to eat the pressed fish that people were made to eat in the countryside. He said he wouldn't eat it and they beat him to death. They beat people to death with sticks and metal poles." I asked about him and his family. "I wasn't married. I just lived in a village and starved. I starved and I worked. Like everybody else. Mostly there was nothing to eat but gruel with five per-cent rice. I don't want to remember those days. Pol Pot was supposed to be close to China, but he killed Chinese just like everybody. And Hun Sen, he's close to Vietnam, but he treats the Chinese better," explained Chen, referring to Hun Sen, the strongman who has run Cambodia ever since the Vietnamese drove the Khmer Rouge from Phnom Penh in 1979 and installed him as their puppet. Chen walked me around the central square, pointing to the old French commercial buildings and the decaying colo-nial homes. "This one, and this one," he said, his finger angling through the heat, "they belong to Chinese." Later that night, as I sat down to a simple Chinese meal at his restaurant, Chen suggested that we drive upriver the next day to see the old *wat* at Sambor and the river dolphins, a chance to see a vanishing species.

Chen procured a red Toyota with a driver the next morning, and we piled into the car with his daughter and one of her friends from school. A narrow track scurried up the east bank of the river, hemmed by stilt houses in bold primary colors, the wealthier households displaying as many as four successive roof peaks, like incoming waves of red tile. We tracked the Mekong north, the river wide here as it fingered around islets clumped with coconut palms and banana trees. An hour of jouncing later, we pulled into a small fishing village, the shoreline jostling with wooden pirogues, some needle-narrow and some of a more bulbous girth. Chen shepherded us down the riverbank, and after a quick conversation with an old man, we climbed into his pirogue and he poled us into the thick current. Our boatman, perhaps in his early sixties, was dressed as many villagers were, a gray cotton *lunghi* wrapped around his waist and a *krama*, a red-checked scarf, knotted around his neck. Half his teeth were missing and a moth-eaten brown fedora was clamped on his head, but it was the very fact of his age that surprised me; in Cambodia, one sees very few old people.

"There used to be a lot more dolphins," the boatman said, propelling us with a single oar at the stern of the pirogue, his wiry muscles stretched over his rib cage. "I've lived here my whole life, and when I was young there were many, many dolphins. During the Khmer Rouge time, they shot a lot of the dolphins, and when the Vietnamese came,[*] they would set up machine guns and shoot at the dolphins for sport. Sometimes they said they would eat them. I ate dolphin once, but it's not very good. Of course, it's a pity the Vietnamese killed so many dolphins, but what could we do."

Here, and a bit farther north toward Laos, live the last remaining Irrawaddy dolphins, nine-foot-long, grayish creatures with bulging fore-heads that lend them a childlike mien. Because they are on the verge of extinction, I doubted we would spy one, but the old boatman insisted we would. We swung into the current, angling toward an island, the boatman twisting the oar rapidly, when suddenly a gray hump with a tiny dorsal fin broke the rippling reddish-brown surface of the river, and then another, and another. I will never know, of course, but it seemed for a moment that the dolphins were romping with the boat, circling us as we flailed about in the current. And then, just as suddenly, the dolphins were gone. "Three dolphins died last year," the boatman said, as he maneuvered us back toward shore, "one in a fishing net and two swam onto a small island and

[*] In late 1978, after repeated attacks by Khmer Rouge forces across the border, Vietnam invaded Cambodia, occupying Phnom Penh in January 1979 and driving the Khmer Rouge into encampments just over the Cambodian border in Thailand. Vietnam continued to rule Cambodia through a proxy government headed by Hun Sen for the next decade. In 1993, the United Nations sponsored elections and though his political party, the Cambodian People's Party, failed to secure a majority in parliament, Hun Sen continued to rule and has retained a steely grip on power ever since.

died. They can't swim backwards, so I don't think they could get off the island once they were on the beach."

There is a certain rush of emotions about seeing what may be the final members of a species, not in any way comparable to contemplating the horror of the genocide committed by the Khmer Rouge, but a sense that a piece of what has made up the ecology of a place is on the verge of being lost forever. I stood for a time looking out across the Mekong, watching the river slip past the clutter of islands, scanning its braided surface hoping for a last glimpse of one of these creatures, but I saw nothing.

We drove north toward Sambor, which had once been a religious and kingly center but is now a small village with a spanking new *wat* in lemon yellow, its golden-tiered roof supported by a forest of willowy lemon columns. The seventeenth-century Dutch trader Gerritt van Wuysthoff described Sambor as the most important kingdom between Phnom Penh and Laos, a territory administered by a monk-king. Chen and his daughter and her friend went off to find a relative, and I wandered around the *wat*, which was deserted in comparison to the teeming temples of Laos. As I sat on the staircase leading to the main prayer hall, a young man in a red-checked *lunghi* sauntered up and in remarkably adept English, considering that we were more than an hour from the nearest electricity pole, and hence a satellite that could bring in English-language television or radio, introduced himself as Pitou Chhay. He laughed when I told him I did not expect to meet an English speaker in such a remote village. "Well, I'm an English teacher," he said. "I teach here in Sambor."

Visibly excited at speaking English with a native speaker, Pitou battered me with questions, including where I was from and what I was doing in Sambor. And then he talked about himself. We sat in the shade of an overhanging roof of the *wat*, little relief from the temperatures that were well above one hundred degrees Fahrenheit. "My father works in Kratie, but after I finished secondary school I was sent here by the government to teach English," he explained. "I live here at the *wat* because I don't have any relatives in Sambor. There's nowhere else to live." He talked a bit about his school. "I know I do not speak English so well, but I have forty-one students. They are ten to fifteen years old. Altogether maybe there are one thousand students at the school," which to me seemed an excessive estimate, given the sparseness of Sambor town. Baby-faced and shorn like a monk, Pitou, who said he had just turned twenty, waggled his crossed legs as he talked. "Most of the people here are farmers, but they still have to pay ten thousand riel per month for each student," a bit more than $2. "And me, my salary is sixty thousand riel each month." And did the pupils have books? I asked. "No books," he said. "We do have paper and pens. I write on the blackboard, and the students copy things."

Even though he was born just as the Khmer Rouge were being driven from Phnom Penh and other Cambodian cities, I asked Pitou about the effects of those years on him and his family. "I don't know what my parents did during the war," he answered. "They never talk about that time with me. I'm not clear about the Khmer Rouge myself. That was many years ago. I remember that we had elections in 1993, but I don't know much about politics. Here in Sambor is what I know—we have no electricity and no telephones." People born after the Khmer Rouge years, I learned, often shied away from talk of those years, or simply denied knowledge of them; often, too, they expressed ignorance of how their parents survived. Indeed, many parents, I was to discover, were reluctant to tell their children much about their life under the Khmer Rouge.* I asked him whether he felt stranded in the middle of nowhere, an hour or more from Kratie, not exactly bright lights and big city, but at least his family's home and a place less somnambulent than Sambor. "Oh, not too much." He laughed. "I guess I'll be here for a long time. We have a little town here, but there is nothing to do. I spend time talking with the monks. There are no old monks. All the old monks were killed and the young monks, I don't think they really know a lot about Buddhism."

I walked with Pitou into town to look for Chen and his daughter, and on the way we stopped in front of a woman selling what in Chinese is called zhuguanfan, sticky rice roasted with yellow beans and coconut milk in a tube of bamboo, an aromatic and slightly sweet snack that passed for lunch. Chen was seated on a wooden bench drinking a Pepsi from a can, a sure sign that tendrils of foreign consumer goods were squirming into even the most remote parts of Cambodia. I said good-bye to Pitou, and we

---

* A growing number of memoirs by survivors of the Khmer Rouge years have appeared in recent years. One of the most moving is by a young woman named Loung Ung, who was five years old the day the Khmer Rouge marched into Phnom Penh. She describes how her father was taken away by soldiers one day, never to return, and her mother, frantic that she could no longer ensure her children's lives, sent them into the countryside in a last, desperate effort to save at least some of her family. Her mother, too, was murdered and, years later, Loung Ung escaped Cambodia and settled in Essex Junction, Vermont.

drove slowly back to Kratie, the road's ruts only occasionally slapping the underside of the car.

A blue-and-white-striped cigar tube of a hydrofoil bobbed by the jetty at Kratie the following afternoon, the fastest river transport down to Kampong Cham, the principal central-Cambodian trading town built originally by the French, a town about halfway to Phnom Penh, the capital, where much of Cambodia's future was being shaped; there were stories of its past that I wanted to hear as well. It was good to be back on the river, although sealed in a banged-up sixty-six-seat tube with a television blaring a Hong Kong kung-fu movie was not the idyllic river journey I had anticipated. Fortunately, one of the hatches in the front was open, and I could squat on a narrow running board, clinging to a handrail as we shot down the river at a steady thirty miles per hour. At times, the boat would arrow toward shore to snare passengers from floating docks. At one village, a group of army officers boarded, one of whom had a patch reading LT. COL. prominently sewn on his uniform breast, and all carrying hard plastic briefcases. A few of them had pistols strapped to their waists. Here the Mekong itself was increasingly corpulent, jostling shorelines as it waddled south, hosting ever larger herds of small fishing pirogues, double-decked tubby wooden cargo vessels and flat-bottomed cross-river ferries.

The scorch was coming off the day as the hydrofoil jiggled up to the metal barge that served as a floating dock at Kampong Cham, from which a flight of concrete steps climbed to the pavement atop the riverbank. Overlooking the river was a newish hotel that beckoned. I slung my pack on my shoulder and trudged into the lobby to find the polished floor evenly scattered with black vinyl sofas and lounge chairs; all were cushioned with young women made up for a night on the town, their skirts shorter than their spiked heels and their tops awfully tight for the steamy weather. I took a room overlooking the river and returned to the esplanade where sidewalk bars had been set up with folding tables and Asia's ubiquitous molded-plastic chairs. I grabbed a chair and a young girl furiously wiped the table in front of me before setting down a can of frigid beer. Downriver a bit, Cambodia's first bridge was being built across the Mekong, and frazzled Japanese engineers in white hard hats were scrambling around trying to get local workers to pour the concrete pilings correctly. At the neighboring table sat six Americans with brush cuts, pumped physiques and scarcely concealed dog tags underneath their T-shirts. They introduced themselves as U.S. Army.

"We're searching a crash site for MIAs," one of them explained as he opened a beer. In Laos, Cambodia and Vietnam, American military teams continue to search for the remains of U.S. soldiers and pilots who disappeared during the Vietnam War. While the United States has been aggressive in extracting cooperation from the three southeast Asian governments in the search for missing Americans, the Pentagon has been notably lackadaisical in providing help to the Hanoi government in its own effort to account for more than three hundred thousand Vietnamese MIAs.

"We really don't expect to find anything," said one of the civvie-clothed soldiers. "People said there are wild pigs up there. You don't believe anyone who says they buried the bodies. And the Khmer Rouge probably killed anyone who knows anything. We'll be lucky if we find a tag." Not a compulsively chatty group, they returned to their own conversation, evidently safer in their huddle from the prying queries of an outsider.

Although its role as a silversmithing center has been lost, Kampong Cham was reviving—its streets were crowded and its markets were busy. The core of the town, like Kratie upriver, was molded from the remains of French architecture, large commercial buildings with ground-floor shops, and farther out, strings of colonial homes, all but a few shored up with new beams, strung with electricity lines and brimming with trade and family life. Once bright pastel walls have long since soured and blackened from humidity and fungus, and the shutters that once hung sprightly from swing hinges sag like eye bags. And spottily, on corners and tucked between early-twentieth-century edifices, new, glass-paned, air-conditioned buildings have sprung up, evidence of some economic pulse. I patrolled the streets, smelling garlicky, gingery dinners being served in shop houses. I watched the ice men grapple with hundred-pound blocks of ice on hand-hauled carts and then saw off slabs for a restaurant or a meat seller. Then I searched for a place that served coffee, from where to watch the town go by. Then I found Mr. Fan's.

In a decaying corner building in what could pass as an arcade, a jumble of worn wooden tables were flung among scarred yellow columns. I picked a sidewalk seat and ordered coffee without the thick base of condensed milk that was customary. Two little girls, I guessed between eight and ten, although given Cambodia's nutritional standards it was tough to tell for sure, scurried about serving customers, flicking rags at the flies that zoomed toward unwatched plates of fried noodles. In the corner, smoking one cigarette after another, a gray-haired man watched the girls and jawed with a couple of younger men. While I worked on my second cup of coffee, a thick, bitter brew, he padded over to my table. "How are you?" he inquired, mopping his face with a handkerchief he yanked from his gray slacks. "What else can I get you?" He smiled crookedly, baring a rampart of gold teeth. His eyes goggled through thick lenses. I introduced myself and asked him to join me. That evening, and over the next several days, he told me his life story, and that of his family.

"My name is Fan Zhengcheng, and I am seventy-two years old," he began, thumping his chest. "There are not so many old people anymore in this country. I am now the lifetime honorary president of the Chinese association." His credentials established, he went on to tell a grim tale.

"I am originally from Kampot," he said, referring to a small southern town on the Gulf of Thailand. "My family has been there for generations. When the Khmer Rouge came, we were all driven from our homes. They made everybody leave the cities and move into the countryside. When the Khmer Rouge came, I had ten children, eight daughters and two sons. When we were forced out of Kampot we had to march with just a few things. I got separated from my sons and their families. I don't know how. But I learned later that they all died, my sons and their families." He dragged on a cigarette, its untended ash tumbling into his lap.

"We were sent to a village in the countryside. For some reason I was made head of a village. I think it was because I knew all the local languages. In my village we had one hundred eighty families and none of them starved. But I know people starved in many other villages. I learned that one of my sons was sent to do hard labor, and he died there. My other son, he had a family of five, they were all beaten to death. We found out from relatives who were in the same village."

We sat, enveloped in silence, for a time. Fan stared out across the square, the harsh memories of that time working within him. "But the gods looked out for our family, even in death," he went on. "We managed to get out of the village, and we escaped to Thailand after the Vietnamese came. But we were able to stay there for only twenty-eight days. The Thais forced us back over the border. We had no idea what to do or where to go. We wanted to go south to Kampot, but the war was going on and the south was still controlled by the Khmer Rouge. There were ten thousand families, and we all were trying to know what to do. So we started to walk. Thousands and thousands of people walked. Many people died on that walk. They died from starvation. Some people died from walking on mines. We walked only at night because we thought it was too dangerous to walk on the road during the day. We tried to stay on the main road because of the mines. We could do about thirty kilometers a day. It took us four months to reach this place. I carried my grandchildren when they could not walk. There were eleven in our family when we did this walk."

This happened in 1979, from May to August, the hottest months of the year. When Fan and his family finally staggered into Kampong Cham, it, like every other city in Cambodia, was desolate, empty, a ghost town. An American journalist, Elizabeth Becker, visited the city in 1978, providing the only account by an outsider of the place under the Khmer Rouge: "There was no one on the streets, no commerce in the markets, no traffic on the roadways."

"When we got here we were starving," Fan continued. "We had no food and didn't know how to get food. Some people said we should go to Vietnam, but the Vietnamese were charging one dollar for each person to cross the border. We had no money, so we could not go. There was nothing here when we came. No markets. Nothing. We built some grass huts to live in.

"Little by little we got better. We fished in the river, and my wife sold the fish. We grew vegetables, and the children sold vegetables. We did whatever we could to survive. I did labor. I worked twelve hours a day. I think for Chinese people, wherever you go, you have to work hard. Everywhere you go there are Chinese people in this world, and wherever there is money to be made we will work our ass off.

"Later on I was able to buy this place. That was in 1986. I think it was June that year, and I bought the building from the government. Some people were talking about destroying this building and putting a new one up. I wanted this just like it is. It's old and falling apart, but basically it's a good building. Now I live upstairs with my family. My wife is sixty-nine." He gestured at the two young girls working the tables, balancing big plates of noodles in their hands as they rushed back and forth between a man behind a steaming wok and customers, all men, hunched over tables, or pulled cans of Coke from a white chest refrigerator filled with ice. "These are my granddaughters. Now I have twenty-two grandchildren. I have two daughters here and four daughters in Phnom Penh and two others in other towns. I think mostly the gods have looked over my family."

I sat with Fan in the heat of the day, in the afternoons, under the tattered canvas awning that stretched over the sidewalk. As he talked I thought I could sense him holding in his sorrow, a habit in Cambodia, in a country where everyone's life has been touched by terror, by the horror of mass murder. Many survivors of the Khmer Rouge tell stories of Communist cadres hiding under stilted huts to listen if people were crying. Weeping was deemed to be a betrayal of the Khmer Rouge, a sign of traitorous intentions toward *angkar*, the faceless organization in whose name society was to be reorganized. There was a saying during the time of the Khmer Rouge, "*Angkar* has the eyes of a pineapple," a phrase that implied that the organization was all-seeing, and all-knowing. "We never showed emotion," Fan told me one day. "No one knew who could be killed next."

But it is true also that many Cambodians skim the surface of their experiences because, in the light of post–Khmer Rouge scrutiny, many people did things they do not want to admit, deeds perhaps small but with awful consequences, actions taken to survive. In the brutality of the Khmer Rouge era, what Cambodians call *samai a-Pot*—the era of the contemptible [Pol] Pot—all social rules were shattered, reverence for parents was forbidden, social mores were obliterated. Survival was a fragile commodity, and what people did to survive may never be fully known. As I listened to Fan, to the tales of suffering he and his family endured, I wondered also at what was not said, what could not be told. After some weeks in Cambodia, I knew I would never truly comprehend what had occurred in this country. There were days and times when Fan and I did not talk of the Khmer Rouge, when we chatted about his life in Kampong Cham. He told me he ran his business, he met with other Chinese businessmen and he kept to himself. "This is Cambodia," he told me on the last day. "In Cambodia, no one is really safe. You can never know for sure."

Across the Mekong from where we sat stood a solitary brick tower, a bit like one of the countless *torre* in Bologna; it even had a slight lean to it. Local lore had it that it was in this tower, or around it, that Hun Sen lost his eye in a firefight with the Khmer Rouge. Fan said that Hun Sen himself had told him the story. Like everything here, I could never be too sure. But I did find a young man with a motorized pirogue who scooted me across the Mekong to the east bank of the river for a look. Though built as a bell tower by the French in the 1940s, there was no sign of a bell when I poked my head through the arched doorway of the three-level brick tower, each level crenellated like a true medieval structure. Concave scars in the brickwork, the permanent tracings of machine-gun fire, pocked all four sides of the tower's exterior. Whatever happened here, it had been furious and violent. I glanced from the tower back toward Kampong Cham, across a river riffled by boat traffic. The town lay low and flat along the river, from a distance just another Mekong town, now at peace.

Downriver the next stop on the Mekong was Phnom Penh, where the aging and erratic King Sihanouk presided at a royal palace, the seat of a government tinged with the aura of the Khmer Rouge, and the emergency room of international relief organizations that stampeded into the country to rebuild it, demine it, rewrite its laws, repave its roads, patch its wounds. I waited on the steel barge for the hydrofoil, crunched under a soft-drink seller's café umbrella. I decided to skip through Phnom Penh for now and head to Siem Riep, the town that has sprung up near Angkor Wat and the other temples and palaces of early Khmer civilization. While Phnom Penh was the heart of Cambodia's rebirth, a place where I intended to stay for some time, it was the country's cultural and spiritual antecedents I sought first, perhaps, I told myself, as a window onto the national soul.

The hydrofoil opened its airplanelike hatch, and I tumbled in along with sixty or so other travelers, all Cambodians heading to the big city. Our pilot wheeled the vessel away from the barge, the ancient engine howling as he poured on the gas. Then, suddenly, just as we were passing the stubby pylons of the bridge construction, the boat whipped sharply to starboard and nose-dived into the muddy current. We rocked abruptly to starboard and then to port, shipping water through open hatches. I was amazed that nobody screamed. I felt like it. With some aplomb, a few passengers unbolted safety hatches and several grabbed for life vests even as we roller-coastered about. Slowly the hydrofoil stopped rocking and we were dead in the water, but at least we had not capsized. I stuck my head out of a safety hatch to try to figure out whether we were ultimately headed to the bottom and what could be saved from my pack. I think I was more alarmed than my fellow travelers. One of the boat hands stripped off his shirt and pants and dove into the current under the boat, a wrench gripped in his right hand. He surfaced a few moments later and hauled himself back aboard, shaking his head. After a conversation with the captain, and the sudden appearance of a flotilla of motorboats, some from the bridge site, the boat hand threw a line to a larger craft that had chugged up and we were towed back to the barge. Someone said that our propellers had snagged a cable line on a warning buoy.

On the barge, the sun was panfrying the passengers on its steel plates. We waited as another hydrofoil was tugged off the shore downriver and pushed toward us. It was dented and rusting, its engine hacked smoke, and one of the cockpit windshields was missing. Once again the passengers piled in, settling onto plasticized cushioned seats in roughly the same order as on the previous boat, and we shuddered out into the river toward Phnom Penh.

From Phnom Penh, there is another hydrofoil that speeds up the Tonle Sap River, past low-lying banks of palm trees and rice fields, past villages of thatched huts ragged in the glare of a noon sun, toward Siem Riep and the temples of the Angkor kingdoms. Angkor is the spiritual and histori-cal touchstone of Cambodian civilization, the place from where for much of six centuries the Angkor empire spread its reign to the sea across what is now southern Vietnam, into what is Laos and well into the central plains of today's Thailand. From the ninth to the fourteenth centuries, Angkor's rulers built immense temples, excavated lake-sized reservoirs, constructed roads and chronicled their exploits in a myriad of stone bas-relief carvings. Even in this century, Angkor lends a cloak of legitimacy and righteousness to government, eerily to both that of the now van-quished Khmer Rouge and its successor.

Now the country's principal tourist destination, Siem Riep brags an opulent five-star hotel for those visitors who hope to remain as far removed from Cambodia's reality as possible, as well as a flurry of smaller, rustic hotels and guest houses; it has become, in truth, a global tourist mecca. And, of course, the French have returned in force, whether as restaurateurs, hoteliers or archaeological restorationists. In part this is because the French lay a certain self-appointed protectionist claim to Angkor's historical treasures, a claim that traces back to one of their nineteenth-century explorers, Henri Mouhot, who "discovered" the ruins of Angkor and penned lengthy descriptions of what he saw. While Mouhot acknowledged the splendor of the temples, he also sought to rein-force for the French their ingrained sense of cultural paternalism. Of a temple overgrown by jungle, he wrote: "One of these temples—a rival to that of Solomon, and erected by some ancient Michael Angelo—might take an honorable place beside our most beautiful buildings. It is grander

Buddhist monks at Angkor Wat

than anything left to us by Greece or Rome, and presents a sad contrast to the state of barbarism in which the nation is now plunged."

Mouhot had no idea when these temples were constructed, surmising that two millennia must have passed since their construction and his arrival in 1860. Though wrong about that—he admitted his inexpertise in archaeology—he was certain of where France's duty lay: "European conquest, abolition of slavery, wise and protecting laws, and experience, fidelity, and scrupulous rectitude of those who administer them, would alone effect the regeneration of this state. It lies near to Cochin China, the subjection of which France is now aiming at, and in which she will doubtless succeed. . . . I wish her to possess this land, which would add a magnificent jewel to her crown." Although he died of a tropical fever in Luang Prabang in 1861 and never saw his hopes realized, France's dominion over Indochina would have warmed his heart; the only hearts not warmed, of course, were those of the Vietnamese, Cambodians and Lao.

For much of the nineteenth and twentieth centuries, Angkor's temples were looted by foreigners, mostly European, who trundled great stone stat-

ues of Buddha, stone friezes of mythological scenes and entire stone temple doorways to the museums of the continent.* Everywhere, the temples
are scenes of vacant alcoves or beheaded Buddhas, gaping spaces where
bas-reliefs were clawed from the masonry. Thievery continues to this day,
some organized, some spontaneous. A Frenchman who deals in Asian
antiquities in Taiwan told me in all earnestness that it was far better for
Angkor's treasures to be kept in private hands than to remain in the heat
and humidity of the jungle. "They will be preserved much better," he told
me, sitting in his Taipei apartment surrounded by a museum's worth of
statuary, including a lovely Buddha from the Angkor period. "Most of us
think this is better than leaving things to decay and neglect. There is a
very big market for these pieces, and we are here to help people find what
they want." Still, it is hard to lug away an entire temple made of sandstone
and larger than the Vatican, and so the great temples of Angkor remain,
monumental, some wreathed in vine-choked mystery, some silent, others
boisterous with the chatter of barefoot children selling water and soft
drinks to tourists fighting off sunstroke—the structures that remain all
evidence of a civilization of power, breadth and endurance.

Although the temple known as Angkor Wat is regarded as the most
magnificent of Angkor architecture—it is the best preserved of the
dozens of great temples and houses the most elaborate and delicate
friezes—I found myself spending more time in the city built by the greatest of Angkor kings, Jayavarman VII, who was crowned in 1181 and ruled
for three decades in what is called Angkor Thom. Surrounded by a moat,
now hardly more than a shallow dip after eight centuries of neglect, and
a towering wall thirty feet high and more than two miles in length on
each of its four sides, Angkor Thom was one of Asia's greatest cities at
the end of the twelfth century. Today, the walls are matted with fungus
and serpentined with strangler figs, but they run straight and true.
Through the soaring gates crowned with the faintly smiling, drowsy-eyed
sculpture of the Buddhist image Avalokiteshvara, a now-tarmacked road
streaks toward the city's center where the great temple, the Bayon, rises.

---

* In 1880, when plundering Asian sites was respectable in Europe, a French lieutenant
named L. Delaporte, who had been on an earlier expedition with Francis Garnier, published a volume detailing a second mission to Angkor Wat in 1873, during which he carried off a trove of sculptures, carved pilasters and friezes so immense that, as he put it,
"even in this day and age there was not a gallery in the Louvre large enough to accommo-
date a collection of this importance."

During the reign of Jayavarman VII Angkor Thom's walls enclosed magnificent palaces, the homes of nobles and military chiefs, the trading quarters and monasteries for the thousands of priests who officiated at royal functions, and the homes of thousands of artisans, traders and bureaucrats who kept the kingdom running. Built from the abundant supply of wood from the jungles of the central plain, these wooden structures are long gone, grown over by forests of soaring *Dipterocarpus alatus*, sometimes called the hairy-leafed apitong, a tree that easily reaches 150 feet in height, with broad, 2-foot-long, deep-green leaves, and the gray-barked *Lythraceae*, which climbs 100 feet to crowns of shiny reddish-brown leaves. What is left are the stone temples, causeways, bathing pools and a magnificent royal reviewing esplanade, the product of mass labor on a scale seldom seen in human history, perhaps only in the building of the pyramids or the temple complexes of Central and South American pre-Columbian cities.

At the end of the thirteenth century, the Mongol dynasty in Beijing dispatched an ambassador to the Angkor court. The envoy, Zhou Daguan, jotted down his observations of Angkor life with thumbnail sketches on the quotidian elements of Khmer society, including bathing, wine making, sexual practices and the organization of the royal court. His accounts remain the only extant description of what life was like at Angkor a full century before the kingdom disintegrated. Although the temples and ruined palaces of Angkor now stand mute, Zhou's keen eye offers a swirl of vivid description that conjures some of the kingdom's pomp and splendor, imagery that still floats vividly before the eye:

When the king leaves his palace, the procession is headed by the soldiery; then come the flags, the banners, the music. Girls of the palace, three or five hundred in number, gaily dressed, with flowers in their hair and tapers in their hands, are massed together in a separate column. The tapers are lighted even in broad daylight. Then come other girls carrying gold and silver vessels from the palace and a whole galaxy of ornaments, of very special design, the uses of which were strange to me. Then came still more girls, the bodyguard of the palace, holding shields and lances. These, too, were separately aligned. Following them came chariots drawn by goats and horses, all adorned with gold; ministers and princes, mounted on elephants, were preceded by bearers of scarlet parasols, without number. Close behind came the royal wives and concubines, in palanquins and chariots, or mounted on horses or elephants, to whom were assigned at least a hundred parasols mottled with gold. Finally, the Sovereign appeared, standing on an elephant and holding in his hand the sacred sword. This elephant, his tusks sheathed in gold, was accompanied by bearers of twenty white parasols with golden shafts. . . .

Among the themes that spurred the Khmer Rouge and underpinned Pol Pot's tyrannical notions of remolding Cambodia was an obsession with mass labor, a theme he directly referenced to his selective reading of Angkor history: "If our people can build Angkor, they can do anything," he once said. During its nearly four years of control, the Khmer Rouge directed massive, and ultimately disastrous, irrigation projects, emulating those of the Angkor kings. In the tenth and eleventh centuries, two mammoth lakes—five miles long and nearly two wide, known as the eastern and western *baray*—were dug to lubricate an intricate web of irrigation channels. Pol Pot's efforts probably exceeded the brutality of Angkor labor and accomplished nothing. Similarly, the prodigious amounts of labor needed to construct the gigantic sandstone temples of the Angkor period suggests a complex social organization of agriculture, labor and slavery, a system that functioned sufficiently well to create these great temples; in the era of Pol Pot, society as a coherent and cohesive entity largely ceased to exist.

At the precise center of Angkor Thom looms the Bayon, which from a distance can appear to be little more than a mountain of grayish stone block. But as I approached it repeatedly over several days, the mountain gave way each time to a vision of tiered arcades, low walls scored with steeply pitched staircases and then, on the third level, as if materializing from a dense fog, rise fifty-four towers, each of their four faces carved with the immense visage of the slightly smiling, half-lidded Buddhist image, the same one that overlooked the gates to the city, the image that has come in popular parlance to be called "the Angkor smile." Everywhere I turned, a face loomed above me, watching and not watching, neither pleased nor angry, both aloof and present. It was the face of omniscience, of ubiquity, of ever-presence. No matter where I walked on the terrace, always a face, two faces, five faces, peered down; there was nowhere to hide to elude their scrutiny. It is understandable that the intimidation of Cambodia by the Khmer Rouge distilled in the phrase about the eyes of a pineapple also found its analogue here, where the great face is thought to be both Buddhist and kingly.

David Chandler, a leading historian of Cambodia, finds disturbing resonances between Jayavarman VII's grandiosity and the megalomania of the Khmer Rouge: "The history of his reign is the story of the imposition of one man's will on a population, a landscape, and a part of Asia, ostensibly in the service of an ideal, Mahayana Buddhism, which in its allegedly 'liberating' fashion bears an ominous resemblance to the ideology of Democratic Kampuchea," what the Khmer Rouge called its regime. "His break with the past, his obsession with punitive expeditions, the impetuous grandeur of his building program, and his imposition of a national religion rather than his patronage of a royal cult all have parallels with recent historical events."

Indeed, the bas-reliefs at the Bayon are an unrelieved account of warfare, of soldiers marching to battle, of naval encounters between the Khmers and the Cham, of victory dinners, of civil war and even of the defeat of the Khmers in 1171 and the sacking of Angkor. The Khmer Rouge, too, celebrated war, feasted on a paranoia regarding the Vietnamese, reveled in sanguinary lust; its national anthem, dedicated to the day its stony-faced, black-pajamaed child soldiers marched into Phnom Penh, tells all, and echoes the historical past:

> *Ruby blood that sprinkles the towns and plains*
> *   of Kampuchea, our Motherland,*
> *Sublime Blood of workers and peasants,*
> *Sublime Blood of revolutionary men and women fighters!*
> *This blood changes into unrelenting hatred*
> *And resolute struggle,*
> *On April 17th, under the Flag of Revolution,*
> *Frees from Slavery!*
>
> *Long live, long live Glorious April 17th!*
> *Glorious Victory with greater significance*
> *Than the times of Angkor. . . .*

Yet Angkor retains a powerfully magnetic quality, a capacity to overwhelm with wonder and mystery. I found the vastness of the Angkor temple structures hard to comprehend. Was there, at the height of the

A woman selling stir-fried water
beetles near Angkor Wat

Angkor empire, a day in a Khmer's life that was not filled with the tap of the chiseler's hammer, the crack of stone blocks being shaped, the sight of elephants hauling raw sandstone or rust-colored laterite from distant quarries? Wandering the Angkor sites today, it is difficult to summon up images of a dense civilization. Even when French explorers first came upon Angkor Wat, there were still monks in great numbers and a surrounding society that supported the monastic community. Today, the sites have been relegated to tourists, save for one or two *wats* of recent vintage that have sprouted in the forests. Village children swarm over the temples, selling cool drinks from ice chests and hawking small drums or musical instruments fashioned from bamboo or rattan. Dancers, musicians and acrobats perform for tourist coins outside the grander sites. Only at the western *baray*, the remaining water-filled reservoir from the Angkor period, are there Cambodians in numbers, local people happily dashing down the embankment to flocks of kids offering immense black inner tubes for rent. Nobody, it seemed, could swim, but everyone was eager to bob about, fully clothed, inside a fat rubber ring. There are beaming young girls selling snacks of stir-fried black water bugs from capacious bamboo panniers, Cambodia's indigenous potato chips. I paid one young girl a few notes, not for one of her water bugs, which I could not quite manage to swallow—in a disgraceful display of cultural myopia—but to take her picture.

I did, however, stumble onto more gastronomically pleasing fare just opposite Angkor Wat. Hidden among trees under a steep, thatched roof supported by stout wood columns, a sign read CHEZ SOP'HÉA. Six or seven tables draped in red-and-white-checked tablecloths hugged wood railings under the thatch, and a magazine carousel toward the back was filled with copies of *L'Express*, *Le Nouvel Observateur* and *Le Monde*. A bamboo bar was crowded with bottles of Beaujolais and Armagnac. And as I strode in, coated in dust and parboiled in a humidity fired by a malevolent sun, a bellied and cheerful Frenchman hurried out to welcome me and help me to an empty table. For several days I stopped here to eat, always fish from the Great Lake, or Tonle Sap, steeped in coconut milk, wrapped in a leaf and baked. When all the tourists were gone and blackness inundated the temples, only the glint of the café's lights punctured the night. During several evenings, I sat and talked with the restaurateur, Matthieu Ravaux, and his Cambodian wife, Sop'héa. A former archaeologist and writer, Ravaux came to Cambodia after the war and the departure of the Vietnamese. After his marriage he decided to open a café, but could not find an ideal location. But as Angkor once again became a tourist destination, he was able to persuade the tourism bureaucracy, not known for its probity, to let him open his restaurant shaded by great trees and in the penumbra of Angkor Wat itself. It was a bit like winning a doughnut concession on the steps of St. Peter's.

"This is my life now," he told me, after pulling a bottle of his favorite Armagnac from beneath the bar. As he did, the skies opened and rain slugged down in heavy pellets, hammering the thatched roof in endless drum rolls. The earth exhaled a heavy, peaty aroma, the fragrance of drenched vegetation, the scent of a tropical night. "It is beautiful here. We are happy. Of course, this is a very, very poor country. Most people have almost nothing. And the government, well, it is better not to say much about the government. But you can guess. Just look at the Angkor tourism board. It used to be run by the government, but so much money was stolen that just this week they are turning it over to a private company to run." All visitors to Angkor must pay for a daily pass, and it was widely believed that the fee, paid in dollars, was going directly into the pocket of Cambodia's minister of tourism. Ravaux paused to sip at his

small snifter of amber fluid. "Many French tourists come here," he continued, pushing another small dollop of Armagnac on me, "so this restaurant
makes them feel a bit like home. It helps with the culture shock."

He chuckled at that. "One of the terrible things about Angkor is that
almost all of the best artifacts have been stolen," he went on. "There is a
conservatory here that is supposed to protect the rarest and best sculptures. But many people want to know why the king's sons have so many
Angkor sculptures. And many people want to know why Hun Sen also
has some of the best pieces." In Phnom Penh, at the National Museum,
two of the finest pieces of Khmer sculpture are accompanied by cardboard
plaques indicating that they are gifts of Hun Sen; not many people here
publicly ask how it is that a former Khmer Rouge officer who defected to
Vietnam and was installed as the head of government on a paltry official
salary came to possess some of the country's most spectacular examples of
Angkor-era sculpture.

As I drove home that night through the forest, a sudden velvety black
blur streaked by our headlights; it was one of Cambodia's rare black leopards. Even the driver yelled in excitement.

Although the historical and architectural grandeur of Angkor remain
central to Cambodia's identity—apart from its prominence on the
national flag, the silhouette of Angkor Wat adorns even the label of the
national brew, Angkor Beer—it is now more a place for foreigners than
Cambodians. In a country as poor as this, few Cambodians can afford the
time or the money to travel here to see the glory of their history. Few care.
Instead, Europeans, and the Japanese who are also here restoring sites,
have appropriated Angkor as a global treasure, almost as good as shipping
the whole place off to the British Museum. One of the strangest feelings
about spending time in Angkor is how divorced one is from Cambodia,
how the experience of these temples and palace sites is so amputated from
the reality of impoverished villages just a mile or two away, from the
recent past that convulsed and brutalized this society. To be sure, Angkor
as a thriving empire slowly expired at the end of the fifteenth century.
Pressed by armed incursions from Thailand, a depleted irrigation system
and the lure of sea- and riverborne trade from China and southeast Asia,
the capital was moved to what is now Phnom Penh. And it is there I was
next to go.

But before I left Angkor, after my last day at Angkor Thom, I had my
driver pull off the main road that led to the temple sites, to what was once

An ossuary for the victims of the
Khmer Rouge near Angkor Wat

a small *wat* and now is a memorial to those murdered by the Khmer
Rouge. I was alone there, unlike at the Angkor temples that were well
peopled with tourists laden with phallic-lensed cameras, away from the
call of children selling drinks and the guides who hurry through a memo-
rized patter about the glories of each temple. A wooden signboard,
cracked and fading and propped against a palm tree, asked for donations
to preserve the "bones that have been collected from nearby fields. These
are from innocent people who died at the hands of the savage Pol Pot
regime (1975–79)." A solitary glass-paned stupa sat on a cement platform
displaying a mound of chalk-white skulls and human bones. I walked to
the stupa, each of its cardinal directions guarded by a pair of cement-cast
stone lions, and stood staring at the stark memorial. Some of the skulls
were punctured by holes, some of the leg bones were cracked or smashed.
Among them, near the top, was the skull of a child.

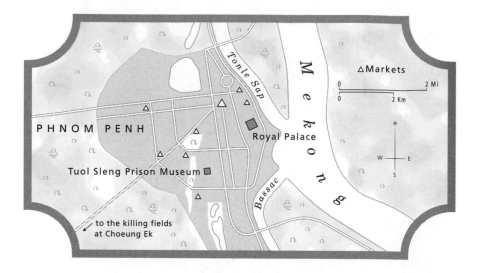

Eight

Memory, the Hill of the Poison Tree, and Hope

We should dig a hole and bury the past and look ahead to the twenty-first century with a clean slate. —HUN SEN

I want these killers to go to court and be tried.
—VANN NATH, ONE OF SEVEN SURVIVORS OF THE
TORTURE AND EXTERMINATION CENTER AT TUOL SLENG

My conscience is clear. —POL POT

J ust south of Siem Riep, what on maps is shaped like a blue gourd, is the Great Lake, or Tonle Sap, and on it floats a vast village of fishermen, a general store, a hardware depot, a couple of gas stations, a cream-colored wooden hospital, a post office and a stretch of houses strapped to oil-drum pontoons. Watery boulevards and alleyways slice and slither between houses, shops, a maroon clapboard school for children, past bamboo-walled fish corrals and the village police station—*Bureau de la police fluviale*—complete with a patrol boat mounted with a machine gun. If it were not afloat, the village would very much resemble a small town in the nineteenth-century American West, a few sparse streets of blue-shuttered wood-plank houses fronted with porches shaded by slanting roofs and hung with pots of flowering plants. Rough-hewn pirogues propelled by a single stern oar glide down the main thoroughfares or out to huddles of fishing scows anchored on the village perimeter.

Tonle Sap is Cambodia's fish basket, the principal source of dietary protein for much of the northwestern part of the country. And for at least two centuries it has also been a fishing ground for Vietnamese fishermen who annually sail up the Mekong and the Tonle Sap River to work the waters of the Great Lake, historically the most abundant fishery in southeast Asia. In the mid-nineteenth century, when Cambodia essentially ceased to exist, torn between Thai and Vietnamese ambitions and military adventurism, Vietnamese fishing fleets dominated the lake, bringing their hauls downriver to the market towns of the Mekong Delta. During the bloodstained years of Pol Pot's regime, any Vietnamese fishermen unlucky enough to have been caught working the lake were summarily slaughtered by the rabidly xenophobic Khmer Rouge. Only after Vietnam's invasion of 1979 and the military defeat of the Khmer Rouge did Mekong Delta fishing boats return to the Tonle Sap. Still, a residual distrust gilds the lake's waters, and the Vietnamese fishing boats cluster in their own ghettoes, removed from the busy town life of the floating village.

What passes for a bus station is a floating jetty reached by water taxis from the shore, a jetty where the Royal Express cigar-tube hydrofoil from Phnom Penh docks on its regular daily run, five hours each way. I stuffed myself and my pack into the back of the vessel, opened *Suttree*, Cormac McCarthy's powerful and wrenching novel of dissolute seaminess and brutality, irony and dignity, and tried to block out the screech of the Hong Kong kung-fu flick on the television in the front of the cabin. The

white-and-blue hydrofoil carried me down the lake to the Tonle Sap
River and toward Phnom Penh, whipping through wide turns, past
quilted paddies tufted by clumps of thatched huts and farmers leading
water buffaloes on slack tethers. Fitful air-conditioning cooled the tube's
interior from the saunalike heat and humidity that sank heavily on the
river. Dusk was chafing the sky when we arrived in the capital, upriver
from the city center, but within sight of a riverbank spangled with light
from streetlamps, cafés and apartment windows.

I came to Phnom Penh burdened by the accounts of the people I had
met upriver while struggling to comprehend what Cambodia had
endured. In the capital, now nearly two decades after the invasion of Vietnamese troops and the retreat of the Khmer Rouge to the country's
periphery, I hoped to understand what lay beneath the monstrous savagery that consumed this land—a task that continues to absorb scholars of
modern Cambodian history and society—and to try to discern the strands
of recovery, the filaments of light leading Cambodia from an unimaginable past. Some fifteen years earlier, working in Nigeria, I was interested
in how that country had reconciled the bitter ethnic war in what was then
called Biafra, a conflict that riveted the world's attention with graphic
pictures of starving babies and mutilated bodies. To my surprise, although
not to that of Nigerians, that conflict had been put behind it, and the Ibo
people, the people of what had been Biafra, were very much part of Nige-
rian national life. (This turned out to be about the only crisis Nigeria was,
in fact, able to grapple with successfully; since the end of that war in 1970,
the country has been mired in a succession of military dictatorships, staggering corruption and apparently irremediable poverty.) Instructive as
well in contemplating the complex and difficult problems of national
recovery, I thought, was the example of South Africa, and the manner in
which Nelson Mandela had managed to reassure white South Africans,
the country's former masters, while radically reshaping the political and
social map of his country, installing a new, black majority South African
government and beginning the process of redressing the country's
grotesque economic inequalities. I wondered whether such hopes were
warranted for Cambodia.

Taxicabs are still a rarity in Phnom Penh, so I hopped on the back of a
taxi scooter and made for a hotel shrouded in tamarind trees across a
broad boulevard from the Royal Palace, the sprawling apricot-colored
compound in the heart of the capital that was built by the French in the

early part of the twentieth century. A mile or so wide here, the Mekong parades past Phnom Penh, a great prairie of barges, rusting pocket river freighters up from the South China Sea, hand-oared fishing pirogues, white-shelled speedboats, a hulking ivory gambling ship strung with lights and an occasional battle gray police patrol boat. The Tonle Sap flows from the north, breeding with the Mekong to produce a river that strains its corset banks. When Pol Pot's army of grim, black-clad teenage soldiers padded silently into this city on April 17, 1975, their vacant and silent faces quelling the initial and spontaneous cheers of welcome, Phnom Penh's population had swollen to well over 2 million people, many of the refugees from American bombing and the battles in the countryside. Then, in just a matter of days, the Khmer Rouge had ordered the entire population to leave the city, some in trucks but the vast majority on foot, carrying whatever possessions could be bundled on their backs. The hospitals were emptied, and those patients who were not ambulatory were simply shot. Members of the defeated regime were taken away and executed. Libraries were burned, and the vaults of the central bank were flung open and the currency of the vanquished government was scattered to the winds. Pol Pot was intent on pounding a new Cambodian society from the clay of an impoverished and war-battered population; murder and terror were the fingers that did the remolding. And Phnom Penh became a dead city, a town of ghosts and memories.

Twenty years on, young families stroll along the riverfront esplanade, their children decked out in a blinding chromatic palette—navy blue sweatshirts and orange pants, sequin-trimmed, flouncy vermilion party dresses, babies in lemon-yellow knit hats, and blue jeans everywhere. On the purely sartorial level, the outrageous colors, the clash and combination of tones and intensities, mark a vivid repudiation of the Khmer Rouge, who demanded that everyone wear black pajamas. Vendors with glass-paneled carts hawk sheaves of translucent dried squid, chicken and rice rolls, skewers of grilled chicken, fresh-crushed sugarcane juice. A balloon man cycled by, coddled by huge clusters of pink and red balloons, like a wad of salmon eggs drifting downstream. An ice-cream cycle followed, its brass bell beckoning customers. On a grassy square across from the main gate to the Royal Palace, families spread grass mats for picnics, piling plastic bowls filled with boiled eggs, fried lotus root and sautéed pork slices in front of them, the air stirring with the aroma of dining al fresco. Beer gardens on the riverfront overflowed with men in short-sleeved white shirts and gray slacks, some chattering into mobile phones, some arguing, some laughing over a business deal gone right, or wrong. And the cafés along the riverfront boulevard—Quai Sisowath, named after a late-nineteenth-century king—were jammed with foreigners, both residents and travelers, and wealthy Cambodians who were dropped off in shiny Toyota Land Cruisers by their drivers. In the swankiest Chinese restaurant in town, flat-faced chandeliers blaze on all three floors, and waitresses in sexy and skimpy outfits massage the shoulders of male customers, cooing in their ears about postprandial possibilities.

New Year's was coming, in April this year, and the Royal Palace was hung with lights like a Disneyland attraction. Behind its walls, King Norodom Sihanouk, a manipulator and dissembler, a man whose ego and spectrum of political coloration would shame a chameleon—over the decades he has promoted himself as a right-winger, a monarchist, a champion of Pol Pot, a Socialist, an abdicator, a restorationist and now "father" of the nation—prepared for the traditional spring plowing ceremony to be held on the grounds of the adjacent National Museum. The British ambassador hosted a small dinner for Hun Sen, the former Khmer Rouge commander who runs Cambodia with a combination of canniness and ruthlessness, a meal of such sumptuousness that the menu became the talk of the town: on satin-white china, a procession of dishes that included smoked salmon, beluga caviar, chilled soup, sorbet, medallions of veal, chocolate mousse and, of course, a bouquet of wines and cognacs. This in a nation with a per capita income of less than $1 a day. Hun Sen, by any standard a man with no compunction about having his enemies murdered, his political opponents beaten up, journalists cowed and his pockets well lined, has become the darling of the Western diplomatic community; "in his heart he is a democrat," an Australian diplomat famously remarked.

On the surface Phnom Penh is, if not thriving, at least recovering. The Central Market, a cavernous four-winged art deco concrete dome built in 1937, is a frenzy. The meat counters hung with defeathered chickens and pig haunches operate alongside jewelry merchants hovering over glass cases drenched in gold chains, pendants and rings. A patchwork grid of streets spreads from the waterfront, and everywhere there are signs promising training in English—PRACTICAL ENGLISH GRAMMAR, or ENGLISH CNN-TV, 6 O'CLOCK TO 7 O'CLOCK, or STREAMLINE ENGLISH. Billboards offer computer literacy—MICROSOFT OFFICE NOW and LEARN SPREADSHEETS. And though government buildings and many streets are labeled in French, there are no classes offered in the Gallic tongue. Chaotic in its layout—Street 55 intersects Street 254, which intersects Street 51, which itself dead-ends at Street 392—it is also a city of construction sites, from the garish, snow-white mansions of the rich and often corrupt to the shantytowns of wood, cardboard and corrugated tin shacks mushrooming throughout the city, neighborhoods of rural migrants seeking economic improvement.

But there are, beneath the lights and balloons, signs as well that the past is not so very far away. On Quai Sisowath, outside the cafés serving frosty Stella Artois beer and foamy cappuccino, beside entrances to riverfront restaurants and at the stairway to the Foreign Correspondents Club, there are men, mostly young men, in wheelchairs, or hunched over crutches, missing a lower leg, or most of both legs, all begging for a handful of Cambodian riel, or perhaps an American dollar. These are victims of the war, of American antipersonnel mines that blew up ten or fifteen years after they were dropped, of land mines laid by the old Cambodian government or strewn by the Khmer Rouge, victims of the millions upon millions of unexploded military devices scattered everywhere in this country. There are people wounded in their souls as well, the crazy man howling at the river, the sporadic instances of women running frantically, naked, through the streets. And among the city's residents, and across Cambodia, still live some of those who were the torturers, the murderers, those who tore this country apart with a deliberate and relentless savagery. And that is the tension that still runs wire-hot through this city, still two decades after Pol Pot was driven into the jungle and, in 1998, to his death. It is a tension that is everywhere, that colors every interaction, that remains inescapable.

Rick Droz arrived at my hotel's courtyard in rumbling two-cylinder splendor, his lacquer-black antique Indian motorcycle shimmying like an off-kilter blender. In a black teardrop sidecar, composed, and I guessed partially deaf by now, sat his wife, Punya. Droz is a big, gentle man, his face partially magnified by oversized lenses in his plastic-framed glasses under a tussle of steelwool hair. The lights on the palace across the street blinked on as the waitress placed two bottles of beer and a Coke on the plastic table. I had heard about Droz from a tiny nonprofit group in London that sent money to his project here—building wheelchairs—and I was determined to meet him.

"I'm from Mendocino," he said, summoning the waitress for his second beer. The heat of the day clung to us like a nasty rash, and the parade of cold beers offered a mirage of relief. "In sixty-seven and sixty-eight I was in the Marines, up by the DMZ," the demilitarized zone between North and South Vietnam at the 17th parallel. "Twelve and a half months." He worked on his beer. "After I got out, I went back to California. I admit that I didn't feel comfortable there. I always wanted to come back to southeast Asia. I had been doing some photojournalism and was in northern Iraq after the Gulf War in 1991 and I met some people from a French NGO working with amputees. They were making prosthetics, and I said to myself, This is something I want to do. So I've been here off and on for nearly ten years. I met Punya, and we got married."

"I was working at an NGO after the Vietnamese left," she explained. "My family, my father and mother and brothers and sisters, everybody was killed by Pol Pot. My father was in the army of the old government. Anyone who was in that army was murdered. I was little then and was adopted by my mother's sister."

Now Droz spoke again. "When I first came, I was working on a project with the Vietnam Veterans of America, building wheelchairs, across the Tonle Sap River on the peninsula there," he said, jerking his head toward the east, toward the spit of land that narrows out as the Tonle Sap runs into the Mekong. "It was funded by AID," the American government's Agency for International Development. "They do good things, but they're a bureaucracy. It's just numbers to them. They have to show a bottom line. So I quit that and went to Nicaragua and Guatemala to build wheelchairs for a British NGO. Then we took a break back in Mendocino and Punya went to a community college."

Droz suggested that we go to a small Cambodian restaurant for dinner, so I climbed onto the back of his motorcycle while Punya eased herself into the sidecar. After some vigorous lashing at the starter lever the cycle burped and coughed to life, and we rattled out of the courtyard into the darkened side streets of Phnom Penh. There are still relatively few cars in Phnom Penh, most of the traffic being made up of locust swarms of high-pitched 100 c.c. Honda and Yamaha motorcycles, for which there are no discernible rules of the road. Apparently it was permissible to drive anywhere on the surface of the roadway, regardless of lanes or the inconvenience of oncoming traffic. For the first time since the terror of Tibet's cliffside dirt tracks, I felt that the probability of a severe maiming on the road had risen dramatically. Droz, however, was unfazed, effortlessly melding with one swarm, then another, dodging a truck here and skimming the fender of a black-windowed four-by-four there. I was relieved when we made the restaurant.

As we ate a mix of grilled meat and fish baked in a banana leaf, Droz continued his story. "After Punya finished college we came back to Cambodia, and I started working with an ILO project," ILO being the International Labor Organization, one of the United Nations' Shiva-like arms that is working here. "We're trying to train handicapped people in three remote areas, but I don't think this is going to work. The idea is that we're training amputees to do a variety of things—to fix motorcycle engines, to be hairdressers, to learn how to be tailors, that sort of thing. But there are so many people who do these things already I don't see how it will work. How can a handicapped person succeed in this society?"

Although I had just met Droz and Punya, I could not resist asking them how they got together. Punya sprang at the question. "You know Cambodians are very, very conservative," she said. "We're not like Thais or Vietnamese at all. After I met Rick we only went on two dates and both times we had an escort from my family." Droz rolled his eyes at the memory of his chaperoned romance. She went on, "This is the way we do things in Cambodia. Now I think things are changing a bit in Phnom Penh. Young kids are not so traditional. But most people in Cambodia still are very conservative. Then we got married. It was a very traditional ceremony. I changed my dress nine times on my wedding day." She laughed at that. "But there was no other way." When coffee came, I asked them what they felt were the repercussions of the Khmer Rouge period. Droz and Punya looked at each other and then he replied.

"I think there's a kind of national posttraumatic stress syndrome at work here. There is this underlying paranoia and fear. Let me give you an example. One afternoon the deminers here decided they were going to detonate all the unexploded mines and bombs they had collected. They had this stuff out near the airport somewhere. The problem was they didn't announce they were going to blow it up. So then suddenly—*bam, bam, bam*—these huge explosions start going off, and they're right by the airport. I tell you, immediately people started leaving the city. Parents were frantic. They drove to their children's schools and grabbed them and left town. People had no idea what was going on. They thought a war was coming. This thing is there. It's deep inside people."

Over the next few weeks I saw Rick and his wife from time to time, or would see them chugging down Quai Sisowath, rakish in an antiquarian kind of way. After a while, they became increasingly blunt about their disgust with the Hun Sen government, about the depths of its corruption, its indifference to the poverty and backwardness of the country, and most of all Hun Sen's unwillingness to confront the past, to confront the crimes against humanity perpetuated by the Khmer Rouge.

While I was in Phnom Penh, the issue of the past kept bursting to the surface like an unwanted guest at a party. Pol Pot, known as Brother Number One, was dead, of suicide or at the hands of his comrades in 1998.* Already, Hun Sen had issued pardons to three of the most senior members of the Khmer Rouge leadership, men who were intimately involved in the movement's policies of forced labor, torture and extermination. Ieng Sary, Pol Pot's closest comrade in arms, had been pardoned in 1996. Then in late 1998, Nuon Chea, a man known for his savagery and as Brother Number Two, and Khieu Samphan, who was the face of the Khmer Rouge abroad, were pardoned and fêted by Hun Sen in the capital—"with bouquets of flowers, not prisons and handcuffs," as he put it—before being allowed to return to their old haunts in western Cambodia where they lived in luxury fueled by smuggling and extortion. And then two of the most vicious of the Khmer Rouge leaders reappeared.

Before that happened, though, I was still struggling to comprehend the scope of Cambodia's tragedy. After a few days in Phnom Penh, I steeled myself for a visit to the torture and extermination center known as Tuol Sleng—a place I knew was visited more by tourists than Cambodians—a memorial not unlike Auschwitz. I found a taxi scooter and told the driver to take me down to Street 103, to Tuol Sleng, in Khmer, "the hill of the poison tree." "Oh yes." He laughed. "I know Tuol Sleng. Everybody goes there." He was clearly unperturbed by the thought of the place, but then he was too young to have experienced the Khmer Rouge.

The rainy season was stirring its first maelstrom on the horizon. Overhead, a broiling sun fought furiously against the fleets of gray-black clouds steaming majestically and ominously toward Phnom Penh, pushing before them a soupy wash of humidity. I was drenched with perspiration by the time we turned into Street 103, a street like any other in the capital, filled

---

* In July 1997, in an extraordinary journalistic scoop, Nate Thayer, a longtime reporter on Cambodia, was asked to witness Pol Pot's trial as it was staged by a faction of the Khmer Rouge. Three months later, Thayer once again returned to Anlong Veng, the Khmer Rouge jungle headquarters, and conducted the first interview with Pol Pot in two decades and, as it turned out, the last before his death. Defiant to the end, Pol Pot expressed no remorse for having murdered as many as 2 million of his countrymen. "My conscience is clear," Pol Pot told Thayer. "We had no other choice."

with two-story white cement houses with broad balconies behind high, barbed-wire-topped walls. These were the houses of Cambodia's wealthy, people who were cashing in on the country's return to normalcy. The slam of hammers and a buzz saw's whine nearby were audible reminders of a construction boom. Bicycle peddlers selling nuts and ice cream wheeled by, indifferent to the gate on their left, the gate that led to Tuol Sleng.

Before April 17, 1975, Tuol Sleng had been a lycée, a three-story, U-shaped grouping of buildings with wooden classroom doors opening onto open-air corridors that overlooked a spacious courtyard. Then, for the three years and eight months of the Khmer Rouge regime, Tuol Sleng was known as *konlaenh choul min dael chenh*, the place of going in and never coming out. More than fourteen thousand people were led in shackles into Tuol Sleng—farmers, teachers, engineers, doctors, journalists, a handful of foreigners and, later, a growing number of Khmer Rouge cadres, low- and high-ranking, and even, at the end, the very torturers of Tuol Sleng themselves. Year in and year out, Pol Pot received files of the "confessions" of those tortured here, confessions that were extracted in a crazed effort to ferret out spies and saboteurs of the new order. Every confession produced more suspects, more torture, more confessions. And when the torturers were finished with their work, the victims were taken in trucks to a field near the hamlet of Choeung Ek. There, they were bludgeoned or shot and dumped into mass graves.

At the door, I paid $2 and received an admission ticket. I was then waved to the left, toward what were once the ground-floor classrooms. As I have worked as a journalist around the world, I have seen horrific things: I once saw a man executed before my eyes in Uganda; I spoke for an excruciating hour with a young Muslim who had been grotesquely tortured by Indian troops in Kashmir; I saw children blown into fragments of pulp in a rocket attack in Afghanistan, and I witnessed the Chinese army's massacre on Beijing's streets and Tiananmen Square in 1989. But still I was unprepared for the visions of horror that Tuol Sleng summoned up.

The bloodstains are gone now, and the schoolrooms where victims were tortured are almost antiseptic. In several rooms a single metal-frame bed with bare springs sits in the middle of the brown-and-beige-tiled floor; on the wall are gruesome poster-sized photographs of the last person to die on that bed—a blackened corpse, an arm distended in a final agony, a pool of blood on the floor, the torturer's hard-backed chair at the

end of the bed. Here, the museum tells us, the last fourteen victims of
Tuol Sleng died, in torture chambers reserved for the senior Khmer
Rouge cadres.

It was numbing and sickening, an exhibit of utter bestiality, of madness.

In an adjoining building, the systematic extent of this butchery is displayed, walls of clinical photos of the victims as they were admitted to
Tuol Sleng, pictures of old men and children just a few years old, wide-
eyed young girls and teenage boys with faces puffy from beatings, a woman
holding her newborn. The Khmer Rouge, not unlike the Nazis, were
meticulous in their record keeping of torture, for it was these records that
documented, in the insane fantasy world of Pol Pot, the conspiracies
being hatched against him and his revolution. There was also a photo of a
man called Duch, a high-cheekboned man with slightly buck teeth and a
pompadour of black hair. Duch had run Tuol Sleng, its chief torturer and
high executioner. At the moment I stood in that place, no one knew what
had happened to him. That was about to change.

Farther on, there are classrooms converted into individual cells,
roughly made brick chambers with steel shackles fixed to the walls. To my
eye, the cells seemed of recent construction, perhaps part of the effort by
the museum keepers to consolidate the exhibits on the ground floor of the
buildings. Where once the museum allowed visitors on all three floors,
now steel gates barred access to the upper levels; those who visited Tuol
Sleng in earlier years describe similar cells above the ground level. On one
wall, a blackboard in Khmer delineated the ten rules to be obeyed by prisoners. Among them, obscenities all, was number six: "While getting
lashes or electrification, you shall not cry out at all."

And in the third wing, there were a series of oil paintings depicting the
methods of torture used in Tuol Sleng—beatings, half-drownings, a
woman having her child ripped from her arms, a man having his finger-
nails torn out. On the far wall, formed in the shape of Cambodia, was a
mosaic of skulls, hundreds of skulls making this country.

I left Tuol Sleng shaking. It is the same reaction I think one has after
leaving Auschwitz, a certain loss of balance in the proximity of evil, at
walking in a place where death was commonplace, casual, indifferent,
where mercy was unknown, where truth was banished, where dignity was
demeaned and tears mocked. Evil was not banal here. Outside the gate a
man with an ice chest sold water and Cokes, perhaps to steady the nerves,
certainly to ward off the heat. I succumbed.

There was still one more place I had to visit before the day was over. My scooter driver waited patiently under a broad-brimmed Australian bush hat. I told him to take me to Choeung Ek. "Okay," he said.

A tarred road gives way to a dirt track on the ten-mile drive to Choeung Ek, spinning quickly out of the city and into newly plowed paddies and clumps of sugar palms. Thatched huts mingled with sturdier cement houses, and schoolchildren in white shirts and carrying canvas book satchels were dashing home barefoot. Water buffaloes, blimplike creatures on spindly legs with horned, flat foreheads and huge, empty black eyes, lolled under palm trees, seeking shade from the afternoon sun. My scooter driver banked into a long, tree-lined drive that ran straight to the killing fields.

I handed over another $2 and was passed through the gate. I could see three boys in shorts kicking a brown soccer ball beyond the fence, their laughter spilling toward me. I could hear as well the call of birds, a high whistle that filtered through the trees. On the far edge of the compound, next to fields that had just been plowed, an array of gentle dimples in the

THE MOST TRAGIC THING IS THAT : _

EVEN IN THIS 20TH CENTURY, ON KAMPUCHEAN SOIL, THE CLIQUE OF POL POT CRIMINALS HAD COMMIT. TED A HEINOUS GENOCIDAL ACT, THEY MASSACRED THE POPULATION WITH ATROCITY IN A LARGE SCALE, IT WAS MORE CRUEL THAN THE GENOCIDAL ACT COMMITTED BY THE HITLER FASCISTS, WHICH THE WORLD HAS NEVER MET.

WITH THE COMMEMORATIVE STUPA IN FRONT OF US, WE IMAGINE THAT WE ARE HEARING THE THE GRIEVOUS VOICE OF THE VICTIMS WHO WERE BEATEN BY POL POT MEN WITH CANES, BAMBOO STUMPS OR HEADS OF HOES, WHO WERE STABBED WITH KNIVES OR SWORDS. WE SEEM TO BE LOO KING AT THE HORRIFYING SCENES AND THE PANIC. STRICKEN FACES OF THE PEOPLE WHO WERE DYING OF STARVATION, FORCED LABOUR OR TORTURE WITHOUT MERCY UPON THE SKINNY BODY, THEY DIED WITHOUT GIVING THE LAST WORDS TO THEIR KITH AND KIN. HOW HURTFUL THOSE VICTIMS WERE WHEN THEY GOT BEATEN WITH CANES, HEADS OF HOES AND STABBED WITH KNIVES OR SWORDS BEFORE THEIR LAST BREATH WENT OUT. HOW BITTER THEY WERE WHEN SEEING THEIR BELOVED CHILDREN, WIWES, HUSBANDS, BROTHERS OR SISTERS WERE SEIZED AND TIGHTLY BOUND BEFORE BEING TAKEN TO MASS GRAVE !

WHILE THEY WERE WAITING FOR THEIR TURN TO COME AND SHARE THE SAME TRAGIC LOT .

THE METHOD OF MASSACRE WHICH THE CLIQUE OF POL POT CRIMINALS WAS CARRIED UPON THE INNOCENT PEOPLE OF KAMPUCHEA CANNOT BE DESCRIBED FULLY AND CLEARLY IN WORDS BECAUSE THE INVENTION OF THIS KILLING METHOD WAS STRANGELY CRUEL. SO IT IS DIFFI. CULT FOR US TO DETERMINE WHO THEY ARE FOR THEY HAVE THE HUMAN FORM BUT THEIR HEARTS ARE DEMON'S HEARTS THEY HAVE GOT THE KHMER FACE BUT THEIR ACTIVITIES ARE PURELY REACTIONARY. THEY WANTED TO TRANSFORM KAMPUCHEAN PEOPLE IN TO A GROUP OF PER SONS WITHOUT REASON OR A GROUP WHO KNEW AND UNDERSTOOD NOTHING, WHO ALWAYS BENT THEIR HEADS TO CARRY OUT ANGKAR'S ORDERS BLINDLY THEY HAD EDUCATED AND TRANSFORMED YOUNG PEOPLE AND THE ADOLESCENT WHOSE HEARTS ARE PURE, GENTLE AND MODEST INTO ODIOUS EXECUTIONERS WHO DARED TO KILL THE INNOCENT AND EVEN THEIR OWN PARENTS, RELATIVES OR FRIENDS .

THEY HAD BURNT THE MARKET PLACE, ABOLISHED MONETARY SYSTEM ELIMINATED BOOKS OF RULES AND PRINCIPLES OF NATIONAL CULTURE, DESTROYED SCHOOLS, HOSPITALS, PAGODAS AND BEAU.. TIFUL MONUMENTS SUCH AS ANGKOR WATT TEMPLE WHICH IS THE SOURCE OF PURE NATIONAL PRIDE AND BEARS THE GENIUS KNOWLEDGE AND INTELLIGENCE OF OUR NATION . THEY WERE TRYING HARD TO GET RID OF KHMER CHARACTER AND TRANSFORM THE SOIL AND WATERS OF KAMPUCHEA INTO A SEA OF BLOOD AND TEARS WHICH WAS DEPRIVE OF CULTURAL INFRASTRUCTURE, CIVILISATION AND NATIONAL CHARACTER, BACAME A DESERT OF GREAT DESTRUCTION THAT OVERTURNED THE KAMPUCHEAN SOCIETY AND DROVE IT BACK ON THE STONE AGE .

The explanatory sign at the killing fields of Choeung Ek, near Phnom Penh earth, shallow concavities, spread before me. These were the mass graves, the place where the victims of Tuol Sleng were taken, most blindfolded, some not, and made to stand on the edge before being shot, or clubbed to death with an iron bar. Of 129 graves, 86 had been excavated and the remains of 8,985 people were exhumed. A coverlet of grass, brilliantly green in the heat, healed each depression, the earth bared only on the paths pounded by human feet that wove among the graves. At the bottom of a depression I saw what looked like a human leg bone and some scraps of clothing. And in another grave pit, a goat foraged through a bunch of yellow wildflowers.

In the center of the compound, rising from a concrete platform, was a tall stupa crowned with a series of compact, tiered roofs, all flared at the ends in a graceful, flamelike gilded wisp. The four walls of the stupa were plate glass, and behind them, piled high above my head, were the bones of those who died here, an ossuary of the victims who were dragged to this place, by then so brutalized they probably were hardly aware of what was happening around them, to them. I wondered: As they stood waiting for death, did they hear the birds sing?

Choeung Ek was hardly Cambodia's only killing field. There were hundreds more across the country, fields where the Khmer Rouge devoured its own people. In a corner of the field here, a café serving coffee and Coke had been erected, and a group of foreign tourists sat in its shade, their conversation hardly a whisper. I left after a time, contemplating how time had eroded the sharper edges of misery, and perhaps memory as well. For younger Cambodians, wallowing in the past seemed to provide neither solace nor apparently much of a prescription about the future. And for those who committed the crimes, there was nothing but denial. Pol Pot, though he had died the year before I reached Phnom Penh, had told his last Western interviewer that he was ignorant not only of what went on at Tuol Sleng but of Tuol Sleng itself.

"I was at the top. I only made big decisions on big issues," Pol Pot told Nate Thayer, an American reporter, shortly before his death in the northern jungles of Cambodia. "I want to tell you, Tuol Sleng was a Vietnamese exhibition. . . . People talk about Tuol Sleng, Tuol Sleng, Tuol Sleng, but when we look at the pictures the pictures are the same. When I first heard about Tuol Sleng it was on the Voice of America. . . . I never heard of it [before 1979]." Eichmann never acknowledged his crimes either.

My driver was finishing yet another Coke as he waited for me, chatting with the young women who dispensed tickets to visitors. As I mounted the pillion on his bike, the clouds that had been steaming toward us reached port, anchored and let loose with walls of water, great, slapping sheets of rain that rocked our little scooter as we jounced through the suddenly muddy ruts in the track. The rain felt wonderful.

At Tuol Sleng, the oil paintings of victims being tortured were the work of a man I had heard about for some days, Vann Nath, who was one of the last seven prisoners in Tuol Sleng and who had escaped in the confusion of the Vietnamese attack on Phnom Penh in 1979. I set out the next day to find him, thinking perhaps he was attached to the Ecoles des Beaux Arts behind the National Museum. The storm of the late afternoon and evening had abated by morning, as it tended to do, and I walked over to the school to ask if Vann Nath was around. Hulking and maroon-colored, it was an old French school of high-ceilinged rooms with doors opening onto arcades, a series of courtyards and wide staircases leading to studios and classrooms. I peeked into rooms where students stood before easels, palettes in their hands, brushes working canvases as at any art school in the world. Sculptors fashioned clay in a studio, a young woman with waist-length hair uncovering the face of a dancer from a mound of tough gray earth. I asked a couple of students and a teacher if they knew of a painter named Vann Nath, but everyone shook their heads.

Across the street from the museum are a row of open-fronted art galleries, the sort of galleries that sell happy art, formulaic pictures of smiling women cooking outside thatched huts with a water buffalo in a soft, hazy distance, or of two girls carrying baskets of oranges—art to order. None of it resembled Vann Nath's work, paintings vaguely primitivist in technique; the perspective in his work is wrong, his figures are not anatomically correct, but the emotions in each of his paintings are unmistakable, intense and compelling. I asked around the galleries, but none of them had heard Vann Nath's name.

That afternoon, I was having lunch with one of the handful of foreign journalists who base themselves in Cambodia and brought up Vann Nath's name. "I've heard of him," the journalist told me, "but I don't know where you'd find him." He did, however, provide a couple of telephone numbers for other reporters in town and finally one of them told me that Vann Nath lived with his family at a restaurant on what used to be called Czechoslovakia Street.

By now I had acquired a regular taxi-scooter driver, and he told me with his usual certainty that he knew exactly where we were headed. Weaving his way through clots of scooters and cars like a barracuda working a school of fish, we raced down what was once U.S.S.R. Street, heading west. I clung to the scooter's grab bar, dimly contemplating concepts of Buddhist fatalism, but unscarred, we made it to Czechoslovakia Street, truly a Haussmannian boulevard in its proportions. I stopped at a couple of restaurants along the street and was met with bafflement. "Vann Nath? Vann Nath?" I repeated. No one seemed to know. The last restaurant, marked by a substantial sign with plastic letters, announced KHEMRA RESTAURANT. Like many eateries in Phnom Penh, the restaurant had no walls, just bamboo drop blinds slung between the building's support columns. A few tables were taken, but the lunch hour was over and most of the staff was seated at the back drinking tea. I asked them if this was where Vann Nath lived. A young woman nodded. "Yes, he is my father."

Vann Nath, a painter who was one of seven
survivors of the torture and extermination center
of Tuol Sleng, in Phnom Penh, Cambodia

I sat at a Formica-topped table, ordered a cup of black coffee and waited for Vann Nath. After I had drunk about half a cup, a slight man approached the table and shook my hand. "I am Vann Nath," he said. "How can I help?" More than anything, I was struck by his thick, completely white hair; very few Cambodians have white hair, and I was surprised by it, particularly because his face was largely unlined by age. But more than his white hair, there was a deep sadness in his eyes, a look not of despair, but perhaps of moments lost. Even his smile, deepening as it did his brow's furrow, seemed painstruck. I explained that I had been at Tuol Sleng and that I was moved by his paintings and the stories I had heard about his survival. He was silent for a time, folding his arms tightly across his chest. "Yes, okay, what would you like to know?" For the next several hours, he told me the story of his life.

He was born in 1946, in Battambang, the country's second-largest city, about 150 miles northwest of Phnom Penh. As a young man, he studied painting and opened a business painting movie billboards and portraits. "I had a bit of talent for painting, so I could make money for my family," he explained, his words uttered in low, almost whispered bursts. "Then in 1975, it was April, suddenly there was shooting and rockets around Battambang. We were very worried what was happening. When the shooting stopped, the soldiers in black pajamas came into the city. I saw people dead on the streets, just shot and their bodies left on the streets. Then they forced all the people to leave the city. We all had to go to the countryside and live in villages. I was with my wife and son, and when we were in the village we had another son. There was no painting then, only working in the fields or cutting rattan in the forest. There was almost no food, just gruel, water and a few grains of rice. Many people starved to death during that time."

He was in the village for two years. Then one day, a day like any other day, he was summoned by the village leader. "This man was called Luom," Vann Nath continued, calling his daughter to bring him another cup of coffee. "He came and made me go with him. They tied me up and took me away to a place where they tortured me. They tied wires to me and shot me with electricity. I thought I was going to die. Certainly I thought I would die. They said I was *kmang*, I was the enemy. That is the worst word."

After his interrogation, Vann Nath was packed into a truck and driven to Phnom Penh. He said that at every stage he thought he was going to be shot. When several days later the truck arrived in Phnom Penh, he was led in shackles into the compound called S-21, the Khmer Rouge code name for Tuol Sleng.

"I had no idea why I was there," he remembered. "Everyone was very scared and very hungry. We were so tired we almost didn't care what happened to us." Vann Nath produced a small photograph of his mug shot from when he was admitted to Tuol Sleng. Sepia-toned, it shows a full face and right profile of a hollow-cheeked man with jet-black hair, thick eyebrows and a ragged goatee; his eyes were dark and desperate; pinned to his shirt was a small board with the number 55. "This was in December 1977. I did not know about this place. They put us on the third floor and chained us to the walls. Every day they took people away, and they never came back. One day, the guards came in and called my name. It was my turn. I thought I was next to die." Vann Nath was taken to the cement blockhouse that served as the administration center for Tuol Sleng. "There was a man sitting on a couch. He looked right through me. He showed me a photograph and asked me who it was. I didn't know. How could I know? He told me to paint a picture from this photo. So I did. I learned later that this was Pol Pot. The guards said it was Brother Number One. Or they said it was *angkar*, 'the organization.' It never had a face. I also learned that the man on the couch was Duch. He was in charge of Tuol Sleng.

"After this I did not go back upstairs but painted pictures of Pol Pot. As long as I painted I could live. Every day people were brought to Tuol Sleng. There were trucks that took people away also. In January 1979, one day there was a lot of shooting suddenly outside, and you could hear artillery shooting in the distance. The guards were running around, and I had no idea what was happening. Then they took seven of us and marched us out of the prison, and the guards marched with us out of Phnom Penh. Of course, now I know that the Vietnamese were invading Cambodia and were taking control of Phnom Penh."

The Vietnamese army swept across Cambodia with remarkable ease and swiftness, sending the Khmer Rouge fleeing for the Thai border. In short order all major towns were under the control of the Vietnamese, a marionette government had been established and a new Cambodian army created. Vann Nath joined the new army and was assigned to paint pictures of what had happened at Tuol Sleng for the museum the Vietnamese were opening to document the atrocities of the Khmer Rouge. "They told me that as a survivor I could see everything and that I could paint what had happened. So I painted pictures of things I saw with my own eyes, things that I had heard about and pictures of friends who had been victims of Pol Pot."

Vann Nath asked me to accompany him upstairs, to the roof where he still paints occasionally. Here, the canvases are not portraits of brutality and death but of elysian villages. In one, a young man in a straw hat reclines peacefully in the shade of a tree playing a bamboo flute, his left leg cocked across his right knee. In an edenic valley below, cows graze, the grass is green and the sky is untroubled. And, if you look closely, you might think the flute player could just be Vann Nath. I asked him why he thought the Khmer Rouge treated the Cambodian people with such savagery. "I don't understand the reason completely," he answered. "Power, for sure. If we talk about people who are so cruel, it is because they care only about power. That is one of my conclusions." And were there still, I continued, ripples of that era that lapped at Cambodia today. "The Pol Pot regime has left a very bad legacy for us. First, he left memories of terrible cruelty. We must ask how could people do these things to each other. I think people don't think about that very much. And second, Pol Pot left so many orphans, people who now have no families at all. Pol Pot destroyed what was good in Cambodian culture. After we overthrew Pol Pot, this is all we have left.

"I want those killers to go to court and to be tried," he went on, "but my dream to bring these killers to trial has up to now not become true. Now it is up to the government. If the government tries them, then I will be happy. As for Pol Pot, several times I heard that he had died. I was not surprised when I heard finally he really did die. But when I finally heard, I regretted that he died. I myself wanted to see him stand trial. Now I cannot see him before the court."* And what of his family, I asked. "My two sons died in the village during the Pol Pot era," he said. "But when the Vietnamese came, I went back to Battambang and found my wife. Now we are in Phnom Penh, and three years ago we built this restaurant. My family runs the restaurant. As for my children now, I just tell them about my

---

* For several years the Cambodian government has vacillated over the question of bringing captured Khmer Rouge leaders to trial. Hun Sen, himself a former Khmer Rouge commander, has obstructed efforts by the United Nations to institute a tribunal to try these leaders for crimes against humanity. In a typical remark, he told a group of local reporters that "we should dig a hole and bury the past and look ahead to the twenty-first century with a clean slate."

life and the people I knew and the conditions during the Pol Pot era. I have told my children I was arrested for no reason, that I never knew why, that one day they sent me to Tuol Sleng without my understanding why. They still wonder why I am alive."

And what, I asked him, of the future for Cambodia. He thought about that for a few moments, tugged the hem of his white T-shirt to straighten it and crossed his arms. He leaned back in his wooden chair. "You know, there are people who want to close Tuol Sleng as a museum," he said. "Fewer and fewer Cambodians come to Tuol Sleng now. That makes me worry. The fewer people who come the less understanding there is. I want to keep it as a museum so that people don't forget. I went to Tuol Sleng last month, just to see again. My only goal is that if we are not careful this will become an ancient story, like history, not like reality. There are some people who think like me. In the Khmer language we say 'broken down,' that people's hearts and minds are broken down. Many people don't want to think about this. But as for me, I am not so sure there will never be conflict in Cambodia again. Maybe something like this could happen again. It's hard to say."

We sat for a while drinking coffee, and I talked with Vann Nath about his paintings, although he said he had not painted much recently. "I'm a bit tired," he told me. From the roof of his house where he keeps his oils and his easel we could see across the city to the west, a crenellated landscape of two- and three-story cement buildings crowned with the scrubby growth of television antennas. Below us, scooter horns squawked and cars and trucks answered back, calls of an urban aviary. I left Vann Nath, discomfited by his lingering anxieties, by his inability to believe that the worst was behind him and the people of Cambodia.

Perhaps it is this uncertainty about the future, the tingly sense of an unsettled present, that lures Westerners, particularly the French, to Phnom Penh, an expectation of fortune, a shiver of intangible danger, a colonial nostalgia. The riverfront, where the Tonle Sap River enters the Mekong, is lined with the architectural residue of French colonialism, what the French once called *France outre mer*, France abroad. Corner cafés serve espresso and baguette sandwiches, the French owner, invariably fat and in his graying years, shuffles about chatting up his regulars, taking orders, while his much younger Cambodian wife works the counter, remonstrating with a member of the staff over a splash of soup when she sets down a bowl. An Australian restaurant serves an eclecticism of cuisine, some German, some Italian—a reflection of Australia's own chaotic culinary traditions—washed down with buckets of Australian beer. And there is a swaggering, glittering Chinese restaurant, a place for food and later, if you wish, assignations with the lithesome girl of your choice. At night, there are the balding, girthsome white men heaving themselves out of white Toyota sedans, then reaching into the car, extending a hand to a well-powdered and lipsticked woman who alights in a tight skirt and needle-heeled slippers; sex tourism is alive and well in Phnom Penh.

So extensive is prostitution here, with young girls from the countryside being purchased for $400 or $500 by brokers from Phnom Penh, that a French NGO attempted to start a project to save these girls and school them in the skills needed for real jobs in the city. A training center was established, and girls were encouraged to leave the brothels and their pimps to learn how to sew or to run a small shop. Six months or so after the NGO started its work, the woman who led the project started to receive death threats from the mafia running the city's prostitution rackets. The woman moved a couple of times, but the threats continued. By then it was apparent that the powers behind the prostitution mafia were the army and the police, who themselves were raking in huge amounts of money from the sex trade. "They're all in it," a worker for another NGO told me. "The police, the army. They will never let anyone try to stop prostitution. And the government will do nothing. It is so corrupt. There is no law here, no law at all. This woman was attacking their source of money. She was a threat and so they would have killed her if she didn't leave the country. So she left the country." And so, prostitution thrives in Phnom Penh.

The central gathering place for Phnom Penh's foreign community is the Foreign Correspondents Club, a bar, restaurant and pool hall that has nothing to do with journalism but does operate out of one of the most magnificent French edifices along the waterfront. Gumdrop yellow, its soaring, beamed ceiling drips lazy ceiling fans, and fat-cushioned lounge chairs are gathered around low tables burdened with beer steins. Cambodian waiters bustle about taking orders, filling mugs, running food to the checkered-cloth-spread tables in the back overlooking the tiered roofs of the National Museum. The clientele is a crosshatch of Cambodia's foreign residents: There are the tall, lean, muscled deminers in T-shirts and crew cuts; the United Nations bureaucrats with their wives in painted toenails and sunglasses propped on their heads who begin every conversation, "Well, in Cambodia . . ."; a gaggle of unkempt stringers trying to flog stories to indifferent editors at newspapers in Sydney or London or Edinburgh, and the occasional clatch of embassy types, undisguised in their polished shoes and starched shirts. On the periphery hang the travelers who drift through Phnom Penh heading upcountry or to Vietnam or back to Bangkok; in their tie-dyes, sandals and mud-flecked backpacks, they are outsiders here.

From the balcony, I watched the slow bruising of the eastern sky, a purple-black swelling on the horizon mushrooming into gray breakers that rolled inexorably toward the city. And then, in an instant, amid a percussion of kettle drums and the crash of cymbals, a stampede of wind carried with it enveloping, swirling curtains of rain, drenching walls of water that avalanched across the Mekong and swept over the city. Scooter drivers huddled under palm trees—no protection from the deluge—and fishermen on the river churned their pirogues toward shore. A wood-wheeled ox cart slopped through the torrent, its driver flicking a shallow whip over the animals' flanks, a waterfall coursing from the brim of his straw hat. The atmosphere, warm and sticky, cools and dries. And then the storm passes, a faint tang of earth and cloud singeing the air.

Cambodia itself, for much of eight centuries, has been convulsed by storms, by the tempest of war, migrations, invasion and, in this century, ecological destruction, genocide and the decimation of the bonds that hold a society together. Violence stalks this country, and in Phnom Penh it is generally accepted that every household owns a gun, often an automatic assault rifle. Over the course of a week, the police blotter for the country is a chronicle of mayhem: a Phnom Penh vegetable seller stabbed to death by two friends; two policemen found shot in the head in Sihanoukville; a thirty-year-old garment worker stabbed in the face after an argument in her village; a surgeon at a local hospital kidnapped for $200,000 in ransom; a United Nations employee shot dead by someone who stole her motorbike; the gunning down of Piseth Pilika, Cambodia's most popular actress, in a suspected revenge killing by a jilted wife.

Among the most thoughtful people I encountered in Cambodia, one who has contemplated the country's condition for many years, was Christophe Peschoux, who worked for the United Nations human rights efforts in Phnom Penh. A slender, sandy-haired Frenchman who spent nearly a decade in the country, he was mercilessly unsentimental about Cambodia, dissecting it in chilling detail. His outspokenness and his unwillingness to temper his criticism of the government led ultimately to his recall to the United Nations offices in Geneva. Peschoux argued, however, that papering over Cambodia's realities—in the very real bureaucratic manner of the United Nations—did nothing to help the country other than bolster the continuing assault on Cambodians' human rights.

"Cambodia is coming from a society that was leveled to the ground to a need for complete reconstruction," he told me one rainy afternoon in his spartan office. "The country's infrastructure needs to be rebuilt—roads, electricity, schools, hospitals, everything. The country's human resources need to be rebuilt—doctors, nurses, teachers, lawyers, engineers, accountants. And, probably most important, there has to be a reconstruction of the social fabric, a rebuilding of relationships based on something other than fear and suspicion. I would say there is some progress on tackling infrastructure, not a lot, but some. But we are bumping into the fact that there are very few educated and trained people in all domains in this country. It will take a generation to have people trained in all domains, two generations to have a really well trained and educated workforce. I would say now there are maybe as many doctors as before the war, but these doctors after seven years of school have the level of knowledge of a nurse in the West. This will be a lingering problem for many years to come, and it will be an impediment to rebuilding the country."

I asked him for his candid appraisal of the government and how it was grappling with the country's immense difficulties. Peschoux was blunt: "The nature of this regime is an obstacle to the rebuilding of human resources and the use of those resources. There has been very little effort—very little effort—by the government on education. We are in an authoritarian political system, and if there is no impetus from the top, nothing gets done. You must remember, these people who rose to the top did so during war and did so by betraying, lying, trampling on people, through deceit. And they are uneducated, so they must rely on technicians who are better educated than they are, and those technicians are a threat, so they are not promoted to positions where they could put the country back on its feet. My impression of Hun Sen is that he is a political animal, a very good tactician. He has outsmarted everyone. He looks at everything in terms of an increase or diminution of his personal power."

This perception of the government as little more than an agglomeration of power and venality is widely held among both Cambodians and foreigners who are working in small-scale development projects across Cambodian society, whether it is work in villages to create small credit institutions, training of social workers, work with amputees or any of the hundreds of other efforts under way by non-governmental organizations. One Cambodian woman who talked to me at length about her work was scathing in her assessment of the Hun Sen regime. "The Cambodian government doesn't learn from the NGOs," she told me. They think we do good work because we have money. They don't realize that we get money because we do good work. I tell people that money is like gasoline. It's worthless unless you have a good machine to put it in. All this government wants is money."

But Peschoux pointed to what he saw as still deeper problems. "This is a country bathed in violence," he told me. "Not only from the war by the Americans but self-inflicted. And there is a growing gap between rich and poor—a gap that is very much the product of the utter corruption of the governing elite—which does nurture a continuing culture of violence. I think there is a risk that if these wrongs are not corrected and these conflicts are not integrated into the political life of the country, then it will go underground and give rise to extremist movements like the Khmer Rouge.

"A leadership rose to power with the idea of a revolutionary project. But the people didn't want a revolution, they wanted to go back to their fields and resume their lives. But that model was imposed, and the leadership discovered enemies at every corner. It's as if you have a size-eleven foot and you want to put it in a size-seven shoe. You cannot, but the Khmer Rouge began cutting off parts of its feet to fit into the shoe. It took the Khmer Rouge five years to take over and three years to self-destruct. The Khmer Rouge phenomenon is very Khmer. There have been these hundreds of years of destruction, depredations. The civilizational varnish has been a very thin layer because it hasn't enjoyed a sufficiently long period to deepen. And so the violence can surface very easily."[*]

---

[*] Scholars of Cambodia offer a range of interpretations for the savagery of the Khmer Rouge, including arguments that it was triggered by a fundamental racism that saw the victims of terror as somehow not being Cambodian, or that it was a reflection of the uncontrolled peasant rage against upper and urban classes. David Chandler, the leading scholar of Cambodia, suggests that the brutality, particularly as evidenced at Tuol Sleng, was "a Cambodian, Communist, imported, twentieth-century phenomenon. As an amalgam, it was unique."

In the weeks that followed, I thought a good deal about Peschoux's comments, thoughts that were riveted by a series of events that happened very quickly. A few days after speaking with Peschoux, the government announced that it had apprehended one of the most feared Khmer Rouge leaders, a guerrilla chief who was still operating out of an enclave along the Cambodian-Thai border. Ta Mok, known outside the Khmer Rouge as the Butcher, had for nearly two decades lived with impunity in Thailand and just inside Cambodia since the Vietnamese invasion of 1979. As part of the Khmer Rouge regime, Ta Mok earned a reputation for appalling brutality, for conducting widespread massacres and for playing a direct role in the torture and extermination of hundreds, if not thousands, of people at Tuol Sleng. The Thai government, for many years with the support of the United States, permitted Khmer Rouge leaders and troops to live and organize resistance against the Vietnamese on Cambodian territory. Even after the departure of the Vietnamese in 1988, Pol Pot and Ta Mok continued to live along the border. The news of Ta Mok's capture, however, galvanized Phnom Penh. For the first time since the defeat of the Khmer Rouge, one of its leaders, and one with an unmatched record of savagery, had been placed behind bars; before his capture, the Phnom Penh government had welcomed as defectors senior Khmer Rouge figures, no matter how bloody their hands, with open arms, and many Cambodians wondered whether any of the Khmer Rouge leaders would ever face trial.

And then, two months later in western Cambodia, Nate Thayer tracked down Kang Kech Ieu, known more commonly by his other name, Duch, the man who oversaw Tuol Sleng. When Thayer published his interview with Duch, Phnom Penh was again roiled by the prospect that the chief torturer of the Khmer Rouge had been identified. But Duch was not immediately arrested.

Still recognizable from his high cheekbones and protruding front teeth, Duch had abandoned his murderous ways, claimed to have converted to Christianity and was working with a NGO called the American Refugee Committee. Then fifty-six, Duch confessed his past to Thayer. "I feel very sorry about the killings and the past," he said. "I wanted to be a good Communist. Now, in the second half of my life, I want to serve God by doing God's work to help people." Again, Phnom Penh was confronted with the sudden appearance of a man who had been at the center of the Khmer Rouge's genocide. But Hun Sen, who was making all decisions about the future of the Khmer Rouge, dithered. In Battambang, where

Duch had been discovered, Western Christian evangelical missionaries who knew him began championing the mass murderer as a born-again Christian who should be forgiven. Daniel Walter, a missionary for the Seventh-Day Adventists, was among the loudest voicing that view. "Viewing it from a Christian viewpoint, when a person shows a complete repentance and shows remorse, that is enough," Walters was quoted as saying in the Phnom Penh papers. For Cambodians who endured the Khmer Rouge, it was not enough.

Finally, several days later, the police arrested Duch and imprisoned him in the capital. In his youth, Duch was first educated under a program sponsored by the U.S. Agency for International Development and one of his teachers at that time was a man named Michael Vickery, who went on to become a well-known scholar of modern Cambodian politics. Duch attended high school in Phnom Penh and scored second on a national examination. Sometime in the 1960s, he joined the underground Communist party even as he was working as a teacher of mathematics at the Pedagogical Institute in the capital. He joined the Khmer Rouge guerrillas in the jungle after being released from jail for leading a riot and very quickly emerged as the movement's chief interrogator. In the three years and eight months that the Khmer Rouge ruled Cambodia, Duch worked in Tuol Sleng, overseeing the torture and execution of prisoners. David Chandler, who has studied in depth the captured files from Tuol Sleng, described its commandant as follows: "His experiences and instincts from teaching were helpful. He was used to keeping records, ferreting out answers to problems, earning respect and disciplining groups of people." Duch was not only a master of the bureaucracy of death, a keeper of files and photographs, a prodigious composer of reports chronicling torture and murder, but in the end, Tuol Sleng's very angel of death. It was his signature that sent each of the people who entered Tuol Sleng to the grave.

I returned to Czechoslovakia Street after Duch's arrest, to see what Vann Nath thought of the flurry of events. When I arrived, he was on his way out to see some friends. He stopped for a moment, though, to share a final word. "Of course this is good," Vann Nath insisted. "Pol Pot is dead, and many Khmer Rouge leaders have been pardoned by Hun Sen. But Ta Mok and Duch should definitely go to trial. Definitely. I want to see Duch spend his life in prison. He is a murderer of the Cambodian people." I watched Vann Nath climb slowly onto the back of a motor scooter, and wondered if now, somehow, there was hope that he would find some sense of repose.

About thirty miles southwest from Phnom Penh down Route 4, a
healthy strip of asphalt laid down by the Americans three decades
ago that now runs past garment factories thrown up by Taiwanese
investors, a petite, dark brown woman with a brioche-sized bun of black
hair shot through with strands of silver-gray hopped off her motorbike.
She wore a traditional long black sarong, a pale blue blouse and around
her neck on a black cord hung a plain wooden cross. "I'm Sister Ath," she
said, shaking my hand. I had driven down to a place called Bayk Chhann
because I had heard that Sister Ath, a member of the Society of Provi-
dent Sisters, was deeply involved in the reconstruction of village society
in this part of Cambodia. I was also intrigued because she was working in
cooperation with a couple of Jesuit priests who were militantly anti-
evangelical in the work they did, unlike the rash of Protestant missionaries who were spending as much time trying to convert people as help
them. I was impressed by the respect they had for the Cambodian people's
own beliefs.

Every day, Sister Ath, who is Cambodian herself, climbs onto her
motorbike and spurts down the dirt tracks that weave through the sparse
trees, heading to one of the 215 villages in which she works. "We're trying
to do very basic rural development," she explained during the course of
one of her seemingly endless days. "In the beginning when I started, this
was in 1991, I just went to villages and started to ask people about the
problems they had. Little by little I realized there was a lack of water for
agriculture, there was a lack of capital for investment, that there was very
little land. There were lots of widows, women separated from their husbands who were killed or somehow died. Many men died during Pol Pot's
time. I would say sixty percent of the women are widows.

"You must remember," she went on, "everybody had to leave their own
village and go somewhere else where they were completely disoriented.
Everything belonged to the party. You were just a number. So we tried to
answer a need. So the first thing we did was to start digging wells, then a
community pond for raising fish and for irrigation. We made dikes and dug
channels and made roads and culverts. To do this we got rice from the
World Food Program as part of a food-for-work project. When people
worked digging we gave them rice. Before this, under the Communist system during the Vietnamese occupation, people didn't get anything for
their work. This was how we got started."

Here, the villages visited by Sister Ath, more often than not, are neat
arrangements of wood-plank houses, the packed-dirt central squares are
swept clean, and the paths between huts are trim and free from discarded
coconut shells or palm fronds that litter the desolate, thatched-hut ham-
lets of northern Cambodia. I remarked on this to her and she laughed.
"When I came to the villages, I said we could use some help with
hygiene," she told me. "I said, we start with twelve women. I want to see
your village cleaner. I want to see people more polite. We need clean
water. So after three months, we began to see a kind of change. Before
this, people ran away, children didn't say hello. This has all changed." I
asked Sister Ath, who was about five feet tall, how she managed to exert
such influence given her diminutive stature, the fact that she was a
woman and that she was a Catholic nun, a pretty rare sight in Cambodia.
She laughed again. "Remember, in the beginning we had the rice to give
out for work. And we never tried to tell people they had to worship my
God. Everybody should be a good Buddhist. And I think people trusted
me because I listened to them and we tried to help them see that there
were solutions to the problems they faced."

Little by little, year after year, Sister Ath and the people she gathered
around her began to change the economic structure of village life. Where
before, rice merchant loan sharks lent out rice in lean times at 100 percent interest, Sister Ath persuaded villagers to start a rice bank. Rice was
contributed by all the villagers to a central silo and drawn out in times of
need at 10 percent interest. "Of course, the people who would lend rice
here were very unhappy about this," she said as she padded down a path to
see a village chief. "We always have to think about what Cambodia has
experienced," she went on. "When people wanted to do something
together they were not very confident. It was hard to get people to do
things together because they have no confidence in each other, they
didn't trust each other. No one ever wants to hear the word *politics*. And
no one wants to hear the word *meeting*. In Pol Pot time, meetings were for
politics. When we started one rice bank and it was effective, the bamboo
telephone is very quick, so in the second year we got a lot of requests to set
up rice banks in other villages."

Some sixty thousand people live in the 215 villages where Sister Ath
works together with a loose group of fifty-two local women. Already,
though, the consequences of economic growth in Phnom Penh are filtering into the villages. As we walked through the village, a couple of young
women, girls really, hurried down a path. Both wore bright sarongs and

blouses seemingly dipped in the juice of tropical fruit. And both wore makeup, their lips bloodred and their cheeks powdered a shade paler than their cocoa-toned arms. "We are seeing this," Sister Ath said. "A lot of girls are going to work in the factories now. So the girls now wear makeup and can dress well. And the boys go to the land. It just starts, and we don't know what these changes will mean for the villages." One of her treasured credit schemes—a cow and oxen bank where villagers could buy a cow on credit and repay it by returning a calf—was falling victim to the burst of inflation that was ballooning prices throughout the region. "We just can't do it anymore," she said. "It's just too expensive for us. We have to try to figure something else out." Over seven years, 1,327 families bought and shared 823 oxen as part of the cow and oxen bank.

Sister Ath entered the open door of an unpainted wooden house to see the village chief, what is called here the *prathienphuum*, and I strolled through the village waiting for her. Beyond the scattered houses, small fields checkered the land, smaller than paddies in western China. Behind a water buffalo, a bare-chested man, a blue-and-white cotton *krama* wrapped around his waist and tucked between his legs, wrestled with a wood-framed plow, urging the beast on. At a village hand-pump well, a couple of women filled aluminum pots and chatted together. As the sun headed west, it was trailed by a frought armada of dark clouds that promised another early evening tempest. Sister Ath hurried from the chief's house and we headed back to her office.

"All these chiefs are chosen by the government," she said, settling down before a cup of milky tea. "I've only seen one place where the village got rid of the chief and put a woman in charge. So we really don't want these chiefs to be involved in our projects, just the people of the village themselves, and they decide who runs the rice bank or the cow bank. But still, I would say that even now many people do not have enough to eat."

She stared off across the fields at the gathering storm. "You know," she said, "we are in the world of human beings, so we have problems."

It was time to begin my journey south, to head to Vietnam and the Mekong's boastful delta, where the Mekong last gasps and where, in some measure, America's history was wrought. The Vietnamese embassy in Phnom Penh was being obstreperous and insisted that my visa was not

valid for entry into the country by boat. I knew that cranky wooden passenger boats headed downriver every day, carrying Cambodians and Vietnamese trading women into the delta, to the innumerable towns and
villages woven together by a mesh of canals and channels, bringing dried
fish and consumer goods not available in Vietnam. After a couple of days
of hunting, I found a boatman who said he would take me to the border, a
trip that would run four hours or so.

Beneath dawn's magenta-pigmented sky we set out, a sturdy outboard
propelling the blue-and-white wooden craft easily through the thick currents. The boat driver and his son sat in the back, smoking Marlboros
from a newly opened package. A small freighter, its corroded hull spattled
by reddish-black sores, limped by in a desultory sulk. A couple of hours
from Phnom Penh we churned past a place once called Neak Luong. On
the afternoon of August 6, 1973, just days before all American bombing in
southeast Asia was to cease, a crewman on an American B-52 bomber
neglected to adjust a switch on a panel in the airplane and dropped its
entire load of bombs on Neak Luong, leaving a mile of utter devastation
right through the center of town and killing nearly 150 people. Two years
later, the Khmer Rouge surrounded the town and launched a bloody and
fiery assault on its starving people, wiping out more than four thousand
defenders and hundreds of civilians, an assault that led to the fall of
Phnom Penh to Pol Pot's forces. Today, this place is known as Phumi
Banam.

Our boat continued south toward the border. The sun climbed above us
and forced me under the shade of the boat's tiny canopy. I was unsure what
awaited me at the border, as indeed was the boatman, who had hinted that
I would not be allowed to cross. I was distressed about that possibility, but
he was evidently cheered by the prospect of my failure, for it meant a double fare at foreigner rates for him. For me it would mean a lengthy detour.
After two more hours we approached the border and swung toward a village on the shore where a Cambodian flag, the white silhouette of Angkor
Wat framed on a field of red and blue, struggled to loose itself from its steel
stanchion. I clambered out of the boat; the boatman followed but headed
off into the market, to look for fruit, he said. I entered the cement hut that
served as a border post and plopped my passport on the desk, pointed
south and mouthed the word "Vietnam." A drowsy official in a dark green
shirt with epaulets and an army patch on his shoulder leafed through my
passport, closed it and slid it back across the desk. He raised his eyes to me.

"No," he said. "No Vietnam." "What do you mean, no Vietnam?" I asked. He fiddled with his rubber stamps. "No Vietnam. No Vietnam."

I briefly contemplated passing him a few dollars but decided against it and left the hut. I found the boat driver standing with a satchel of oranges and a clear plastic bag of nuts. He shook his head. "No foreigns," he said. "No Vietnam." I was beyond argument, weary and resigned. We returned to the boat and turned north, back to Phnom Penh, pushed gently by the tide from the South China Sea.

As we ran north I found myself absorbed less by the river and more by reflections on the fate of Cambodia. Although two decades had passed since the holocaust of the Pol Pot era, almost every conversation I had had pivoted on memory and mourning. Official efforts to bury the past, whether out of self-interest or a genuine determination to start afresh, were belied by what seemed a broad popular desire for some degree of accountability. But whether a handful of trials would expiate the demons that still lurked here, I was not so sure. Cambodians, cursed in the twentieth century with a succession of monstrous governments, were subjugated yet again with an authoritarian regime of venal megalomaniacs. How would it ever be possible for Cambodia to develop the institutions that would lead to reasonable politics and governance? From where would the resources come, human and material, to haul the country from a poverty so intense to a better future when anxieties over a reversion to the extremism and savagery of the past would no longer be so vivid? People like Sister Ath offer that glimmer of hope. But then I recalled her final words to me. "I don't know how long we'll be able to stay here," she said from the simple compound where she worked, where amputees were trained as sculptors or engine mechanics, and where the Jesuit community lived. "Some government officials really want this land. They say it is very valuable."

I drove out to Pochentong Airport and took a plane to Ho Chi Minh City, what they used to call Saigon.

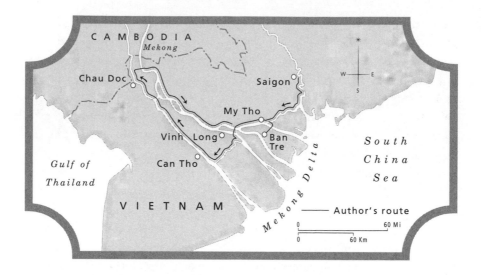

Nine

Nine Dragons

Oh, hey, the Mekong River is a nine-headed dragon
Love is sometimes muddy, sometimes clear
Oh, I love you, oh, I love the girl with the rosy cheeks
I love you, oh, because you are virtuous
Oh, hey, I love you because you were born into a scholarly family.

—A MEKONG DELTA LULLABY

Vietnam Airlines flight 812, a squeaky-clean white-and-blue Airbus, banked slowly and purred down toward Ton Son Nhut Airport, for more than a decade the major airbase for the American military efforts in Vietnam. As someone for whom the war was a daily, vivid event during my college years, landing at Ton Son Nhut summoned up images of the final days of the American presence as North Vietnamese troops moved relentlessly toward Saigon. A quarter of a century earlier, on April 28, 1975, North Vietnamese troops began a terrifying final mortar barrage of the airfield, an attack that ended the desperate shuttle of lumbering C-130 cargo planes ferrying escaping southerners out of the country, a country that had two days of life left.

But as the plane schussed onto the runway under graying skies, surrounded by paddy fields that glinted like polished zinc, there were no visible scars of that conflict; the glass-walled terminal building was new and as many arriving passengers carried briefcases as backpacks. Though Hanoi's victory over the south gave it the right to rechristen the defeated capital, and the name they chose—Ho Chi Minh City—memorialized the founder of the Communist state, most people still called their town by its old name, Saigon. My taxi driver, a skilled flim-flam artist, hollered "Welcome to Saigon" before trying to foist a series of cut-rate hotels, seedy bars and working girls on me, all during the scant fifteen-minute dash into center city.

Disheartened by not being able to float over the border into Vietnam, what I had hoped would be an appropriate start to the final leg of my journey, I was intent on heading immediately into the Mekong Delta, what the Vietnamese call Cuu Long, or Nine Dragons, for the mythologized nine mouths of the Mekong. I had heard that there might be puddle jumpers or charter flights into one of the delta towns, but I could find no one at the airport who had heard similar things. So I checked into a grand old hotel overlooking the Saigon River, the aptly named Hotel Majestic, an edifice out of the first arrondissement, a chalk white cake studded with wrought-iron balustrades on the balconies and an arched, corner entrance bathed by a shimmering chandelier, a 1929 temple of French hotel architecture. Across the riverfront park, I spied a signboard for the Green Line, a ferry service that ran hydrofoils into the delta every day. I bought a ticket for the early morning boat and then set out to savor Saigon's streets.

Over the last decade, I have visited this southern city frequently and at first wanted little more than a good meal and sufficient rest for the journey through the delta. Now, I reflected as well on the breadth of the journey I had taken so far. Nowhere in Laos or Cambodia had the hand of foreign invaders and intruders not been visible. Whether the French, or the Americans who followed them, it was the foreign presence that had largely underpinned the course of events in twentieth-century southeast

Asia, mostly for the worse. Both the Pathet Lao and the Khmer Rouge found fertile ground in appeals to nationalism, to resistance against colonialism and the undeclared American war over their lands. And while both movements emerged victorious, they proceeded to assault their own cultures in a wholesale manner seen only in China, in Mao Zedong's vandalization of China's past. I left Laos more pessimistic than I did Cambodia, although neither country seemed likely to emerge from their own darknesses anytime soon. I hoped that my travels through Vietnam's Mekong Delta, although just a fragment of the country itself, would reinstill some optimism in my view of the region.

Though I had been traveling the better part of a year by now, I found myself invigorated by returning to Vietnam. The wrenching emotions of Cambodia that left me exhausted at times had dissipated in a flurry of expectations. Since the mid-1960s, I have steadily read both fiction about, and the history of, Vietnam, from the atmospheric moodiness of Marguerite Duras's novels to Neil Sheehan's darkly written account of U.S. Army colonel John Paul Vann and the American experience in Vietnam. I brought with me as well my own history of antiwar activism. So there was a rush of intellectual passion mixed with the emotions stirred by memories of the effects the Vietnam conflict had on my generation. In a strange way I felt a personal attachment to Vietnam.

Saigon becomes more alluring each time I visit. An 1899 opera house, also of French provenance, has been restored, a beige and taupe palace like a fresh mint regally enthroned at the heart of what used to be rue Catinat (and was renamed Tu Do, or Freedom Street, by the South Vietnamese, and now is called Dong Khoi, or Uprising Street), a musical theater appropriate for what had been the French capital of Cochin China. Other colonial structures abound, and some, like Saigon's City Hall, glow a radiant gold in the early evening silky gray mist. But what is equally striking is the procession of glass-walled office towers that have sprouted like the giant kapok trees one can still see in Saigon's parks. Dazzled by visions of an untamed and virgin economic landscape, multinational companies stormed into Vietnam in the early 1990s, convinced that the booming economies of southeast Asia were the template for a rapid transformation of Vietnam's stodgy Socialist economic planning. Oil drillers, car manufacturers, computer assemblers, sneaker makers, bankers—all rushed through Ton Son Nhut Airport clutching investment plans, construction diagrams, marketing strategies, all intended to pluck Vietnam from its somnambulence and not coincidentally get rich in the process. But Vietnam was not so easily budged. Bureaucrats remained obdurate and enigmatic. Plans withered like unplucked grapes. Undeterred, though, the multinationals remained, as they put it, "upbeat," although their jargon-filled pronouncements—"this is a win-win for everybody" being a favorite—were fraying discernibly at the edges. Still, buildings went up, their glass walls were polished and foreign executives moved in, settling into cushy chairs behind big wooden desks. And they waited for the deals, for the sales, for the factories. And they waited.

The great boom never happened. The executives spent more time in bars, or perfecting their chip shots. Five-star hotels were halted in mid-construction, leaving rusting, cartilaginous remains behind sagging plywood walls. And the hotels that had been finished emptied. When I checked into the Majestic, the lobby was empty, an air of desolation echoing across the polished marble floors. The posted room rates started at $150 a night, and moved quickly higher, but when I asked for the lowest rate available, a desk clerk asked me, "Is sixty dollars a night too much?" Vietnam has stalled, sputtering to a stop on the shoulder of Asia's economic highway. Up north, in Hanoi, Communist leaders tear their hair out over the conflicting demands of ideological purity and the need to embrace an economic strategy that can drag the country from its mire of poverty.* Roughly put, the Communist party is still controlled by old men who accord Marx and Lenin a kind of biblical reverence, regardless of the consequences for the Vietnamese people. The blindingly apparent success of economies like those of Thailand, Malaysia, Korea and Taiwan poses for these Communist dinosaurs not challenges and opportunity, but a threat to their faith. And so, while the dithering continues, Vietnam languishes. A disconsolate Singaporean businessman summed up the situation to me with undiplomatic bluntness: "The economy is a catastrophe."

American culture, the pulse of rock 'n' roll, blue jeans, long hair, just looking cool, never caught on in Hanoi, but fifteen years of American

---

* Vietnam, with 78 million people, is among the most densely populated countries on Earth. It is also among the poorest, with a per capita gross national product of $330 per year, poorer than Ghana, Albania, Bangladesh and Syria. More than half the population lives below the poverty line, a line Vietnam itself establishes. Still, unlike most countries in Africa, 95 percent of primary-school-age children are enrolled in schools, and literacy remains high.

presence in Saigon planted an indelible, and evidently ineradicable, fever here.* In a country that boasts its Communist credentials, the cafés and bars burst with hip young women and men cruising for dates. The latest American rock music roars from open windows. Boys in jeans, tight T-shirts and wraparound sunglasses (even at night) rocket by on motor-bikes, heading to the next club. And even the postcard sellers, the flocks of children who hawk their cheap card packs to tourists, display an ease with English argot. "Buy a postcard?" they ask, and when you shake your head, they shoot back, "Why not?" In an effort to purify the country, Communist hacks tried to ban the use of English on restaurant signboards and billboards—only Vietnamese, they insisted—but it never worked, and English is back with a vengeance. On the battlefield America lost the war, but on Saigon's streets they can't wait for Uncle Sam to return.

Aware that I was in for weeks of rustic delta cuisine, even if the food in Vietnam is perhaps the best in southeast Asia, I trundled down a few alleyways toward a recommended restaurant, a glamorous affair with silk-clad waitresses, a foreign maître d' and a wine list that would make a Parisian bistro blush. I ate perfect scallops sautéed in garlic and served on the shell; light, crisp *cha gio*, a sort of dainty egg roll; succulent beef rolls with ginger and vinegar; delicately fried wedges of bean curd with rock salt and garlic; and a fragrant steamed squid. It was a meal of miraculous qualities, a feast that obscured the previous months' privations. A bottle of Gevrey-Chambertin did nothing to inhibit the experience. Afterward, content as I have ever been after a meal, I wandered over to one of Saigon's storefront Internet shops, small businesses that let foreigners check their e-mail but that mostly train young Vietnamese in the myster-ies of the global information network. It is a business that skirts the edges of legality, with party bureaucrats periodically announcing crackdowns on the Internet to "correct mistakes and bias," or to block "negative" infor-mation. Prices demanded by the government for access to the Internet are

---

* A month or so after its victory, the new rulers of South Vietnam published an edito-rial lambasting American culture. "Every regime has its own way of life," the *Saigon Giai Phong* wrote. "American neo-colonialism produced, nourished, and left behind a bar-barous, American-style way of life. . . . This way of life has been the law for several years in the regions controlled by the Americans and the puppets, and has destroyed the fine tradi-tions of our culture." Twenty-five years later much of Saigon lusts after this "barbarous, American-style way of life."

steep, high enough to keep most Vietnamese unconnected, but somehow the little Web shops are thriving, with every computer busy until well into the night.

Also busy, thunderously so, was a longtime nightclub named after the Francis Ford Coppola Vietnam War epic, *Apocalypse Now*. Pool players were stacked around a bank of tables like sharks in *The Hustler*, the bar was eight-deep with Vietnamese and foreigners, all clutching icy bottles of Heineken or the local 333 Beer, and on the dance floor beneath rotating mirrored balls and strobe lights firing like antiaircraft batteries, young people in skanty outfits steamed the room. The wail and screech of Jimi Hendrix's guitar peeled the paint off the walls, and young women, willowy, long-haired, with alpine cheekbones and eyes that would make Buddha weep, sidle up and whisper, "Can I be your girlfriend?" In a studded leather vest, a beefy American the size of a television wrestler with a hurricane of gray hair and a Santa's beard spun and whirled on the dance floor, hanging on to his beer bottle like a talisman; he pounded around in his cowboy boots, sending the slighter Vietnamese dancers scurrying and giggling from the path of this frenzied barbarian, this apparition of American looniness. It was all in a night's fun. It was America, America without war, an American dream.

I woke as dawn's light creased the horizon. Already the Saigon River was swirling with water traffic, slow and not so slow, the hulking and the nimble, all still silhouettes against the morning's glaze. Along the riverfront, joggers in black socks and rubber shoes bounced along, stealing through dawn's coolness, cheating the incoming avalanche of heat and humidity. Three-wheeled bicycle rickshaws, the *cyclopousses*, floated by, their pilots languidly pedaling before the morning rush. Downriver, a ship's basso horn trumpeted its arrival. I hoisted my pack and dodged cars and buses across the boulevard tracing the river and headed for the Green Line. The streetlights blinked off.

Lashed to the dock was a white aluminum hydrofoil, and passengers hurried onto the dock for the ride into the Mekong Delta. Almost exactly the size of the Netherlands and with roughly the same population, not to mention a similar abundance of water, the delta historically has been Vietnam's rice basket. It is the place where the Mekong River, after traveling nearly three thousand miles, swells its chest and splays its might in nine powerful sinews—fat, wide rivers in their own right, woven together by a web of canals and channels, rivulets and water alleys. Some 2 million years ago, a first ancient delta was formed, what geologists call a Pleistocene Delta, which, in turn, was followed by periods of alluvial sedimentation, a process that led to the basic structure of the Mekong Delta today. As recently as 11,500 years ago, the sea was substantially higher around the delta than it is now, and only within the last few millennia have sea levels subsided to the waters familiar to today's delta residents. At the end of the thirteenth century, contemporary writers spoke of a region of dense forests—terrain that has been completely transformed in the seven centuries since—a place, as one writer noted, "where herds of hundreds and thousands of wild buffaloes are found." Still, the delta was not overrun by Vietnamese until the fifteenth century, and it was not until the eighteenth century that major canal building began. And with the canals came villages, and with the villages came the felling of the forests and the rise of agriculture, an abundance of rice as well as a myriad of other crops—beans, corn, potatoes, melons, sugarcane; that and more is grown in the delta today.

At 7:30 sharp, the hydrofoil eased from the dock, wheeled slowly about and began creeping south, feeling its way through the clotting riverine traffic. Two hippolike, pot-bellied, wooden grain boats with upswept prows daubed with large, unblinking red and black eyes and rudders worthy of a Viking warship waddled upriver to a Saigon grain silo. Wooden canoes skittled across the river, skulled rapidly, and seemingly effortlessly, by women in *non la*, the woven-palm-leaf conical hats worn throughout rural Vietnam. Freighters from Thailand and Bangladesh with names like *Challenger* and *Hub Trader*, their flanks powdered in cinnamon rust, were roped to river docks as two slate gray Japanese destroyers arrived for a port call, their crews picket-fenced along the port side in their snow white uniforms. After ten minutes or so, the hydrofoil accelerated, rising on its submerged wings until it was ripping down the river, its klaxon hammering the riverbanks and sending stern-poled sampans fleeing for shelter. Constructed in the old Soviet Union—all the labels on the vessel were in Cyrillic—the boat more than made up in sturdiness for its abundant lack of elegance.

As we hurtled downriver, capillaries of manmade canals and natural rivulets snaked away from the river, toward delta villages and towns. Then abruptly we banked to starboard and roared down a canal, the boat's horn a deafening battering ram. Waterfront villages, strings of huts banged together from unpainted boards and roofs of corrugated metal, leaned over the brown water. Wooden grain boats with distended bellies plied the canals, either low in the water with mountainous loads of rice or bobbing almost like rubber duckies atop the surface returning from the granary; these are the trucks of the delta highways, the long-distance haulers bearing both the captain and his family in quaint wood houses propped high on the stern, all hung with lines of laundry and trimmed in potted plants. Phalanxes of palm trees line the banks, hiding beehive-shaped brick kilns spewing black smoke from conical chimneys or village sugar-palm refineries.

And then we were on the Mekong, or rather one of the Mekong's Nine Dragons, and the water blinked from the canal's brown to a roof-tile red, a clay-red boulevard more than a half mile wide spackled with pirogues and fishing trawlers, dispirited freighters and the ubiquitous, grain-laden big bellies. Our captain roared across the river, occasionally touching speeds of forty miles an hour, and then yanked the wheel hard to port to dodge down yet another canal. Then, as suddenly, we ground to a halt, the boat slipping from its subsurface wings and settling onto the water. The engines were heaved into reverse, and we began backing slowly down the canal, like a circus elephant angling out of its trailer. I wondered if we were lost but dismissed that thought; a map on the cabin wall was clear enough about our route. And then we clunked into forward gear and in seconds we were once again flying down the canal. Later, after three or four more of these procedures, I determined that the vessel's propeller system was not designed to cope with the floating vegetation of the Delta, much of it from soggy shoreline mangroves and lotus plants. Again, it was apparent that sturdy Russian design did not necessarily mean unalloyed nautical success in tropical waters.

We swept past a delta cowgirl, a young, conical-hatted woman paddling a skiff around a flock of white ducks, herding them onto the shore into a wire pen. Steel barges stacked with crates of beer, sacks of cement and piles of lumber were being towed upriver by straining tugs. Four hours later we turned up yet another spindle of the Mekong and tacked toward shore, toward a flourish of a town ruffling the riverbank, the town of Can Tho. It is the largest of the delta towns, now a major administrative center for the region, and during the war it was a center of American military

activity. As the South Vietnamese regime was collapsing in on itself during those final days in April 1975, a victim of its own corruption, greed,
nepotism, megalomania and palace politics, the last American consul
general to serve here, Francis McNamara, frantically organized a flotilla of
tempermental landing craft to spirit the few remaining Americans and
their local Vietnamese employees to the safety of the Seventh Fleet lurk-
ing off Vietnam's coast. With a helmet liner clamped on his head emblazoned COMMODORE CAN THO YACHT CLUB, McNamara piloted his
two landing craft past anxiety-ridden South Vietnamese patrol boats and
through a final ambush by local guerrillas—the "last shots fired against the
enemy," a Marine on board said later—and steamed into the South China
Sea and safety. For Vietnamese desperate to flee the triumphal victory of
communism, Can Tho became for a time a departure port, the town from
where fishing boats and the big bellies, as well as smaller, unseaworthy
sampans, chugged out to sea and refuge. Over the years, tens of thousands
of Vietnamese fled Communist rule by boat, earning the appellation "boat
people," ending up in Malaysia, the Philippines, Singapore and Hong
Kong; after more than a quarter of a century, the last fourteen hundred
boat people in Hong Kong, unable to find asylum anywhere else in the

A floating market at Can Tho, in the Mekong
Delta, in Vietnam, with delta water ferries
moored on the right

world, were finally accorded residency there in early 2000 and, at last, a shaky sense of permanence.

At Can Tho's wharf there are no refugees assembling anymore; those days are long over. Instead, the docks and jetties are crowded with skiffs filled with bananas, oranges, longan, custard apples, coconuts, rice, spices, mushrooms and fish in a vast floating market, the women of the market boats, all in the de rigueur *non la*, bargaining over prices, weighing their produce, all the time bobbing in the wakes of the upriver ferries that ply by. At the far end of town, a ten-foot-tall silvery statue of Bak Ho, Uncle Ho Chi Minh, Vietnam's version of George Washington, peers south, his right hand raised in salute. Alleys of commerce stretch away from the port, with open-air shops seemingly sandbagged with cartons of Sony and Panasonic televisions, others bushy with racks of Japanese watches, sunglasses and watches from Thailand, and endless markets of spices, fish sauces, dried squid, sacks of rice and dried shrimp the size of collar buttons, and even a shop selling, of all things, exercise treadmills.

In rural Vietnam, in the delta particularly, there is a traditional oral poetry called *ve*, lyrics sung to an even, sprinting beat that has been all but lost in a younger generation more interested in pop songs. But the older generation still holds to the *ve*, both for its roots deep in the culture and its witty play on words. A well-known *ve* about markets in the delta,

A market lady at Can Tho's floating market

markets like that in Can Tho, runs a bit like this, with the puns added in
brackets:

> *Doing business is good at Ben Thanh* [*thanh:* successful]
> *You can't tie something well at Ben Suc* [*suc:* to unravel]
> *When you push someone, that's Ca Mau* [*mau:* to go faster]
> *In the country there's a lot of sedge at Lach market* [*lach:* sedge]
> *Selling pots, selling pots, that's at Tri Ton* [*ton:* pot-making tin]
> *Studying well is at Truong Binh* [*truong:* school; *binh:* clever]
> *The drum beats suddenly at Chau Doc.* . . .

Older village people still sing these poems, but the young kids in Ellesse
hats have no memory of them. In Can Tho's cafés, older men linger over
Vietnamese coffee, a concoction of thick coffee strained through an aluminum filtering contraption into a glass a quarter filled with condensed
milk and then poured into a beer mug of ice; it tastes a bit like a coffee
milkshake and does wonders in the swelter of the day. And toward
evening the riverfront promenade fills with the sauntering sashay of
strollers, couples holding hands, men in deep conversations, giggling
schoolgirls peeking at young boys kicking soccer balls, and all attired in
pajamas; not the black pajamas of Vietcong guerrillas, but pj's with bunny
rabbits and pink bears on them, yellow-striped numbers with scarlet piping, white ones with plate-sized blue dots. It is as if a big slumber party has
broken up and everyone has decided it is time for their evening constitu-
tionals.

I stopped in Café Bière to watch the world go by, and the young man
who placed my icy bottle of 333 on the table started practicing his English
on me. "I'm at the university studying English," he told me. "I have an
older brother who is in Long Beach in California. He left Vietnam ten
years ago. I hope next year I can go to Long Beach, too." As he talked, the
Sony boom box at the bar was belting out Don MacLean's "American
Pie." I asked my waiter why he wanted to go to California. "No future
here," he said. "Nothing to do here. Vietnam is very poor. America is
great. America is the best country in the world."

In all Vietnam, Saigon and the delta were the most resistant to the
advent of Communist rule. American influence in Saigon was profound,
but in the delta, the indigenous religions of Hoa Hao and Cao Dai carried
with them a deep undercurrent of anticommunism. And when, in the

years after 1975, Hanoi embarked on the colossal, and ultimately futile, effort to collectivize agriculture as part of its adherence to Socialist ortho-doxy, resistance among farmers in the delta was ferocious; the north never really succeeded in imposing its will on farmers here, and today farmers till their own land. Even so, I marveled at my waiter's earnest conviction that life was inevitably better on the eastern shore of the Pacific Ocean. I asked him whether he knew how hard life could be for new immigrants to the United States. "Yes," he said. "I know I must work very hard. But American people are free people. Vietnamese people are not free people."

Later, as I wandered the markets, I stopped to buy a new belt, mine having eroded under the onslaught of heat, water and an unspeakable fungus. A stalk of a man, bespectacled, crew cut and crisp in a pressed white short-sleeved shirt, spun a rack of leather belts for me. As I contem-plated my choices, I asked him about life in Can Tho. "Well, you can see this is a big commercial center," he explained, settling onto a stool amid piles of cheap handbags, racks of shirts of artificial fibers and a case of black leather wallets with plastic windows for the national identity card. "People come from all over the delta here to buy and sell things. Farmers bring food here to sell, fruit. You can get any kind of fruit here." I chose an innocuous but reasonably sturdy cinch and handed over 18,000 dong, about $1.30. The salesman introduced himself as Ouang Mu Nghu as he punched holes in the leather, but he spoke Chinese so I presumed he was ethnically Chinese. "Yes," he told me. "My parents came here in the 1940s, from Dongguan in Guangdong Province. That was during the war, World War II." I told him that I had thought that most Sino-Vietnamese had fled after 1975. "Yes, that's true," he said. "But there are still many who stayed. One problem for the Chinese here is that many Vietnamese don't like Chinese.* But I'd say things are better now. Things are all

---

* After its victory, Hanoi gradually began a purge of ethnic Chinese from the Commu-nist party and from administrative positions in the south, even purging Chinese who had fought with the Vietcong for many years. As a result of this growing ethnic discrimination and hostility, many ethnic Chinese either fled or were deported to China or the West. Even ethnic Vietnamese who were members of the National Liberation Front, the formal name of the Vietcong, were quickly sidelined as virtually all government jobs, down to the level of engineers and hotel managers, were handed to northern cadres; southerners called this *Dao Chinh*, "the coup." The result is a widespread bitterness in the south toward the north, even among those who originally supported the defeat of the South Vietnamese regime.

right." And what about life here, after twenty-five years of Communist rule? He rubbed his chin and answered, "Well, I'd say that it isn't so bad here now. For my family, we're not rich but we're not poor either. We can send our kids for half the day to Chinese school and half the day to Vietnamese school. I don't talk about politics because there's no point. The government makes the political decisions, and we just run our business."

In the morning, the distinct scent of salt water washed my nostrils for the first time. From just downriver, the tides of the South China Sea were pushing up the delta, infiltrating the estuaries with seawater, prodding boats on, tipping mooring buoys unexpectedly upriver. Across from Can Tho town, a clutter of shacks, the homes of boatmen and fishermen, perched on stilts. Amid the shanties, though, a handful of three-story pink and white and lemon houses protruded like new dentures, cement-walled buildings with ornate riverside balconies, auburn-tile roofs and brown-glass windows. They were, I learned later, the mansions of a group of fishing-fleet magnates, men who owned the steel-hulled trawlers that were moored downriver at fish-processing plants.

On my daily meander along the water, several people, men and women both, had asked if I wanted to rent a boat. I shook my head each time before finally settling on a middle-aged woman in a *non la* and pink pajamas with white dots. We sat on a bench one evening watching the sun shatter among the palm trees. I explained that I wanted to head up toward the Cambodian border, to wander the canals, to stop wherever seemed interesting, that basically I did not want a boat for a few hours but for a couple of weeks. She looked at me as if I had suddenly gone mad. "Why?" she asked. "That's not possible." I told her I was willing to pay a reasonable amount, in dollars, for the boat, and that I had an unlimited amount of time. She shook her head at the notion that someone would want to travel the delta without any plan, without hauling cargo or without a destination in mind. She told me she would talk to her brother who had a boat and would meet me in the morning.

Every morning seemed hotter than the day before, and I woke in a dawn that would poach an egg. I trooped back down to the waterside and found my boat broker who, again in her pink pj's, waited on a bench. "Okay," she told me. "My name is Ninh. My brother Phuong will take you." We walked down to the pier, beside the floating market, and she introduced me to her brother and his boat, a thirty-four-foot narrow wooden canal runner painted industrial blue with two plank benches and a rough wood canopy. In the stern, a steering wheel poked from the wooden crate covering a small engine. It wasn't glamorous, but it would have to do. Phuong's seven-year-old son sat on the boat's bottom, playing with the remains of a toy truck. I returned with my pack and a plastic sack full of bottled water and climbed into the boat. Phuong adjusted his black baseball cap, waved to his sister and we putted out into the river, poking our nose northeast into the morning current.

The boat's engine clattered like a bag of aluminum pots, the craft's wood frame vibrating. We hung close to shore, out of the way of the bigger vessels that plodded up- and downriver. A white car ferry yo-yoed back and forth across the river here, carrying trucks, a few cars and mostly bicycles; there are few roads of substance in the delta and the lacing of canals and rivers still remains the region's network of thoroughfares, main streets and byways. Steel barges piled with sand funneled from the chain buckets of dredgers were towed downriver by tugs, part of the effort to keep the two broadest rivers in the delta open for small freighter traffic. Big bellies, their holds swollen with golden, unhusked rice, trundled to delta granaries; on the stern of one, a woman bathed from a bucket lowered by rope into the river. And everywhere, delicate pirogues, the delta's gondolas propelled by women standing upright on a stern spit manipulating the long, crossed oars in deep rhythmic motions eased silently into channels ferrying passengers to or from villages beyond the fringe of sugar palms. Along the banks, fishermen pulled in lengths of netting left overnight to catch river-running fish. A bit farther on, two freighters, the rusty *Yu Kang* from Xiamen and the black-hulled *Thor Skipper* from Bangkok, unloaded huge bags of cement into lighters tied up alongside. Incised by wakes and striated by currents, the river, here called the Hau Giang, flattened out from shore to shore like a swath of taffeta the color of freshly butchered beef.

And then we were panting by villages, handfuls of thatched huts sprouting among clutches of banana trees and roughened pineapple groves. The duck herders were out in their pirogues, and fishermen lowered elaborate bamboo cantilevered fishing nets into the river, the sort seen from Kerala in southern India to China. Above us, the sun steamed the river and cooked the boat like a string bean in a pan. I retreated under the canopy and guzzled bottled water; Phuong's son swayed in a hammock strung from the canopy's stanchions. By evening, we had reached Chau Doc, the border town with Cambodia that had been overrun by the

Khmer Rouge in the late 1970s and before that had been a center for American special forces operations in the delta. We eased off the main river and into a feeder channel along which the main town hovered, many of the buildings propped on stilts over the water. I spied a sign announcing a hotel, and Phuong swung the boat toward a flight of wooden steps that descended from the bowels of the hotel to the river. I clambered up the fractured timber ladder to claim a room. Here in Chau Doc I was but a few miles from where the Cambodian border guard had turned me back a few weeks earlier.

A ruler-straight two-lane strip of asphalt runs out of Chau Doc across the top of a dike toward the highest promontory in the delta, a mountain—more of a substantial hill really—called Nui Sam, or Sam Mountain. I rented a motorbike and scootered out to the mountain, a mound rising from a quilt of water-logged paddy fields. Legend has it that in the early nineteenth century, villagers discovered an ancient marble statue of a woman near here. They named the woman Ba Chua Xu, or "country woman," and built a temple in her honor to bless their crops. Every year a ceremony is held at the temple at the end of the fourth lunar month, during which the statue is bathed and its robes changed; the old robes are then cut into swatches and distributed as amulets to pilgrims who travel here for the ritual.

A gauze-masked woman oars a water taxi in Chau
Doc, in the northern Mekong Delta in Vietnam

Here, too, is the tomb of Thoai Ngok Hau, the first and most celebrated of the delta's canal builders. Born in 1761, he was appointed by the first emperor of the Nguyen dynasty, Gia Long, the emperor who first unified Vietnam, to move here to Chau Doc and begin weaving the delta together with canals as part of the effort to settle this remote and heavily forested region. When he visited here in 1821, the second emperor of the dynasty, Minh Mang, declared, "Chau Doc is a strategic area, and you must be skillful with the surroundings to unite, pacify and reassure the local people. Above all, we must enlist traders, build neighborhoods and villages and create for our sons a community that grows with each day. . . ." Thoai Ngok Hau, with a force of fifty-five thousand laborers, built the canals—including the first canal, the Vinh Te, which cut through to the Gulf of Thailand—that made that dream possible, and today Vietnamese pilgrims and tourists venerate him as one of the key figures in the country's unification, a man who was in a way the Robert Moses of the delta, the man who saw that infrastructure development, canals and transport were the keys to the settlement of the delta.

Although there are a series of winding, sometimes stair-stepped paths etched into the flanks of the mountain, I buzzed up the hill on a scooter to find the summit crowned with a thick-walled concrete bunker and trenches. From here, I was told, Vietnamese troops battled invading Khmer Rouge forces; I was not told whether they successfully held off the assault. Today the guns are gone and only a few unarmed soldiers lounged by a casual outpost. The summit mostly swarmed with Vietnamese tourists—a woman in a shocking pink Tommy Hilfiger T-shirt, a young man with sunglasses and a Head Ski baseball hat (he told me he'd never seen snow and didn't know what skiing was), a profusion of people wearing Nike polo shirts who had visited the Country Woman Temple and then climbed the mountain to relish delta panoramas and, beyond a fringe of palm trees, Cambodia. They lit joss sticks and planted them on the hill's ramparts.

In the mornings here, wading through a spongy mugginess, flocks of raven-haired young schoolgirls in cloud white *ao dai*, a long, tight dress with slits up each side that is worn over pajama pants, padded gracefully, their hems billowing in milky wavelets, to a little cross-river ferry that scooted back and forth all day long, while boys in white shirts and dark pants moved in their own chattering herds; all the students lugged canvas briefcases stuffed with texts and notebooks. Here and there, faded Vietnamese flags, a red banner emblazoned with a single five-pointed yellow star, dangled from poles fixed to wooden houses. I watched a blur of lagging schoolkids dash through the school gate as I paid my hotel bill. Phuong was waiting in what I had come to call the Blue Arrow, bobbing beneath the hotel. In the back of the boat he had stashed a chicken, its legs trussed but its wings flapping desultorily, and a plastic sack with spinach, a bunch of scallions, some lemons and a bag of rice; he had also acquired a kerosene burner, a couple of aluminum pots, a red plastic bucket, bowls, chopsticks and an industrial-sized bottle of *nuoc mam*, the fermented fish sauce that is used copiously in Vietnamese cuisine. We had a long way to go that day, and I figured it would be easier to have dinner al fresco.

We set off heading north to find a canal that would take us to the other main branch of the Mekong, the Tien Giang. As we glided down one canal and then another, the lushness of the delta obscured whatever scars the now distant war may have left. Unlike in northern Vietnam, where the evidence of intensive bombing from B-52s is apparent as one flies into Hanoi over endless chains of water-filled craters, most of which have been converted to fish ponds, the effects of bombing in the delta have been eroded by intensive and bountiful farming practices. Papayas, bananas, pineapples, and golden and rose-colored dragon fruits are all grown here effortlessly. Rice springs from paddies in envious abundance and a cornucopia of vegetables ensures the most varied diet in the country. But it is also a place where human muscle is the most valuable commodity; whether it is plowing fields, rowing boats, heaving about sacks of rice, washing clothes, flinging circle fishing nets or sawing lumber, the delta remains a labor-intensive rural society. Even children three or four years old work here, some hoeing vegetable gardens, some helping their mothers scrub clothing in the river, some learning the art of mending nets. There are no fat people here.

By late afternoon, with the temperature pushing 104 degrees, we were famished and tied up along shore. Phuong lopped off the chicken's head, defeathered the bird and sectioned it faster than your hometown butcher, fired up a burner and, in what amounted to some nifty culinary legerdemain, produced a rice soup with chicken and scallions that was as good as any I had eaten in Vietnam. We dipped the chicken pieces in a small plastic bowl of salt, pepper and lime, and spit the bones overboard. I ate until I thought I would burst. Phuong's son lolled on the boat bottom sucking on a chicken leg and Phuong stretched out for a nap. Contentment reigned.

While there was still daylight, we shoved off and resumed our rackety progress. Suddenly, an hour later, with the sun beginning its nocturnal retreat, a sharp bang fired from the engine box and a vicious eruption of black oil and smoke belched from the exhaust pipe. I grabbed a paddle, and we managed to prod the Blue Arrow to shore, a rather forlorn vessel now that it was stripped of its primitive system of propulsion. Phuong raised the lid of the engine compartment, peered in and then fished a disposable plastic lighter from his pocket, which he promptly lit and lowered into the engine box to get a better look at things. I expected an explosion and hollered at him to extinguish the flame. Then I hovered over him holding my flashlight.

The engine was lathered in grease like a California sun worshiper. I had no clue what had gone wrong, but Phuong opened a small kit of tools, more a collection of discarded screwdrivers and odd wrenches than an organized assemblage of engine-repair implements. He began unscrewing various bits of the engine, looking in tubes, tapping on its black epidermis like a practicing physician. He rummaged around some more in the toolbox until he found a piece of scrap metal that he proceeded to bend and cut. He held his handiwork up for inspection—it looked pretty much like a scrap of steel to me—and then proceeded to insert it into the engine. By now darkness had trampled over us, and I could see nothing as he conducted surgery on the engine. After some screwing and banging he raised his head, extracted his arms and keyed the engine. And to my utter astonishment, it turned over and fired up. Phuong cleaned his arms in the river and we putted off, proceeding up the first canal we could toward Cao Lanh. Then, just as we entered a thread of a canal that a fisherman told us led to the town, the engine seized up again. We drifted to the bank and I told Phuong I would hitchhike into town and see him in the morning; I was sure he would find me.

Nudging the shore as night gripped the delta, I remained surprised at the ease of my meanderings here. There were no police, no checkpoints, no apparent restrictions on my movements; in Communist societies, one expects at least the occasional glance from some authority. But then, apart from the small pile of entry and exit stamp papers in each Laotian town I visited, no one paid much attention to me there either. But more than this, I found a certain pleasure in drifting through a landscape, both physical and social, that seemed to bear few scars of the decade-plus war that swept through here twenty-five years ago. For me, the memories of the war lingered in my imagination—Nick Ut's seminal photograph of nine-year-old Phan Thi Kim Phuk running naked, screaming, down Highway 1 after a napalm attack on her village of Trang Bang in 1972; Eddie Adams's photo of the South Vietnamese general Nguyen Ngoc Loan nonchalantly executing a prisoner; the television pictures of Americans clambering into helicopters on the roof of their embassy as North Vietnamese soldiers entered the city; those and hundreds more. Yet, all of that seemed so distant, so much part of another time, another place. The Vietnam through which I floated now was looking elsewhere.

I scrambled up the canal bank with my pack, waved to Phuong and settled down next to the road to wait for some traffic. A couple of trucks jolted past, uninterested in picking up a wayward foreigner. Then one of the country's micropickup trucks appeared in the darkness and stopped. I said, "Cao Lanh," the driver nodded his head and we were off.

For its part, Cao Lanh lived up to its billing as the most depressing town in the Mekong Delta. Built after the war according to precepts of Socialist town planning—the two principal elements of which are broad, treeless boulevards and concrete blockhouse architecture—Cao Lanh was deserted at eight o'clock at night. I checked into a monstrous hotel, both in design and bulk, and then headed down the block to what I was told was the only restaurant open in the city at that hour. The town's abundance of concrete complemented the day's ovenlike temperatures, roasting the night air. I collapsed into a plastic chair at the empty restaurant and polished off three ice-cold cans of Phong Dinh beer so fast it left the owner's daughter gaping.

Somehow the next morning Phuong appeared in the lobby of the hotel with news that he had repaired the engine with actual manufactured parts instead of his own handiwork. Both he and his son were in new shirts and pants and the Blue Arrow was tied up three blocks from the hotel. I told him to take a *cyclopousse* with my pack down to the boat and I would meet him after a quick walk to the end of the main boulevard, which was punctuated in an exclamatory fashion by a massive cement bandshell-shaped war memorial. At the entrance to the memorial—Martyrs for the Motherland—stood a gigantic cement sculpture of a North Vietnamese soldier charging forward with his assault rifle, joined on each side by a peasant in pajamas and a worker with his fist thrust into the air. In bold bas-relief on the inner curve of the shell, figures of soldiers frozen in triumph, muscled peasants beaming in their labors and the wreckage of an American helicopter told of Hanoi's version of history. And spread around the shell in a fan of cement markers were the graves of 3,112 soldiers who had lost their lives fighting the Americans and its South Vietnamese regime, a handful of the 2 million Vietnamese who died over the thirteen years of war. A solitary stooped gardener tended yellow daffodils that edged a flagstone walkway.

By late morning, the Blue Arrow was clanking downstream again, its engine noisily, but consistently, driving a new propeller Phuong said he had attached. We made for Vinh Long, where we planned to rest for a few days. A sleepy market town, Vinh Long squats on yet another of the delta's estuaries, the Co Chien River, and is moated by canals that straggle off toward tiny villages. It was here I met Hoang, a man who belongs to the category of human Vietnamese disdainfully call *bui doi*, dust of life: Hoang, in his flattop crew cut, a heavy-link gold bracelet and chain, and occasional bombast, is the son of an American father and a Vietnamese woman, the son of a soldier who came and went, like thousands upon thousands of others, leaving behind the results of their sexual escapades.

"People hate us," Hoang told me loudly. "They say we are worse than dirt. They say we are Americans. They say we have no rights." Across southern Vietnam, but particularly in Saigon, children, now in their twenties, of American soldiers are a frequent sight. "I don't care. I have relatives in the U.S. so I'm okay." Hoang insisted I join his table where some twenty friends and family, well into their cups, sat around a long table in an open-walled restaurant down a backstreet. Hoang boasted of his business deals one moment, lamenting slights against him the next. "When I was a kid, they made me sleep with the pigs," he said. "I had to sleep in a pigsty. I was seen as the enemy, just because of who my father is." I asked him about his father. He pushed his chest out under his black T-shirt. "My father was an army colonel," he said. "He was high rank." Hoang's English was fluid and colloquial, a product, he said, of his mother's patience and the recent visits of relatives from the United States. He introduced one of them, a sturdy Vietnamese in a yellow polo shirt and pressed khaki shorts who sat quietly in the corner. "This is my cousin Manh," he shouted. "He's from New Jersey."

It was evident that most of the twenty or so people at the dinner did not speak English, and so I moved to an adjoining table to chat with Manh. "I've been back to Vietnam three times so far," said Manh, whose American diet was evidenced by a paunch that sagged over his belt. "My father was a sort of middle-level officer in the old government. He was sent to reeducation camp, and he died there.* My mom lives here though. Even though I escaped to the U.S. she doesn't want to come. All her friends are here. She's happy, or at least as happy as anyone is here." Manh lounged in his chair in the easy body language of an American suburbanite, a contrast with the more contained postures of his Vinh Long relatives who sat, if not primly, more self-consciously than Manh. "After college I started out in San Diego. I worked as a manager for Nordstrom's and was transferred to the East Coast. New Jersey isn't so bad. I think there's about seventeen thousand Vietnamese in the state, so that's nice. When I first started coming back, there were some problems. The government wanted money. But that stopped." I asked him about his family here. "What can I say?" he answered. "You can see that everybody's pretty poor here. If you didn't get out and you're stuck living here, there's not a lot to do. I mean, the economy's a complete disaster. So I help my mom out, and she's doing all right. After a while you begin to wonder whether Vietnam will ever get its act together. For a country that won the war they act like losers."

Hoang was putting away beer at a prodigious rate, fueled by his cousin's generosity, all the while spewing sporadic denunciations of Vietnam in a near-American patois. "These guys suck," he hollered, waving a hand across the room. "They're Communists, these guys. Hey, America's the greatest." I worried about Hoang, not that I thought any secret police were going to haul him away, but that he was so clearly a prisoner of his Americanisms, American aspirations and American conspicuous behavior, and yet was anchored to this backwater place tempered by the rigors of rural life. (Backwater though it be, the previous year two lesbians had married each other in a noisy, glitzy ceremony here even though the local authorities refused to issue them a formal marriage certificate.) Like other *bui doi*, he was despised by the politically correct for wearing the face of the American oppressor, for being taller than other Vietnamese, for being the product of an impure union, for being, in the end, not really Vietnamese. Yet Hoang could not escape being Vietnamese either: He spoke Vietnamese as his first language, walked more like a Vietnamese who grew

---

* After the fall of Saigon, the Hanoi government rounded up as many as 200,000 officials, police and members of the army of the defeated regime and sent them to reeducation camps for various lengths of time, some as long as fifteen years. Of those 200,000, about 6,000 died while in detention.

up wearing flip-flops than an American who wore sneakers or leather shoes his whole life, and despite the crew cut, the gold chain and the exaggerated American slang, he seemed at heart deeply Vietnamese, at the same time, though, a Vietnamese discarded by his own society. It is a cruelty of victory.

I left the restaurant that night serenaded by Hoang and Manh singing along with their friends, their off-key, soulful song trailing me down the darkened streets. For the kids at the table that night, there had never been an American war; their lives were by any standard peaceful and, with Manh's periodic help, a bit easier than it would have been. But like many, many Vietnamese, bits and pieces of their family had sunk roots in the United States, shedding their culture little by little; despite the neighborhoods in Los Angeles and San Jose where Vietnamese is still the lingua franca, overseas Vietnamese return to their homeland more as strangers every year. As Manh put it before I left, shrugging his shoulders, "Hey, I'm American."

A few days later, with the Blue Arrow rested and Phuong and his son refreshed by lazy days in Vinh Long, we returned to the river, chuttering among small islands as we made our way toward the Song My Tho, a delta branch that would funnel us toward the town of My Tho. Near My Tho was the old American base of Dong Tam, which served among other things as a helicopter and patrol-boat base for operations throughout the delta against Vietcong guerrillas. Now, though, only big bellies bearing mounds of rice and swarms of pirogues stirred on canal waters until we putted into the Song My Tho. Here, river trains of gasoline barges pulled by tugs moved upriver, sprays of water playing across the metal decks to keep them cool in the sun's broiler. Then, creeping along the shoreline, an old American patrol boat, what the Americans dubbed "Tango Boats," in a coat of fresh gray appeared, a red one-star Vietnamese flag planted on its stern; it meandered aimlessly downriver, a couple of shirtless soldiers smoking on the foredeck as they played cards.

A ragged town of eroding colonial houses and Socialist blockhouse architecture cracking at the edges, My Tho plays second fiddle to Can Tho as a market town and regional center. I checked into an empty but new riverside hotel and wandered into the market, where I bought a baguette and a bottle of water. Even in the delta, crusty, although often airy, baguettes are available in the larger towns and make for a quick snack. As I sat on a cement bench watching the river churn with traffic, an older gentleman strolled over, sat down next me, introduced himself in mellifluous English as Nguyen-thanh Chan and asked if I wished to join him for lunch. I was somewhat surprised at his forwardness, but accepted his offer. We made our way down the lip of a canal to an open-front Vietnamese restaurant. "This is Truc," my host told me, "my son." Of course. The father was drumming up business for his son's eatery. I accepted anyway, curious at the old man's command of English and his evident willingness to talk. His son flipped the caps off the tops of two bottles of 333, and we ordered a couple of plates of food. I leaned over the railing to look down the canal. Crumbling concrete pylons of an old bridge—"that was built by the French, but it was wrecked in the war," Chan told me—sulked on either bank and a flatbed ferry metronomed passengers back and forth across the canal. A plate of snake in a spicy oyster sauce arrived, followed by a pile of sautéed spinach greens. As we ate, I asked Chan where he had learned English.

"I learned in school," he said. "I'm sixty years old now, and when I was in school we could learn English or French. When the war came, I worked with the American army for seven years at Dong Tam. That's where the army base was. Just upriver. You can go there if you want. I can get you a boat." I thanked him and said I'd think about it. I asked him what he did for the Americans. In a taut safari shirt, Chan seemed fit and his whitening head of close-cropped steely hair and slightly vulpine features lent him the cast of a former military man, but he denied it. "I wasn't actually in the army. But when there were briefings about what was going on or what plans they had, the Americans didn't speak Vietnamese and the Vietnamese officers couldn't speak English well, so I would translate. I worked as a translator.

"Then one day the Americans left," he continued. "They just left one day. They left in the black." I asked what he meant by that. "They just left. They didn't tell anybody they were leaving and suddenly they were gone. What could we do? The Vietcong came and that was the end. I was sent to a reeducation camp for three years. I wasn't very important, so I wasn't there for a very long time." And what happened at the camp? I wanted to know. "Every day was the same," he said. "In the morning we got up at five o'clock. We had fifteen minutes to wash up and then fifteen minutes for a bowl of rice with fish sauce. We worked all day digging irrigation canals." I asked him where his camp was. "I stayed here in the Mekong Delta. Mostly there were lieutenants, captains and majors from the South Vietnam army in my camp. High-ranking officers or people in the old government, they were sent to different parts of Vietnam. Some of them stayed for ten years or more." I asked him about the political aspects of his so-called reeducation. Chan spat over the rail into the canal.

"It was shit," he said. "They would read Stalin to us. Or Mao. Or Ho Chi Minh. Then they would ask us questions. It was shit. But I never said shit. I said 'bible.' Every time I thought it was shit, I just said 'bible.' If you said it was shit, you could have another six months added on to your sentence. But everybody knew it was all shit." We ordered another round of beers in an effort to vanquish the lava of heat and humidity that oozed down the canal. "The conditions were terrible in the camp," Chan continued. "We drank the Mekong River when we were thirsty. We called it 'raw water.' I was very skinny in reeducation camp. We didn't eat much. But now I look all right." Then he spread his hands in front him, in almost a gesture of hopelessness. "When I was in there, my wife left me. What could I do? I could not support her when I was in the camp. When I got out, I worked as a laborer carrying bags of rice. There were not very many jobs for us at that time. The government wouldn't let people like me open businesses. Only in 1991 did the government finally let us run our own businesses."

Truc finished clearing our table and sat down with us. I asked him how things were in the restaurant business, but his father interrupted. "He doesn't really speak English," he explained. Truc grinned and shrugged. "I tell you, the government here is very, very corrupt," Chan continued. "It always wants money. Even so, this is not such a bad place. But in the 1980s, there were a lot of people who wanted to take boats from here and go to Hong Kong or the Philippines or to Malaysia. They had to pay a couple thousand dollars for each person. Usually they had to pay in gold. That's a lot of money for a Vietnamese. For most people I think that was impossible. So I taught the people who were leaving some English. I had a little business teaching them basic things; just some words and phrases so they would be able to talk a little. There were lots of boats that left from here. Many, many boats." So why, I asked, did he not leave. "I don't know," he said slowly. "I'm Vietnamese. I don't like this government. But I am Vietnamese and I want to live in Vietnam. I also think the Americans did not treat us well. They just left. When it was very difficult, they did not stay and help us. They gave up. I think many people think like this." He paused and stared across the canal at the shanties that backed up onto the trash-strewn water. "I did not have money, of course. But I am Vietnamese. So I said I will stay."*

I paid for our lunch and thanked Chan for our talk. He was gazing across the canal as I walked out. Chan's profession of his Vietnameseness, his deeply felt, although simply articulated, passion for his homeland is something that many Westerners either do not understand or refuse to believe. There is, particularly in those American political circles with little real understanding of the world, an unshakable conviction that everyone in Vietnam (and Cuba, China, indeed any Communist country) would flee to the United States if they could. In fact, life is far more complex and nuanced than this. Chan's emotional links to the delta are not unlike the thousands of Chinese graduate students—all of whom know acutely Beijing's reprehensible human rights record—who nonetheless eagerly return to China to make their fortunes, take care of their parents, speak their own language, live lives as Chinese. Are they happy about the absence of democracy in their country, about the controls on what they read and see on television? No. But they have a bond to their homeland, and it is a powerful one.

Along the street there were a few new shops opening, a shoe store fronted by a window stacked with polished leather shoes, and a women's dress store, its window display akin to a Des Moines shop in the 1950s. But what was interesting was not the antiquated appearance of the shops

---

* Although data on the number of Vietnamese who have either fled or left the country is somewhat imprecise, W. Courtland Robinson, an associate at the Center for Refugee and Disaster Studies at the Johns Hopkins University School of Hygiene and Public Health, has conducted the most detailed study of data issued by the United Nations and other organizations. He maintains that between 1975 and 1997, a total of about 3 million refugees fled their homelands in southeast Asia, with 1,513,179 people having left Vietnam, either by boat or through what was called the Orderly Departure Program, an agreement between the United Nations and the Vietnamese government to facilitate the emigration of those Vietnamese who sought to leave the country. Altogether, 1,017,317 Vietnamese have settled in the United States, with the remainder scattered across Europe, Australia, Canada and Japan.

but that they were not the traditional shop houses, open-front emporiums with goods piled willy-nilly in the day only to be converted to the family home at night. These clothing stores were laid out like those on shopping streets in spiffier Asian towns, with attention paid to the arrangement of the clothes or shoes in the window, a departure from the more common practice of piling clothes in heaps on flimsy tables; and in the shop, dresses were hung on racks and mirrors were on the wall. And more, the dresses were not the traditional *ao dai*, but frocks that would have cheered the eyes of a midwestern woman some five decades ago.

Over the next days Phuong and I took the Blue Arrow around My Tho, upriver and down, dodging islets and skirting palm-topped islands that jeweled the river, running past farms of trees beaded with the white-fleshed longan fruit, sapodilla trees pendulant with dull reddish softball-sized fruits, endless parades of banana trees and soaring coconut palms. After a few hours of wiggling down canals canopied by water palms, we tied up in the small town of Ben Tre. I left Phuong and his son and walked off into the town, although it was hardly that. Skewers of packed dirt streets led into palm-shaded neighborhoods of single-floor cement houses tucked behind manicured vegetable gardens. At a far intersection, a white temple rose from behind a cracked and faded wooden fence and behind it a barracklike building with a red-tile roof. An ancient man in a long white robe, a flat black turban and a scraggly beard sat under a capacious rambutan tree eating a handful of its hairy, gumball-sized fruits. I wandered into the compound and tried to make sense of the Chinese calligraphy incised into the temple's red lacquer pillars adorned with writhing golden dragons and the two steeples capped with Buddhist swastikas. Then a younger man, also in a white robe and bearded as well, emerged from the barracks and hurried over to me, his skirts flapping. "How do you do," he said in labored English. I asked him what temple I was in. "This is Cao Dai Temple," he answered, gesturing for me to follow him inside.

Among the globe's religions perhaps none is as gloriously syncretic as Cao Dai. Founded in Saigon around 1925 by a group of Vietnamese bureaucrats who worked for the French colonial administration, the religion melded beliefs in Taoism, Buddhism, Confucianism and Christianity with nativist folklore, and leavened it with a reverence for classical learning. The temple was in a parlous state with holes in the roof and the wall. "That is from Tet war," the young Cao Dai priest said, pointing at the bits of sky that peppered the roof. "People were here to be safe. But guns still came." In 1968, the Vietcong and North Vietnamese armies staged attacks throughout the south, capturing for a time many urban centers and, in a sustained and bloody assault, almost occupied the American embassy in the heart of Saigon. The Tet Offensive, as it was called, was deemed a military defeat for the north by American officials, but the surprise and breadth of the attacks forever dispelled the notion that the United States was winning the war, or indeed could ever win the war. Here in Ben Tre, the Cao Dai temple bore the wounds of that offensive.

The young priest escorted me back to the temple's main altar, three tiers of glazed ceramic figurines embracing the entirety of the Cao Dai religious cosmos. At the center stood the figure of the Jade Emperor of Vietnamese folklore, here representing Thuong De, or God. Around him were clustered statuettes of the Buddha, Laoze—the philosopher whose ideas gave birth to Taoism—and Confucius. Below them stood Quan Am, the Vietnamese representation of the Chinese female Buddha Guan Yin; Ly Thai Bach, the Vietnamese name for the eighth-century Chinese poet; Li Po, perhaps the greatest poet of the Tang dynasty and a devout Taoist adept; and a red-faced Quan Thanh, the Chinese god of war. And finally, on the lowest tier, a figurine of Jesus stood next to one of Khuong Thai Cong, the chief of the genies in Vietnamese lore. Cao Dai flourished in the 1930s during a period of great economic hardship in Vietnam, attracting well over 1 million adherents. In later years, it developed a reputation for anticommunism and after 1975 was regarded with suspicion by the new Socialist regime. Today, it is tolerated at best.

I asked the young priest how many people believed in Cao Dai. He looked around and asked another priest who had by then joined us. "I think three hundred thousand," he said. That seemed to me an enormous number of people in this area, but I let it pass. Did young people come to the temple as well? He looked at his fellow priest again. "No," he said finally. "Not many young people. Today young people not so interested." I was having trouble communicating with the priest, so I read the Chinese on the columns to him, but he could not follow and did not seem to be able to read the calligraphy himself. We walked back outside and he presented me with a small plastic bag of rambutan fruits.

Back on the Blue Arrow, I asked Phuong to see if he could figure out how to find the Dong Tam military base where Chan had told me he had worked, to see if any traces of the American military effort remained here. He asked a few other boatmen and glanced at the labyrinth of canals facing us. I handed over a piece of paper and a pen and one of the boatmen sketched out a rough map for Phuong, although from my vantage point I could not easily extract a clear route from the scratchings he made. Phuong seemed uncertain, but we set off anyway, feeling a bit like pioneers. The traffic of pirogues jaded our pioneer spirit somewhat. A few hours later we crept up a canal with Phuong asking each boat he passed. Suddenly a woman in a pirogue gestured toward shore, toward a mud bank under a bridge. Phuong nodded and said that we should tie up here and that I should find a scooter to take me down to the camp. I slipped and clawed my way up the bank to the road and waved at passing scooters. Finally one came by and let me climb on back; he dropped me at the entrance to the old base.

A rust-eaten sign half tucked in overgrown bushes warned: KHU VUC CAM RESTRICTED AREA NO TRESPASSING, a shard of the American presence. To the left, a well-kept road ran down to what a sign told me was now a snake farm. And straight ahead was an open gate with a sleeping guard. A placard warned that it was now a base for the Vietnamese army. I wandered down to the snake farm, paid a couple of dollars to get in and poked my head in buildings filled with cages of alarmingly large pythons. In smooth-walled cement pits in back were small islands of shrubs and grass that rustled with the slither of cobras and other varieties of snake that my guide—her badge said her name was Emerald—promised me would "kill in ten seconds," or "kill in thirty seconds." At the snake farm shop, she tried to sell me a bottle of snake liquor, that is, a glass bottle stuffed with a snake and filled with the local fire water. I demurred, but when she offered me a glass of the stuff I shrugged and chugged it back. "Good for sex," she told me.

My thumb got me a ride back to the Blue Arrow, and I skiied down the bank to the boat. Phuong was asleep but bounced up when he saw me nearly land in the canal. I told him to take us back to My Tho. We were back on the river. The sea was in sight.

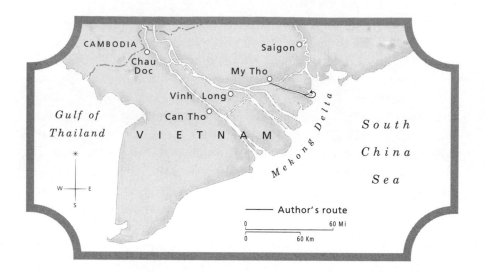

Ten

"Bien Dong, Bien Dong . . ."

On the day I was to take the Blue Arrow to the sea I woke early, almost in blackness. Only filaments of gold traced the eastern horizon as I headed for the jetty, a clutch of baguettes under my arm and a few bottles of water dangling from my wrist in a plastic bag. I knew I would be early for Phuong, so I sat on the riverbank watching dawn's brocade and reflected on the Vietnam I had seen and that had affected my own life.

In 1968, at the height of American involvement in the war in southeast Asia, I was studying Chinese at the University of Wisconsin, in Madison. For many college students and other Americans, myself included, there was a deep sense that the war was utterly misguided and immoral, although the scenes of horror that trickled onto television sets from Vietnam perhaps stirred us emotionally far more than they prompted dispassionate analyses of administration policies. Already, reporters like David Halber-

stam and Neil Sheehan had written extensively about the lies, the bum-
bling, the absence of purpose that permeated American policy, and more,
of the corruption, deceit and crass megalomania of the South Vietnamese
leaders the American government kept propping up. For young men turning eighteen in those years, the prospect of war was far closer than the television screen: the law required all eighteen-year-olds to register for the
draft.

By the time I turned eighteen, in the summer of 1968, I had already been
involved in antiwar protests, had been tear-gassed on the campus at
protests against the Dow Chemical Company, the company that manufactured the napalm that we saw on our televisions being used with such horrifying consequences on Vietnamese, and was certain I would not fight in
the war. And so, almost without much internal debate, I declined to register for the draft, a position that placed me in violation of the law and put me
in some jeopardy of imprisonment. I certainly did not regard the decision as
particularly brave; indeed I was, whenever I thought about it, petrified by
the thought of prison, but I also felt that it was a choice that genuine opposition to the war dictated. (I could have avoided the entire issue and risked
neither prison nor the army by registering, certain that my near blindness
in one eye would have deferred me from serving, but that clearly was a step
smeared with disingenuousness.) Over the next year, I was increasingly
active in antiwar protests and worked with poor people in Milwaukee as
part of a group called Catholic Worker. In due course, as I've said, I was
arrested for failure to register for the draft and wound up spending a bit
more than two years in a federal prison in Kentucky, a rather less than salu-
brious experience. During my residency in Kentucky, I watched the intensity of the war mount, the spread of bombing into Cambodia and Laos, the
arrogance and mendacity of Nixon's and Kissinger's public posturing and
their unmasking with the publication of the Pentagon Papers, the Rand
Corporation's detailed history of the war and policymaking, and enjoyed a
frisson of schadenfreude as the first act of the Watergate saga opened.

As I sat on the concrete steps that led down to the Mekong in My Tho
that morning, memories of that time tumbled over me. The television
images of war that assaulted our eyes in those days, the powerful writing by
journalists who dissected and eviscerated American policy, all that
seemed very distant* as dawn brought the first red and blue wooden delta

---

* Lee Lescaze, who covered Vietnam for the *Washington Post*, wrote a gripping
account of My Tho in the wake of the Tet Offensive. "My Tho still smells of death," Lescaze

ferries from villages and towns. Market boats—narrow, stern-rowed pirogues, filled with baskets of thick-skinned oranges, yellow-red pomegranates, glossy pink and red bell fruits, the juicy and violet jambolan, brown billiard-ball-sized lichees—mingled with vegetable skiffs packed with onions, garlic, long beans, bouquets of broccoli; it was a scene that transpired before the war convulsed this country, and it is a scene that has returned. But my conversations with those who were its victims also spoke of the costs of victory by the North; national unification brought with it peace, certainly, but it brought also a rigid authoritarianism that has stunted the lives of the Vietnamese. Even so, Vietnam is in no way the murky, paranoid place that is Laos, nor the traumatized land of Cambodia. It is a country, especially here in the south, that retains a sense of its culture and identity mixed with a yearning for the world beyond.

For the most part, the United States has moved beyond the Vietnam era, so far beyond it that when, in occasional lectures at American universities, I mention the Vietnam War, I am met by vacant looks. A war that ended twenty-five years ago, especially one that was not fought on American soil and that ended in defeat, is not the stuff of popular legend, and strikes most college students as no more relevant than the Battle of Hastings. Part of this is due to a thorough and prevailing provincialism that inheres in American life. A well-known American television anchorman, defending the absence of foreign news on his network, expressed this parochialism succinctly once. "I defy anyone," he told a friend of mine, "to name one foreign story that is of any relevance to our viewers." Relevant, instead, are stories about hurricanes, cures for baldness, presidential pets, the life and doings inside Washington's capital beltway, and, when they happen, conflicts that involve American soldiers; the massacre of Tutsis in Rwanda does not measure up, neither does ethnic conflict in Indonesia, the war in Chechnya, European integration. The best American newspapers have covered these events exhaustively, but most people in the United States, alas, receive the bulk of their news from their television sets.

Such myopia is a luxury not shared here. Each of the countries along

---

wrote. "Most of the bodies—Vietcong and friendly—have been removed from the streets, but some remain. In the wreckage of their homes, people are looking for things to save. There is little emotion and less noise. For a crowded area in Vietnam it is almost impossibly quiet." Today, talk and shouting and laughter have returned.

the Mekong has been indelibly stained by that war a quarter of a century ago, a stain that is all too visible. That stain is what, in contemplating the American role in southeast Asia and opposition to it, is most troubling for me today. The austere, cloistered paranoia of Laos, the Khmer Rouge holocaust in Cambodia, the stringency of Hanoi's vision of the future, all are incompatible with any reasonable hope for a just and democratic society, for a society that will be part of a larger Asia, and the broader world. During the war there was a tendency by some on the American left to romanticize North Vietnam (and by a handful of the truly deranged, the Khmer Rouge or the Pathet Lao), a proclivity induced by the hypocrisies of the Nixon administration, the vivid pictures of carpet bombing and napalm attacks on villages, and a lingering admiration for pajama-clad Vietnamese battling the world's most powerful military. There was little discussion of atrocities committed by the North and its counterpart guerrilla armies in the South, and little interest in analyzing what victory by the North would bring. But there is also no question that the southeast Asian regimes promoted and propped up by American policy were brutal, corrupt and utterly without popular support. I juggled these competing ideas, as I have repeatedly over the years, and returned to those moments of hope I had encountered, particularly in Cambodia where, after the worst of crimes against humanity, semblances of normal life were returning, and in Laos, where solace was found in the oldest of the country's tradition, Buddhism. The collapse of the Soviet Union, and with it any pretense that socialism and authoritarianism constituted any path toward the future, has confirmed the mortality of communism; what remains is for the aging leaders in Laos and Vietnam to give way to that realization, to a future not dictated by them but by their people.

While I was wrapped in these thoughts, Phuong jogged up with his son, and behind him came his sister Ninh, her daughter and a cousin. "They have come to see the sea." Phuong beamed. "And we have new boat. No more Blue Arrow." No more Blue Arrow? Our not-always-trusty craft, beloved by me alone, was being dispatched with scant sentiment by Phuong. I asked him what had happened. "Last night I call Ninh," he explained. "She said she come, too. And she bring big boat." Now a sizable group, we scuttled down the wharf to where the new vessel was tied up, a bigger boat with a heftier engine, not quite the same as the monsters on which I had rocketed down the Mekong in Laos, but clearly capable of pushing us along at a decent clip. It, too, was blue-hulled, so I silently dubbed it Blue Arrow Redux, a moniker I kept to myself.

We settled into the bigger craft, and Phuong cranked the engine, which caught with more authority and throatiness than the old boat's motor, a rumble of some confidence. Phuong pointed us out into the current, a red rash that was running east, toward the South China Sea. On the shore, fruit trees crowded the banks, trees that figured in southern Vietnamese versions of Genesis. Vietnamese folklore embraces two creation myths, one common in the North and one told in the South, here in the delta. The southern myth tells of two celestial beings, a man and a woman, who descend to Earth, to a deserted, forested island with a solitary ancient tree at its center. Beneath this tree the earth exuded a fragrance of intoxicating sweetness and delicacy, so intense that these heavenly beings could not but taste it, and then consume some more. As night came, they tried to return to heaven but having eaten of the earth they found, weighed down by the soil they had eaten, that they could no longer fly. And so, they settled on the island, built a house and in time had twenty-four children, twelve boys and twelve girls. In heaven, the king of the genies saw these heavenly beings prosper and in reward sent them a peach tree to nourish them. The parents instructed the children to stay away from the peach tree, not to eat its fruit when they were away gathering wood in the forest. But the children disobeyed and ate peaches from the tree until they were stuffed. Upon returning from the forest and seeing that the tree had been stripped of its fruit, the parents were furious and banished the children from the house, sending them in pairs in all directions, where they became the ancestors of other human races. Only the two youngest boys and girls understood their parents' displeasure and admitted their disobedience, and so they were permitted to remain. It was these two pairs who were the progenitors of the south, the youngest pair of children becoming the ancestors of the Khmer people, and the second-youngest pair became the ancestors of the Kinh people, the Vietnamese.

It is not entirely clear from where this folktale emanates, although it is widely known here, celebrating the origin of humanity in southern Vietnam, probably here in the delta through which we were traveling. In the North, a different myth is recited, one of the fairy Au Cao and the water dragon Lac Long Quan, who gave birth to one hundred humans who became mankind's ancestors. But no one told that tale here.

A rice grain boat pushing through a Mekong Delta
canal on the way to a granary

At My Tho, the river bloats like a python that has swallowed a pig, and
we whipped into this bulge, arrowing toward the southern flank of our
dragon. Phuong, energized by a mightier engine, chicaned among islets,
powered past the big bellies fighting the current as they labored upriver
and made for the white sun rising fast on the horizon. Though it seemed
we were reckless in our progress, a quick check of my GPS showed that we
were racing along at only a shade more than fifteen miles per hour. There
were no towns here, just clusters of stilted huts, most with corrugated
roofs, some sprouting awkward, elbowed television antennas. Two fishermen rocking in a pirogue were hanging a fence line of nylon netting tethered to the surface by discarded spray cans. Children splashed in the
clay-stained water as a woman in her conical hat scrubbed away at a pile
of clothing. A filigree of streams and canals adorned the delta here, and
pirogues drifted like chips of wood on a mountain brook, others in chase
of rowdy flotillas of white ducks.

Then the river opened its mouth, its lips now rimmed in sandy banks,
and Ninh shouted, "*Bien Dong, Bien Dong*," "Eastern Sea," what the Vietnamese call the South China Sea. Before us, a cobalt sky bent and kissed
the sea, an infinity of aquamarine, water of hope and pleasure, of possibilities unknown. A briny aroma washed over us, and I dipped my hand in the

sea—or was it still the Mekong?—raised my fingers to my lips and tasted salt. Here, the Mekong leaks its last strength, and even then it is not suffi- cient to hold the sea back from its daily tidal march upriver. I looked around me, at Phuong, who arced our boat around an island tip toward another dragon, at Ninh, who pointed to the sea for the children, and grinned myself at the sight of absolute vastness at river's end. From these estuaries, the dragons that opened onto the sea, thousands upon thousands of Vietnamese fled this land, although many more did not or could not.

In a moving collection of reminiscences of Saigon's last days compiled by Larry Engelmann, a Californian writer, he records the tale of a young girl named Nguyen Thi Hoa who managed to get on a final boat leaving the delta. Of her escape, she tells the following:

> The name of the boat was the *Tan Man Viet*. It was a big boat and it carried about five or six hundred people. . . . I was very scared when we went down the river. Some of the people on the boat stayed on the deck to get a last look at Vietnam. . . . But I did not look back. I was so sad. I was leaving everything behind. And I didn't know where I was going or what would happen to me. . . .

There were no patrol boats to stop us now, no one took an interest in our outing and we were passed by two steel-hulled trawlers that churned out into the fecund sea, great reels of stowed dragnets clamped to their sterns. My maps showed us at a mouth of the Mekong called Cua Dai, and my GPS told me I was 1,789 miles from the mountain crevice on the Tibetan plateau that gave birth to this river. A breeze of delicious coolness rippled from the sea, defying the sun's blistering designs. We bobbed and shuffled some, creeping around the island, unwilling to leave immensity around us. But then Phuong throttled us on, and we turned slowly, north and finally west into the Cua Tieu, back toward My Tho.

For nearly a year of travel, I had been wedded to the Mekong, following its progress from infancy to its final exhalation, watching its might and its fury, its tempering and its play, its bounty and its majesty. But more than that, I had traced this river through culture and history, through the black glass of memory and loss, mazes of expectation and disillusion, into the lives of dozens of people who revealed their worlds to me. It was not with- out some sadness that I watched our boat's wake slice away from the South China Sea, carving a froth-edged course back upriver toward My Tho.

Once again, palm trees shaded the riverbanks, ribbons of sunlight fluttering through the green fronds splashing the river with sequins of yellow and gold.

I could not tell, although perhaps a river hydrologist could estimate, when the water now under me first left that spot on the Tibetan plateau where my journey had started a year ago. Putt-putting gently upstream, images of the Mekong's first early stampedes through Tibet's great gorges flashed through my mind, a tumult that after nearly three thousand miles was transformed into the placidity beneath the Blue Arrow Redux. At the most basic geological level, the Mekong traces the history of the Asian continent, from the breath-stealing plateau formed by India's relentless drive northward, to the alluvial fan of the Mekong Delta itself, from arid cold to tropical forest. In places I could, and did, toss a pebble across the Mekong; here in Vietnam, traversing its breadth takes days.

It was a year that coursed through a landscape of language, dress, habits, food, a terrain of hope and despair, expectation and resignation, and above all change. I saw a sturdiness in Tibet I had not expected, and a determination from the Chinese to impose their will about which I knew too much. Ominously for Tibetans, however, it is what happens in Beijing so many miles away that will determine their future, not their own stubborn adherence to their culture and traditions. If Beijing wants to build a railroad into Lhasa—tracks that will carry more Han Chinese into the Tibetan heartland, and a project now being undertaken—it will do so, and there is little Tibetans can do about it. Will the Khamba horsemen two generations from now still sing their tribal songs? Or will they raise their voices to some Chinese ditty? I didn't find the answer to that. Even the reconstruction of Gyalthang's monastery—originally destroyed by the Chinese—did not provide certainty of Tibetan Buddhism's vitality; I could not envision a thriving religious culture without the Tibetan theologians who fled Chinese persecution.

But there, and forcefully in Cambodia, I was confronted with the very meaning of survival, with how people rebuild lives that have been decimated in ways few of us raised in the West can imagine, about how societies struggle to bring themselves back from the brink. No matter how much I read before visiting Cambodia, there was no way to appreciate the true horror, the true breadth of evil that lay upon that country until I had met people like Vann Nath. What is stunning to realize as well is that the suffering of the Cambodian people went virtually unreported until Vietnamese troops invaded the country. (Indeed, the American government, mired in a residual antipathy to Vietnam and a convoluted notion of geopolitics, supported the Khmer Rouge regime as Cambodia's legitimate government after it was forced from power.) Survival, though, means more than going on. It means understanding the past and finding a way to subdue it, to reconcile it, to overcome it. In a sense, building a monastery does that. And in a sense, demanding that the murderers of the Cambodian people face justice does that, too. But, just as the Mekong never ceases in its rush to the sea, but only passes through Tibet and Cambodia, there is no final certainty to such questions.

On the riverfront at My Tho, I ate a final meal of steamed fish, garlicky frogs' legs and rice with Ninh, Phuong and the rest of his family. Ninh, whose English was the best, talked as we ate. "Our father is a fisherman," she said. "I think our family always was fishermen. But now with big fishing boats, it is difficult for people with small boats to make money. So we rent our small boats to people. Or we use for carrying rice bags. We are poor people. But we are not very poor. I think we are like most people." I asked Ninh where she had learned English, and she laughed. "I learn from tourists," she said. "There are tourists who come to Can Tho. And I have English books. I study the books. So I can speak English a little." Then I asked her about the war, what she remembered. "I was a little girl. I don't remember the war. Of course, my father talks about the war, that it was very bad. Many people died then. But it was long ago. Today, nobody talks about the war. We talk about making money." She laughed. "Like we make money from you."

Ninh and Phuong's family met me to say good-bye the next morning, the Blue Arrow bobbing on a painter attached to the stern of Blue Arrow Redux. I presented the children with a yellow-and-orange plastic dump truck, a junior-sized soccer ball and baseball hats embroidered in white with "Ellesse." Ninh hugged me shyly, and I shook Phuong's hand. Then they stepped into the blue boat. In a moment they were gone, their wake quickly devoured by the silent current.

Like everywhere on this trip, my moments with Phuong, and later his family, were all too brief. Traveling truncated friendships; following the river meant moving on. If I were a sociologist, I could have remained on the Tibetan plateau, learning in depth the way of yak herders, their songs, their prayers. Or if I were a musicologist, I would certainly have remained in Lijiang, learning from Xuan Ke and his musicians, learning the way of the Naxi. In Luang Prabang, there was still much that I yearned to know about Buddhist life. And it was impossible to spend too much time in Cambodia. Had I yielded to my impulses to linger more, I would never have finished my journey. Many incipient friendships never flowered; always, the river beckoned to me.

I spent a few more days in My Tho before gathering my pack and returning to the jetty to catch the Russian hydrofoil back to Saigon. A couple of enterprising women, shaded by their conical *non la,* sold bottles of chilled mineral water from a plastic cooler; they had a captive market of us who, slowly charbroiling under an early summer sun, waited for the ferry to arrive. Waiting with me was a young woman, scarcely five feet tall, with a full moon face and a well-scissored page boy haircut, quite out of common with most Vietnamese women, who wear their hair long. She wore designer blue jeans and a tailored khaki jacket over a snowy cotton blouse; it was for her the adjective "pert" was coined. Leaning against her chair, equally uncommon for women in the delta, was a briefcase. I interrupted her from the newspaper that lay across her lap and asked her, in English, on the chance that her appearance indicated some multilingual talents, what she was doing sweltering on the dock in big-city duds. She burbled with laughter.

"I was here on business," she replied. "I work in Saigon, but I had business here." Not only was her English effortless, but it was clear that the language was part of her daily life. The hydrofoil, the same blue-and-white tube that had brought me to the delta weeks before, jogged to the floating dock, and we grabbed two adjoining seats. I asked her what she did in Saigon. "I work for a big American company," she said (the name of which is unimportant). "I'm in marketing. We sell consumer cosmetics, soaps, hair-care products. I'm an assistant brand manager and was in the delta talking to my sales force." It turned out that she oversaw three hundred men and women who scootered around the delta hawking shampoos and rinses. "I was here because we're launching a new product and I wanted to brief everybody on it." Then she introduced herself as Nguyen Pham Thi Diem Huong. "Call me Huong," she said, as I struggled with the tonal intricacies of Vietnamese pronunciation.

"My hometown is Ha Tien," she told me, after I had presumed her to be a modern Saigon woman. "Ha Tien is in the delta, on the Cambodian border." Indeed, the great nineteenth-century builder Thoai Ngok Hau, whose tomb I had seen at Chau Doc, dug the Vinh Te canal from Chau

Doc to Ha Tien on the Gulf of Thailand, linking the formerly Cambodian settlement to the Vietnamese towns in the delta. It is a town that was subject to periodic attacks by the virulently anti-Vietnamese Khmer Rouge in the late 1970s, forcing the entire town's population to flee. But Huong was untouched by the war, and her memory of the Khmer Rouge attacks is faint.

"When I was young, my mother used to tell me not to go play with the frogs in the paddy fields. We used to pull their legs off. We were terrible. My mother said we would be killed by the Khmer Rouge if we were in the paddy fields." I asked about her father. "My father was an official, actually a translator of English," she said, "and he was sent to jail. He died in jail." Did she mean a reeducation camp? I asked. "Yes, they called it a reeducation camp. But it was really a jail." Still, her father's association with the previous regime did not hinder her own education. "I got a scholarship from the Catholic Church to go to college in Saigon, and went to the College of Agriculture and Forestry. They gave me the scholarship on the condition I returned to Ha Tien to teach. But after you've been in Saigon, how can you go back to a little delta town?

"So I stayed in Saigon and got this job. By now I've worked my way up five levels to management. But, of course, it's still low-level management. And I'm only twenty-six." And how was business going? I asked. "Well, you know the economy is not so great. The government has really got to get its act together or the whole economy will collapse. A lot of foreign investors have pulled out because they're finding it's just too hard to work under these conditions." I wondered aloud if she felt a tangible cultural divide between the North and the northerners who ran the country and the South and the attitudes and culture of southerners.

"Absolutely," she said. "One of the problems is that there is a very different mentality between northerners and southerners. The northerners run the government. They set the policy. They're very set in their ways. I myself really don't like northerners. They're not friendly. They're not straightforward. They're not straight talking. They use all this jargon that means nothing. There's never a yes; there's never a no. Everything is very vague. It's impossible to have a real discussion with them. They don't understand what it means to cut a deal or to compromise or to be flexible. This is alien to them. And these are the people running the country." I told her that even twenty-five years after the war's end, the government seemed to be shackled to a relentless drum-banging about how it won the war and defeated the Americans. She shrugged. "It's all they have. The economy is a disaster. The Communist party is corrupt. The country is poor. So they repeat over and over that they won the war, as if that will make everything okay."

To some degree, at least in the South, the government has acknowledged the absolute failure of its efforts to impose Soviet-style Socialist notions of economic development: farms are private now, state-owned industries in the delta—small brickworks, sugarcane mills, breweries, rice mills, fishing fleets—are now in private hands for the most part, and markets flourish free of state meddling, save for the bribes collected by the police. Although large swathes of the delta were regarded by the Americans as under the sway of Vietcong guerrillas during the war, an influence that manifested itself in a smoldering antipathy for the Saigon regime and a resentment of the American presence in the country, whatever loyalty delta residents had for the guerrillas did not extend to the troops from the North and did not translate into uncritical acceptance of northern dictate. For all of the northern polemics about the "liberation" of the South, there remains, a quarter of a century after the war's end, the scent of occupation here.

No one has expressed this sense of betrayal by the North better than Truong Nhu Tang, a French-educated founding member of the National Liberation Front, the South's quasi-Communist resistance organization during the war. He was named the Vietcong's minister of justice during meetings in the jungle as American bombers roamed overhead vainly searching for the NLF headquarters and, after the occupation of Saigon on April 30, 1979, moved into offices as justice minister for the South's new government. Very quickly, however, it became apparent to him that Communist cadres from the North held the real reins of power in Saigon and Truong was eased from his post. Scarcely a year after victory, Truong observed in his memoir that:

> Arrests and uncertainty had generated hostility toward the government, but the breathtaking rapacity of the Northern soldiers and cadres filled the Saigonese with contempt and brought out their talent for scurrility. . . . For days at a time, it seemed, I heard nothing but scathing complaints, mixed with reports of the most disquieting personal and family tragedies. I couldn't walk down the street without friends of mine, old school-fellows and former colleagues,

accosting me. Finally I couldn't stomach it anymore. I shut myself up in my house and refused to go back to the office.

In August 1978, after a year of preparation, Truong and his wife crept aboard a wooden river freighter, a big belly, at the delta town of Long Xuyen and slipped out of Vietnam to the South China Sea, and ultimately to refuge in France.[*] On the final page of his memoir, penned in Paris in 1984, Truong lamented that "instead of national reconciliation and independence, Ho Chi Minh's successors have given us a country devouring its own and beholden once again to foreigners, though now it is the Soviets rather than the Americans." One could accuse Truong of naïveté, but he met Ho Chi Minh, suffered in southern prisons and worked with northern cadres for years; the worst one could say is that Truong's optimism was misplaced and that he and other southerners were crassly manipulated by the North. And now, with the collapse of the Soviet empire, Vietnam is adrift on its own, gingerly in its dealings with the world, even with China, the last of the Communist behemoths, with whom it clashed over their border two decades ago. But whether it was betrayal or merely inevitability, the North's dominance of the South is thorough and resented.

Huong stewed a bit after venting her frustration, and then I asked her how often she got back to Ha Tien. "I try to go home twice a year," she said. "On Tet and one other time. It's funny. I've changed tremendously from when I lived in Ha Tien. I'm a big-city girl. I've been to New York on company business. My friends in Ha Tien think of me as some kind of an alien, like from outer space." She also had an American boyfriend, which set her off still more from the provincialism of her hometown, and from mainstream Vietnamese society, even in somewhat cosmopolitan Saigon.

I saw Huong and her very Yankee boyfriend a couple of times in Saigon in the days that followed and was buoyed by her indomitable optimism, her certainty that despite the obduracy of the government, the poverty of the country, the spread of corruption, Vietnam would emerge from its extended torpor. "We are Vietnamese," she would say to me. "There are a lot of smart people in this country. Not everybody is an old Communist. There are many people like me here in the South. We're not afraid of the

---

[*] In fact, so many of My Tho's fishing boats were used by escaping Vietnamese after 1975 that the entire fishing fleet of the area had to be rebuilt.

world. We want to be part of this world." But the commissars who still run the country are very much afraid of the world, afraid of what it could do to them and afraid that if the Vietnamese people are allowed to know the world beyond, the party's control would evaporate. As I headed out one morning to meet some friends in Saigon, I picked up a day-old copy of the *Bangkok Post* and, sure enough, an article about Vietnamese dissidents had been blacked over with a Magic Marker by the censors. No news is good news.

That night, I sat in the aerie on the roof of the Hotel Majestic watching my last southeast Asian sunset, a tempura of pinks and purples, of shot gold and rouge haloing a melting, liquid sun. Beneath me, the Saigon River tiptoed past, its waters stirred by the day's dying traffic, three stubby white ferries bungeeing from shore to shore, carrying commuters home, a weary freighter blaring its way past, a blue-hulled big belly making for a granary, pirogues like dragonflies, darting amid the bigger craft, and the last hydrofoil of the day from the beach resort in Vung Tao. On the main roof of the hotel, a wedding reception unfolded. A young woman with shimmering onyx hair that fell to her waist floated across the floor in a white satin gown and delicate veil, lightly fingering her new husband's tuxedoed arm, flowing among guests—sylvan women in *ao dai* and men in loose white shirts and dark slacks—who held glasses of champagne aloft at the couple's passing. This was Saigon's new elite, a celebration of a rite of passage draped, though, in the cultural finery of the West; and faintly, gently, the music drifted toward me, the plaintive sounds of traditional Vietnamese folksinging. To the west, a final golden gleam torched the air, and then it was the ruby violets that reigned.

This had been a journey that consumed a year of my life, a year like no other, a year that took me from the globe's highest plateau to its greatest delta, from a land colored in earthy hues—browns, grays, greens, blacks—to the kaleidoscopic spectrum of the Mekong's expansive release at the sea. It was also for me a journey away from the constraints of salaried life, although the constraints on a foreign correspondent are far looser than perhaps in other vocations. I had sought to linger, to listen, to loll about, and I did. My notebooks filled up as I traveled, rather a lot of them, and I shot nearly a hundred rolls of film. Nowhere did I have to rush. I never wore a tie and rarely used the telephone. I did not even carry a computer, an appendage most correspondents could not do without.

For a year I was untethered, a remarkable experience. I owed no editor a story, no one an accounting of my travels. I had no guilt over reading too many novels. There are not many times in one's life that one can spend a year following an idea, totally removed from the world of the familiar, visiting places where a rat eating your stash of crackers is not an unhappy experience. It was a year, too, in which I sought to link together different phases of my life, my years as an antiwar activist, my graduate school years as an historian, my work as a journalist and my passion for Asia. Somehow, elements of all these experiences surfaced at times, coalescing in a small odyssey of intellectual exploration and personal discovery. As all-consuming as the journey was—worries about transport (and the seaworthiness of my vessels), about border crossings, occasionally about the police, more often about food, coupled with the intensity of the conversations and the lives of those I encountered—there were at times pangs of solitude. As a newspaper correspondent, one could on a whim pick up the phone and call a friend anywhere in the world for companionship; on the Mekong, there were few phones, at least up north, and when there were, the cost was often prohibitive. Yet solitude prompts reflection and a willingness to spend more time than one should trying to understand. Perhaps it was solitude, or whim, that led to tossing a half dozen plastic bottles with notes in them—with a telephone number and an address—into the Mekong at various stages. I never did get a response.

It is fashionable, and not utterly unrealistic, to celebrate what is called "diversity" in the United States; a year traveling across America, roughly the distance I traversed on or along the Mekong, would unveil the textured social fabric of America. Yet, there remain broad commonalities in the United States that supercede ethnicity, language, skin color, certain binding principles and values and expectations that inhere in most of the country, not always to the same degree or in the same way, but which are discernible, palpable, indeed admirable.

Along the Mekong, from northern Tibet to Lijiang, from Luang Prabang to Phnom Penh to Can Tho, I moved from one world to another, among cultural islands often ignorant of one another's presence. Yet each island, as if built on shifting sands and eroded and reshaped by a universal sea, was re-forming itself, or was being remolded, was expanding its horizons or sinking under the rising waters of a cultural global warming. It was a journey between worlds, worlds fragiley conjoined by a river both ominous and luminescent, muscular and bosomy, harsh and sensuous.

I confess to a mix of intellectual romanticism combined with a conviction that it is precisely the emanation of cultural differences—culture in the broadest of senses, the rituals, the literature and music, the political forms and ideas of a people—that adds meaning and fullness to the story of humanity. Indeed, official China's own uneasy appreciation of Han culture itself has led, for example, to an evisceration of the Chinese language—witness the complexity and sophistication of Chinese spoken and written in Taiwan and Hong Kong, in comparison to mainland China— an attempt to flatten and homogenize mainland culture. Insecure in their own cultural overcoat, it has been impossible for the Chinese to accept or appreciate these strange peoples who inhabit China's border regions— better to absorb and change them, the thinking goes.

South of the Yunnan border, south to the sea, the brush of Europe and America is still visible, brushstrokes largely painted over in Tibet and China. In southeast Asia, though, the baguette-stacked golden pyramids echo a Gallic empire, proof perhaps that even if French ideals of *liberté, egalité, fraternité* (ideals hardly encouraged by the colonial regime) did not flourish, their breakfast loaf did. *"Vive la baguette"* as a rallying cry, however, is not much of a legacy. The result is that apart from this sacred bread, and the occasional street sign in French—France, it seems, will tolerate any tyranny as long as the tyrants ensure the roads are *rues*—the culture longed after, for better or worse, is American, at least in more urban arenas. I find this remarkable, for the United States destroyed far more of southeast Asia than did France, the French to their dismay lacking the capabilities for carpet bombing, deforestation and napalming.

The irony of this is striking in a multitude of ways. France, which expends formidable energies promoting its culture and language, both at home (where there are even rules on the precise percentage of French-language songs a radio station must play) and abroad, has done so in particularly politically odious countries, places like the Central African Republic, Laos, Gabon, Congo, Cambodia, Haiti, Vietnam. And it seems that the greater its effort, the more meager its results. At the same time, I found that American culture, a disorganized, continually evolving, linguistically flexible, universally accommodating pastiche of music, literature, ideas, business attitudes, relentless innovation and, in recent years, commitments to principles of human rights and democracy, has insinuated itself throughout Asia, not by design, but by what many people see as its plain appeal. I say this reluctantly, because I would rather live in Paris than any city in the United States, but it is no coincidence that the hottest club in Saigon is called Apocalypse Now, an evocation of the American war experience; nobody cares, or remembers (except for propaganda writers in Hanoi), the French getting walloped at Dien Bien Phu in 1954. Despite more than 3 million people being killed,* swathes of the country being defoliated or carpet bombed, there remains, at least in the south of Vietnam, a yearning, perhaps an uncritical yearning, for things American. The hamburger has not replaced the baguette, but Coke and Pepsi are everywhere, and English is the second language of choice. As Phuong told me, "I want my son to go to America." Why? I asked him. "America is best country" was all he could say. He meant it.

Everywhere along the Mekong I felt as if I were moving through history, through a tale of Asia's transformation. I retain intense images in my mind of this journey across history, the debates by saffron-clad Tibetan monks, rituals that are millennia-old; the old Naxi lady smoking a stained long-stem pipe in her elaborate cape of night and day, the stars and the moon; the sturdy Akha woman asking for coins for her headdress; Vann Nath, the white-haired painter who survived the Tuol Sleng torture center; the sight of young high school girls in shimmering white *ao dai* floating toward school.

There is an intense beauty along the Mekong, among the people who rise each morning to offer incense to Buddha, who, silhouetted against a glowing dusk, fling circle nets into a slow-dancing current; of a woman washing herself on the back of a delta big belly. And the river itself, one of Asia's central sinews, slings itself south in torrents and placidity, in a youthful, roaring energy through gorges as startling as anywhere, in pan-flat repose fingering islands like a magician's coin trick, in a splay of final glory and abundance. At journey's end, I turned to a page of my well-thumbed copy of Marguerite Duras's *The Lover*, a novel of Vietnam and

---

* Between 1954 and 1975, 1.1 million North Vietnamese and Vietcong (southern National Liberation Front fighters) died while 250,000 soldiers of the South Vietnamese regime were killed; altogether, 2 million Vietnamese civilians died during the same period, of whom between 300,000 and 400,000 were southerners. There were 57,605 Americans killed in combat. More than 300,000 Vietnamese soldiers are designated as missing in action, with approximately 2,200 Americans described as MIA.

love and loss, and read of the light and night that touches this river, this river in its last moments:

> . . . I can't really remember the days. The light of the sun blurred and annihilated all color. But the nights, I remember them. The blue was more distant than the sky, beyond all depths, covering the bounds of the world. The sky, for me, was the stretch of pure brilliance crossing the blue, that cold coalescence beyond all color. . . . The light fell from the sky in cataracts of pure transparency, in torrents of silence and immobility. The air was blue, you could hold it in your hand. Blue. The sky was the continual throbbing of the brilliance of the light. The night lit up everything, all the country on either bank of the river as far as the eye could reach. Every night was different, each one had a name as long as it lasted. Their sound was that of the dogs, the country dogs baying at mystery. They answered one another from village to village, until the time and space of the night were utterly consumed. . . .

Boats on the Mekong Delta, heading home at sunset

Sources

CHAPTERS ONE AND TWO

Bacot, Jacques, *Introduction à l'histoire du Tibet* (Paris: Société Asiatique, 1962).

Barnett, Robert, ed., *Ancient Tibet: Research Materials from the Yeshe De Project* (Berkeley, Calif.: Dharma Publishing, 1986).

———, *Resistance and Reform in Tibet* (Bloomington: Indiana University Press, 1994).

Carrasco, Pedro, *Land and Polity in Tibet* (Seattle: University of Washington Press, 1959).

Goldstein, Melvyn C., *A History of Modern Tibet, 1913–1951: The Demise of the Lamaist State* (Berkeley: University of California Press, 1989).

Goldstein, Melvyn C., Cynthia M. Beall, and Richard P. Cincotta, "Traditional Nomadic Pastoralism and Ecological Conservation on Tibet's Northern Plateau," *National Geographic Research* 6(2) (1990):139–56.

He Daming and Hsiang-te Kung, "Facilitating Regional Sustainable Development Through Integrated Multi-Objective Utilization, Management of Water Resources in the Lancang-Mekong River Basin," *The Journal of Chinese Geography* 7 (4) (1997).

Hilton, James, *Lost Horizon* (New York: Grosset & Dunlap, 1936).

MacGregor, John, *Tibet: A Chronicle of Exploration* (London: Routledge & Kegan Paul, 1970).

Norbu, Jamyang, *Warriors of Tibet: The Story of Aten and the Khampa's Fight for the Freedom of the Their Country* (London: Wisdom Publications, 1986).

Peissel, Michel, *Cavaliers of Kham: The Secret War in Tibet* (London: Heinemann, 1972).

Penick, Douglas J., *The Warrior Song of King Gesar* (Boston: Wisdom Publications, 1996).

Snellgrove, David, and Hugh Richardson, *A Cultural History of Tibet* (New York: George Weidenfeld and Nicolson Ltd., 1968).

Ward, F. Kingdon, *The Land of the Blue Poppy: Travels of a Naturalist in Eastern Tibet* (Cambridge: Cambridge University Press, 1913).

———, *A Plant Hunter in Tibet* (London: Jonathan Cape, 1934).

Winn, Peter S., "Observations about the Geology and Geography of the Mekong Headwaters Area, Southern Qinghai, China," http://users.aol.com/pswinn/ese.html, October 1999.

CHAPTER THREE

Gao Xingjian, *Soul Mountain* (New York: Flamingo, 2000).

He Liyi, *Mr. China's Son: A Villager's Life* (Boulder, Colo.: Westview Press, 1993).

Hill, Ann Maxwell, *Merchants and Migrants: Ethnicity and Trade Among Yunnanese Chinese in Southeast Asia* (New Haven: Yale Southeast Asian Studies, 1998).

Miller, Lucien, ed., *South of the Clouds: Tales from Yunnan* (Seattle and London: University of Washington Press, 1994).

Prasertkul, Chiranan, *Yunnan Trade in the Nineteenth Century: Southwest China's Cross-boundaries Functional System* (Bangkok: Institute of Asian Studies, Chulalongkorn University, 1989).

Renard, Ronald D., *The Burmese Connection: Illegal Drugs and the Making of the Golden Triangle* (Boulder, Colo.: Lynne Rienner Publishers, 1996).

Rock, Joseph F., "The Land of the Yellow Lama: National Geographic Society Explorer Visits the Strange Kingdom of Muli, Beyond the Likiang Snow Range of Yünnan Province, China," *National Geographic*, April 1925.

———, "Experiences of a Lone Geographer: An American Agricultural Explorer Makes His Way Through Brigand Invested Central China en Route to the Amne Machin Range, Tibet," *National Geographic*, September 1925.

———, "Through the Great River Trenches of Asia: National Geographic Explorer Follows the Yangtze, Mekong, and Salwin Through Mighty Gorges, Some of Whose Canyon Walls Tower to a Height of More Than Two Miles," *National Geographic*, August 1926.

———, *The Zhi mä Funeral Ceremony of the Na-khi of Southwest China* (Vienna-Mödling: St. Gabriel's Mission Press, 1955).

———, *A Na-Khi-English Encyclopedic Dictionary* (Rome: Istituto Italiano per il Medio ed Estremo Oriente, 1963), two volumes.

Smith, Nicol, *Burma Road: The Story of the World's Most Romantic Highway* (Garden City, N.Y.: Garden City Publishing, 1942).

Winn, Peter, and Han Chunyu, "Earthshaking Adventures in the Middle Kingdom," http://users.aol.com/pswinn/ese.html.

Zhu Liangwen, *The Dai or the Tai and Their Architecture & Customs in South Asia* (Bangkok: DD Books, 1992).

CHAPTERS FOUR, FIVE AND SIX

Chang, K. C. *Food in Chinese Culture* (New Haven and London: Yale University Press, 1977).

Etherington, Dan M., and Keith Forster, *Green Gold: The Political Economy of China's Post-1949 Tea Industry* (Hong Kong: Oxford University Press, 1993).

Gagneux, Pierre-Marie, *L'Art Lao: présence et signification* (Vientiane: Ambassade de France au Laos, 1969).

Garnier, Francis, *Travels in Cambodia and Part of Laos: The Mekong Exploration Commission Report* (1866–1868), Vol. 1 (Bangkok: White Lotus Press, 1996).

———, *Further Travels in Laos and Yunnan: The Mekong Exploration Commission Report* (1866–1868), Vol. 2 (Bangkok: White Lotus Press, 1996).

Hutchison, Charles S., *Geological Evolution of Southeast Asia* (Oxford: Clarendon Press, 1989).

Isaacs, Arnold R., *Without Honor: Defeat in Vietnam & Cambodia* (New York: Vintage, 1984).

Joel, David, and Karl Schapira, *The Book of Coffee and Tea* (New York: St. Martin's Press, 1975).

King, Victor T., ed., *Explorers of South-East Asia: Six Lives* (Kuala Lumpur: Oxford University Press, 1995).

Kremmer, Christopher, *Stalking the Elephant Kings: In Search of Laos* (Chiang Mai: Silkworm Books, 1997).

Lebar, Frank M., Gerald C. Hickey, and John K. Musgrave, *Ethnic Groups of Mainland Southeast Asia* (New Haven: Human Relations Area Files Press, 1964).

Lewis, Paul, and Elaine Lewis, *Peoples of the Golden Triangle: Six Tribes in Thailand* (London: Thames and Hudson Ltd., 1984).

McCoy, Alfred W., *The Politics of Heroin: CIA Complicity in the Global Drug Trade* (Chicago: Lawrence Hill Books, 1991).

Nguyen Van Huyen, *The Ancient Civilization of Vietnam* (Hanoi: The Gioi Publishers, 1955). This is a reprint of the 1944 edition, *La Civilisation Annamite*.

Pingali, Prabhu, and Mahabub Hossian, eds., *The Impact of Rice Research* (Los Banos: International Rice Research Institute, 1998).

Stuart-Fox, Martin, *Buddhist Kingdom, Marxist State: The Making of Modern Laos* (Bangkok: White Lotus Press, 1996).

———, *A History of Laos* (Cambridge: Cambridge University Press, 1997).

Ukers, William H., *All About Tea*, Vols. I and II (New York: The Tea and Coffee Trade Journal Company, 1935).

United Nations Development Report (New York: Oxford University Press, 1999).

Warner, Roger, *Back Fire: The CIA's Secret War in Laos and Its Link to the War in Vietnam* (New York: Simon & Schuster, 1995).

Wilding-White, Charles F. B., "Luang Prabang and Its Temples," *Arts of Asia* 6 (1) (1976).

Workman, D. R., "Geology of Laos, Cambodia, South Vietnam and the Eastern Part of Thailand," in *Overseas Geology and Mineral Resources* (London: Institute of Geological Sciences, Natural Environment Research Council, 1977).

World Bank, *World Development Report 1999/2000* (Washington, D.C., 1999).

CHAPTERS SEVEN AND EIGHT

Becker, Elizabeth, *When the War Was Over: The Voices of Cambodia's Revolution and Its People* (New York: Simon & Schuster, 1986).

Chandler, David, *Brother Number One: A Political Biography of Pol Pot* (Boulder, Colo.: Westview Press, 1992).

———, *A History of Cambodia* (Boulder, Colo.: Westview Press, 1996).

———, *Voices from S-21: Terror and History in Pol Pot's Secret Prison* (Berkeley and Los Angeles: University of California Press, 1999).

Chou Ta-kuan, *The Customs of Cambodia* (Bangkok: The Siam Society, 1987).

Curtis, Grant, *Cambodia Reborn? The Transition to Democracy and Development* (Washington, D.C.: Brookings Institution Press, 1998).

Delaporte, L., *Voyage au Cambodge: l'architecture Khmer* (Paris: Librairie Ch. Delagrave, 1880).

Ebihara, May M., Carol A. Mortland, and Judy Ledgerwood, eds., *Cambodian Culture Since 1975: Homeland and Exile* (Ithaca, N.Y., and London: Cornell University Press, 1994).

Jensen, Michael, *Trees Commonly Cultivated in Southeast Asia: An Illustrated Field Guide* (Bangkok: FAO Regional Office for Asia and the Pacific, 1995).

King, Ben F., and Edward C. Dickinson, *A Field Guide to the Birds of South-East Asia* (Glasgow: William Collins Sons & Co., 1975).

Loung Ung, *First They Killed My Father: A Daughter of Cambodia Remembers* (New York: HarperCollins, 2000).

Mabbett, Ian, and David Chandler, *The Khmers* (Oxford: Blackwell, 1995).

Martin, Marie Alexandrine, *Cambodia: A Shattered Society* (Berkeley, Los Angeles, London: University of California Press, 1994).

Phoeun, Mak, *Histoire du Cambodge de la fin du XVIe siècle au début du XVIIIe* (Paris: Presse de l'École Française d'Extrême-Orient, 1995).

Vann Nath, *A Cambodian Prison Portrait: One Year in the Khmer Rouge's S-21* (Bangkok: White Lotus Press, 1998).

CHAPTERS NINE AND TEN

Chanoff, David, and Doan Van Toai, *Portrait of the Enemy* (New York: Random House, 1986).

Druiker, William J., *Vietnam Since the Fall of Saigon* (Athens: Ohio University Center for International Studies, Monographs in International Studies, 1989).

Engelmann, Larry, *Tears Before the Rain: An Oral History of the Fall of South Vietnam* (New York: De Capo Press, 1997).

Herr, Michael, *Dispatches* (New York: Alfred A. Knopf, 1977).

Kamm, Henry, *Dragon Ascending: Vietnam and the Vietnamese* (New York: Arcade, 1996).

Kolko, Gabriel, *Vietnam: Anatomy of a Peace* (London: Routledge, 1997).

Le Ba Thao, *Vietnam: The Country and Its Geographical Regions* (Hanoi: The Gioi Publishers, 1997).

Nguyen Cong Binh, Le Xuan Diem, and Mac Duong, *Van Hoa va Cu Dan Dong Bang Song Cuu Long* ("The Culture and Population of the Mekong Delta") (Ho Chi Minh City: Nha Xuat Ban Khoa Hoc Xa Hoi Publishers, 1990).

Reporting Vietnam: Part One, American Journalism, 1959–1969 (New York: The Library of America, Library Classics of the United States, Inc., 1998).

Robinson, W. Courtland, *Terms of Refuge: The Indochinese Exodus and the International Response* (London and New York: Zed Books, 1998).

Sheehan, Neil, *After the War Was Over: Hanoi and Saigon* (New York: Random House, 1992).

Son Nam, *Lich Su Khan Hoang Mien Nam* ("The History of the Settlement of the South") (Ho Chi Minh City: Nha Xuat Ban Tre Publishers, 1997).

Terzani, Tiziano, *Giai Phong! The Fall and Liberation of Saigon* (New York: St. Martin's Press, 1976).

Thu-huong Nguyen-vo, *Khmer-Viet Relations and the Third Indochina Conflict* (Jefferson, N.C., and London: McFarland & Company, Inc., 1992).

Truong Nhu Tang, *A Vietcong Memoir: An Inside Account of the Vietnam War and Its Aftermath* (New York: Vintage, 1986).

Werner, Jayne Susan, *Peasant Politics and Religious Sectarianism: Peasant and Priest in the Cao Dai in Viet Nam* (New Haven: Yale University Southeast Asia Studies, 1981).

Acknowledgments

Few books are solitary efforts. I have been treated with astonishing generosity by many people during the travel, research and writing of this book, gifts of time, energy, spirit, ideas and cuisine. At the summit of generosity has been Lulu Yu, whose patience and unquestioning hospitality in Hong Kong over more than two years is unparalleled. Luo Jianhua, a painter of depth and sensitivity, opened his home and thoughts to me during my trips to Kunming. Dakpa Kelden was a stalwart friend on several trips to Tibet and Qinghai, easing obstacles with humor and aplomb. At the Yunnan Institute of Geography, Zhou Yue shared his time and ideas, despite the best efforts of the bureaucracy to impede him. Jennifer Wang, for several years my assistant in Hong Kong, was a good friend and thoughtful traveler. In Saigon, Nguyen Pham Thi Diem Huong guided me to collections of folktales and local histories of the Mekong Delta. At the Center for Chinese Studies at the University of California, Berkeley, its director, Yeh Wenhsin, provided resources to make the writing of this book possible and overwhelmed me with an abundance of ideas; the staff of the Center for Chinese Studies is to be thanked as well for their help. Frederick Wakeman encouraged me to present some of my ideas at the Institute of East Asian Studies as part of the Shorenstein lecture series. Mary Jordan and Kevin Sullivan read much of the manuscript and chastened me with my inadequacies, a laudable exercise. Molly Moore and John Ward Anderson leavened their critiques with humor and encouragement and the promise of fine wine. Helen Winternitz was penetrating in her observations during her reading of the early parts of this book. Blaine Harden was a severe critic who made me see and write things I wished to avoid. In Boston, Irwin Schwartz kept versions of the manuscript under electronic lock and key but, more important, paddled with me in the Mekong Delta for a time. My agent, Flip Brophy, somehow never abandoned her faith in me and kept me going. Jonathan Segal, my editor, mingled praise, suggestions and criticism in dosages sometimes difficult to swallow, but which in the end made this a far better book than it would have been without his guidance. And last, but far from least, I want to thank profusely my research assistant in Berkeley, Courtney J. Norris, a scholar of Vietnam, whose prodigious research talents gave this book dimensions it otherwise never would have had. During the writing, she uncovered books and essays I thought did not exist, translated voluminous tales from and histories of Vietnam and never flagged under my mounting pile of demands and needs. This book would not have happened without her.

Index

Page numbers in **bold italics** refer to illustrations.

A Note About the Author

Edward A. Gargan has worked as a foreign correspondent and bureau chief for the *New York Times* in West Africa, China, India and Hong Kong, as well as a magazine writer for the *Los Angeles Times*. The author of *China's Fate*, he divides his time between Beijing and Martha's Vineyard, where he is working on his next book.

A Note on the Type

The text of this book has been set in Goudy Old Style, one of the more than one hundred typefaces designed by Frederic William Goudy (1865–1947). Although Goudy began his career as a bookkeeper, he was so inspired by the appearance of several newly published books from the Kelmscott Press that he devoted the remainder of his life to typography in an attempt to bring a better understanding of the movement led by William Morris to the printers of the United States. Produced in 1914, Goudy Old Style reflects the absorption of a generation of designers with things "ancient." Its smooth, even color combined with its generous curves and ample cut marks it as one of Goudy's finest achievements.

Composed by North Market Street Graphics,
Lancaster, Pennsylvania

Printed and bound by Quebecor World,
Fairfield, Pennsylvania

Designed by Iris Weinstein